The Impact of Macroeconomic Policies in Trinidad and Tobago

International Finance and Development Series

Published in association with the Institute of Social Studies

General Editor: **E. V. K. FitzGerald**, Professor of Economics, Institute of Social Studies, The Hague, and Director, Finance and Trade Policy Research Centre, University of Oxford

The International Finance and Development Series reflects the research carried out at The Hague and associated centres in Europe, Asia, Africa and Latin America on the relationship between international capital flows and the process of structural adjustment in less-developed economies. The studies in this series share a common analytical approach based on the use of advanced social accounting techniques and the explicit modelling of the economic behaviour of institutional sectors, which in turn permit a new approach to macroeconomic policy design.

Titles include:

Alemayehu Geda
FINANCE AND TRADE IN AFRICA
Macroeconomic Response in the World Economy Context

Philomen Harrison
THE IMPACT OF MACROECONOMIC POLICIES IN TRINIDAD AND TOBAGO
The Firm under Adjustment

Karel Jansen
EXTERNAL FINANCE IN THAILAND'S DEVELOPMENT

Karel Jansen and Rob Vos (*editors*)
EXTERNAL FINANCE AND ADJUSTMENT

Luis Carlos Jemio
DEBT, CRISIS AND REFORM IN BOLIVIA
Biting the Bullet

Joke Luttik
ACCOUNTING FOR THE GLOBAL ECONOMY

Rob Vos
DEBT AND ADJUSTMENT IN THE WORLD ECONOMY

Rob Vos and Josef T. Yap
THE PHILIPPINE ECONOMY
East Asia's Stray Cat?

Howard White (*editor*)
AID AND MACROECONOMIC PERFORMANCE

The Impact of Macroeconomic Policies in Trinidad and Tobago

The Firm Under Adjustment

Philomen Harrison
Deputy Programme Manager
CARICOM Secretariat
Georgetown
Guyana

palgrave
macmillan

ISS
Institute of Social Studies

First published 2002 by
PALGRAVE MACMILLAN
Houndmills, Basingstoke, Hampshire RG21 6XS and
175 Fifth Avenue, New York, N. Y. 10010
Companies and representatives throughout the world

PALGRAVE MACMILLAN is the global academic imprint of the Palgrave Macmillan division of St. Martin's Press, LLC and of Palgrave Macmillan Ltd. Macmillan® is a registered trademark in the United States, United Kingdom and other countries. Palgrave is a registered trademark in the European Union and other countries.

ISBN 0–333–99315–2

This book is printed on paper suitable for recycling and made from fully managed and sustained forest sources.

A catalogue record for this book is available from the British Library.

Library of Congress Cataloging–in–Publication Data
Harrison, Philomen.
The impact of macroeconomic policies in Trinidad and Tobago: the firm under adjustment / Philomen Harrison.
p. cm. — (International finance and development series)
Includes bibliographical references and index.
ISBN 0–333–99315–2 (cloth)
1. Structural adjustment (Economic policy)—Trinidad and Tobago. 2. Business enterprises—Trinidad and Tobago. I. Title. II. Series.

HC157.3 .H37 2002
339.5'0972983—dc21

2001058219

10 9 8 7 6 5 4 3 2 1
11 10 09 08 07 06 05 04 03 02

Printed and bound in Great Britain by
Antony Rowe Ltd, Chippenham and Eastbourne

For my mother

Contents

List of Tables

List of Figures

List of Boxes

Acknowledgements

I would like to express my most profound appreciation to Professor E. V. K. FitzGerald for his comments and encouragement along the way and for being instrumental in enabling the publication of this book. I also extend thanks to the government of the Netherlands, without whose support this work would not have been possible. This book is based on my PhD thesis, the research for which was carried out at the Institute of Social Studies (ISS) in The Hague, the Netherlands. Along with Professor E. V. K. FitzGerald, my supervision team also comprised Professor Marc Wuyts and Dr. Howard White and I thank them warmly for their support. I must also express my appreciation to the staff and other personnel at ISS. In particular I thank Professor Rob Vos, Dr. Karel Jansen, Professor Ashwani Saith and the programme administrator of the economics of development programme for their assistance and support.

Special thanks to Paula Bownas, who managed the production aspects of this book and to the editor, Vilma Linares, who painstakingly and diligently edited the manuscript, as well as my contact person Michelle Luijben, an important link between the editors and myself. There were many friends in Trinidad & Tobago, The Hague and the rest of the world who supported me throughout the research and whom I would prefer not to list, for fear of leaving out anyone, but they know who they are and my fondest wishes go out to them. Finally I would like to thank my family in Trinidad & Tobago for their self-sacrificing and unstinting support.

Series Editor's Preface to *The Impact of Macroeconomic Policies in Trinidad & Tobago*

Countries such as Trinidad & Tobago that gained their independence from colonial rule after the Second World War had great hopes of overcoming poverty and gaining a respected place in the concert of nations within a generation. However, the hopes of the peoples of small states were soon dashed by a cycle of external debt, forced devaluations, social service retrenchments and defensive reactions to external trade shocks that characterized the 1970s. The dream of planned industrialization and balanced development – which had been shared by all political parties – had been shattered. However, international and national policymakers held out a new promise in the 1980s – that a shift from state-based to market-based development strategies could achieve the original objectives of development planning, only more quickly and less wastefully. A central feature of life for island states – and for developing countries as a whole – in the closing decades of the century has thus become the experience of 'structural adjustment'.

From the very outset of the design and implementation of structural adjustment policy in developing countries, international financial institutions such as the World Bank held the position that private sector response to such policies was central to their success. Indeed, the approach that came to be known as the 'Washington consensus' was designed to promote private investment through the increased incentives provided by the reduction of government claims on resources, the liberalization of domestic markets and integration to the world economy. This key assumption was a matter of economic doctrine rather than empirical experience, as no studies had been carried out of how, whether and when the private sector might respond to such policies. This doctrine was reinforced by the evident failure of the previous state-led economic strategies, from which it was deduced that the markets could only do better.

More surprisingly still, after two decades' experience with such policies, there is still little detailed evidence of private sector behaviour during structural adjustment. Almost all the evidence produced is of three kinds. First, there are computable general equilibrium models which 'test' the effects of policies (usually relative prices) under a set of arbitrary assumptions about sectoral behaviour. These tell us little about private sector behaviour because their initial assumptions, usually imputed supply elasticities, have not been empirically established. Second, there are econometric exercises on macroeconomic data such as output growth or trade performance, which attempt to show how those countries which have successfully adjusted perform better than those which have not. Third, there are detailed surveys of household expenditure that attempt to gauge the effect of adjustment policies on income distribution and poverty. None of these actually address the central question of how firms themselves respond to structural adjustment.

There is thus an urgent need for more studies of private sector behaviour under adjustment. Further, such studies should differentiate clearly between large and small firms on the one hand, and domestic and foreign firms on the other. Small firms are the main providers of employment, so their nurture is a central part of a pro-poor adjustment policy. The support of domestic firms so that they can compete internationally without the benefits of scale or natural protection may be necessary if a poor small country is to maintain some degree of autonomy in an increasingly hostile global economic environment.

Small business has particular problems with lack of credit, information and agency asymmetry, as well as with lack of skills in the family firms or lack of scale to compete effectively. Modern investment theory indicates that uncertainty is one of the major determinants of the decision to invest because the option value of delaying investment is high. However, this option value depends on two factors: the ability of the firm to acquire and use information effectively on the one hand, and the degree of competition – i.e. the likelihood of a competitor moving into the market if investment is delayed – on the other. Small firms are not in such a position because they have little information (particularly about technology) and cannot afford to wait due to intense market competition. As a consequence, they are often forced to invest badly and too soon.

The affiliates of foreign firms in small poor countries are disproportionately large in relation to domestic firms, a fact which is recognized in international trade rules which provide for national treatment only 'in like circumstances'. Modern finance theory indicates that banks will tend to lend to foreign rather than domestic firms (and still less to small firms) because of the lack of collateral in the latter and the high unit cost of administering loans. In a context of credit constraints brought about by stabilization policy and financial liberalization widening the investment options for banks, it is commonly observed that small as well as domestic firms find it more difficult to adjust than large or foreign firms do.

Amidst this dearth of rigorous research on firm behaviour under adjustment, the original doctoral research by Philomen Harrison at The Hague, upon which this volume is based, is a particularly valuable contribution to our understanding of the process. She was originally drawn to the Institute of Social Studies by our critical work on structural adjustment and came to form part of the 'International Capital Flows and Economic Adjustment' research programme. The work of our group at The Hague – which emphasized that the response of the economy to external shocks depends critically upon the distinct production, investment and savings decisions of economic agents in the private sector (foreign corporations, domestic firms, small business and households) – seemed to her to offer an approach which could combine institutional specificity with econometric rigour.

Her study of Trinidad & Tobago is the fourth country monograph in the International Finance and Development Series, having been preceded by studies of the Philippines (R. Vos and J. Yap *The Philippine Economy: East Asia's Stray Cat?* 1996), Thailand (K. Jansen *External Finance in Thailand's Development: An Interpretation of Thailand's Economic Growth*, 1997) and Bolivia (L. Jemio *Crisis and Reform in Bolivia: Biting the Bullet*, 2001). A number of other cases are summarized into our comparative studies of development assistance (H. White (ed.) *Aid and Macroeconomic Performance: Theory, Empirical Evidence and Four*

Country Cases, 1998) and of adjustment policies (K. Jansen and R. Vos (eds) *External Finance and Adjustment: Failure and Success in the Developing World*, 1997). Philomen's approach shares many of the principles upon which the other case studies are based, particularly the notion that the heterogeneous and constrained nature of the different constituent parts of the private sector would mean that similar macroeconomic and liberalization policies could have quite distinct effects in different countries. More specifically, this implies that the private sector may not be able to respond to 'shock therapy' because of its own financial, technological and organizational weaknesses. However, she also made her own special contribution to our work as a group by embarking on an ambitious but ultimately fruitful exploration of detailed survey data at the firm level. This econometric analysis confirmed many of our hypotheses, but in ways different from those we had expected – defining much more clearly the linkages between profitability, finance and investment.

Furthermore, Philomen was also concerned that the tradition of 'dependency theory' in the Caribbean had been based on an important historical insight, but she was hampered by a lack of rigorous economic analysis to support her concern. In contrast, the neoclassical approach, while manifestly inappropriate to a small poor economy with weak institutions and a powerful neighbour, had become ascendant because of its domination of modern analytical techniques. In this book she has demonstrated that a view based ultimately on political economy rather than general equilibrium can be tested rigorously using modern techniques, and it can lead to greater understanding of how the private sector behaves in small island economies. It is only upon this understanding that sound policies, which enable poor people to enhance their welfare within a hostile global economy, can be built.

In Chapter 9 of her study, Philomen draws a number of valuable and practical policy implications for Trinidad & Tobago. But what wider policy lessons for island states – or more generally for vulnerable open economies – can be drawn from this book? One, of course, is methodological: that even in a small economy, firms can be highly heterogeneous. Thus, policy design must be based on a thorough understanding of institutional behaviour, which requires dedicated research and careful consideration of local history. International financial institutions do this when considering a large economy such as Brazil or India, but it is just assumed that a 'one size fits all' policy is adequate for smaller economies.

The second lesson is that financial markets remain highly segmented even after financial liberalization, and discriminatory credit allocation can continue by banks against firms based on criteria of size, ownership, ethnicity and 'social connections'. Public intervention in the form of prudential oversight may thus be necessary, not only to ensure solvency but also to guarantee all forms of equitable access to available financial resources. A third lesson is that the financial structure of firms may make them more (or less) vulnerable to external shocks. Thus, in order to protect shareholders the prudential oversight of company solvency in small open economies, employees and other stakeholders must include currency exposure. The fourth lesson is that firms that invest perform best in the adjustment process. In consequence, support for macroeconomic adjustment policies should involve not only foreign investment promotion but also low real interest rates, credit availability and tax incentives for domestic firms.

In sum, this book forms a valuable contribution not only to the research literature on structural adjustment in developing countries, but also to the policy debate on economic strategy for island economies in general and the Caribbean in particular.

Valpy FitzGerald
Oxford and The Hague
Series Editor

December 1999

Introduction

The Objectives of the Research and Location of the Problem

This research falls under the problem area of the effects of structural adjustment policies on the development of the private sector. Despite more than a decade of adjustment, investment performance in many developing countries has shown significant decline.[1] Empirical studies show that total investment was adversely affected by factors such as external indebtedness and macroeconomic instability which led to a lack of investor confidence . Private investment, in turn, was affected by a fall-off in public investment due to the complementarity of these two components, with the effect of the real exchange rate on private investment being complex.[2] The lack of private investment response to macroeconomic adjustment pointed to a need to explore the heterogeneous behaviour of firms in developing countries as well as the financial constraints on private investment (FitzGerald 1992a & 1992b).

The adjustment policies of the International Monetary Fund (IMF) and the World Bank are supposed to be favourable to producers in the private sector, specifically in the traded goods sector, through the creation of a stable macroeconomic environment for entrepreneurs. Under this framework, the use of market-determined price incentives is considered essential to promoting the volume and efficiency of private investment, to improving international competitiveness, to increasing efficiency in production, and to stimulating the expansion of exports. These policies were thought to be necessary to assist the recovery of developing countries faced with macroeconomic problems derived from domestic policy causes, as well as external shocks such as deteriorating terms of trade and oil price shocks. While in some regions adjustment followed many years of persistent economic decline, in other regions adjustment was implemented in response to external debt crises and not as a form of development.

The current research therefore undertakes a study of firms in the private sector, specifically the manufacturing industry of Trinidad & Tobago over a period of years (1983–1994) within which falls the implementation of stabilization/adjustment policies of the IMF and World Bank. Like many developing countries, Trinidad & Tobago found it necessary to approach the IMF and the World Bank in the late 1980s for financial support and assistance in economic recovery. Despite being the recipient of commodity booms in the 1970s, the early 1980s saw the appearance of fiscal and external deficits with increased unemployment and indebtedness, which was followed by other macroeconomic disturbances leading up to the need for adjustment loans beginning in the late 1980s. The formal implementation of these policies can be pinpointed to 1988 even though preparatory work for qualification started as early as 1987.

The significance of the research is that it challenges the treatment of the private sector in the analysis of macroeconomic adjustment policies as a homogeneous entity in which firms are expected to respond flexibly to relative price changes. The approach to the research is to present a microeconomic perspective of the macro policies of adjustment and it is expected to contribute to the literature on the effects of adjustment policies on private investment and on the profitability of firms, with particular reference to specific macroeconomic policies identified later in this research. In particular, the intention is to examine how firms in the private sector of a developing country have been affected by these policies, how they have responded to them and what are the factors contributing to or affecting their capacity to respond under adjustment. Essentially, the question that is asked in this research is:

> *With reference to the private sector in a developing country and specific policies of adjustment, what has been the response of private investment and its profitability given what these policies ought to achieve?*

The specific objectives of this research are:

(i) to evaluate specific policies of adjustment from the perspective of how firms in the private sector of a developing country have been able to cope with the changed macroeconomic environment;

(ii) to evaluate specifically the effect of the policies on profitability and the investment response of firms;

(iii) to investigate the mechanisms through which the effect of the policies have been transmitted to the variables in (ii) above, and which necessitate the restructuring process of firms;

(iv) to understand some of the factors that contribute to differences in the response of firms to the policies under review;

(v) to evaluate specifically with respect to (iv) whether size/ownership and industry differences of firms matter;

(vi) to derive some policy implications based on the findings of the research.

The research addresses the question as to what has happened to firms under adjustment rather than what should happen. Underlying the policies of adjustment is the assumption of a representative firm capable of responding to market-determined price incentives. Essential aspects of this approach are the role of markets and the complementary role of governments in ensuring an enabling environment inclusive of competition, infrastructure requirements and institutions thought necessary to assist the functioning of markets. This enabling environment is viewed as the mechanism through which confidence in the private sector can be reinstated in order to achieve sustained economic progress.

The justification of the emphasis given to the role of the private sector is interwoven in the debate on the state-market dichotomy. Under conditions of perfect competition, the existence of market equilibrium, rationality in the behaviour of consumers who maximize utility and producers who maximize profit, the belief is that the allocation of resources by the market will be optimal. The *World Development Report 1991* stated:[3]

> ... getting the prices right, and creating a climate which allows businesses to respond to them, can raise the rate of return on investments by half – even double it where distortions had been particularly large... (WDR 1991: 70)

While the 1991 report also acknowledged that markets are not enough to ensure the promotion of economic growth and the alleviation of poverty, it also stressed that the role of the state should be viewed as one which involves minimal and market friendly intervention. The *World Development Report* (1997) revisited the issues surrounding the role of the state relative to the demands of globalization, with emphasis on state effectiveness and capability as important ingredients in economic and social development though not as a direct provider of growth as illustrated in the following:

> Development – economic, social and sustainable – without an effective state is impossible. It is increasingly recognised that an effective state – not a minimal one – is central to economic and social development, but more as a partner and facilitator than as a director... (WDR 1997: 18)

While acknowledging a role for the state, this approach still does not delve deeply into the issues related to the impact of the market-oriented policies given the heterogeneous nature of the private sector in many developing countries and the differential effect on firms. The lack of homogeneity in the private sector is manifested through differences in firm size, firm behaviour, resource availability and use, with the historical evolution and positioning of the firm affecting the response of firms to changes in the macroeconomic environment. The recovery of the private sector through increased productive investment may not therefore be an immediate response.[4] The aggregation of efficiency at the individual level also may not equate to a social optimum for the economy. The underlying assumption of a homogeneous private sector comprising profit-maximizing firms which can achieve microlevel efficiency in the presence of perfectly competitive markets is questionable. FitzGerald & Vos (1989) argued that:

> ... there is little convincing empirical evidence available to support the claims by the New Orthodoxy that market-oriented solutions will lead to more efficient resource allocation, automatic stabilization and renewed economic growth... (FitzGerald & Vos 1989: 25)

The Theoretical Framework of the Research and the Approach to the Study

The approach to the study attempts to integrate the micro and macro aspects of adjustment. At the macro level, the research focuses on specific aspects of monetary, exchange rate and financial policies in adjustment, with the implications of the effect of changes in relative prices – the real exchange rate, interest rate and to some extent the wage rate on firms. The literature on financial liberalization in developing countries, notably that of McKinnon (1973) and Shaw (1973) as well as issues surrounding the targeting of the exchange rate and the use of monetary policy are reviewed in the study though not exhaustively.

In order to understand the firm under adjustment from the angle of what the policies ought to achieve, the neo-classical theory of the firm is explored, incorporating an assessment of the possibilities of restructuring in response to macroeconomic policy changes as well as its relevance in Less Developed Countries (LDCs). Under the neo-classical framework, the private sector is viewed as consisting of a homogeneous mass of firms whose objective is profit maximization under the existence of perfect competition, facing similar demands, cost-free entry and exit and ease of substitution of factors of production.

Partly due to the unfeasibility of these assumptions, the process of adjustment to changing macroeconomic policies may lead to adverse consequences in micro-level restructuring. Furthermore, the inherent lack of historical awareness in neo-classical theory, factors such as ownership and the process by which a state of equilibrium is achieved are other drawbacks of this approach relative to the analysis of adjustment policies on firms.

After careful analyses of the drawbacks of neo-classical microeconomics in understanding the process of adjustment, a Structuralist/Post-Keynesian approach was adapted to analyse the impact of adjustment policies on the firms in the private sector. This framework is useful in the understanding of the importance of history and the process of change, of structural features in the production and capital accumulation processes, and in making allowances for segmented markets, the presence of heterogeneity in firm behaviour, and so forth. The Structuralist/Post-Keynesian approach is also useful in understanding the micro-level processes of macroeconomic changes in the sense of the dynamics of adjustment of economic agents. In this context, the micro foundations do not assume aggregative, profit-maximizing behaviour of economic agents.

The study, however, does not have as an overriding aim the testing of competing approaches, as to whether the neo-classical or Structuralist/ Post-Keynesian approach offers the better explanation in adjustment implementation. Instead, based on the objectives outlined above, this study seeks to analyse (in the context of the structural and historical constraints of firms) the effects of the macro policies on the firms and the process of micro-level restructuring. Nonetheless, the discussion shall cast some light on the policy relevance of the competing theoretical approaches.

The strategy of the research is to analyse the historical and structural constraints which affect the capacity of firms to restructure. The study identifies channels in the cost and asset structures of the firm through which relative prices of adjustment policies affect profit and investment. For selected sectors, an investigation of the relationship of structural factors and price relatives is performed to reinforce the argument of the relevance of structure.

The research is also concerned with the structural heterogeneity that arises out of the historical experience, specifying the context under which the process of firm restructuring occurs. While issues such as market orientation are highlighted in the research, the problem surrounding access to credit by firms is emphasized. Less focus therefore is given to related though separate problems of access to foreign markets, technology acquisition and so on.

The data sets include quantitative firm level data through which the impact of relative price changes on the structure of the firm and the effect of these variables on profit and investment can be measured.[5] Arranged as pooled cross-section time-series, the data enables analyses of structural changes over time in which the main focus is on the variability of different types of firms, with allowances for variability within and between groups. Hence, there was a comparison over time of changes in variables pertaining to items in the cost and asset structures of firms, profit, investment, employment, output, etc. for specific categories such as size, ownership and industry.

A point of departure of this study from most of the others on issues of adjustment is its focus on the issue of variability of firm behaviour, albeit at the level of categories or groups of firms, relative to the presence of heterogeneity. In support of the evaluation of the processes involved in restructuring, the analysis also makes use of qualitative data on a small sample of firms relative to the effects of adjustment policies and their patterns of adjustment.

The analysis therefore attempts to integrate qualitative data on firm behaviour and response under adjustment with quantitative aspects of the cost/asset structure using a combination of exploratory data analysis, econometrics and reports of interviews conducted. The theoretical framework and approach to the study including issues on the use of cross-section data over time are elaborated in the chapters that follow.

Outline of the Study

The study is presented in nine chapters that follow this introduction. Chapter 1 contains a discussion of the private sector's role in adjustment, looking at the origins of enterprise development in economic liberalism, the role of the market versus the state, efficiency and private ownership, and the neo-classical and Structuralist/Post-Keynesian approaches to understanding markets and the dynamics of adjustment. Given that there are spaces in the development process for both the state and the private sector and given the prominence of private sector investment, this chapter looks at the role of the private sector in the process of economic development and its capacity to fulfil this role through understanding the determinants of private investment.

Chapter 2 is critical to the depiction of the private sector in a developing country because it begins the focus on Trinidad & Tobago, the country case study used to analyse the research problem. This chapter contextualizes the study from a historical perspective with a view of deriving the dynamics of the experience of firms. The highlights of this chapter include: the common experience of Caribbean economies and the structural features that explain the nature of the economy and the firm today; the policy framework of the industrialization thrust in Trinidad & Tobago; insights into the performance of the economy and the emergent industrial structure and aspects of the firm which concern access to credit/market orientation. The thread of the argument in Chapter 2 shows that history, institutions and theory influence policy and give rise to a determinate structure, pattern of behaviour, and performance of the economy, industry and firm. Ultimately, it is this last unit that the chapter seeks to articulate.

In Chapter 3, the discussion centres around the macro and microeconomic framework of adjustment with a discussion of specific adjustment policies and their impact on firms. Selected adjustment policies, the theory of the firm/markets and alternative approaches are the foundations used to formulate an understanding of the firm under adjustment. The relevance, if any, of these alternate models and the neo-classical theory of the firm to LDCs and the implications of the neo-classical firm in the understanding of adjustment are discussed. Exploratory in nature, the chapter seeks a framework from which to understand the micro-level effects of macroeconomic policies of adjustment, in the absence of any well-articulated and integrated theoretical approach.

Chapter 4 discusses the technical aspects of the framework relative to the analysis, summarizes the argumentation of the research, and presents the hypotheses. The chapter includes: descriptions of the official survey data and narrower qualitative inquiry; other sources of data; the sampling designs and methods of data collection; the survey objective; the questionnaire design and changes over time; quality control procedures and an overall assessment of data limitations and quality; and the rationale for using pooled cross-section time-series data. The chapter also presents selected profiles of the sample data critical to the categories that are analysed.

The core analyses of the research are presented in Chapters 5 through 8. Chapters 5, 6 and 7 focus on structural changes over time of key variables such as ownership, size and industry respectively, with connotations relative to access to credit. Chapter 8 describes regression analyses based on models of profitability and investment at the firm level relative to the effect of the macro policies on the cost and asset structures of firms within categories of firms. Some regressions on structural factors incorporating price relatives are also shown. Tables with the results, which also give an idea of the sample sizes of the different subgroups, along with some graphical representations of the regression diagnostics, are included at the end of this chapter.

Finally, Chapter 9 summarizes the main findings and conclusions of the research – its limitations, policy relevance and the implications for further research.

Main Findings of the Research

The main themes tackled in this research are:

(a) the relevance of structure, history, heterogeneity, and openness in the process of micro adjustment to macro policies;

(b) the structure of production of the firm – dependence on imports, the inherited debt structure as affected by key relative prices;

(c) the functioning of financial markets/credit rationing in a developing country context and the links to ownership, size of firm and industry.

The main findings of the research are:

1. At a broad level, the research has shown that the historically and institutionally determined structure of the firm and of the environment within which it operates influence its ability to deal with external changes.

2. Related to (1) – the processes by which change is achieved bears relation to the underlying features that evolve in the economy and the firm, including the heterogeneity present in the private sector; consequently, the nature of these processes must be understood in context.

3. More specifically, an economy which was historically developed along the lines of import-dependent industrialization as reflected in the structure of production of the material inputs, and in which the monetary system was historically not geared to the development of indigenous firms, should expect relative price changes to impose cost constraints on firms in a differential manner that limit/enhance the options of different types of firms in the process of restructuring.

4. Additionally, in the context of a financial market structure that is notably segmented (manifested through credit rationing behaviour of financial institutions that discriminate between loan applicants in the allocation of credit and the charging of interest rates), financial liberalization policies will not automatically or decisively result in

increased financial efficiency and private investment improvement for all categories of firms.

5. Furthermore, the nature of credit rationing and the functioning of the interest rate in a process of financial liberalization may not lead to improved credit access for all categories of firms.

6. Specifically, the expectation of greater availability of credit to small firms under financial liberalization based on a criterion of efficiency is not necessarily realized. There were negative effects of interest expenses on investment in the adjustment years in which the variable (interest expenses) was significant, with some exceptions for years of high liquidity, and mixed results on profitability for small firms.

7. Thus, since the allocation of credit to the private sector is historically and institutionally determined by the commercial banking sector and possibly by companies/families with interests in that sector, the question of credit is interwoven in a criteria based on characteristics such as size, ownership, cutting across industry in the process and causing differential effects of macroeconomic polices.

8. The inherited liability structure of the firm under conditions of credit rationing has important consequences for the adjustment patterns of firms such that small firms that can borrow are caught in a trap of high indebtedness, resulting in a largely negative effect of leverage use on profitability. It was shown that very large or highly leveraged firms with ease of access to credit experienced declining profitability. Thus, the advantage of credit was really a disadvantage for some firms. A narrowing of the gap in leverage use between foreign and local firms was one of the changes brought on by adjustment.

9. While the devaluation of the exchange rate may result in increased cost of raw materials, one of the restructuring mechanisms of firms was to implement measures which limited wage increases relative to increases in the real exchange rate or to impose wage freezes. Variations occurred in the degree of implementation of this measure across firm categories.

10. In light of the disadvantages faced by small firms relative to finance, forced productivity increases appeared to have been their only recourse for survival under adjustment. Productivity increases in foreign firms seem to be more related to increased capital intensification than to increased productivity of labour.

11. Patterns of adjustment practised by firms included wage suppression, employment and raw-material purchasing reduction, switching from traded to non-traded activities, switching from labour to capital-intensive technology, investment in financial assets, real investment reduction, and for some firms, mainly large/foreign ones, a pro-active strategy of export expansion.

12. Thus, devaluation led to cost-cutting measures detrimental to labour and while it might have facilitated the export thrust of some of the larger firms, it did not necessarily trigger it.

13. The performance of investment and profitability under structural adjustment in Trinidad & Tobago, in general, depicted a declining trend, tending not to show any sustainable signs of recovery in the adjustment period. In light of the above, the expectations of macroeconomic policies based on the neo-classical theory of the firm, the functioning of competitive market system and on relative price response were not necessarily realized.

14. As a result, an understanding of the historical structural features, the inherent heterogeneity that exists as manifested through the patterns of production and financing at the micro level in Trinidad & Tobago are crucial to effecting change through macroeconomic policies.

More details of the above are found in Chapter 9 and in general throughout the book.

Notes

1. See Corbo, Fischer & Webb (1992), Thomas et al. (1991), Serven & Solimano (1992), Benjamin (1992), Bleaney & Fielding (1995), and World Bank – Adjustment Lending and Mobilization of Private and Public Resources for Growth – 22-Country Economics Department (1992), for studies on investment response under adjustment.

2. See Serven & Solimano (1993).
3. See *World Development Report* (1991, Oxford University Press for the World Bank) for the expectations of how the private sector should develop under adjustment.
4. See Thomas et al., *Restructuring an Economy in Distress* (1991, Oxford University Press for the World Bank).
5. This data also includes some characteristics of the firm relative to ownership, activity, employment size and so on. The data was analysed as pooled cross-section over time in which there was some elements of panel data later discussed.

1 The Private Sector's Role in Adjustment

1.1 Introduction

> Sensible people do not get involved in arguments about whether economic progress is due to government activity or to individual initiative; they know that it is due to both, and they concern themselves with asking only what is the proper contribution of each. (Lewis 1955: 376)

> ... competitive markets are the best way yet found for efficiently organizing the production and distribution of goods and services. (WDR 1991: 1)

> ... An effective state is vital for the provision of the goods and services – and the rules and institutions – that allows market to flourish and people to lead healthier lives... (WDR 1997: 1)

The above quotations are perspectives on the role of the state relative to that of the market/private sector which are elaborated in this chapter within the context of the origins of enterprise development. In the macroeconomic policies of adjustment, a pivotal role is given to the recovery of the private sector. These policies are aimed particularly at increasing the volume and efficiency of private investment in the traded goods sector.[1] The removal of domestic market distortions and of barriers to trade are viewed as enabling factors for economic agents to respond to market-determined price incentives. The role of the state is diminished in favour of a market-driven private sector. Guided by the market, private sector investment is viewed as the mechanism through which sustainable growth ought to be achieved. In adjustment there is an implicit understanding that ownership implies efficiency.

The underlying philosophy behind the view that the market can deliver what is best for the individual (or firm) as well as for society (or the economy) can be traced back to the doctrine of economic liberalism. Justification for the faith in the market and perfect competition finds support in welfare economics, with perfectly competitive factor and product markets seen as achieving Pareto optimality optimality.[2] The maximization of social welfare assumes that there are no increasing returns to scale, no technological external effects and no uncertainty or informational asymmetry, all of which can lead to market failure.

In this chapter, the focus is on the role of the private sector in adjustment: its origins, its theoretical justification and its effect on private investment. Section 1.2 discusses the origins of enterprise, the functioning of markets, the claims to efficiency and the role of incentives. Alternate views on market functioning are contained in sections 1.3 and 1.4, which look at the Structuralist (including the neo-Structuralists) and Post-Keynesian perspectives, respectively. The role of the private sector in adjustment and its capacity relative to private investment is discussed in section 1.5. A comparison of the Structuralists and other traditions is contained in section 1.6. Conclusions follow in section 1.7.

1.2 The Background of Adjustment

1.2.1 The origins of enterprise development

The general economic approach to adjustment is neo-liberalism, which was a resurgence in the late 1970s of the tradition of economic liberalism.[3] Dating back to classical political economics, neo-liberalist ideas reflected an opposition to state intervention.[4] This tradition held that a free competitive market was the most efficient means of guiding resources into production. In this system the pursuit of individual interests and that of society are thought to be in harmony. One of its main themes as expressed by Adam Smith was the process of surplus extraction and capital accumulation in economic growth (Walsh & Gram 1980).[5]

Productive capacity was seen as dependent upon the accumulation of capital whose source was the profits of production.[6] Increasing demand ensured that capitalists continued to invest, increasing the intricacy of specialization and leading to higher productivity, profits, wages and capital accumulation. Implicit in this process was a representation of a typical firm (Hunt & Sherman 1972).[7]

With respect to ownership of the means of production, there was an enlarged role for the private over the public sector. Economic liberalists argued over the delineation between private and public enterprise and ownership as well as possible mixtures. Issues of efficiency and corruption are used to explain the marginalization of the state today as was done during the advent of economic liberalism (Lewis 1988: 35). Hence, the origins of the development of enterprise and the process of capital accumulation can be traced back to this early classical tradition.[8]

Neo-classical theory emerged as an offshoot of the classical political doctrine. [9] While supporting the *laissez-faire* doctrine of the classical tradition, the neo-classicists' analyses were embedded in the achievement of equilibrium, and a theory of exchange based on marginality analysis and optimization theory. They focused on topics such as price and output decisions, market forms, allocation of resources and economic welfare. There was little regard for empirical support and historical and institutional factors in the neo-classical paradigm. Its claim to the effectiveness of the market resting on the standard theorem of welfare economics. The theory of the firm which arose from this tradition was in reality the functioning of markets, output and price determination to satisfy the objective of profit maximization. The same degree of flexibility in the response of economic agents to price changes and free mobility of factors were assumed, irrespective of country (Deane 1978).

Despite the depression of the 1930s and the challenge of Keynes, who advocated active government through fiscal and monetary policy, the neo-classical doctrine flourished. Keynes had argued, among other things, against the inevitability of achieving a classical equilibrium position, against the neo-classical techniques of rational economic decisions and the omission of expectations (Deane 1978). Kalecki, while reaching similar macroeconomic conclusions to Keynes, focused his theory on linking macro and microeconomics. He looked at the effects of imperfect competition on firm behaviour with respect to their pricing practices, in particular monopoly pricing, linking also the degree of monopoly with capacity under-utilization (Feiwel 1975).

Development economics came into prominence in the late 1940s with an approach that was against the price mechanism of the market and in favour of state planning (Knight 1991). LDCs were said to be different from developed countries and required analyses other than a neo-classical type.[10] Critics of the neo-classical paradigm emphasized the deficiencies of the product and factor markets (which were seen to be segmented or rudimentary); the inflexibility present in developing countries that inhibit the process of economic change; the inelastic supply of most goods and factors; trade pessimism and inequitable income distribution. These structural problems were seen as impediments to the development process and pointed to the need for selected government intervention.[11]

The beginning of the counter revolution in development theory and policy in the late 1970s was seen as a reaction to the impact of the interventionist economic policy of Keynes (Toye 1987).[12] The failure of developing countries, in particular ex-colonies, to develop under the *laissez-faire* doctrine led to the tendency of governments to intervene in an effort to achieve economic independence and social well-being.

In the late 1970s and early 1980s, writers such as Lal (1983), Bauer (1976), Balassa (1978), Kreuger (1974), Little, Scitovsky & Scott (1970) set the basis for the return of mainstream economics in the form of neo-liberalism and influential attacks on development economics. They argued that massive government intervention in developing countries contributed to severe economic distortions. The notion of the inapplicability of neo-classical theory in LDCs was thought to be wrong. They placed emphasis on the need for perfectly competitive markets for LDCs' economic growth, and on an outward-oriented strategy based on comparative advantage. Lal (1983)[13] contended that 'dirigiste' intervention involved less welfare than *laissez-faire*.[14] These arguments set the basis for the greater role given to the market over the state. The next section goes on to discuss arguments for and against the market.

1.2.2 Theoretical justification for the market under adjustment

The WDR (1983: 41–46), while expressing the view that efficiency entails both 'technically optimal solutions' and a political process, went on to define efficiency as follows:

> … efficient resource allocation – through prices, markets and administrative intervention … and operational efficiency – to maximize the use

> of labour and capital through sound management of enterprises, projects in both the public and private sector ... (WDR 1983: 42)

> Efficiency therefore requires capital and labour to be priced according to their marginal productivities at international prices. In other words labour costs per unit of output must be kept internationally competitive and interest rates should reflect the cost of foreign borrowing ... countries will invest and expand in ways that reflect the relative scarcity of capital and labour ... This view of efficiency is consistent with government goals for alleviating poverty and meeting basic needs ... (WDR 1983: 43)

Thus in this report the question of efficiency is couched not only in terms of efficiency in production but is also broadened to incorporate economic efficiency relative to a more equitable distribution of income. The choice of relative prices that reflect the relative technological scarcities is seen as a dynamic element underlying sound macroeconomic management. This section discusses the theoretical justification of the belief that a socially optimal result is realizable under a perfectly competitive market and the assumptions under which such a situation can hold.

The shifting focus in economic thought from the classical to the neo-classical tradition meant a transition of the preoccupation with the dynamic process of capital accumulation to that of the derivation of conditions of efficiency for static resource allocation. A free market economy in which a perfectly competitive equilibrium prevails ought to produce an efficient allocation of resources under assumptions of constant returns to scale, homogeneous factors of production which are also indivisible, no information problems and no externalities.[15] In this setting, individual efficiency in consumption, production and a product mix defined in terms of Pareto optimality optimality can be also socially optimal when equity is simultaneously satisfied.[16] Other assumptions are: utility maximization of consumers who are assumed to be rational, cost minimization and profit maximization of producers, and an equitable distribution of factors of production, all of which make it possible to maximize social welfare.[17]

Under these assumptions, prices determined by the forces of supply and demand in a perfectly competitive market act as incentives in the maximization of utility and profit by consumers and producers where the law of one price for all economic agents ensures that productive efficiency is the outcome. Thus entrepreneurs invest, purchase inputs, and hire workers responding in the process to the monetary incentives determined by the market, once these prices are allowed to correctly reflect the scarcities of the relevant economic goods. Hence the wage rate, the relative price of tradables and non-tradables and the interest rate are key incentives that ought to direct production and consumption into efficient means.

The above framework is criticized for its static nature in which there is no allowance made for uncertainty and where perfect knowledge is assumed to prevail (Nath 1969). There are, in the real world, instances where the above assumptions do not hold such that there are non-constant returns to scale of factors of production, externalities and information asymmetries. Increasing returns to scale imply that an equal proportional increase in all inputs will lead to a more than proportional increase in output, i.e. the average cost of output falls as output increases. Hence, this situation places larger firms in advantageous positions over smaller firms since the former can produce at a lower average cost, which enables their ability to set prices.

In the presence of technological external effects, the decision of one economic agent can directly affect the output or utility of another beyond any indirect effects that are channeled through relative prices.[18] Under these conditions an economic agent derives utility or relies on an activity of another in such a manner that the resultant costs/benefits that are imposed on, or received, are done so without payments. i.e. the derivation of the utility/activity is not marketable. In the presence of positive (negative) externality, the true cost of production is not taken into account in the production and utility functions and this results in outcomes which are not socially optimal.

The assumption of perfect knowledge in a perfectly competitive system implies that firms are able to maximize profits with the knowledge of relevant prices about its outputs and inputs. However, in the presence of rapid technological change or fluctuations in demand, it is possible that the law of one price will not hold.[19]

Differences relative to firm size, foreign/domestic ownership and industry type may imply that price may not equate to marginal cost due to increasing returns to scale. In addition, a unique price may not be guaranteed due to imperfect knowledge. Hence producers may not respond in a rational way to market prices when faced with uncertainty.

Differences in ownership and size can also contribute to distributional problems in access to resources affecting the process of investment. For example, in the presence of segmented financial markets there would be differential effects among firms relative to obtaining loans for working capital and investment. In effect, firms or categories of firms may face different market prices with implications for the impact of changes in macroeconomic policies.

Hence, the efficacy of the market and perfect competition in achieving a social optimum may not be realized in the presence of conditions such as externalities, imperfect knowledge and uncertainty, increasing returns to scale and type of ownership. In effect, the ability of relative prices to reflect the scarcities of various economic goods and, in the process, to provide incentives for firms and individuals can be impaired. Below the discussion looks at the Structuralist and Post-Keynesian traditions, their insights into the functioning of markets and their implications for the allocation of resources for private investment.

1.3 The Structuralist Tradition: An Overview

The Structuralist tradition has as key issues the historical and institutional basis of the functioning of markets and the structural characteristics that accompany the allocation of resources. This tradition argues for the structurally heterogeneous nature of developing economies including 'a more plausible portrayal of firm behaviour' and a more realistic representation of the structure of developing countries. FitzGerald & Vos (1989: 28) state that this representation should be based on each country's own innate specificity relative to 'technological, organizational and social heterogeneity'.

The Structuralist approach is also noted for the study of macroeconomics that reflect precisely the 'features of the agents and the markets within which they operate' (ibid. 1989: 28). Thus, the projection of this approach as being concerned with specific rigidities, lags and market failure versus the state, omits overriding themes on the 'determinate' structure of economies as fashioned by institutions, history and technology as they impact resource allocation and the capacity to adjust (ibid.: 28).[20] Hence in the provision of macroeconomic policy options for developing countries, specificities about the realities of the conditions and behaviour of economic agents and the markets in which they operate can contribute integrally to successful policy outcomes.

Noted for an adherence to a planning approach, an early Structuralist explanation of the term structure in developing countries was presented by Eckaus (1955), who identified features such as market imperfections, limited substitution of factors of production, limitations in the structure of demand, etc.[21] Governments as well as individuals were seen as having a role to play in economic activity, an approach which was also stressed by Lewis who stated:

> … some planning is necessary, since the results of demand and supply are not socially acceptable in their entirety; but planning can be confined to those spheres where it is considered most important to modify the results that market forces acting alone would yield … (Lewis 1955 : 384)

The question of resource mobilization for capital formation entered into the Structuralist debate on overcoming underdevelopment. Basic to this approach is the concept of economic dualism which originates from the presence of uneven growth in development both within and between sectors of the economy and which featured prominently in product and factor markets in developing countries. One of the most influential formulations of this problem is that of Lewis (1954) whose exposition included a model comprising capitalist production (using capital) and subsistence production (using no-capital) and labour supply that was elastic at a conventional wage.[22] In this research, distinctions are similarly made on firms in the private sector in a developing country based on foreign/local ownership or large/small firms, which cut across industry. These distinctions can reflect the ability of firms to acquire resources for capital investment.

The presence of complementarity in demand which underpinned the models of balanced growth, is another important feature of early Structuralists. These models included formulations such as the dependency of consumer demand on food and clothing and income, rather than on relative prices.[23]

Yet another foremost concern in this tradition was expressed in the Structuralist theory of inflation which was viewed as 'a natural accompaniment of growth' and in which the passivity of the money supply is seen as an integral part.[24] In the Structuralist explanation of inflation, propagative elements such as rising wages, increasing cost of living, increasing cost of production in industry and lowering of agricultural productivity transmit inflationary pressures in the economy through relative price changes. In this transmission process, a passive money supply is assumed (Canavese 1982).[25] In the presence of supply rigidities, the Structuralists saw tight monetary policy as leading to unemployment and lower growth.

Another concern of the early Structuralists was expressed by Singer (1950) who questioned the development effects of international free trade using a centre-periphery argument. He showed that the production of raw materials by the periphery (developing countries) and manufactured goods by the centre (developed countries) subjected the former to deteriorating terms of trade contrary to the expectations of free trade. Thus, rather than raising the welfare of all trading partners, the gains from trade were concentrated in the centre(s). He argued for a change in the structure of comparative advantage through the investment of the periphery in industrialization.

The above issues are but a few representations of the concerns of the early Structuralists which were used to produce analyses that were more realistic relative to the structural features inherent in developing countries. These features can affect the efficiency of the market and private investment recovery, as recommended by international institutions.

From the neo-Structuralist perspective, the structure of an economy is defined as:

> An economy has structure if its institutions and the behaviour of its members make some patterns of resource allocation and evolution substantially more likely than others ... (Taylor 1983: 3)

The themes of heterogeneity and the historical and institutional approach to the study of the functioning of markets and developing economies are emphasized in the neo-Structuralist as in the early Structuralist tradition. There is recognition that development entails economic transformation that can be achieved through innovation, 'economies of scale, distributional changes, financial deepening and institutional shifts' (Taylor 1992: 51–52).[26] Taylor (1992) also saw the significant strength of the Structuralist tradition in its awareness of 'historical observation' and the ways in which macro-economic failure can occur. Some of the features of Structuralist modelling are discussed in the following section.

1.3.1 The Structuralist approach: Modelling of and mechanisms of adjustment

The neo-Structuralist approach to modelling, in which the work of Taylor (1981, 1983) stands out, uses models that incorporate structural features of developing countries, and related patterns of behaviour of economic agents.[27] Features of this modelling include: the determination of prices as a mark-up over prime cost which includes labour, intermediate imports and working capital finance costs; saving propensities that differ by class; the dependency of the growth rate of capital stock on the profit rate, or on the rate of growth of capacity utilization. The ability of the firm to mark-up price is indicative of the presence of oligopolistic firms with monopoly power being present in some sectors.

Another feature identified by Taylor (1983) states that excess capacity occurs through quantity adjustment.[28] Sectoral adjustment occurs through price and quantity changes while financial variables are assumed to affect the real side of the economy. Neo-Structuralist formulations therefore incorporate adjustment through 'flexprice-fixprice' routes. Also included in this modelling are differences in demand elasticities by industry with some industries having inelastic demand with respect to price and income.

The structure of production of firms is said to consist mainly of labour payments and imported intermediates, the cost of raw materials obviously being a key factor in production. The exchange rate therefore comes in as a prime factor in the cost structure of the firm relative to the imported aspects of production. In the case of developing countries, capital imports are also needed for the production process since these are not produced locally.

With respect to differences in saving propensities by class, profit earners have a higher propensity to save than wage-earners. This view is derived from Kalecki (1933–1970 [1971]) who saw wage-earners as non-savers and the capitalist class as savers.[29] This point was also articulated by proponents of the early Structuralist school such as Lewis (1954) who viewed savings as being done by the people who receive profits with workers having very small savings.

Following Lewis (1954) in neo-Structuralist modelling, the wage is determined institutionally through a process of class conflicts. Like the exchange rate, the wage rate comes in as a key relative price in the determination of the cost of production of the firm. Producers can therefore adjust through wage reduction or cutting back output or reduction of the purchases of raw materials, which may imply the presence of excess capacity. In the short run, they contend that the production structure is inflexible because the technology which it comprises cannot be easily altered. Therefore, the question of ease of substitution amongst factors of production is not realistic.

For sources of capital, large producers are thought to rely on self-financing through retained profits for investment, while small producers depend on their saving capacity. Firms can borrow at variable rates of interest for working capital purposes. The interest payments (and therefore the interest rate) enter the cost of production of the firm to cover its operating expenses, since it produces in advance of the receipts of sales. This feature is indicative of the overlap between the real and financial sector of the economy (Taylor 1983: 8–9). The ratio of working capital to total cash flow is thought to be large.

There is also an overlap between savers and investors. Informal credit markets are widespread in developing countries while stock markets are not well developed or non-existent. Costs are pushed by interest rate and wage increases through trade union pressure, while devaluation raises the cost of production through its effect on imported intermediates. In essence, Taylor (1983) concludes that adjustment policies, with relative prices and tight money, can have adverse effects on poor economies due to the structural features omitted by the neo-classical model.

Essentially, the neo-Structuralists seek to incorporate in their analyses inherent structures in developing countries that give rise to heterogeneity in economic and social behaviour. As will become apparent later in this research, the analysis of investment and profitability of firms uses as its basis, heterogeneity and structural features inherent in the economy and the firm that determine the pattern of production, and access to and differences in cost of resources for investment.

In another approach found useful in describing semi-industrialized economies, FitzGerald (1993: 36–37) identifies four actors which depict the private sector as:

- *Wage-labour households*, which comprise the poor and unskilled whose entire income is spent on wage goods, and the skilled administrative with savings that is disposed off in the acquisition of housing;

- *Small-household production* and trade units, which are unincorporated enterprises mainly petty traders and artisans, peasants etc. in which there is no separation of the unit within which consumption, production and savings occurs. These functions are based on total household income derived mainly from enterprise profit, and imputed own account/family labour. There are constraints on the financing of investment, the sources of which are surplus income from the enterprise, informal sector credit and some state credit;

- *Private corporate firms*, which consist of modernized companies operating at a large scale and with market power to influence prices but with constraints relative to size of market. Investment financing for the private corporate firms is through depreciation and retained earnings with bank credit that is easy to access used primarily for working capital needs. Access to credit in this group is also through established linkages between banks and financial enterprises with family ownership existing in the latter. Profitability is therefore the major constraint to investment for these firms;

- *Foreign firms*, which form part of a global network including banks and companies, in which there is a reliance on price control such as intra-group sales to mark-up price. Their major source of finance for investment is profits but they are able to procure favoured access to local banks as well as international bank credit. In addition, these foreign firms are also known to borrow internally from their parent or affiliate company abroad.

The above features of developing economies depict a heterogeneous private sector with implications relative to the structure of production, patterns of financing investment and working capital, as well as labour market dynamics. Links are also suggested between ownership and size of firms, access to credit, and type of technology utilized. Structuralism does not deny the market but projects themes that are aimed at having a more realistic approach grounded in institutions and history that are country specific. Out of the patterns of behaviour and changes in micro units, structural features can arise that can inform macroeconomic policies.

Another perspective that looks at the functioning of markets and has some degree of similarity with the Structuralist approach is the Post-Keynesian tradition.[30] Some aspects of this tradition such as the importance of history and institutions, uncertainty, the role of money, and linkages between real and financial variables will be discussed in the next section.

1.4 Elements of the Post-Keynesian Tradition

1.4.1 An overview of the Post-Keynesian approach

As in the Structuralist approach, there is a role for the state in economic progress with the process of historical change deemed to be an important feature. The nature of the market and its regulatory function is a relevant issue to be addressed in this process, due to its role in industrial development (Galbraith 1978).[31] Different writers in this tradition identify various themes as being core to the Post-Keynesian approach. Some of these themes are discussed below.

Main themes identified as forming the basis of this tradition are: the historical process of the economy; the existence of uncertainty which implies that expectations are a necessary part of economic outcomes; and a significant role for economic and political institutions (Davidson 1981).[32] Factors identified by Eichner & Kregel (1975: 1293–314) as being distinctive features of Post-Keynesian economics include: growth and its dynamics, distribution, Keynesian constraints and the microeconomic base.

Institutions have an important role to play in Post-Keynesian economics as in the Structuralist tradition. There are two ways in which institutions feature. First, in the 'transformational growth' that Nell (1994) relates to the development and institutional structure of capitalism as it concerns innovation, problems of the market, etc. Second, the specific nature and roles of institutions are addressed such as the monetary and financial system, conditions of liquidity, wage contracts, etc in a particular era.

Relative to a theory of money, Moore (1979: 120) states that while there is no formal Post-Keynesian theory of money there are distinguishing features which include the recognition of historical time as opposed to general equilibrium, the centrality of finance for investment behaviour, the unique role of labour markets in price determination and the endogeneity of the money stock which is derived from and affects economic processes. The endogeneity process has its roots in Kalecki's treatise on investment financing using 'outside' funds.

Eichner (1979: 34) sees the essence of Post-Keynesianism as the 'relationship between the savings and investment plan of businessmen' also derived from Kalecki (1943 [1971]), who saw the determinants of fixed capital investment decisions as being related to the internal accumulation of capital – undistributed profits and depreciation – which he termed the gross savings of the firm, and from outside funds (debt). This relationship does not however suggest that savings determine investment at the micro level with the interest rate being the equilibrating mechanism but emphasizes the self-financing nature of investment.

The theory of aggregate demand and distribution of Kalecki (1942, [1971]) and Kaldor (1955/56) is identified by Palley (1996: 465) as forming the core of Post-Keynesian analyses.[33] The distribution of income is shown in this construct to be important for the level of aggregate demand and is in turn determined by the saving propensities of capitalists. Thus, the centrality of effective demand is viewed as being linked to the issue of a demand-determined equilibrium through the adjustment of output. This feature is in contrast to the neo-classical supply constrained notion of equilibrium in which aggregate demand features in determining the interest rate (Palley 1996: 12).

The microeconomic basis of this tradition, as is the case with the neo-Structuralist, relies on the significant contribution of Kalecki who as earlier stated reached similar conclusions as Keynes relative to macroeconomic outcomes in which the micro-foundations are used to enrich the understanding of macro processes.[34] These micro-foundations do not, as for the neo-classical economists, assume profit-maximizing economic agents.

Kalecki's work also implies the determination of prices as being based on a mark-up of margin over costs out of which investment is financed. Similar to the neo-Structuralists therefore, firms are oligopolistic in nature; they are not price-takers as in the neo-classical tradition but have the ability to mark-up prices depending on the degree of monopoly they possess.

As in the Structuralist approach, markets are both 'flexprice' – clearing by prices, or 'fixprice' reflecting adjustment through changes in output. Sectors in which there are 'fixprice' markets are mainly oligopolistic in structure. The static oligopolistic structure that depicts this market form as one in which mutual interdependence occurs accompanied by profit-maximizing behaviour, is rejected in this approach.

Another significant aspect of Kalecki's work that has contributed to Post-Keynesian thought is the role of capacity utilization in determining the price mark-up. In the resulting model, the expected rate of capacity utilization becomes the basis for estimating total costs upon which the margin is estimated.

Some of the methodological principles of Post-Keynesian economics were derived from major issues that conflicted with Orthodoxy. Davis (1987: 553) identified three such instances as that of Sraffa's 1926 economic journal, Keynes' marginal efficiency of capital, and the 'Cambridge-Cambridge' capital controversy.[35] The capital controversy disputed the contention that marginal productivity was the basis for distribution in the neo-classical production function.[36] Supporting arguments included the lack of substitutability of capital based on changes in relative prices and the heterogeneity of capital such that a fall in the price of capital may imply switching to another technique that is less capital intensive.[37]

An implication of this controversy is the neo-classical contention that high interest rates can lead to increased investment and that growth in tradables may not be realized because new investment may imply the 'switching' of technology rather than expansion. Additionally, new investment is more likely to be a firm's response to the cutting of costs or increasing of efficiency in order to cut processing time and not necessarily growth-oriented relative to increased employment (Robinson 1973a & 1978, Harcourt 1972).[38]

Hence, this tradition brings to the fore some limitations of the neo-classical approach while highlighting issues surrounding the determinants of private investment, the notion of and behaviour of the firm, and the process by which equilibrium can be achieved. Below specific aspects of the Post-Keynesian tradition are further discussed.

1.4.2 Time, equilibrium and uncertainty

Kaldor (1972) puts forward the view that there is an unawareness of history in general equilibrium analysis of an economy. Markets function in a sequential manner under the constraint of a set of exogenous variables, which determine the equilibrium position, notwithstanding the nature of the initial situation. The process of change is therefore based on the notion of the achievement of a state of equilibrium over time with no analysis of how the equilibrium position was achieved. There is no allowance for analyses outside of a state of equilibrium since the system always moves towards this state.

One level of criticism of this state of equilibrium discussed earlier is based on issues surrounding the presence of increasing returns to scale. Furthermore, a distinction is made between historical and logical time. In the former, time is viewed as reflecting changes in economic structure and institutions, and the irrevocable and unidirectional nature of the past and the uncertainty of the future (Sawyer 1988).[39] Logical time, on the other hand, can move both backward and forward such that decisions/structures created in the past can be easily reversed.

In historical time, history and expectations impact the decisions made by economic agents. In discussing the concept of logical time, Joan Robinson (1980) argued that historical events were introduced into a situation of equilibrium which is void of time.[40] She saw the movement from one point to another in the process of attaining an equilibrium under a framework of comparative statics as being equivalent to a comparison of their positions rather than as a temporal sequence.[41] historical time is therefore linked to the notions of history, uncertainty and expectations relative to investment decisions which cannot be revoked.

The concept of uncertainty, in contrast to risk, implies that there is 'no scientific basis on which to form any calculable probability' about the occurrence of future events (Keynes 1957 [reprint of 1936]: 66). The unpredictability of the future due to uncertainty when linked to the irreversible nature of time can affect the commitments made by businessmen in their production and investment decisions (Arestis 1988: 42). In the course of economic activity, a businessman can obtain debt based on the expectations of future earnings from the sale of production. Uncertainty therefore allows for the disappointment of expectations relative to past investment (Kregel 1976: 209).[42]

In the Post-Keynesian approach ignorance about the future is recognized, unlike the neo-classical approach earlier described in which decisions are made with the assumption of perfect knowledge though there is some allowance for calculable risk. In the neo-classical approach, knowledge about the future is based on rational expectations which ensures that stable prices prevail and social welfare is maximized (Davidson 1991).

Allowing for uncertainty implies that expectations of profitability may not be realized. In deciding to invest, a firm must therefore consider its contractual obligations, in light of uncertainty about the returns to investment. This view goes back to Keynes who reasoned that since production took time, the liquidity position of the firm is crucial for the understanding of how it is able to withstand unfulfilled returns to investment. The introduction then of money transactions, historical time and uncertainty undermined the neo-classical market equilibrium analysis which was based on pure exchange and on perfect foresight in reversible time.

The significance of these concepts to the discussion on adjustment and the private sector is the awareness that, at the time of adjustment, firms in the private sector have a given structure of production, a given debt structure and capital investment which cannot easily be reversed. Firms may have entered into these expenditures based on expectations of future profitability. Since the future is clouded by some measure of uncertainty and expectations may not have been realized, it then becomes necessary for firms to reposition themselves in response to changes in the macroeconomic environment. This re-positioning occurs in historical time not in logical time.

The irreversible nature of investment implemented in the past (to be discussed later) is one factor that militates against the ease of positioning of the firm. The capital investment, the inherited cost/debt structure, labour force and so on may render flexible adjustment futile. The notion of equilibrium implies ease of positioning of the firm, while the notion of historical time makes one aware of the initial conditions faced by the firm based on its historical experience, and the process that restructuring entails. Below, the discussion centres on issues surrounding money and finance, related financial institutions and markets; and provides another angle on the functioning of markets in Post-Keynesian economics.

1.4.3 The endogeneity of the money supply

In IMF-supported adjustment policies, the approach to analysing the balance of payments is viewed as a monetary phenomenon in which emphasis is placed on the specification of the demand for money and the money supply process in an open economy. The custom in this approach was to consider the money supply as exogenous, being determined by the monetary authorities. There are different ways of expressing the equation of exchange in the quantity theory of money. The modern-day version of the quantity theory popularized by Milton Friedman in the foundation of the theory known as monetarism states that ' money is all that matters for changes in nominal income in the long run and in real income in the short run' (cited in Froyen 1993: 71).

Kaldor & Trevithick (1988) see this *modern version of the quantity theory of money* as an integral part of classical and neo-classical economic theory. They state that the monetarists' argument on the effectiveness of control of money income through controlling the money stock was based on a stable relationship between the money stock 'however measured' and national income, and the exogeneity of the former (ibid.: 102–3).

A distinctive feature of Post-Keynesian economics (which allows for a more realistic understanding of the functioning of institutions) is that of the endogeneity of the money supply, which is explained in terms of accommodative and structural endogeneity. Both approaches start at the position that the rate of growth of money supply and credit availability are determined by demand-side pressures within financial markets and that banks extend credit creating money in the process while looking for reserves later. Related debts such as credit for working capital purposes, for the purchasing of durables in the process of production and consumer borrowing are therefore mechanisms by which money is created (Arestis 1988).

This question of the relationship between money and debt was also recognized by Keynes and Kalecki, the former stated that money and debt came into existence simultaneously as contracts for deferred payments.[43] Kalecki posited that deposits created money in his argument on the self-financing nature of investment. He stated that the financing of additional investment by bank credit implies that 'the spending of the amounts in question will cause equal amounts of saved profits to accumulate as bank deposits …' (1942 [1971]: 84).

The divergence in the two views on money supply endogeneity lies in the process by which the banks look for reserves (Pollin 1991: 367). In the accommodative approach, the base money needs of the banking system is accommodated through expansionary open market operations or through the discount window for non-borrowed and borrowed reserves. Thus, there is an absence of quantity restrictions on reserves required by banks (Pollin 1991: 367). In structural endogeneity, full quantitative accommodation is not recognized, in which case private banks practise liability management to permit the growth of lending that need not be matched by accommodative reserves. Efforts by central banks to affect the growth of non-borrowed reserves will impose quantity constraints on the availability of reserves. These quantity constraints occur regardless of the political leanings of the governors or administration in power.

While these quantity constraints are recognized as contractionary, more problematic concerns that necessitate quantity restrictions are inflationary pressures or downward pressures on the exchange rate value to national currencies (Pollin 1991: 374). Thus, in the face of restrictive open market policies, the theory of structural endogeneity holds that the practice of liability management as a means of attracting funds into deposit accounts that require lower reserve requirements enables banks to expand the possibilities of loans and deposits.[44] Private banks are able to generate needed reserves through financial innovations, and the influence on the interest rate is not only under the direct jurisdiction of the central bank but also of the commercial banks.

In the accommodative approach, the Central Bank determines the interest rates (particularly short-term rates) through its influence over the discount rate and open-market operations. Thus, as Kaldor (1982: 24) summed up, the money stock is determined by the private/commercial banks while the interest rate is determined by the central bank which is in contrast to the view of the monetarist school.[45] Under these accommodative circumstances, variations in demand for money by businesses and individuals affect the ability of the authorities to control the money supply. Accordingly, it follows that an increase in bank-lending (deposits) which is accommodated by reserves can affect the ability to control the money supply through open-market operations and the rediscount rate without exposing private banks to the risk of being unable to pay depositors (Kaldor & Trevithick 1981). Two main points of departure between accommodative and structural endogeneity in banking practices are the ability of banks to generate credit without risk exposure relative to their depositors and the manner of determination of the interest rate.[46]

The discussion above not only provides background information on money supply concerns and an understanding of financial sector institutions but is also concerned with monetary and financial policies relative to the availability and cost of credit to firms for investment and working capital, given the nature of the banking institutions. Arising from the above concerns, are issues on the question of banking practices, bank exposure and the lending policy of banks as they may impact on private investment financing and affect the functioning of financial markets. The study, however, does not undertake an in-depth analysis of financial institutions as economic agents.[47] Nevertheless, by identifying aspects of their lending practices to firms, the analysis will attempt to show how these practices affect the performance of firms under adjustment focusing mainly on the availability and cost of credit in financial markets in a developing country. In particular, a critical issue in the research is that of credit-rationing and how it impacts investment financing. This issue is discussed below.

1.4.4 Implications of money supply: credit-rationing[48]

The need for credit to finance investment and working capital needs arises out of the time lag between production and sales. Firms therefore enter into arrangements with respect to debt from the financial system. Credit-rationing is a key contribution to understanding the functioning of financial markets which may not clear by relative prices to produce a social optimum. In segmented financial markets or even within the formal financial system, differentials in the granting of credit can occur. In the next paragraphs, the approaches to credit-rationing as portrayed in the New-Keynesian literature is contrasted with that in the Post-Keynesian literature.

In the New-Keynesian literature, credit-rationing under the assumption of asymmetric information arises out of the inefficiency of the interest rate as a market-clearing device, in which the bank is unable to distinguish between high and low-risk borrowers (Stiglitz & Weiss 1981). New-Keynesians aimed to show the existence of credit-rationing in equilibrium loan markets. Banks, they state, are concerned with receiving interest and also with the riskiness of loans. Since the behaviour of the borrowers cannot be monitored costlessly by the banks, the effect of the interest rate on borrowers are taken into account. The interest rate is therefore used as a screening device to sift out high-risk borrowers who, they argue, are willing to pay high rates of interest with the knowledge that their probability of repaying is low. This feature in which the interest rate is used to sort high- and low-risk borrowers is described as the 'adverse selection effect'. Hence, the interest rate in financial markets under these conditions does not reflect the relative scarcity of capital, nor would it necessary lead to more efficient private investment.

Secondly, the action of borrowers is affected in that – at higher interest rates – the rate of return on successful projects is decreased. At the same time, firms may choose to invest in riskier projects with high returns but low probability of success. In efforts to attract low-risk borrowers, the bank may not lend to identical borrowers even though they are willing to pay above a stipulated 'bank-optimal' interest rate. As a result, risky projects may permeate the loan portfolio of banks while borrowers with more efficient projects are discouraged. This effect is referred to as the 'incentive effect'.

The Stiglitz approach which comes under the agenda of the new neo-classical approach still has at its base the view of economic agents as maximizers but with different behaviour pattern in the absence of perfect information relative to the use of the interest rate. The quality of the resulting private investment projects is therefore affected in this approach either through the discouragement of potentially viable projects or the approval of potentially infeasible ones. Thus, in an era of macroeconomic adjustment the recovery of private investment may not be an automatic outcome of interest rate changes if past investment projects were assessed in this manner. The whole notion of a market determined rate of interest is discredited.

Another approach to the problem of asymmetric information which comes under the New Keynsian tradition is from the perspective of the lender, focusing on the ability of the banks to overcome the problem of incomplete information due to their expertise in gathering information about borrowers, evaluating projects and monitoring loans. Credit-rationing comes into the picture due to the inability of some borrowers to receive loans from one bank though they can receive loans from others.[49]

In the Post-Keynesian approach, the issue of credit-rationing is reflected in the following factors: the presence of a fringe of unsatisfied borrowers, the concept of lender's risk versus borrower's risk, uncertainty, and asymmetric expectations. Also considered are the lending decisions and institutional aspects of banks such as pricing of loans, rationing of credit and the establishment of bank-firm relationships (Wolfson 1996).

Thus, while some aspects of the Post-Keynesian models on money and finance assume well-developed and organized financial markets *vis-à-vis* stock markets, liability management, etc. This approach to credit-rationing typifies a less-developed capital market where retained earnings and bank credit rather than stocks and bonds are the instruments used to raise finance (Studart 1995).

Aspects of this approach are derived from Keynes (1936 [1957]) who saw the presence of the fringe of unsatisfied borrowers as a means by which banks can influence the volume of investment. He also saw the bank's determination to grant loans as based on the relationship between the borrower and the bank. Therefore, a client of long standing with the bank will be less rationed. Borrower's risk and lender's risk also go back to Keynes. These risks affect the volume of investment and are viewed by Post-Keynesians as being related more to uncertainty about the future than to asymmetric information.

The resulting asymmetric expectations imply that both borrower and lender can arrive at different conclusions about the profitability of a particular project, which again may lead to credit-rationing, by the bank. Relative to the institutional aspects of credit-rationing the ongoing relationship between the bank and the lender has been mentioned above. Thus, well-established borrowers with a successful borrowing record may not be rationed as one without a record of borrowing.

Firms are also affected by a lack of objectivity in risk assessment by banks. While it is assumed that there is some objective means of assessing risk, macroeconomic changes may lead to changed perceptions by bank managers resulting in credit-rationing. As is to be expected, borrowers with established 'ongoing' relationships suffer neither from credit-rationing nor increased price and non-price terms. Those borrowers who in the judgement of the bank are deemed to be high-risk or not creditworthy are either denied loans or are charged higher price and non-price terms. This subjectivity by bank managers that leads to credit-rationing may be a systemic aspect of the economy and not just a feature of changed macroeconomic circumstances (Dow & Dow 1989).

In comparing the two traditions, the New Keynesian approach is based on the notion of risk and asymmetric information while the

Post-Keynesian approach introduces the concepts of uncertainty and asymmetric expectations, and the institutional aspects of bank-lending and financial markets.[50] They both provide a more realistic foundation to understanding the problems with respect to credit-rationing and how it can affect access to credit by firms for investment and working capital purposes.

Credit-rationing of firms by banks creates an aspect of firm heterogeneity which is based on the ability of firms of different size/ownership and industry characteristics to be able to access credit or the differential costs of credit to firms. This feature also has implications for the ability of firms to be able to access other resources such as technology, foreign exchange and foreign markets due to financial constraints. One application of credit-rationing is that large or foreign firms or those belonging to key economic activities may be favoured by banks relative to loans for working capital and investment purposes. Small local firms without established and long-standing relationships may, on the other hand, find it more difficult to access credit even though their investment projects may be as viable or better than those of large local or foreign firms.

Like FitzGerald (1993), Sikorski (1996) also identifies a classification of borrowers integrated in a system of risk-sharing relationships with governments. This system often took the form of the imposition of credit ceilings and directed credit policies which favoured some borrowers (priority in development policy) over others (non-priority firms and small urban, informal fully credit-rationed firms). The relevance of these classifications to the country study will be discussed later in the research.

The above concludes issues on the functioning of markets and alternative views based on Structuralist and Post-Keynesian approaches. The next section continues with the role of the private sector under adjustment and its capacity to fulfil this role through private investment.

1.5 The Private Sector: The Basis for Its Role in Adjustment

The focus on private sector development is in part a reaffirmation of the belief in the efficiency of the market mechanism discussed earlier. While there is no clear-cut justification in microeconomic theory for the belief in the superiority of private over public ownership, the argument is intertwined with the debate on market efficiency versus that of the state. From an ideological perspective, the concepts of property rights and residual claimant are used as justification for private ownership along with the belief in individual freedom.[51]

The promotion of economic recovery in adjustment policies through focusing on the recovery of private investment is also aimed at strengthening the private sector to withstand the effects of external shocks arising from the global economy. For example, trade liberalization which shifts the economy from being inward-oriented to export-oriented through the removal of trade restrictions, is aimed at shifting resources from non-tradables and the protected import-competing activities to tradables. This policy should lead to the growth of exports and efficient import substitutes.

The process of adjustment therefore entails a movement in the relative price of tradables to international prices allowing increased international competitiveness of private sectors in developing countries and enabling them to withstand the effects of global changes. Hence, adjustment programs are undertaken partly to enable countries to be able to adapt to changes in the globalization of the world economy. Thus, from the position of a minimal role for the state in the 1983 WDR, the WDR of 1997 highlighted the need for an effective state, albeit to let the market flourish. Some of these views on the state and market relative to the role of the private sector in adjustment are discussed below.

1.5.1 The state-market dichotomy as a justification for private ownership

The focus on a state-interventionist approach within the development paradigm of the post World War II era was related to the market failure that was thought to be prevalent in LDCs. Instances of market failure and inefficiency in allocation and distribution were discussed earlier. State involvement in economic activity in the 1980s was discussed in the context of the relative efficiency properties of market versus non-market resource allocation (Clarke & Pitelis 1993).

In addition, public investment was also thought necessary to enable industrial growth, to redirect capital due to poorly developed financial markets, and to assist in the provision of utilities and of inputs of imported raw materials at concessionary terms (Clarke & Pitelis 1993).

There was also need for the state to intervene towards achieving a more equitable distribution of resources aimed at alleviating poverty. The relationship between public and private investment is also discussed in terms of the crowding in/out controversy. Investment in public infrastructure can facilitate private investment projects which is one of the main channels for 'crowding in'. Alternatively, it is argued that public sector investment in activities that can also be undertaken by the private sector lead to competing claims by the public sector for resources such as finance and skilled labour, therefore crowding out private investment.

The reassessment of the role of the state in the late 1970s was due to the perceived failure of development-planning in LDCs with the belief that governments had contributed to severe economic distortions. Relative to targets that were set, public sector investment projects were said to have performed poorly with a dismal failure of the import substitution strategy (Cook & Kirkpatrick 1988). Therefore, minimizing the state *vis-à-vis* the market was appealed to on the grounds of economic inefficiency of the nation states reflected in bureaucratic delays, incompetence, lack of access to information, corruption etc.[52] Hence, the shift in emphasis back to the market and private enterprise was grounded in the above perception of state inefficiency versus market efficiency.[53]

In line with the above, privatization of state-owned enterprises (SOEs) is seen as a mechanism in adjustment to expand the role of the private sector and to diminish that of the state. One rationale for privatization is the belief that the private sector is capable of superior economic performance than the state (Cook & Kirkpatrick 1988). The focus on private ownership is explained through higher and more consistent profitability, better managerial supervision, greater incentives to perform, absence of political interference, etc. These factors are said to lead to higher output levels, better quality and allocative efficiency (Adam et al. 1988).[54] The presence of incentives is assumed to drive managers in the private sector to profit-maximizing behaviour within constraints of competition, the likelihood of takeovers, etc, which is absent among SOEs.[55]

It is argued that microeconomic theory while making claims of superior efficiency based on perfect competition, does not really deal with or cannot really support the link between ownership and efficiency (Commander & Killick 1988). In general, the arguments for the key role of the private sector are therefore said to be ideologically-based, with no definitive proof or theoretical foundation from the perspective of ownership. The claims to the efficiency of private ownership are linked to the efficiency arguments about the market.[56]

Concerns were however expressed as to the feasibility of a mix of the state and the market. Polyani drew reference to the early period of economic liberalism in which the state played the role of regulating the market because of the inability of the latter to provide society with that which was needed. He therefore advocated a role for both the market and the state emphasizing that one should not be 'eliminated in favour of the other'.[57] In developed countries, private ownership was supported by inherited institutional structures that existed over centuries while the backdrop in developing countries consists of conditions such as the lack of a capital market and other institutions. Therefore a mix of both the state and the market should aid successful restructuring (Rider 1994).[58]

Globally, however, the philosophy that prevailed since the late 1970s called for a reduced state (Cook & Kirkpatrick 1988).[59] The policy of privatization was therefore part of a broader framework of economic liberalization recommended by the World Bank in the 1980s following on policies of public sector reforms. This measure was seen as leading to increased efficiency in resource use. However, in the presence of segmented markets and informational problems, the processes of capital accumulation, allocation and distribution, if left to the market, may not lead to the recovery of investment. This is because the benefits may accrue individually or solely to firms in the private sector that possess certain advantages over other forms relative to capital, technology and economies of scale, preventing the achievement of a social optimum.

There is continued significance given to the private sector in macroeconomic adjustment policies aimed at creating an enabling environment for new and efficient private investment to thrive. Yet the link between private ownership and efficiency is not a convincing one nor does it fully depict the capacity of the private sector to respond under adjustment. The importance given to private investment in structural adjustment leads to the discussion in the next section on its determinants.

1.5.2 Capacity of the private sector: The determinants of private investment

The performance of private investment in the 1980s is comprehensively surveyed in Servén & Solimano (1992, 1993). Among their conclusions were: (a) that both public and private investment rates declined, with the decline in the latter being more severe; and (b) that in many countries there was not any marked response in private investment to adjustment, while other countries were able to restore profitability and correct imbalances only through heavy cuts in real wages. The current study attempts to understand some of the processes involved in firm restructuring in the private sector in the context of macroeconomic policies. From the wide variety of literature on investment, a selection of approaches are discussed, including the accelerator approaches, the neo-classical investment model, Kalecki, Keynes and Keynesian, and the issue of irreversibility of investment.[60]

The accelerator approaches

The accelerator approaches look at investment in fixed capital relative to changes in output. The naive accelerator principle relates the level of net investment to the rate of growth of output. A contraction in demand should therefore decrease investment. A basic form of the accelerator model is:

$$K^d = \alpha Y \tag{1.1}$$

where K^d is the desired level of capital stock which is shown as a constant multiple of output, Y. The flexible accelerator model takes into consideration lags in demand and production in which investment is derived as a function of current output level and lagged capital stock. Another interpretation of the accelerator models considers expectations about future output and incorporates a cash flow variable to represent future profitability which is assumed to have some bearing on future output levels.[61] These models, however, do not consider supply constraints such as capital and raw material unavailability as is often the case in LDCs.

The neo-classical investment model

The neo-classical investment model is based on the concept that factor inputs are optimally utilized when they are functions of their relative prices under conditions of perfect competition. The desired stock of capital is related to the level of output and the user cost of capital, with the latter being dependent on the price of capital goods, the interest rate and the depreciation rate. This model therefore relies on the concept of the 'representative firm' that is responsive to market prices, with all firms facing equal access to credit, with external and internal funds being perfect substitutes, and real and financial decisions being independent. Versions of this model pioneered by Jorgenson & Siebert (1968) considered desired investment as being a function of the ratio of output to the price of capital services.[62]

$$K_t^* = \frac{\alpha\, p_t Q_t}{c_t} \tag{1.2}$$

where $c_t = \left[q_t (1 - u_t w_t)\delta + r_t - \frac{q_t - q_{t-1}}{q_t} \right]$

Equation (1.2) gives a version of the neo-classical model in which the desired capital stock K_t^* depends on the value of output $p_t Q_t$, deflated by the price of capital services c_t, which in turn depends on the price of investment goods q_t, the rate of replacement δ, the cost of capital r_t, the rate of corporate income u_t, and the proportion of replacement cost deductible for income tax purposes w_t.

The assumption of perfect substitutability of factors of production implies that if the cost of capital is low then firms would shift from labour-intensive to capital-intensive production.[63] This approach does not take into consideration the asset-specific nature of some forms of investment and the sunk costs (discussed under irreversibility of investment) which render it impossible to shift from capital to labour-intensive production and vice-versa. This model is also criticized with respect to the static nature of its assumptions and the absence of expectations. Investment is futuristic in outlook, with the uncertainty of the future vis-à-vis relative prices not guaranteeing successful response. In the context of developing countries, the structural rigidities that are present may hinder the smooth mobility of factors of production assumed in the neo-classical investment model.[64]

Kalecki and the determinants of investment

The relationship between gross savings and gross investment at the economy level was such that 'investment once carried out, automatically provides the savings necessary to finance it' (Kalecki 1942 [1971]: 83), i.e. investment is self-financing and is related to the internal accumulation of capital of the firm or its gross savings – which is savings out of current profit and depreciation (Kalecki 1943 [1971]: 83 & 111]).[65] Hence, the equality between savings and investment will be independent of the interest rate traditionally thought in economic theory to equate these two variables. Kalecki saw the use of liquid reserves by some capitalists to increase their investment, as increasing the profits of other capitalists *pro tanto*.[66]

Kalecki's view that loans generate deposits is also a reflection of the self-financing nature of investment (Kalecki 1943 [1971]): 84). This view further lends support to the contention that the rate of interest cannot be determined by the demand and supply of new capital. In his view, the decision to invest is related to the internal accumulation of capital and the increase in profit per unit of time, and is adversely affected by the net increment of capital equipment. With regard to this last determinant, Kalecki saw an increase in the stock of capital equipment of firms as leading to a reduction in its investment plans, basing his argument on the view that that firms are unlikely to utilize the capital market to its fullest potential because risk increases with the amount of capital invested (Kalecki 1942 [1971]: 112).[67]

Keynes and Keynesian approaches

Keynes linked the demand for investment with the marginal efficiency of capital which in turn depends on the prospective yield of a durable asset and its replacement cost or supply price. The inducement to invest will be up to the point where the supply price of a capital asset is such that the marginal efficiency of capital is equal to the rate of interest. Keynes saw the marginal efficiency of capital schedule as the main link through which expectations about the future can influence the present, with the level of confidence being a relevant factor.[68]

Other approaches to investment

The irreversible nature of investment recognizes that outlays entail sunk costs which cannot be recovered in the face of uncertainty about the future. [69] A sunk cost is defined as a visible expenditure that has already been made and cannot be easily recovered (Pindyck & Rubinfeld 1992: 200). The concepts of sunk costs and irreversibility are inextricably linked. The notion of irreversibility contrasts with the neo-classical investment models which are consistent with the reversibility of the investment decision, such that 'the firm faces no sunk costs, no intertemporal profit trade-offs and no irreversible debt burden' – i.e. a reversible investment decision implies reversing the financial commitments used to finance them (Crotty 1992).

Servén & Solimano (1992) emphasized the relevance of uncertainty to the investment decision when one considers the notion of irreversibility. They stated that in the face of uncertainty, firms may find that productive capacity today may lead to excess capital that cannot be costlessly eliminated. Servén (1996: 14) discusses another form of uncertainty in the context of imperfect credibility of policy reform. He stated that uncertainty about the likelihood of policy reversal in adjustment programs may lead to an 'investment pause' by investors faced with irreversible investment projects.

Rodrik (1991) incorporates sunk costs of entry and exit in his model, in which he shows that a reform that favours investment but which is not fully credible, will stimulate an investment response only if the return on capital can compensate investors for losses that may occur if the policy is reversed. With allowances for both uncertainty and irreversibility, the decision to invest is delayed or the projects are 'downsized'. In the face of adjustment therefore the decision to invest is weighed into the amount of confidence that the investor has in the future.

In the disequilibrium models, investment is modeled as a function of profitability and output demand. Firstly, the decision to invest is related to the level of productive capacity and uses as a proxy the degree of capacity utilization, which is indicative of demand. Secondly, the capital intensity of the additional investment that is required is considered as a function of relative prices such as labour and capital costs. While the investment decision takes into consideration current and expected constraints of sales at the firm level, these models are criticized for their simplistic representation of expectations (Servén & Solimano 1992).

The literature on investment and finance looks at various financial constraints on firms in capital markets in the presence of imperfect information and as a result of controlled interest rates and credit-rationing. Hence, in addition to the possibility of investment being affected through the interest rate channel, allowance is made for the practice of credit-rationing (Tybout 1983). The issue of the faultiness of the interest rate and collateral requirements in sifting out borrowers was discussed earlier. The implication is that investment is negatively affected by credit-rationing in the presence of information asymmetry (Stiglitz & Weiss 1981).[70]

Credit-rationing arising from disequilibrium interest rates implies that the rate of investment will depend on the amount of investible funds that the firm has at its disposal. The cash flow of the firm is therefore an essential feature under credit-rationing. Models that depict links between finance and development comprise variables such as retained earnings, bank credit and similar variables representing internal and external funds. Variables from the models discussed above are often incorporated with financial variables such as the ratio of sales to capital stock. Below a few of the empirical studies on investment are highlighted.

1.5.3 Empirical investment studies: Macroeconomic policies and firm studies

In this section a selection of empirical studies on investment are briefly discussed starting with some that relate to macroeconomic policies and also firm-level studies. Studies by Greene & Villanueva (1991) and de Melo & Tybout (1986) found that restrictive monetary policy led to reduced investment because it increased the interest rate and the cost of bank credits. In a macro model by van Wijnbergen (1983), focus was given to the transmission of monetary policy in LDCs through working-capital costs. He depicted firms in LDCs as financing investment, fixed capital stock and working capital using short-term bank credit, retained earnings or loans from the unofficial money market. Bank loans were said to be used almost exclusively for financing working and fixed capital requirements of firms and are therefore directly linked to production. Under these conditions he showed that tight money may initially increase inflation, slowing down production in the process. In addition, the current account may increase but at the expense of investment. Furthermore, a sustained policy of tight money was shown to reduce capital stock and financial wealth in the long run.

Dailami & Giugale (1991) developed a model of firm investment to illustrate the impact of credit availability and price. They showed that both factors should be considered jointly when assessing the impact of credit policy on investment. Estimating the impact of aggregate credit supply and the interest rate for five developing countries, the results show the joint contribution of credit volume and cost to investment.

In studies on exchange rate policies and investment, ambiguity is present in the results; Servén & Solimano (1993) argue that this reflects theoretical ambiguity relative to the net effect of investment given that investment goods contain both domestic and foreign components. A real depreciation of the exchange rate was seen to have reduced investment in studies done by Musalem (1989), Faini & de Melo (1990) and Solimano (1989). Some of the studies conclude that the long-run effect of devaluation may be positive. Relative to fiscal policy it was found that some aspects of government expenditure such as in infrastructure is complementary with private investment (Greene & Villanueva 1991 and Musalem 1989).

Table 1.1 lists a few studies that bear some relation to firm-level investment. The studies by Fazzarri & Mott (1986/87), and Fazzarri, Petersen, Hubbard (1988) focus on links between financial and real variables in developed countries.[71] The main conclusions from these two studies are that financial factors are important determinants of firm-level investment.

The study by Fazzarri & Mott (1986/87) used a large pooled cross-section time-series sample and obtained significant results relative to the effect of internal liquidity and sales on investment. Their results support the position of Keynes and Kalecki that effective demand and financial factors are prime determinants of investment. Fazzarri & Mott (1986/87) also found that the interest expense variable used for cash payment commitments had an adverse effect on investment, i.e. committed cash flow used to service debt acts as an investment constraint. The significance of the sales variable implies some relevance of the accelerator model in explaining investment.

Table 1.1 *Selected firm-level studies on investment/structural adjustment*[72]

Study/Method	Findings
Fazzarri & Mott (1986/87)	
Empirical study of firm data using pooled time series cross-section sample to test the relation between investment and: (i) capacity utilization; (ii) internal finance; & (iii) cash payment commitments.	+ve with sales, +ve with internal finance -ve with interest expense
Fazzarri, Hubbard & Petersen (1988)	
Firm data to test conventional investment models incorporating capital market imperfections and disparities in credit access of firms analysing differences in investment, based on earning retention practices, credit access of firms, sources of funds – internal/external.	(i) For q, neo-classical and accelerator models, the investment of firms that exhaust all their internal finance is more sensitive to cash flow changes than high-dividend firms. (ii) There were differences across firms in the sensitivity of investment to liquidity measures. (iii) Financial effects on firms are greatest in the presence of severe capital market information and for high retention firms.
Steel & Webster (1992)	
Survey of 82 manufacturing firms to analyse the response of small, private enterprise to adjustment; focusing on differences across firm size, subsector and age looking at trends before adjustment and during adjustment focusing on output, employment and investment.	(i) Approximately 50% of micro-enterprises were new firms. (ii) 38% and 44% respectively entered in 4–9 and 10–29 categories to supply low-cost local raw material substitutes such as paints, agricultural implements, etc. (iii) 50% of the sample had purchased new equipment.
Dawson (1994)	
A sample of 210 small enterprises in a study to identify whether structural adjustment has opened up opportunities for them	(i) Devaluation appeared to have pushed prices of some capital equipment beyond the purchasing power of most entrepreneurs; (ii) 25% of the sample had less operating equipment by 1986 adjustment period. Only 5% had more equipment; (iil) few linkages were developed between the informal and formal sectors.
Aryeetey et al. (1994)	
A survey of manufacturing enterprises in urban areas focusing on the impact of liberalization policies	Main results on investment: (i) lack of credit for purchase of capital equipment as suggested by 37% of the entire sample. (ii) 21% of the respondents thought that it was the greatest obstacle to expansion.

In an extension of the above, the study by Fazzarri, Hubbard & Petersen (1988) used alternative theoretical models to study firm investment behaviour under the assumption that internal and external funds are not perfect substitutes. They also assumed the existence of capital market imperfections such that firms have differential access to credit markets. In their results, higher leverage use is thought to lead to increased marginal cost of new debts and to agency problems. It is thought that because of the limited liability nature of the debt contract, the greater the debt-equity ratio the stronger the incentive for managers to act in the interest of the equity owner rather than of the creditors. To pre-empt conflict of interests with managers, creditors may stipulate debt equity ratios or working-capital requirements which limit the investment behaviour of managers. As a result of favouring equity owners, increased financial costs to firms result from failure to pay the principal and interests.

In their model, firms were classified according to degree of retention of dividends, the assumption being that faced with high-cost disadvantage of external funds, the retention practices of firms contribute to differences in the impact of financial variables on investment. Firms may pay low dividends if they need finance for investment while those with high retention ratios have the ability to access funds internally and externally. In general, the results showed that the investment of firms that use all or most of their internal funds are more sensitive to fluctuations in cash flow than those that are able to pay high dividends. Liquidity has a greater effect on investment for low-dividend than for high-dividend firms.

The results above point to two important issues: the importance of heterogeneity of firms and their access to capital markets, and the relevance of financial factors such as internal versus external finance for investment. To the extent that it incorporates features of developed economies such as the application of the Tobin q model and principal-agent practices, the model presents limitations for consideration in developing countries. However, the concern with differential access to credit is quite appropriate to LDCs.

In the Steel & Webster (1992) study in which the firm size comprised those with 4–29 employees, the focus was on constraints that would affect firms' ability to respond to changing incentives of adjustment. They hypothesized that new firms (reflective of new investment) would emerge and existing small firms would be more responsive to incentives. They found that investment took place 'at least among small firms' through the emergence of firms that supplied low-cost substitute as a result of increased import costs. Approximately 50 per cent of the firms had purchased some capital equipment since adjustment. Aryeetey et al. (1994), in an expansion of the study above by Steele & Webster, found that firms had problems with accessing credit for purchase of capital equipment.

In the Dawson (1994) study, the main finding on investment was that devaluation appeared to have pushed prices of capital equipment, tools, etc. beyond the reach of entrepreneurs. There were also few linkages developed between smaller firms and more formal entrepreneurs.

Of the models and factors that were discussed, the accelerator model can be modified to consider lags in response for use in developing countries. As emphasized earlier, the financial factors need further examination in a developing-country context, relative to the imperfections in capital markets and credit-rationing behaviour by financial institutions. Empirical studies that consider constraints of finance or capital-market imperfections on investment in developed countries seem to suggest that financial factors act as constraints to the capacity of the firm to invest. The survey by Servén & Solimano suggests that the recovery of private investment was not realised and therefore questions the capacity of the private sector to fulfil its designated role in adjustment policies through the recovery of private investment. The context, however, in which firms in a private sector adjust vis-à-vis the performance of private investment is not altogether clear.

1.6 Structuralism and Other Traditions – Comparison

This section attempts to synthesize the earlier discussions on the varying approaches to economic development in order to clarify how the Structuralist approach differs from the other approaches, particularly the neo-classical, with regard to adjustment and private sector investment. Some of the major tenets in these approaches are contrasted below:

Market, structure and history

In the Structuralist tradition a central theme is that economic development should be rooted in the structural, endogenous and historical features that exist on a case by case basis. Fundamental structural features of developing countries and areas include: the existence of persistent unemployment and underemployment, the coexistence of modern capital-intensive technique side by side with labour intensive traditional modes of production; differentials in capital returns in different sectors limitations in the structure of demand, and rudimentary financial markets. These features result from factor market imperfections, limited technical substitutability of factors of production, divergences between demand and supply under conditions of full capacity utilization, and income distribution differentials.

On the other hand, the neo-classical approach holds the view that the market provides the basis for resolving resource allocation problems while at the same time achieving economic welfare. In the presence of perfect competition there exist markets for foreign exchange, labour, capital and commodities that will clear through a particular set of prices. In the process of adjustment there are winners and losers based on a criteria of efficiency. Firms or activities that are not efficient will not survive.

Relative prices and factor substitutability

In the neo-classical tradition, ease of factor substitutability is assumed in maximizing efficiency and achieving economic growth. The achievement of optimal resource allocation for investment is through profit-maximizing behaviour. The policy framework which has the neo-classical tradition as a base emphasizes relative prices, which include the use of a competitive exchange rate which encourages exports, a positive real interest rate which encourages savings, the liberalization of foreign and domestic trade through the reduction of barriers, the removal of price controls, general deregulation, the creation of incentives to promote the entry of foreign capital, the reduction of the budget deficit and the practice of prudent fiscal and monetary policies which will control inflation and encourage savings into productive investment.

Structuralism does not accentuate the use of relative prices. It does not see that the application of liberalization emphasizing relative prices will lead to optimal resource allocation in every single case.

Role of the state

In the application of adjustment, the neo-classical perspective does not recognize any structural rationale that will imply a difference in the size and role of the state in LDCs as compared to industrialized countries. Neo-classicists advocate a reduction of the role of the state as a producer of goods and services; and they view government intervention as leading to market failure rather than being a solution to the inability of the market to fulfil the efficient allocation of resources. Hence, public investment is viewed as crowding out private investment.

Strucutralists, on the other hand, believe that where there is pervasive market failure due to structural and historical problems, there is a role for the state to intervene by promoting and stimulating those markets which are incomplete or are in need of strengthening. Liberalization policies of adjustment may not have the desired effect of increasing the volume and efficiency of investment in the presence of initial conditions that are country specific and of structural heterogeneity based on size, ownership, and industries with implications for the allocation of resources. These conditions may preempt exchange and interest rate liberalization from expanding exports, and achieving efficient allocation of investible funds in response to market determined relative prices.

Heterogeneity versus homogeneity

The concept of a representative firm facing identical prices and market conditions, cost free entry and exit, and ease of factor substitution as mentioned above, is the basis of the assumption of homogeneity in economic behaviour which is embraced by the neo-classical tradition. In the presence of perfect competition and profit-maximizing behaviour, economic welfare is maximized.

This view is disputed by the Structuralists who allow for differences based on structure and history. More precisely, the notion of a representative firm facing identical prices and market conditions is rejected in favour of firms facing differential access to resources, different market prices and conditions. As a result, heterogeneity in economic behaviour underlies the approach of this tradition and is a key point of difference between the two traditions

Post-Keynesian and Structuralism

While both the Post-Keynesian and Structuralism approaches have common themes, there are areas of differences. Both perspectives agree that the understanding of the process of economic growth in developing countries is linked to insufficient productivity growth in the wage good sector, particularly food processing. Money supply is viewed as endogenous in both schemas. They both emphasize the role of income distribution in the growth process.

Subtle points of difference lie in what the Post-Keynesians see as the causes of the problems of economic development. For example, while the structuralists state that the labour-saving nature of technology implies that more labour using technology should be applied to achieve an appropriate balance between capital stock and labour; Post-Keynesians see the unemployment problem as arising from the use of more capital intensive technology and insufficient investment.

While structuralists identify population growth as a major cause of under-development, Post-Keynesians see population growth as intensifying rather than causing underdevelopment. Structuralists stress the need to insulate the primary producing sectors from the adverse effects of international trade; Post-Keynesians see that improving the terms of trade will not necessarily improve unemployment.

In light of the above comparison, the hypotheses to be articulated should shed some light on the various ways in which economies successfully adjust and on how features such as the pattern of ownership, the access to resources (such as adequate credit and technology), and export market access can make a difference during adjustment.

1.7 Conclusions

This chapter considered the role of the private sector in adjustment. Starting with the origins of enterprise development, the changing emphasis in analyses from the classical political economy to the neo-classical tradition fashioned the view of adjustment relative to the achievement of a market equilibrium with individual efficiency being seen as socially optimal. The Keynesian challenge, the contribution of the early Structuralists and neo-Structuralists, and the Post-Keynesian approach provided a more realistic portrayal of the market based on historical, structural and institutional settings, which can be useful in depicting the existing conditions in LDCs.

Thus, issues relative to finance, historical and institutional structures, etc. were discussed from the perspective of the Structuralist and Post-Keynesian traditions. In this context, the resulting heterogeneity of firms that determines the access to resources as fashioned by history and institutions was identified as a key issue in the analysis of adjustment. Some patterns of heterogeneity that can be identified are foreign/domestic ownership, size of firms, activity which also reflects access to credit and differences relative to technology used in production.

Linked to the debate on the efficiency of the market versus the state, the justification on claims of efficiency of private ownership was found to be essentially ideologically-based. The capacity of the private sector as examined from the potential for investment looked at the determinants and models of investment which could be applied in developing countries. The performance of private investment was shown to be generally poor over time, based on a comprehensive survey of issues and studies surrounding private investment. This research is therefore an attempt to understand the dynamics of the private sector – the pattern of firm behaviour relative to production and investment activities and their reaction to macroeconomic adjustment.

The WDR (1997), in discussing the 'appropriate' mix of market and government, expressed the view that the state should enhance its role in making markets grow:

> ... these policies help position an economy to benefit from competitive market forces. These forces provide the right signals and incentives for economic agents to accumulate resources, use them efficiently, and innovate. Over time ... getting the basics right can have a dramatic effect on living standards... (WDR 1997: 46)

The role of the state, its capability and effectiveness is of course relevant. However, the failure of private investment over time can also be investigated through microeconomic responses to macroeconomic policies of adjustment, taking into consieration the structural problems of developing economies. It is this issue that the current study seeks to address. The next chapter brings into focus the private sector in the case of Trinidad & Tobago.

Notes

1. References to the role of total investment or private investment in adjustment include: Thomas et al. (1991), Meier & Steel (1989), Corbo et al. (1992), Oshikoya (1994), Benjamin (1992), Servén & Solimano (1993) and several others.
2. A competitive equilibrium is said to be Pareto optimality optimal, with such a criterion implying that there is no other feasible allocation which would make some individuals better-off and no individual worse-off.
3. Influential neo-liberal writers include Kreuger (1974, 1981, 1985, 1990), Balassa (1978, 1984), Lal (1983, 1984), Bauer (1976, 1984, 1991), Friedman (1980), and Little, Scitovsky & Scott (1970).
4. This reference includes Adam Smith, Ricardo, Malthus, Bentham, Say, Senior and Mill. Concerns with the theorizing of capital accumulation is also identified with Marxism – Marx, Blanc and Kingsley. In a broad sense, therefore, these persons come under the umbrella of classical political economics. Preceding this tradition, however, was the work of the Physiocrats – of note is Quesnay (Walsh & Gram 1980).
5. A major role was assigned to capital accumulation by Adam Smith who saw labour being put into motion by capital with the rate of progress of an economy being seen as proportional to its rate of investment (Meir 1984: 107). Ricardo and Marx were also main contributors to this theme. Ricardo, with his theory of value and distribution, showed the changes in the relative shares of land labour and capital in the accumulation process. Marx, starting with a critique of Ricardo, focused more on the income distribution and the detrimental consequences of the capitalist system (Oser & Brue 1988).
6. Production of everything that was needed for oneself was thought to be inefficient, which led to a coordinated division of labour and increased productivity (Hunt & Sherman 1992).
7. An instrumental feature of economic liberalists' contribution to economic theory were laws which they held to be universal, such as: the law of comparative advantage, the law of diminishing returns, Say's Law and the Malthusian theory of population (Oser & Brue 1988).
8. See also Meier (1984: 106–29).
9. The neo-classical school began with independent writings by Jevons, Menger and Walras, and Marshall in the 1870s (Walsh & Gram 1980, Deane 1978). There were, however, differences between these economists. Walras, for example, used marginal analysis in the application of markets and the conditions for general equilibrium. Menger concentrated his use of marginal analysis on the problems of price determination.

10. Sen (1983) argues that the concern that neo-classical economics 'did not apply terribly well to developing countries' should come as no surprise – since 'it did not apply terribly well anywhere'. Dudley Seers (1964), arguing on this same point, presented one alternative model tailored to suit an underdeveloped economy.
11. As expressed by Lewis (1955: 384) 'the results of demand and supply were not socially acceptable' which warranted some measure of government intervention.
12. Early focus on economic growth as distinct from economic development was the Harrod-Domar analysis in the late 1940s. Developed within a Keynesian framework, the model depicts net investment through its addition to the capital stock leading to an increase in the productive capacity and in potential income.
13. Lal (1983) argued that peasants have been shown to respond to relative prices, with the factor substitution of inputs being the same for developing and developed countries. Hence trade restrictions were viewed as leading to rent-seeking behaviour and welfare loss. While market imperfections were recognized, it was thought by the neo-liberals that imperfect market mechanisms were better than imperfect planning, with the label 'dirigiste' being used by Lal to include those critics who question the validity of neo-classical economic theory in the Third World.
14. The general theorem of the second best states that if there is introduced into a general equilibrium system a constraint which prevents the attainment of one of the Paretian conditions, the other Paretian conditions although attainable are in general no longer desirable. Lipsey & Lancaster (1956–7) showed in their exposition of the theorem of the second best, that in the presence of imperfect markets with more than one distortion, the result of removing any one distortion is ambiguous.
15. Mishan (1960: 210) argued that '... perfect competition is neither a necessary nor a sufficient condition for meeting the allocative rule, or the optimum conditions ...'. The relationship between the perfectly competitive system and a Pareto optimality optimum holds only under a situation of equilibrium. For the firm, profit maximization occurs where marginal revenue equals marginal cost with price equal to the latter under perfect competition.
16. Efficient consumption assumes that all individuals place the same relative values on all products and is explained through the notion of the positioning of indifference curves. A basic concept in welfare economics is that of value judgement which embodies ethical connotations about an individual's welfare, utility or satisfaction, and is also the basis for the prescription of 'desirable' or socially acceptable policies (Nath 1969).

17. Pareto optimality optimality though necessary is not sufficient for welfare maximization. To satisfy the latter an explicit welfare function that states the objectives of a society is required.
18. The construction of a factory by one producer may harm the drinking water of villagers (negative externality) or on the other hand may provide an outlet for the sale of home production for others (positive externality). See Nath (1969).
19. Additionally, uncertainty brings with it information costs as well as factor costs.
20. See Chenery (1975: 310) and Little (1982: 20–22) for exposés of structuralism that stress these issues as being the main concerns.
21. Chenery (1975) also places Paul Rosentein-Rodan, Ragnar Nurske, W. Arthur Lewis, Raul Prebisch, Hans Singer and Gunnar Myrdal among the early pioneers in the formulation of the Structuralist hypotheses.
22. Blomstron & Hettne (1984: 18) describe Lewis' exposition as the most influential, while Meier (1984: 152) sees Lewis' dual economy model as the 'simplest in construction yet the richest in perceptive insights'.
23. This follows from Engel's Law.
24. Campos (1961) cited in Arndt (1985).
25. Also see Olivera (1970) for a discussion on passive money.
26. Also identified as being the concern of development were innovation, economies of scale, and distributional and institutional changes over time (Taylor 1992).
27. The focus on the neo-Structuralist approach is due to its strong microeconomic base.
28. This may also be the case in developed countries.
29. This work which spans the period 1933–70 was a selection of essays that were published in 1971.
30. Chakravarty (1987) discusses the similarity and differences in these two traditions.
31. From a more pragmatic angle it is argued in the Post-Keynesian tradition that in an effort to escape from, or reduce the influence of the market on their lives, individuals attempt to have control over their incomes (Galbraith 1978: 8–11).
32. Cited in Sawyer (1988).
33. See his diagrammatic depiction of the centrality of aggregate demand in understanding a range of issues in Post-Keynesian economics in Palley (1996: 17). These references to Kalecki and Kaldor were cited in Palley (1996).

34. For example, Kalecki's micro-analysis was used primarily to formalize his understanding of the development of output and the trade cycle (Kriesler 1987).
35. Among the issues raised by Sraffa was the assimilation by the neo-classical tradition of diminishing and increasing returns, into a single law of non-proportional returns to scale. He also took issue with the assumptions of atomistic competition and self-interest on the grounds that interdependence in decision-making was pervasive (Bienfeld 1991).
36. The capital controversy arose out of the search for a model suitable enough to allow for the analysis of accumulation and distribution between wages and profit (Harcourt 1972).
37. Queries were also directed at the concept of capital and its financing and the issue of what it comprises (machine, equipment, etc) from which arose the problem of aggregation.
38. A few references exist by Joan Robinson on this topic (1973a, 1973b, 1978, 1980).
39. A distinction is also made by Setterfield (1995) between 'irreversible' time, in which the sequence of actions cannot be inverted to restore the initial conditions even though these conditions can be restored by a subsequent process, and 'irrevocable' time, in which the sequence of actions cannot be inverted nor any subsequent process be used to restore those initial conditions.
40. 'Time in Economic Theory', reproduced in Sawyer (1988).
41. Joan Robinson argued: 'When a mathematician says "*y* rises as *x* falls", he is implying nothing about temporal sequences or saying anything different from "When *x* is low *y* is high"' (Robinson 1980: 34). This quotation from Joan Robinson was explained to her by Professor Samuelson.
42. Keynes argued that in the formation of expectations it is more reasonable to attach more weight to facts about which there is more confidence than uncertainty (Keynes 1957: 148 reprint of 1936).
43. Outside money is seen as comprising gold and silver. Keynes argued that money came into existence along with debt as cited in Arestis (1988). Palley (1996) also presented a model of inside debt and its effect on aggregate demand.
44. Minsky's seminal article (1985) stressed that liability management is seen as exerting upward pressure on interest rates but for an indefinite period such that quantity constraints on reserves may not impose further increases on interest rates.

45. Pollin (1991: 370) also sees as key points in the accommodative argument the notion of proportionality between the relative changes in loans and reserves; the close substitutability between borrowed and non-borrowed reserves supplied by the central bank; and causality in the interest rate from the central bank to the financial markets.
46. A more radical approach is given by Nell (1984: 65) who argued that the real balance effect in the neo-classical argument necessitated money holdings to consist of 'outside' money, i.e. money that is not another economic agent's debt (inside money). Since most money is in fact bank obligations, or that of government and other financial intermediaries, then a change in the real value of an agent's money has repercussions for the money of another agent. The real balance effect therefore does not consider that both household and firms have financial obligations and claims denominated in money.
47. Palley (1996) makes a distinction between debtors and creditors in a macroeconomic model exploring the foundations of price adjustment. Sikorski (1996) looks closely at financial institutions relative to the application of monetary policies in developing countries. See also Studdart (1995) for some insights into the banking firm and related literature on finance in a monetary production economy.
48. A useful piece of literature in this area is written by Wolfson (1996).
49. This approach like that of Stiglitz & Weiss (1981) is said to be derived from the New-Keynesian tradition (Wolfson 1996).
50. See Pollin (1991) for further insights into similarities and differences of the two approaches to the endogeneity of the money supply in Post-Keynesian economics.
51. The residual claimant concept views private ownership of firms as essential for the purpose of a residual claimant for the income-generating assets (Clarke & Pitelis 1993). See Eggertsson (1990) and Barzel (1989) on property rights and economics. Lensink (1996) makes reference to the neglect of property rights by neo-liberals.
52. A few references on this question of the state versus the market include: Brett (1988), Savas (1982), Dutt et al. (1994) and Colclough (1993).
53. The explanations of the immense growth of the state were: from a neo-classical perspective relative to the demand for state services by sovereign consumers; public choice theories which focus on utility maximizing policies of state officials, who benefit from enhanced state activity. The state was organized to serve special interest groups such as businessmen and officials which resulted in rising administrative costs (Friedman 1969 and Wolf 1990, both cited in Clarke & Pitelis 1993). The Marxist explanation of the size of the state was one of increasing concentration and centralization in

a sector in which labour was unproductive and was linked to the falling rate of profit.

54. Allocative efficiency is defined as a situation in which consumers' needs are met at prices which reflect the cost of provision (Cook & Kirkpatrick 1988).
55. The scale of operations of some private firms may have bearing for take-overs and may form an argument for public ownership, since private monopolies can insulate themselves from competition.
56. One criticism is that competition is often equated to ownership and may not therefore be sufficient justification for opening up the private sector, in contrast to increasing the scope of the public sector (Cook & Kirkpatrick 1988). Problems of managerial capitalism and principal-agent, where divergence exist between objectives of owner-manager or principal-agent, can occur irrespective of ownership.
57. Karl Polyani and the contradictions of the 1980s in Bienefeld (1991) – Polyani's concept of a 'double movement' of the market and society heralded the emergence of a modern state. See also Mendell & Salée (1993) for the concept of Polyani's 'double movement' of state and the market.
58. In the context of transition economies, Rider (1994) also argued for a pragmatic approach to the process of restructuring since these economies 'moving through real historical time are not simply to be regarded as laboratories for a static allocation exercise'.
59. There were concerted efforts in the late 1970s by Thatcher in Britain and Reagan in the United States to minimize the state through privatization and subcontracting of activities. Some references of the privatization experience in the UK include: Pirie (1988), Savas (1982), Nell (1984).
60. See also Clark (1979), Evans (1969), Crotty (1992), Jorgenson (1971); and for studies in developing countries, see for example: Benjamin (1992), Blejer & Khan (1984), Khan & Reinhart (1990), Servén & Solimano (1992), Greene & Villanueva (1991).
61. See Clark (1979) on investment behaviour and performance.
62. The concept of the capital structure describes the assets – fixed and current – that a company owns and the method of loans or risk capital that has been used to obtain the assets.
63. See Jorgensen & Siebert (1968) for a variation of the neo-classical model and arguments countering some of the neo-classical assumptions by Stiglitz (1988); Crotty (1992) and Gordon (1992) on the substitutability of internal and external funds.

64. Competing with the neo-classical model was the concept of the marginal Q in which financial policies and events affect aggregate demand by changing the valuation of physical assets relative to their replacement costs.
65. From his proposition that workers do not save, and that capitalists gain what they consume or invest, Kalecki (1933 [1971]: 79–80) established that real gross profits in a short period are determined by decisions made by capitalists about consumption and investment in the past.
66. Additional investment can be financed by bank credit, 'outside funds' – loans from banks based on entrepreneurial capital.
67. This was based on his principle of increasing risk in which lenders demanded higher interest rates as the investment level of the firm increased.
68. The Keynesian disequilibrium approach uses determinants of investment which incorporates profitability, the demand for output, capacity utilization and the capital intensity of additional capacity with the latter dependent on the relative prices of labour and capital (Servén & Solimano 1993).
69. See Pindyck (1991), Bernanke (1983), Servén & Solimano (1992), Caballero (1993).
70. Tybout (1983) also looked at cost and liquidity effects in a model of credit-rationing.
71. Because of the lack of firm-level information in developing countries, a couple of firm-level studies from developed countries are included.
72. See Servén & Solimano (1992) for a comprehensive survey of the effects of macroeconomic adjustment on investment.

2 The Private Sector in Trinidad & Tobago

2.1 Introduction

This chapter describes the context of the study relative to what constitutes the private sector in a developing country, Trinidad & Tobago, focusing on the environment in which the firm operates and the patterns of behaviour and structural features that characterize the economy and the firm. These structures and patterns have been influenced by the historical processes and institutions through which the economies of many developing countries have evolved, giving rise to a heterogeneous private sector. Thus, the aim of this chapter is to provide some insights that can afford a better understanding of the impact of macroeconomic policies in a developing country context. Some of the main issues discussed in this chapter are:[1]

- intellectual traditions, policy frameworks, and institutional settings that have influenced the economic structure of Trinidad & Tobago with focus mainly on monetary/financial considerations;
- economic performance during the different phases of the policy thrust;
- emergent industrial structure of the economy; and
- development of the firm with focus on the manufacturing sector.

In examining the historical processes, the interest is on influences that still affect firms today, to see whether fundamental features of firm behaviour from the past still persist.

Section 2.2 contains a brief overview of the main intellectual economic traditions that influenced both the industrial structure and government policy in Trinidad & Tobago. Section 2.3 looks at some aspects of the industrial policy framework arising out of these traditions, including the incentives that were created for the development of the private sector. The economic performance and industrial structure of Trinidad & Tobago for the period 1966-98, subject to the availability of data, are presented in section 2.4. Section 2.5 looks at issues surrounding the development of the firm in Trinidad & Tobago, mainly access to credit but also market orientation. Conclusions follow in section 2.6 with annexes providing additional tables and other relevant information.

2.2 The Intellectual Tradition: The Origin of the Firm

2.2.1 Main traditions in Caribbean economic thought

The past experience of economic development in the Caribbean fashioned an economic structure that determined the pattern of production and firm behaviour that evolved and is common to many of the countries of the region. An examination of the intellectual traditions that influenced the policy framework and the economic structure of Trinidad & Tobago is best understood in the context of Caribbean economic thought. Four distinct theoretical intellectual traditions were identified by Bernal et al. (1984) as:

- neo-classical and Keynesian economic thought,
- Lewis' strategy of development,
- radical economists, largely the plantation school and other Structuralists, and
- Marxist political economy.

The neo-classical/Keynesian synthesis instructed the period of colonization which was the pre-1962 era (Trinidad & Tobago became independent from British colonial rule on 31 August 1962).[2] The initial colonial period, beginning in the late 15th century, was one of expansionary mercantilist policy in Europe. Following World War II, the movement to independence and the development of trade links with the USA, the debate over the post-war economic development of the British West Indies culminated in Lewis' theses on industrialization for this region.

This strategy of Lewis was eventually subjected to ideological criticism by the radical economic tradition which explained problems of backwardness and underdevelopment in Caribbean economies through the historical processes under which they were formulated during European expansion in the mercantilist period. While Lewis' strategy formed the intellectual basis of attempts at industrialization in the Caribbean region, it was not necessarily applied in its entirety. Sections 2.2.2 and 2.2.3 explore these two economic traditions relative to the insights that they provide on the current structural features of Trinidad & Tobago's economy.[3] The implications of these traditions to the industrial structure that emerged are further explored in section 2.2.4.

2.2.2 Lewis' strategy of development: Insights into the theoretical base

Post-war industrialization in the Caribbean is understood primarily through the challenge made by Lewis to the colonial authorities. After a series of articles on this issue, Lewis based his case for rapid industrialization on overpopulation, citing a population growth rate for the region of about 1.5–2% per annum and the inability of agriculture – which was already shedding labour – to absorb more people.[4] His model depicted a case of economic dualism relative to the presence of 'capitalist' and 'subsistence' sectors in Caribbean economies with the former sector using reproducible capital from which income accrued to capitalists, while the latter sector was noted for low labour productivity and for the absence of reproducible capital.

While one interpretation of Lewis' model is in the context of agriculture-industry, the economic dualism described above cuts across this sectoral breakdown such that there were highly capitalized industries or mechanized plantations side by side with primitive techniques/peasants (Lewis 1954: 408). The wage at which the surplus labour was available was set institutionally.[5] Limitation of size based on a small domestic market meant that industries were to be geared towards exports. His model also identified the following features: a low savings rate due to the low share of capitalist profits to national income. Other sources of capital were credit creation and inflation.[6] The process of growth and employment creation depended critically on the reinvestment of capital, i.e. the use that is made of the capitalist surplus (Lewis 1954: 412).

Prior to the formal presentation of his model in 1954, Lewis had recommended a resource-based strategy for the industrialization of the British West Indies.[7] Eventually he shifted his position to a combination of import-substitution industrialization for home consumption and an export-oriented strategy geared to employ labour (St Cyr 1980). Due to the shortage of capital the suggestion was for the use of foreign capital.[8] The role of the state was to facilitate the transfer of foreign capital through the passing of ordinances which provided incentives such as duty-free concessions on imports of capital goods and tax exemption.

2.2.3 The radical tradition: The plantation school and its contribution [9]

The radical tradition partly centred on the foreign domination of the economy by firms which, it argued, distorted the development consciousness; kept the decision-making process abroad; led to a misallocation of resources; and discouraged internal dynamism of the economy (Best 1968).[10] Sugar production was organized in 'total economic institutions' known as 'plantations' and was almost exclusively for exports with very little economic exchange between the 'plantations' that existed in the hinterlands since they were all producing the same crops and all depended on external dynamism (Beckford & Witter 1980).[11]

The dual economy feature was identified as foreign and residentiary sectors, the latter being the domestic economy.[12] There was little value added accruing to the domestic economy since there was negligible sugar processing with the bulk of the processing being done abroad, i.e. production was largely in the form of 'the raw material' (unrefined sugar). Resources that were realized from the staple production were not used for the creation of profitable production elsewhere in the economy, which constrained the expansion of the residentiary sector.[13]

With the introduction of mercantilist capital, joint stock-trading companies emerged, consistent with the provision of initial venture capital, shipping and supplies from the metropolitan as well as chattel slavery. These joint stock companies were comprised of proprietors, planters, merchants, bankers and others who put up joint stock (Best 1980). Available capital fueled the growth of the foreign-oriented plantation sector. The residentiary sector used little or no capital, producing mainly for subsistence. There were little backward or forward linkages towards further processing and accrual of value added to the local economy.[14]

Characteristic features of production as depicted in this model included the following: the dependence by the plantations on imported raw materials, supplies and capital goods from the metropolitan countries; dependence on metropolitan demand; absence of backward and forward production linkages within the economy; and a financial system biased against the funding of projects for the development of domestic enterprises. The folding-up of plantations due to indebtedness of planters to foreign merchants led to the development of the domestic sector: cultivation of cash crops, provisions for domestic consumption, and crafts, the appearance of artisans and petty tradesmen. The plantation system was so deeply entrenched in the economic and social fabric of these economies that the behaviour of the firm was said to be reflective of the institutional framework – the resources, the production structure, the markets and so forth. (Best 1968: 323).[15] Some of these patterns are discussed further in the next section relative to the contribution of these traditions to understanding the industrial structure.

2.2.4 The intellectual traditions and the emergent industrial structure

The theoretical exposition of Lewis' theses on industrialization in the British West Indies identified features in the structure of Caribbean economies similar to those discussed under the Structuralist tradition in Chapter 1. The main structural features that emerge are: heterogeneity in the economy through the presence of economic dualism, which is reflected in segmented capital markets leading to unequal access to credit; differences with respect to technology – capital-intensive versus rudimentary tools; income distribution biased in favour of capitalists; domestic-market size limitation; low saving rates; and profit and debt-financed investment for industry.

Relative to the plantation school, the following features come to the forefront: an externally-propelled economy with an industrial structure comprising larger foreign enterprises with highly specific, capital-intensive and modernized technology; a small share of wages relative to profit; a pattern of production/ consumption tied to imported tastes and imported intermediate and capital goods, imported managerial personnel and organizational procedures; the absence of lateral linkages with local firms due to parent-affiliate relationship. The large share of profit relative to wages did not accrue to the domestic economy but to the parent company abroad.

The existence of profits was the rationale for the existence of the foreign firm in the hinterland with the perpetuation of this parent-affiliate relationship posing barriers to the emergence of indigenous enterprises. The local enterprises that developed were depicted as differing from the foreign firms relative to the capacity of the latter to be able to have ease of access to cheaper raw materials and capital, to credit and foreign exchange, to technology and to foreign markets. All these aspects were facilitated to the foreign firm through the parent-affiliate arrangements including for the provision of venture capital from abroad.

In Lewis' strategy of industrialization it was assumed that local people would have learnt 'the tricks of the trade' relative to the techniques of production, marketing, the use of resources and so on (St Cyr 1980: 20). The plantation criticism of this strategy was that the excessive openness of the economy and the addition of more foreign capital reinforced the old mercantilist ties rather than the achievement of economic transformation. The strategy of branch plant manufacturing led to the residentiary sector engaging in 'import-replacement' activities, as against 'displacement', taking the form of the importation of parts and components which were assembled rather than the importation of the finished product (Best 1980: 181).

The assembly-type industries created new rigidities in imports through the heavy reliance on imported components. The result was therefore a private sector, producing similar products, placing a high burden on the import bill, producing for domestic consumption, at a high unit cost, not absorbing masses of surplus labour and contributing negligibly to government revenues (Levitt & Best 1975: 36).[16]

Apart from the repatriation of profits by foreign firms, the lack of capital for the development of indigenous industries was reinforced by the banks through their loan policies. This feature served to hinder the development of indigenous enterprise. As a result, the issue of ownership differentiated between firms that were foreign or locally-owned or firms owned by white and non-white residents. Under this interpretation, ownership was critical as far as access to capital in this period and remains pervasive over time.

The persistence of some of the features of the past experience in Caribbean development manifested itself in the form of a 'fractured and partial capital market' in which the financial system was noted for the transfer of funds from affiliate to parent company in the metropolitan country and discriminatory credit policy to the disadvantage of domestic firms.[17] Consequently, the situation with respect to the pattern of extending credit by metropolitan banks was that, in general, credit was not made available to local entrepreneurs despite the receipt of savings of local persons with high incomes. Instead, the banks favoured credit to the distribution sector, directly or indirectly, for the purchasing of consumer durable goods (cars, etc), either imported or locally assembled. Loans by these banks to industry showed a bias in favour of foreign firms, or joint ventures between local and foreign companies (Levitt & Best 1975: 57).

The appearance of a shortage of capital was therefore treated as a constraint, but the real issue was said to be the unavailability of the surplus that was generated in the staple sector or from the banks for the use of the other sectors in the economy. Best (1980) argued that the economy generated surpluses which accrued in specific sectors such that there was capital available for investment but it was not available to the sectors that needed to develop. The question of financial constraints to industrialization is also disputed by St Cyr (1981) who argued that consistently throughout the years the economy was generating surpluses, part of which were being reinvested.[18]

Given the diagnosis of structural financial constraints there was a need for financial institutions to transfer funds from sectors that generate surpluses to those that did not or to indigenous entrepreneurs that could not generate the required finance needed for investment. Given the above backdrop in the evolution of Caribbean economies, the focus below turns more specifically to Trinidad & Tobago and its policy framework.

2.3 Industrialization in Trinidad & Tobago: The Policy Framework

The post-World War II period, particularly the post-independence period, saw the emergence of active governments in the Caribbean region in an effort to promote economic growth and employment. In the early periods, as discussed above, the economy of Trinidad & Tobago was dominated by sugar, which was followed by the domination of petroleum after its discovery in the early 20th century. In this section, the distinction is made in phases of government policy to highlight the pre-independence and pre-oil boom phase (1950s to 1973), the oil boom period (1974–81), and the post-oil boom and adjustment period (1982–94). It is of course impossible to give in this study a comprehensive picture of government policies and performance in its entirety. Because of data limitations, adjustments are made in a later section in depicting the performance of the economy. Elements of the industrial policy of Trinidad & Tobago are discussed highlighting where possible the main policies implemented in each period.

It was stated above that the development of indigenous manufacturing pursuits was at a distinct disadvantage initially due to a colonial-based monetary system and production that was geared to satisfying external demands, technology and so forth. In addition, the colonial policy did not favour industrialization in the British West Indies including Trinidad & Tobago. This policy formed the basis of Lewis' challenge.[19]

The manufacturing sector as it eventually emerged was of an import-substitution nature but, as Best (1968) noted, with high import content. Changes at the political level in the 1950s/independence period, the oil boom of the 1970s and the post-oil boom/structural adjustment periods further conditioned the process of industrialization in Trinidad & Tobago. In what follows, elements of the policies implemented in the different phases of industrialization are discussed.

2.3.1 Pre-Independence to pre-oil boom period: The 1950s to 1973

The colonial response to the calls for industrialization in Trinidad & Tobago resulted in the recommendation for the setting up of 'secondary industries' with aid from government. A number of incentives were sug-

gested such as: releasing of foreign exchange for purchasing duty-free imports on capital equipment; protective tariffs and the removal of barriers to exports through agreements with foreign governments; and tax exemption and assistance in procurement of raw materials (St Cyr 1981). Legislation to this effect was implemented through the creation of the Aid to Pioneer Industry Ordinance and the Income Tax Act, which officially entailed:
- duty-free concessions on imports of capital equipment;
- exemptions from payment of income tax for five years;
- unlimited carry-over losses from one year to the next;
- tax-free distributions of profit.

The Income Tax Act was further amended in 1955 to provide manufacturers with accelerated depreciation in the post tax-free period. The Trade Ordinance of 1958 offered protection to local industries against unfair practices. Also in that same year, a Customs Duties Dumping and Subsidies Ordinance was introduced. These were but a few ordinances geared towards the industrialization thrust of investment promotion and employment generation.

Active planning by the government was intensified with the coming into power in 1956 of the People's National Movement (PNM) government, headed by Eric Williams, who attempted to implement the strategy of Lewis. There were three five-year plans aimed at industrialization for satisfying the employment needs and diversifying the economy away from the dependence on petroleum.[20] The objective of the First Five-Year Plan (1958–62) was the promotion of manufacturing through the investment of public capital and the development of skills. The industries were not only to be domestic users of resources but were also to brely on the advantageous presence of fuel in the economy. They were also to be geared for local consumption. While Lewis suggested a mix of exporting and import-substituting industry, the latter was actually implemented.

With the establishment of the Industrial Development Corporation (IDC) in 1958, the government put in place some amendments to the existing incentive legislation and provided new legislation to guard against unfair practices.[21] Incentives created and monitored by the IDC and other arms of government included income tax holidays, duty-free concessions on raw material imports, factory shells, the provision of infrastructure in the form of industrial sites with roads, electricity and water. Other measures aimed at protecting infant industry included the setting-up of a negative list which limited imports of products that were manufactured locally, protecting these sectors from external competition.

The implementation of this First Five-Year Plan, while improving the social and economic infrastructure and giving development incentives to enterprises, led to a fiscal squeeze (St Cyr 1981). The strategy as implemented failed to reduce unemployment and income inequality in the country. The diversification of the economy away from the dependence on oil as articulated in the Third Five-Year Plan (1969–73) was not achieved.[22] The establishment of the Caribbean Free Trade Area (CARIFTA) in 1968 also saw an amendment to the Customs Act of 1973 to implement higher import charges for goods from outside the Caribbean region.

The economic framework for the achievement of a diversified economy was a mix of fiscal, monetary and financial policies aimed primarily at the mobilization of domestic financial resources through increased local ownership of financial institutions, the encouragement of investment and the penalization of consumption. The Central Bank was instituted in 1964, assuming functions such as the management of government accounts and the establishment of reserve requirements for commercial banks. During the 1960s, exchange controls on foreign currencies were put in place, at which stage the Trinidad & Tobago dollar was convertible into sterling and could be affected by the devaluation of the pound.

Commercial policy was used to protect potentially viable industries, encourage manufactured exports, strengthen regional integration, and develop and widen ties with Latin America. National participation was to be deepened into productive sectors and inter-industry linkages were to be developed such as agro-processing and petrochemicals using revenues from oil to build up the petrochemical industry (St Cyr 1981).

Impatience with the slow pace of changes promised in the Third Five-Year Plan by the PNM government led to political and social upheavals in 1970 and brought about some measure of change in the complexion of business. In 1970, Trinidad & Tobago was the scene of Black Power demonstrations. One of the underlying causes for the marches was economic disenchantment with the policy of industrialization which was seen as having failed to reduce unemployment significantly.

Calls were made for the government to nationalize the sugar, petroleum and banking industries. In the wake of these demonstrations, which almost led to an overthrow of the government, a foreign bank was nationalized and major equity was acquired in the sugar industry.[23]

This upheaval saw the increased emergence of non-white businesses. To wit, the establishment of a small business unit in 1970 as part of the IDC was aimed at correcting some of the anomalies that prevented persons of African and Indian descent from entering the business sphere. The Black Power uprising was therefore the backdrop for the thrust towards nationalization, which was articulated but not implemented in the Third Five-Year Plan.

Essentially, despite gaining independence and moving towards industrialization, there were still structural factors relative to credit access, ownership and so on, that influenced economic development and affected industrial performance. The oil boom of the 1970s enabled the implementation of the move towards nationalization as well as the strategy of resource-based industrialization. This period is discussed below.

2.3.2 The oil boom period: 1974–81

With the oil boom of the 1973/74 and 1978/79 years, the nationalization thrust proceeded with the acquisition of companies in the oil industry as well as ailing enterprises in the manufacturing sector which were on the verge of bankruptcy. During the period of the oil boom, the government further proceeded to invest in oil-based industries or those requiring heavy energy consumption of raw material inputs such as petrochemicals – including methanol, urea and ammonia production. Changes were made in both the pattern of ownership and the activities, with greater emphasis given by government to resource-based industrialization strategy, either wholly government-owned or as a joint venture with international firms.

Consequently, the role of government in economic activity was intensified. This role was reflected in increased public sector employment and the nationalization of firms in almost every sector including the purchasing of ailing private enterprises to preserve employment. Government also acquired minority interests in several other enterprises. From the 1960s to the early 1970s, the classification of persons with jobs showed that government workers comprised approximately 18% of persons with jobs as compared with over 30% in the 1980s.[24] Additionally, there was heavy state investment, which at times overshadowed that of private investment. Available figures show, for example, that in 1982 public sector gross capital formation was 58.5% of total capital formation and about 50% in 1985 (Republic of Trinidad & Tobago National Income Report 1981–91).

During the oil boom period there was a continuation of the protection offered to local industry in the non-oil manufacturing sector, the development of heavy energy export-oriented industries in steel and petrochemicals, and massive government participation through these energy-based industries. With investment in the construction of roads and public buildings, the state expanded its role in economic activity.

The boom in the petroleum sector was, however, accompanied by declining production in this sector. While there was positive growth in both the traded and the non-traded sectors; the rate of growth in the traded sector was less than that of the pre-oil boom growth and also that of non-traded sector growth in the oil boom period. In effect, expansion of the traded sector, a reversal of 'Dutch disease' effect, was at a declining rate compared to the pre-oil boom period. The textile industry, in particular, experienced negative growth. Assembly experienced positive but lower growth rate than the pre-oil boom period. The oil boom, its sectoral effect and the management of the boom marked the beginning of the problems relative to the need for structural adjustment in Trinidad & Tobago (Harrison 1994).

2.3.3 The post-oil boom and adjustment period: 1982–94

The 1970s were a period of rapid economic growth, fueled by oil price increases, the implementation of resource-based industrialization and intensive public investment programmes. These factors contributed to the drain of foreign exchange reserves and increased external indebtedness. With the end of the oil boom, the reduction in government revenues left the economy with fiscal and external deficits which will be discussed more fully in section 2.4.2.[25] Exchange controls were introduced to limit demands on foreign reserves. For example, a ban on garment imports other than for personal use was applied in 1987 to protect this industry. Container-loads of garments were particularly targeted and subjected to Customs Duty.

The 1980s saw the start of efforts at economic restructuring. Efforts were made to streamline public expenditure and capital, but they resulted in increasing unemployment. The incentive structure of the private sector also changed. The deteriorating balance of payments and foreign reserves position, which led to the appearance of fiscal and external deficits in 1981, culminated in a 33% devaluation in 1985 when a dual exchange rate regime was introduced. In 1987, with a change of government close to the end of the previous year, the new government embarked on a medium-term adjustment programme. Some details of the early and later adjustment measures are discussed below.

Adjustment policies: 1982–94 [26]

Officially, the adjustment programme relative to receipt/commitments of loans from the international financial institutions started in 1988/1989. However actual adjustment measures started in 1987, with cuts in salaries of public officers, a devaluation in 1988, tightening of liquidity and other measures. Consequently, it can be said that official commitment towards the medium-term economic programme leading up to official financing occurred in 1988.[27] The first phase of finance for the official start of adjustment was received in 1989. The adjustment programme for the initial period was supported by two (2) Stand-by Arrangements in 25 January 1989 and 27 April 1990 with the IMF and Structural Adjustment Loan.

The rescheduling of the external debt also formed part of the measures that were recommended by the international institutions. Some details of the events of adjustment are given in Annex II with the sources of the information in the references. The policies for the immediate pre-adjustment and adjustment period are outlined in Boxes 2.1, 2.2 and 2.3.

Monetary and financial policies, which had bearing on private investment, were among the earliest measures used in the application of adjustment. Some specific elements of this policy are highlighted in Box 2.2 for the period 1982–88. Restriction of the money supply growth rate and the movement towards positive real interest rates were two key measures used to tighten liquidity.

The 1989–94 period of adjustment saw the continuation of the implementation of policies relative to trade liberalization, exchange rate

Box 2.1 Main adjustment measures, 1982–88

- A devaluation of 35% in 1985 was followed by unification of the exchange rate and a further 17% devaluation in 1988.
- Monetary and financial policy (see Box 2.2).
- Reduction of exchange controls on visible trade items.
- Tax reform which included the reduction of both personal and income-tax levels and the implementation of a 15% value-added tax (VAT).
- Tighter control of public expenditures to reduce the fiscal deficit; tighter management of public sector investment programmes; divestment, liquidation and restructuring of state-owned enterprises (SOEs); increases in public utilities tariff.
- Rescheduling of a portion of the external debt payments.
- Relaxation of the exchange control policy.
- Liberalization of the trade regime – dismantling of negative list, removal of 40% of items in 1988.
- Reduction of transfers and subsidies.
- Improvement of the private sector incentive framework through trade reform measures.
- Reduction of price controls.

devaluation, and monetary and financial policies aimed at stabilizing the level of foreign reserves. A devaluation of approximately 35% along with managed floating of the dollar in 1993 was one of the highlights of this period. Removal of most of the items on the negative list that debarred imports of these manufactured products continued during this period. At the end of the 1994 period, the actual implementation of trade liberalization continued with a decrease in the import duty tariff to 60% in 1994 and scheduled reductions of 30% in 1995 and 1996, and 20% in 1997.[28] The Common External Tariff (CET) with the Caribbean region was also to come into effect by 1997. These tariff rates were pushed back and the CET was to be implemented by the middle of 1998.

2.3.4 The private sector: The policy thrust

During this adjustment period, the private sector's role was defined relative to a new role for the state, which reduced its participation in manufacturing and related activities, and focused its investment in the provision of infrastructure such as water and sewerage, health and edu-

Box 2.2 Specific measures of financial and monetary policy, 1982–88

- The cash reserve requirement of non-bank financial institutions was increased by 5%.
- In 1984, the statutory reserve requirement that commercial banks were required to hold was increased to 17% of their deposit utilities from a requirement of 9% and marginal reserves of 15% of any increase. Other adjustments to this instrument were made in 1986 and 1987 - in the latter year through a directive from the Central Bank that resulted in an increase in the reserve requirement.
- Relatively contractionary monetary policy through reduced growth rate of money supply, particularly in 1988.
- Restriction of credit to state enterprises in 1988.
- Increase of rediscount rate in 1983 and 1988.
- Maintenance of positive real interest rates from 1984.
- Financial support arrangement between Central Bank and commercial banks because of tight liquidity conditions.
- Modification of selective credit controls relative to consumer loans.
- Greater transparency through introduction of financial reforms – Companies Act, the Insurance Act, Banking Act, etc. – to increase competitiveness, capitalization, regulation and institutional capability.

cational services. Essentially, the objectives of restructuring were to create an incentive framework for a more competitive private sector for the increase of private investment and exports and to be in keeping with movements towards trade liberalization.

The policies toward the private sector therefore fitted into the overall objectives of this period, which was the attainment of sustainable growth via income reduction. Thus, private sector framework incentives were improved primarily through financial, monetary and trade policies: exchange rate devaluation to fuel the export thrust through increasing international competitiveness; trade liberalization to remove the barriers to trade such as removal of export bias through tariff reductions; disbanding of import restrictions; and tax reforms. The dismantling of trade barriers and the focus on export-oriented growth were to ultimately achieve closer integration into the world economy and a more diversified economy.

In effect, the policy goal of the Medium-Term Policy Framework 1994–96 (MTPF November 1993) was to increase the participation of

Box 2.3 Main adjustment measures, 1989–94

- Increase of the rediscount rate.
- Other measures aimed at the tightening of liquidity.
- Removal of directives to commercial banks with respect to credit policy.
- Devaluation of the exchange rate by 35% and managed floatation thereof.
- Removal of exchange controls.
- The holding of foreign exchange accounts was made more widespread.
- Removal of most items from the negative list by second quarter 1992.
- Introduction of import surcharges and anti-dumping legislation.
- Increased liquidity in the system 1994/95.
- Phased reduction and revision of tariffs, reform and implementation of Common External Tariff (CET) with CARICOM – the period 1994–98 were scheduled to reach set targets.

the private sector as the primary source of incremental investment and growth, including the promotion of exports as the 'foundation of economic growth and employment generation' (MTPF 1994–96: 2).

From the angle of state-labour relations and private sector response, Maharaj (1991) described the dismantling of the welfare state in Trinidad & Tobago with business associations backing the liberal policies of adjustment and labour being emasculated. She argued that in the process of adjustment there were changing patterns in labour control, which became employer-dominated and with features such as political party loyalties and class-consciousness becoming prominent aspects of existing state/labour/private-sector relationships. Links between the business elite and the political directorate are other facets of the differentials in business response that are perpetuated in the application of adjustment policies in Trinidad & Tobago. Further insights into the response of business groups will be discussed under market orientation in section 2.5.3.

In the sections that follow the focus is on government policy in trade and finance as they have affected the environment within which firms in the private sector operate.

Further insights into monetary and financial policies: Evidence of financial repression

Monetary and financial policies were some of the main adjustment measures implemented during the early stages of adjustment. The policy instruments throughout the years from 1966 onwards included targeting of the reserve requirements through specifications of cash reserve balances of commercial banks, and persuading the commercial banks to hold secondary reserves of a specified percent of total deposits. Between 1966 and 1973, there were also alterations of the rediscount rates in order to relate domestic interest rate structure to that of the UK bank rate. Changes in the Central Bank rediscount rate were signals for commercial banks to alter their rates accordingly.

From 1973 to 1983, the rediscount rate was inactive as a policy instrument, given that the commercial banks did not need to borrow from the Central Bank, but it was reactivated after 1983. In 1978, the Central Bank Act gave the President of Trinidad & Tobago the power to fix the level of interest rates payable on deposits and chargeable on loans and advances which, however, was not exercised as a direct measure to control interest rates. In so far as there was a prolonged variation of the rediscount rates, it served the purpose of suppressing the interest rates to a low level.

Selective credit controls were also instituted during the 1970s and early 1980s because of the Central Bank's concern with lending for consumer purposes and the guiding of finance into productive activities; however, they were not implemented by the direct imposition of interest rate ceilings to selected sectors. Credit controls therefore took the form of directives relative to the lending of loans to foreigners or to owners of companies who were foreigners. Other measures included variations in the minimum down-payment on loans for consumer durables, and directives relative to the extension of credit for non-businesses. To the extent that there were exchange controls on capital transactions which were applied over a long period, there was a policy of financial repression in the form of financial restrictions on the interest rate, which did not reflect international rates and thus resulted in negative real interest rates.[29]

While it is argued that financial repression was not acute in the case of Trinidad & Tobago, there were credit guidance with respect to loans, changes in reserve requirements, rediscount rates and exchange controls, which indirectly led to a situation of financial repression.[30] For example, directions were given relative to the percentage down-payment on consumer loans. These measures were aimed at the fulfillment of the government's development goals to control inflation and to manage the exchange rate.

Furthermore, an indicator of financial repression is the presence of negative real interest rates. Table 2.2 and Figure 2.2 show negative or very low positive period averages for both the real lending and deposit rates which provide evidence that there was some measure of financial repression or restriction. It is argued that the appearance of negative real interest rates over a prolonged period from 1972–84 was not due just to a policy of repression but was more a reflection of high liquidity, administrative regulation and the setting of the interest rates by banks. While the negative interest rates may not have resulted through deliberate policies of imposing ceilings, the outcome was the same as having these ceilings in place.

Hence, in the case of Trinidad & Tobago the interest rates were said to be set collectively by the commercial banking system (Bobb 1986). The passing of the Central Bank Act of 1978, the use of moral persuasion, the varying of the rediscount rates and bank rates, collusion between banks, and discriminatory interest rates all served to produce a rate of interest that was not – in a strict sense – market-determined. In the context of Trinidad & Tobago, financial repression therefore did not take the conventional form of interest rate ceilings or the direction of credit to particular sectors or groups of firms as is normally articulated in the literature on financial liberalization versus repression.

In assessing the conduct of the monetary policy of development, a gap was noted between theory and practice in the policies put in place by the Central Bank of Trinidad & Tobago (Farrell 1989). For example, in the 1969/71 period, one of the articulated policies said that interest rates should be higher than those in the UK. In practice, the interest rates were consistently below the UK level. The reasons given for this policy divergence were very high liquidity (despite a rapid expansion in Trinidad & Tobago of loans, advances and investment in government securities) and pressure from the government to keep interest rates low. This last reason lends supporting evidence to the presence of final repression.

The Central Bank's position on interest rate policy was that savings, including financial savings, was related to income. The view that real interest rates must be positive in order to increase savings for investment

Table 2.1 Summary of selected policies by phases of industrialization

Period	Policy/Area	Main elements
Pre-Independence to pre-oil boom: 1950s to 1973	Import substitution industrialization	An incentive framework was created with the following features: – Protective tariffs – income tax exemptions – duty-free imports on plant equipment & raw materials – setting up of an IDC – encouraging of Joint Venture Schemes with foreign partners – trade & custom ordinances
Oil boom phase: 1974 to 1981	Resource-based industrialization; economic diversification; intensified public sector participation	– continuation of incentives to industry and protectionist policies – protection of regional industries – investment wholly or joint government to government arrangement in energy-based/heavy energy-using industries
Post-oil boom to pre-adjustment period: 1982 to 1988 and	Reorientation of industry to international focus; reduction in public investment	
Adjustment period: 1989 to 1994	Tight monetary policy, financial policy – Exchange rate policy, devaluation and managed floatation	Devaluation of 35% in 1985; devaluation of 17% in 1988 and devaluation of 34% and floatation of the currency in 1993
	– Efforts towards trade liberalization Privatization of state enterprises	Dismantling of the negative lists except for a few selected items

Note: Other details in Boxes 2.1 to 2.3

was not supported. In an era of adjustment to higher positive real interest rates, the reliance of the business community on bank loans would prove burdensome to business activity (Farrell 1989).

Efforts at trade reforms: Private sector reorientation

Measures included under trade reforms were highlighted above. The aim of these measures was to re-orient the private sector and the economy towards becoming internationally competitive through facilitating and promoting exports and encouraging foreign investment. Adjustments to the exchange rate were partly efforts to facilitate access to international markets. Other policy measures to facilitate the export thrust are discussed below.

Changes in the legislation and institutional framework also supported this thrust. One of the key institutional changes was the merging of organizations that were geared to assist business development into one body.[31] In this context, the former Industrial Development Corporation (IDC) which was set up in the 1950s was streamlined and merged with the Export Development Corporation (EDC) to form the Tourism and Industrial Development Corporation (TIDCO). The Small Business Development Company Limited (SBDC) was established to enhance small business development. With the advent of TIDCO, special trade facilities were also established to assist firms. One of these is Trade Point – a trade facilitation centre aimed at increasing participation in internal trade by small and medium-sized producers and to reduce transaction costs. Services that are offered include: statistics on foreign market, customs information, country and company profiles, commercial contacts, and internet advertising; however, no assessment has been done on the success of this venture.

Assistance to businesses also came from the World Bank-funded Business Expansion and Industrial Restructuring Loan (BEIRL). Scheduled to start in 1992, this programme actually started in 1996. One component of this package was the setting up of the Export Technical Assistance Facility (ETAF) located under TIDCO. The objectives of ETAF are to assist exporters, actual and potential, in searching and penetrating export markets. Thus, firms are given assistance with export expansion plans to enter new markets through a provision of a 50/50 cost sharing grants, i.e. exporters qualify for 50% of the expenditures that are incurred in entering eligible export markets up to a maximum of

$US60,000 per firm or $US100,000 for companies within the same group of firms. Activities that qualify for assistance are all manufacturing export activities, agriculture including livestock, service exports such as entertainment and tourism, and exports to all markets supported.

Initial information available on the performance of ETAF showed approximately 700 exporters listed. Since ETAF is open to sectors other than manufacturing, such as livestock, agriculture, and entertainment, it is difficult to assess what these 700 firms represent relative to the manufacturing sector. However, out of this number approximately 30% are small firms (<10 persons employed or an asset base of less than $TT250,000), 50% were medium-sized firms (classification by asset size was not clear). In addition, 10% of these firms were new exporters, while the remaining 90% already had experience in export markets. Another aspect of this project is the assistance of firms in obtaining ISO certification, which clearly puts them in an advantageous position in negotiating export markets.

While this programme started outside of the period for which data in the study is analysed, it however gives an idea of efforts to aid the private sector beyond 1994. In this context, given that the majority of firms in operation are small firms, ETAF appears to have made little inroads into the problem of market penetration for these firms. In addition, only a small percentage of firms assisted were new exporters.

In the context of the policy framework discussed, the next section briefly reviews the performance of the economy.

2.4 An Overview of the Economic Performance of Trinidad & Tobago

2.4.1 Relative price movements

Table 2.2 shows the price incentives under which the private sector operated over time. The real exchange rate defined as the price of traded to non-traded goods appreciated during the periods 1974/80 and 1981/87, primarily through 'Dutch disease' effects of the 1970s oil boom.[32]

The real depreciation in the period 1988/94 reflected the devaluation and supporting measures such as wage reductions during that period. The managed floating of the exchange rate reflected a depreciation of approximately 8.6% in the period 1995/98. Closely related to the de-

Table 2.2 Selected price relatives and changes in the CPI

Variable	1966/73	1974/80	1981/87	1988/94	1995/98
Real exchange rate (RER)	149.9	125.4	93.3	105.2	136.8
Minimum wage rate	43.5	125.4	396.2	472.8	533.5
– real lending rate (RLEND)	2.5	–4.5	1.2	3.8	8.5
– real deposit rate (RDEP)	–1.3	–9.9	–5.4	–2.6	1.4
Inflation rate (INFL)	6.1	14.8	10.6	8.9	4.6

Source: Own worksheet based on data in various statistical reports of the Central Statistical Office, Trinidad & Tobago (base year 1985=100 for indices).

valuation is the movement in real wages. While there was an increase in the minimum wage in the 1988/94 period of about 19.3% over the previous period, this was offset by the devaluation of 15 and 33% during 1988–94. In the more recent period (1995/98), the real lending rate increased from 3.8% in 1988/1994 to 8.5% while the real deposit rate finally became positive but at a very low level (1.4%). These real rates of interest were supported by a low inflation rate in this period of 4.5 % rather than by decreasing nominal rates that in fact increased (See Figure 2.2). Figure 2.1 below shows the movement in the RER in which real devaluation seemed to have lagged behind nominal devaluation for the years 1985 and 1988 but was realized for the devaluation of 1993.

Figure 2.1 Bilateral RER with the US

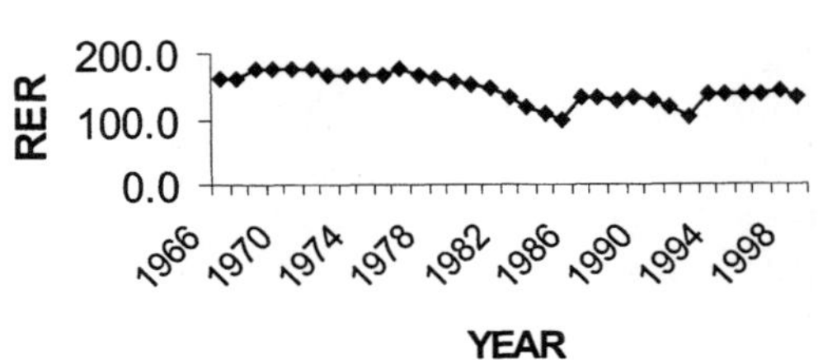

Figure 2.2 Real lending and deposit rates and the rate of inflation

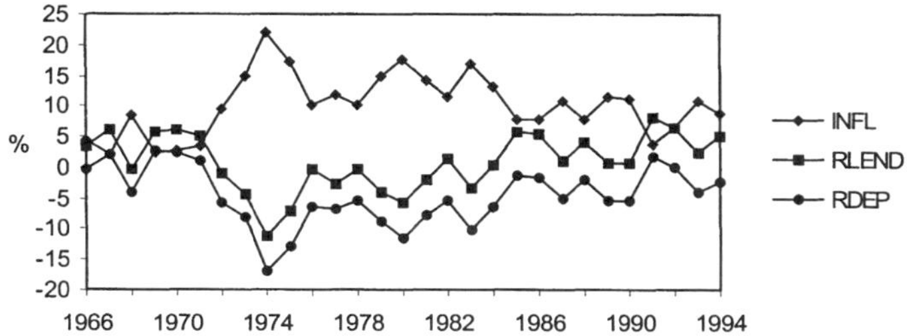

Nominal interest rates on loans and deposits were slightly higher during the 1998–94 period compared to the period preceding adjustment. The rate of inflation (measured by ΔCPI) was at its peak of 22% in 1974 during the first oil boom, contributing to high negative real lending and deposit rates of interest in that year. Pre-oil boom (before 1974) rates of inflation ranged from about 2 to 10%, approximately, to average 6% for the early period of 1966/73. While in the 1981–87 period, prior to the start of adjustment, the rate of inflation was on average 10.6%, decreasing to approximately 9% during the period of 1988/94.

Increases in nominal lending and deposit interest rates, and single digit inflation for some years of the adjustment period contributed to the occurrence of positive real lending rates of interest. The difference how-

Figure 2.3 GDP growth rates by period

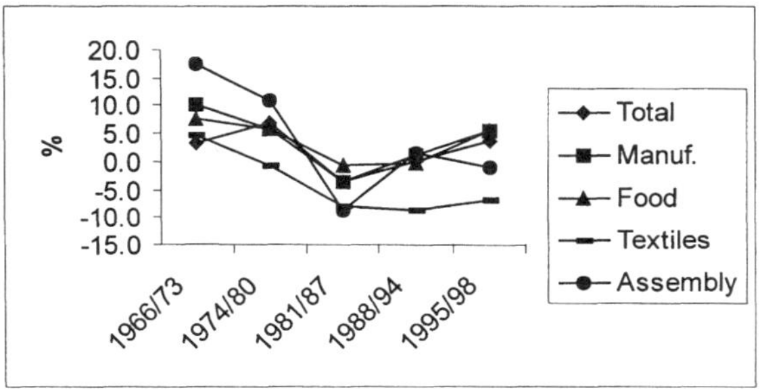

ever between the nominal lending and deposit rate (interest rate spread) is a contributing factor to negative deposit rates for most of the years as reflected in all the period averages, and is evident in gains made by banks.

2.4.2 Other macroeconomic indicators[33]

There was negligible but positive growth rate in real GDP in 1988/94 as shown in Table 2.3 and Figure 2.3. Traded sector growth rate was 2.1%, with agriculture showing approximately 4% and manufacturing 1%, with some sectors such as textiles contracting by as much as 8% (see Table A2.1 in Annex 1). While there is evidence of improved performance during this period, the movement in GDP for the individual years shows that the apparent improvement was not sustainable during the 1988/94 period. Tables A2.1 and A2.2 provide further details such as the GDP growth rates for the 1988/94 period.

In the period of application of adjustment policies, there were mixed performances in the sectors. Increasing exports can be attributed to increased revenue from oil, ammonia and urea production. Comparing the pre-oil boom period (1966/73) with the post-oil boom/adjustment period (1988/94), the growth rates of the latter are far removed from that of the former. Given that declining oil prices was the reason behind the economic collapse, the adjustment measures to date have failed to restore growth rates that existed during or prior to the oil boom period. The unemployment rate as shown in Table A2.1 also worsened

Table 2.3 GDP growth rates by sector (1985=100) [34]

Sector	Period				
	1966/73	1974/80	1981/87	1988/94	1995/98
Agriculture	0.8	–3.2	0.9	5.3	–4.5
Petroleum	0.2	–2.6	–2.0	–0.3	0.7
Manufacturing	10.1	5.6	–3.9	1.1	5.5
Traded	6.4	3.3	–2.8	2.3	2.7
Non-traded	3.7	11.4	–4.6	–0.4	4.8
Total GDP	3.1	7.0	–3.5	0.0	3.5

Source: Central Statistical Office, Republic of Trinidad & Tobago, National Income Reports 1966–85, 1981–91, 1990–94.

during the period of adjustment, with a period average of 22.1% of the labour force.

Data for the 1995/8 period shows the more recent economic performance of the country. Real GDP rose to 3.5%. There was also some recovery in the manufacturing sector which increased in this period by 5.5%, largely due to the food processing industry (5.2%), while textiles (–6.8%) and assembly (–1.2%) experienced negative growth. The chemical and non-metallic minerals sector, which is closely aligned to the construction sector (cement, bricks and blocks) also contributed to the growth in manufacturing with 10.8%. Hence, the economy has been rolled back to period growth rates that existed approximately 20–30 years ago.

Total investment to GDP and public and private investment worsened during 1988/94. Both public and private investment to GDP fell in the period 1988/ 1994 compared to the previous period as shown in Table 2.4. Netting out state enterprises from private investment, the available figures for savings and investment for the periods 1981–87 and 1988–94 (respectively) show: private savings at 17.6% and 19.3%; private investment at 11.6% and 9.0%; government savings at 0% and –1.4%; and government investment at 12.2% and 5.5%.[35]

In the 1995/98 period, investment increased largely due to foreign direct investment in the energy sector and other government projects such as the airport expansion and other public construction. During this same period, both private and public savings improved with the former increasing marginally (Table 2.4).

The rate of growth in the money supply (Ma) increased at a declining rate in the periods 1981/87, 1988/94 and 1995/98 as compared to 1974/80 (the oil boom period). The rate of growth of domestic credit to

Table 2.4 Savings and investment to GDP (current prices)

Variable	1966/73	1974/80	1981/87	1988/94	1995/98
Sp	10.9	24.6	17.6	19.3	20.8
Sg	4.0	9.0	0.02	-1.4	2.8
Ip	13.5	15.0	11.6	9.0	15.3
Ig	10.9	12.1	12.2	5.5	11.2

Source: Republic of Trinidad & Tobago, Central Statistical Accounts-National Accounts Reports-several years, own worksheets.

Figure 2.4 Private and public investment to GDP (current prices)

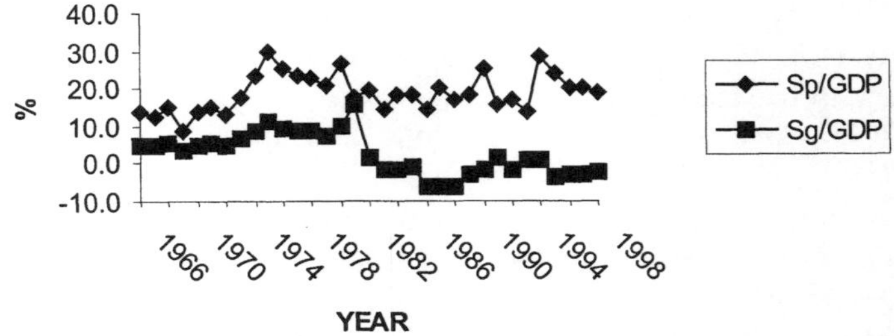

GDP for the public and private sector shows the effect of the oil boom in 1974/81 when government was the recipient of revenue from oil. However, in the subsequent periods, domestic credit to the public sector grew but below that of the private sector.

The debt ratios increased during the immediate post-oil boom and adjustment periods, reflecting the economic problems facing the country (Table 2.5). The fiscal deficit, which reflects a broad definition of the government accounts, was negative throughout all four periods.[36] For the general government accounts, only the 1974/80 figure for the fiscal deficit was 12.6% . Hence, the figure of –3.2% for the same period for the entire public sector accounts reflects major problems with the state enterprises and utilities which contributed to the erosion of the oil wealth. The improved current account deficit in the 1988/94 period was

Figure 2.5 Private and public saving to GDP (current prices)

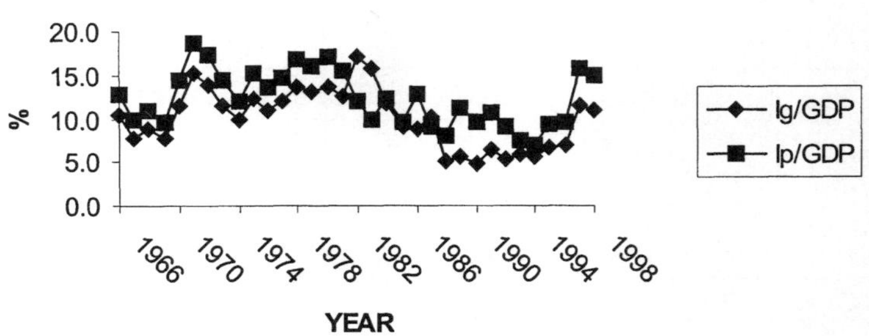

Table 2.5 Debt ratios, monetary variables, fiscal and current account deficits

Item	1966/73	1974/80	1981/87	1988/94	1995/98
DCg/GDP growth	5.3	–25.7	1.1	18.5	9.5
DCp/GDP growth	18.7	21.5	30.6	31.9	29.3
M2 growth	17.1	27.6	9.1	2.9	8.2
Fiscal deficit/GDP	–6.9	–3.2	–12.1	–6.1	–11.8
Current account deficit/GDP	–9.5	6.4	–6.1	3.5	–3.4
Total debt/exports (%)	27.0	19.4	63.3	110.6	106.2
Total debt/GNP (%)	12.5	10.6	23.8	50.1	61.7
Debt service/exports (%)	3.9	3.5	11.9	18.2	17.5

Source: International Financial Statistics several Years; Republic of Trinidad & Tobago-Central Statistical Office Annual Statistical Digests and National Income Reports (several years); World Debt Tables.

due to favourable oil prices in the 1990s as well as the sale of some state enterprises.

The 1995–98 period saw the current account in deficit. Total debt to exports and the debt service ratios showed slight improvement in 1995–98. The total debt to GNP ratio worsened and the ratios in general remained relatively high.. Changes in critical variables underscore the problems that the economy is still facing despite some positive indicators.

2.4.3 The emergent industrial structure

The sectoral contribution

The economic structure of Trinidad & Tobago reflects the dominance of the petroleum sector and of energy-based production in general. Table 2.6 shows the sectoral contribution to GDP by period. The petroleum sector is the largest single contributor to GDP for all the periods, reaching a peak of 41% in the oil boom period of 1974/81.[37] In the initial period (1966–73), petroleum also contributed 38% of total government revenue and 79% of total exports while in the oil boom period these figures were 68% of government revenue and 90% of exports. The contribution of the services sector has been consistent, with transport, distribution and government being the main contributors of these sectors to GDP.

Table 2.6 Sectoral contribution to GDP

Industry	Period				
	1966/73	1974/80	1981/87	1988/94	1995/98
Agriculture	5.6	3.6	2.2	2.4	2.2
Petroleum	25.0	41.0	26.9	26.3	26.6
Manufacturing, of which:	10.2	7.0	7.1	8.9	7.8
– Food processing	4.5	2.5	2.9	4.2	3.2
– Textiles	0.8	0.6	0.5	0.3	0.2
– Printing	0.7	0.5	0.6	0.7	0.8
– Wood	0.5	0.5	0.3	0.2	0.3
– Chemicals	1.3	0.9	1.0	1.3	1.3
– Assembly	2.1	1.7	1.6	1.8	1.7
– Miscellaneous	0.4	0.3	0.2	0.4	0.3
Traded	15.7	10.6	9.3	11.3	9.9
Non-traded	59.2	48.3	63.8	61.1	63.5

Source: Central Statistical Office, Republic of Trinidad & Tobago, National Income Reports, 1966–85, 1981–91, 1990–94.

As the figures in Table 2.6 show, the contribution of the non-oil manufacturing sector remained minimal. The sectoral growth rates described earlier also show the difficulty in economic transformation for the country. As St Cyr (1981) argued, the manufacturing sector never really had the dynamism that should have resulted from development strategies and plans, leaving the economy still heavily dependent on a staple for export earnings and government revenues. In general, it cannot be said that there has been sustainable economic recovery and diversification despite the improvement in the growth rate from a decline of –3.5% for the 1981/87 period to 0.1% for the period during the structural adjustment programmes of 1988/94. Largely, the significant contributors to GDP in the manufacturing sectors are: food-processing, assembly and chemicals – in that order.

The small increase in the manufacturing sector in the 1988/94 period arose from the food processing industry with a few large firms penetrating export markets abroad and also from a large firm in the iron and steel sub-industry of assembly. There were some gains from adjustment even though the sustainability of these gains are questionable in light of the decline in the contribution of these sectors in 1995/98. These gains are largely related to the increased activity in the energy sector including the area of natural gas.

Economic openness and direction of trade

With the shift in focus from sugar to oil in the 20th century, exports of petroleum products to the USA surpassed sugar exports to the UK. It was also the case that most of the direct foreign investment no longer came from the UK but from the USA, which was the main source of imported intermediates and consumer goods. Table 2.7 shows the direction of trade with some selected countries including the Caribbean Community (CARICOM) region.

Table 2.7 Direction of trade exports to selected countries and years

Years	Country (%)		
	United States	United Kingdom	CARICOM
1955	3.3	44.5	8.7
1965	34.3	17.6	7.3
1975	69.7	4.0	9.4
1985	61.9	3.9	11.5
1992	47.0	1.7	13.8

Source: Republic of Trinidad & Tobago, Central Statistical Office, Annual Statistical Digests (several years).

Figure 2.6 Exports and imports, 1966-80, constant prices (1970=100)

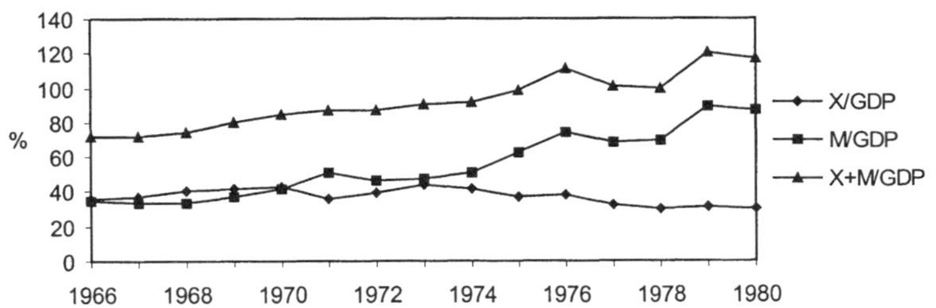

Table 2.8 *Exports by commodities out of total exports (selected items)*

Year	Petroleum	Commodities sugar	Urea/ammonia
1955	63.9	10.8	–
1965	59.5	12.7	6.7
1975	72.2	7.1	2.7
1985	82.2	1.0	10.4
1992	62.1	1.8	11.8
1996	54.7	–	16.8

Source: Republic of Trinidad & Tobago, Central Statistical Office, Annual Statistical Digests several years.

The degree of openness in the economy is shown in Figures 2.6 and 2.7 which show exports (*X*), imports (*M*) and the sum of exports and imports to GDP at constant prices for different periods.[38] The ratio of the sum (*X* + *M*)/GDP was over 70% for all the years shown in Figure 2.6, while the pattern from 1974 to 1978 shows some deviation in the individual ratios with imports to GDP being higher. This was the period of the oil boom. In Figure 2.7, which is not strictly comparable with Figure 2.6 because of differences in base year, the post-oil boom period shows the narrowing of the gap in the individual ratios *X* and *M;* while the adjustment period showed a contraction of the imports ratio relative to the export ratio, which moved almost parallel to the sum of the two to GDP. The tables corresponding to these figures are in Annex I (A2.3 and A2.4).

Figure 2.7 *Exports and imports, 1981–94, constant prices (1985 = 100)*

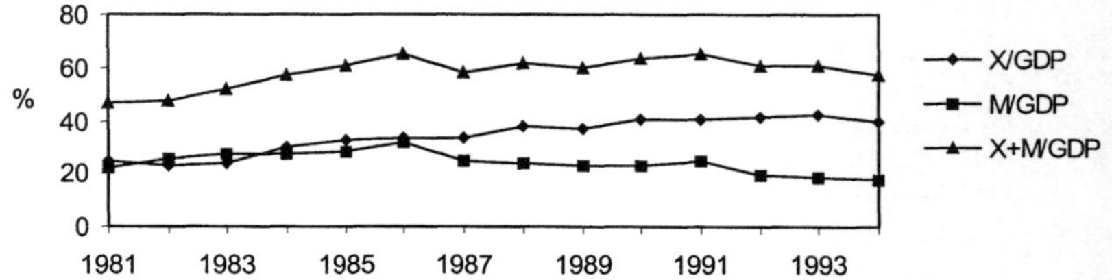

Table 2.9 Imports by sections (selected)

Year	Sections (%)				
	Food, bevrgs, etc.	Mineral fuels	Chemicals	Manufac'd goods	Machinery & transport
1955	19.3	28.3	5.4	20.4	17.0
1965	20.7	1.5	8.2	24.5	30.5
1975	18.7	0.7	9.3	28.3	33.1
1985	21.3	3.3	9.5	20.2	30.4
1992	15.1	1.0	12.6	21.8	31.5
1996	15.3	5.3	13.0	19.5	38.8

Source: Republic of Trinidad & Tobago, Central Statistical Office-Annual Statistical Digests-several years.

Petroleum, sugar and urea/ ammonia were the dominant export items with the major export market being the USA for most years (Table 2.8). Non-oil manufacturing exports for most of the years were approximately 1–2% of total exports. Excluding imports of petroleum from Venezuela and other Arab countries for further processing, imports are mainly from USA, Canada, the UK and other European countries. These imports are mainly manufactured goods, machinery and transport equipment, and food and beverages (Table 2.9).

Figure 2.8 Imports by economic end-use (percentage of total imports)

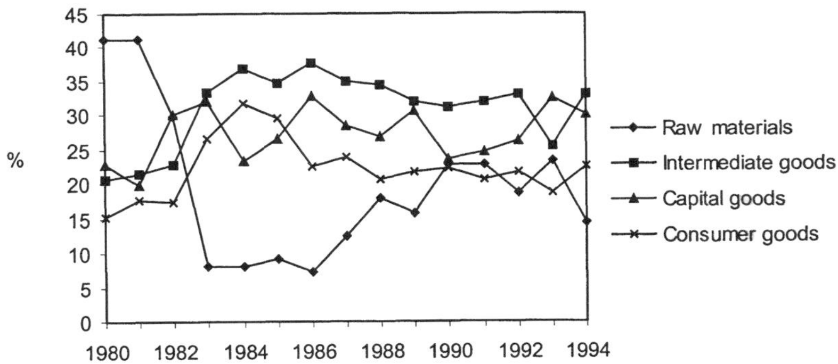

Looking at imports by economic end-use from 1980–94, these figures show that in 1980 and 1981, 40% of total imports were raw material imports (Table A2.5, Annex I). For the 1983–86 period, this figure dropped to less than 10%, with the percentage for 1987–94 ranging from 12–23% of total imports. These lower percentages of raw materials to total imports reflect the post-oil boom slump in manufacturing. Overall for all industries, raw material, capital and intermediate goods were always over 68% and as high as 80% or more for some of the years in the 1980–94 period. Figure 2.8 shows the relationships between these categories of imports.

The past pattern of reliance on a staple, in this case petroleum, and petroleum and natural gas-based products, on imports of intermediates and capital equipment, and on imported manufactured items still exists today. The situation with respect to imports and exports reflects the high degree of openness in the economy and its vulnerability to external shocks.

While the adjustment policies should in principle improve the lot of the non-oil manufacturing sectors, the performance above suggests that these activities have not contributed consistently or significantly to the economy. Hence, there have been low or negative growth rates for some manufacturing sectors and the contribution to GDP has been less than 10% as a whole throughout all the years. These features go along with the disappearance of some activities and the closures of firms. The chapter continues with a micro-level discussion of the firm and its environment.

2.5 The Firm: The Influence of History and Institutions

From a historical perspective, indigenous firms assumed a minor position relative to foreign firms. The industrial structure which evolved shows: a lack of access to capital through a banking system that was geared to satisfying metropolitan concerns of profit repatriation and loan repayments; heavy reliance on imported inputs; and an orientation towards the domestic market with little access to external markets for exports. The role of the indigenous firm in the private sector was clearly secondary to that of the foreign firm. In this section we take a closer look at indigenous businesses, by which is meant businesses that are not foreign-owned.

This account begins by looking at firm response and gives an idea of firm retrenchment and receivership (reported) in the period bordering and including adjustment. Some structural features of the firm are given for selected years relative to items of operating expenses and sources/uses of funds. Some elements regarding the effect of economic development on firms are then discussed including the question of credit access, bank-firm relationship and market orientation.

2.5.1 The response of business in the post-oil boom period

Retrenchment and business failure – available evidence

The economic downturn which resulted from the oil price decline in 1980 saw the failure of many businesses by the mid-1980s. While figures are not well documented on the number of failures, some insights can be gained in the available data from official and other sources.[39]

Failure to heed early warning signs saw many firms committing themselves to irreversible expenditure during the boom period, and suffering the after-effects of foreign exchange shortage, decline in domestic demand, structural changes in production and marketing failures. This failure, however, was not specific to any particular business, it cut across firm size, activity, ethnicity as well as foreign/local ownership, limited liability or unincorporated businesses. While some of the larger businesses were able to restructure their debts, other large and small businesses were forced into receivership.

Approximately 500 businesses in the manufacturing sectors *are known* to have gone into receivership in the post-1985 to 1994 period, of which approximately 56% were in the 1989–94 period during the height of adjustment policies. While it is not clear how many manufacturing firms were actually in operation at the beginning of that period, assuming that there were approximately 2,000–2,500, then the 500 businesses suggest that about 22% went into receivership.[40] However, it is not unlikely that numerous firms (unincorporated ones) which went out of operation may not be included in these sources.[41]

An estimate of the number of persons retrenched in the post-oil boom and pre-adjustment period for this sector is in Table A2.6 in Annex I. These figures are also expressed as a percentage of the average number of persons with jobs for the respective sectors over the period shown.[42] For the 1982–86 period, the number of persons (all industries) who became unemployed through retrenchment represented approximately 6% of persons with jobs and 3% for the 1987–94 period. The manufacturing sector accounted for 35% of the total persons retrenched in 1982–86 and 26% in 1987–94.

The breakdown of retrenchment for the manufacturing sector shows that the textiles/garments (31%) and the assembly and related (29.7%) industries had high percentages of retrenchment relative to the persons with jobs in those sectors for the 1982–86 period. In 1987–94, assembly and related (15.8%) and chemical and non-metallic mineral (14.1%) industries showed high percentages of retrenchment.

Tables 2.10 and 2.11 look at the firm, relative to selected items in its cost structure (wages/salaries, raw material purchases, interest expense) for two years: 1974, which was an oil boom year, and 1990, which is a post-oil boom and structural adjustment year.[43] These tables bring out structural aspects of the costs faced by firms in the context of relative price changes.

For 1974, the clothing and printing sectors had the highest percentage of raw material to total expenses at almost 60%. With the exception of the distilleries and miscellaneous manufacturing, most of the other sectors showed a raw material to total expenses ratio of approximately 30–40%.

Wages and salaries comprise another significant factor in the cost structure. With a couple of exceptions, for most activities this percentage was a little over 20% of the total expenses. Interest expenses varied from around 2 to 7%. The relatively higher percentages for chemicals and assembly could reflect that credit is directed to these sectors more than others, or that the cost of credit is relatively higher, or that increased use of leverage was necessary for these activities to remain viable. In any case the question of indebtedness in these sectors should be taken into account as reflected in the interest expenses.

Although identical firms are not represented in both years, there are some similarities and differences by activities between and within years. For example the wages/salaries to total expenses figures in 1990 show most sectors falling below 20%, with wood and chemicals being an exception. Clothing, printing, chemicals and assembly show reduced raw

Table 2.10 Selected components of operating expenses, 1974 (row per cent)

Industry	Wages/salaries	Raw materials	Interest etc.
Rum distilleries	21.9	23.7	1.9
Food	15.7	46.5	1.6
Clothing	21.2	59.3	1.5
Printing	34.1	59.3	2.0
Wood	23.7	48.7	2.4
Chemicals	23.9	33.0	7.4
Assembly	23.1	44.3	4.7
Miscellaneous	22.1	19.3	3.1

Source: Central Statistical Office Survey of Business Establishments, own worksheets

Table 2.11 Selected components of operating expenses, 1990 (row per cent)

Industry	Wages/salaries	Raw materials	Interest etc.
Food	13.9	40.0	1.8
Clothing	17.4	46.9	4.9
Printing	16.2	37.6	2.7
Wood	26.2	45.5	5.0
Chemical	24.5	29.5	4.6
Assembly	9.1	23.6	2.1
Miscellaneous	17.1	37.5	6.0

Source: Central Statistical Office Survey of Business Establishment, own worksheets.

material ratios – particularly in the last case the ratio was noticeably lower. The assembly sector experienced a decline in demand after the oil boom.

Interest expenses ranged between 2 and 5% in 1990 almost similar in range to 1974, but with differences by sector. For example, the interest expenses ratio fell for assembly and chemicals in 1990 as compared to 1974 with the ratio increasing for wood and clothing. It could be that these increases reflect the increases in the real lending rate discussed above. The fall-off in the ratios for assembly possibly reflect firm closures in this industry.

Given the above picture it can be seen that the post-oil boom period, including the period of structural adjustment, was one of business failure and retrenchment. An idea of the size of the manufacturing sector from the register of business establishments shows in the vicinity of 1,800 firms up to and including 1993, and 2,300 firms in 1994, of which approximately 29% and 21% (for 1993 and 1994 respectively) were firms with employment size greater than or equal to 10. Thus the majority of the firms had less than 10 employees.[44] The next section looks at the literature on business development in Trinidad & Tobago from a more socioeconomic perspective but also incorporating highlights into issues surrounding market focus, credit access and so forth.[45]

2.5.2 The financial environment of firms

In general, the literature on businesses in Trinidad & Tobago classifies them by ownership based on ethnicity.[46] It is argued that ethnicity affects business performance and results in problems for some ethic groups with respect to access to credit, establishment of a business support base and so on. While our main interest is not to analyse businesses by ethnic groupings, these features are considered insofar as they influence the performance and behaviour patterns of firms during the process of adjustment.[47] Thus this section looks at two major issues emerging from the available literature (access to resources vis-à-vis land ownership and bank-firm relationships), along with information from other sources on firms.[48]

Factors affecting access to resources: Land ownership

In the context of Trinidad & Tobago, the question of land ownership is a contentious issue. The control over the agricultural resources that persons of European descent had in the 19th century was the basis for their dominance in commercial and manufacturing activities. This factor enabled them to expand capital and wealth while investing in other sectors to the point where interest in agriculture waned (Sebastien 1982: 207).[49]

Ramsaran (1992), in a study on entrepreneurial practices, found that the historical development of Trinidad & Tobago and factors governing the distribution of wealth in colonial times had a significant impact on the structure of entrepreneurship which emerged. He argued that the disproportionate number of entrepreneurs of European descent over time was based on the advantage of landownership.[50] Relative to entrepreneurs of Indian descent, it is argued that the basis for savings accumulation was the entitlement of this group to land in exchange for the return passage to India (Stewart 1994). Hence, they were able to obtain savings out of agricultural pursuits. Other groups, such as the Syrian-Lebanese who arrived later, were alleged to have an orientation of thrift to accumulate capital for business expansion. Their experience did not include the domination and discriminatory practices of the plantation system (Ramsaran 1992). To a certain extent, he argued that the capacity to save is cultural and related to the ownership of land.

Nevertheless, it is also argued that persons of African descent did own land and were also involved in businesses in the past. Institutional factors, however, worked to their disadvantage, resulting in loss of property and business failure (Reddock 1980). For example, Reddock (1980) argued that persons of African descent had established retail shops in a market niche that catered to late-hour customers/workers who were paid at night. This attempt at entrepreneurship was destroyed through the Shop Hours Ordinance of 1938 which limited the hours of operation of these establishments. Although the question as to why these businesses could not cope with the existing competition was not examined, it could have been due to the scale of other businesses and their ability to sell at lower prices.

The issue that people of African descent did not own or have land at their disposal is also disputed by Ryan & Barclay (1992).[51] There was declining land ownership among persons of African descent for reasons that included: the depression of the late 1930s, increased indebtedness and forfeiture, abandonment of cultivation in favour of urban migration in search of education and paid employment, abandonment of intestate properties, and problematic multiple-family ownership.[52] Since persons of African descent experienced difficulties in obtaining loans directly from banks, they acquired debt from merchants who had access to bank loans and who re-loaned at exorbitant rates. Lower prices as well as crop failure also led to foreclosure and the loss of land in cases where it was used as collateral for these loans.

Hence, cultural explanations for the success or failure of particular ethnic groups (such as thrift orientation), without an exploration of the issues for a particular occurrence, seemingly boil down to a case of 'blaming the victim'.[53] On the question of ownership and ethnicity, some emphasis is placed below on financial factors that acted as constraints to business development.

Access to capital

The importance of the discussion on land ownership concerns its use as collateral for loans. One implication of the lack of land ownership was thought to be a lack of access to bank loans which resulted in getting loans from usurious merchants, indebtedness and loss of property. Multiple ownership of family land was also problematic. Ramsaran (1992) contended that it was not merely that family ownership of land proved to be an obstacle to entrepreneurship, but that it was also the unwillingness of the state and credit institutions to accept as collateral land held under multiple ownership which exacerbated the problem.[54] Having access to land in order to get credit was seen as an important factor in starting a business. In his survey of 168 entrepreneurs, Ramsaran found that 70% of the respondents had access to land. Forty-five per cent of those who had access to land utilized it as a means of establishing businesses.[55] However, his data (given in Table 2.12) show that access to capital from banks did not vary much across the different groups.[56]

Worrell (1985: 120) in looking at monetary mechanisms in Trinidad & Tobago and other Caribbean economies, focuses on the cost of credit, since his view is that credit-rationing is determined by institutional norms. Those firms who do not meet the conventional credit standard never qualify for credit. His contention therefore is that it is the costs of loans as reflected by the loan rate that varies based on the bank's cost in providing the resource. He sees the loan rate as affecting the production

Table 2.12 Percentage distribution of respondents by source of initial capital and ethnicity

Ethnic origin	Source of capital			
	Family	Bank	Own funds	Other
African descent	–	37.5	46.9	15.6
Indian descent	30.4	42.0	23.2	4.4
Mixed descent	25.8	41.9	19.4	12.9
Other	25.0	41.7	16.7	16.6

Source: Table 4: The Future of The Caribbean Culture and Entrepreneurship in the Caribbean (Ramsaran 1992) ISER.

schedule of real output as well as the expenditure of consumers and firms. However, he notes that there are some Caribbean economies in which credit-rationing is important.

Farrell & Crichton (1986) found evidence that loan allocation to businesses in Trinidad & Tobago was such that small and medium-sized firms faced undue restrictions with respect to credit allocation by commercial banks. This factor points to the use of credit-rationing based on a criterion that does not reflect the efficiency of the investment project, which implies that the allocation of credit is not performed in a socially optimal manner.

The views of Worrell (1985) and Farrell & Crichton (1986) lend support to the emphasis placed in this study on the systemic problems in the economy relative to firms' access to credit.

Table A2.7 in Annex I shows the loans outstanding to the private sector. Assuming a relationship between loans outstanding and allocated, the assembly and related, food processing, and chemicals industries appear to be the ones that have consistently received the largest share of loans combined over the period. Printing and paper converters, wood and related products and textiles/garments received lower percentages of loans. Detailed breakdown of the total number of firms by sector for the years shown are not available except for 1993. For this year, the sectoral breakdown shows that food processing/drink/tobacco had the highest proportion of firms with 24%, followed by wood and related with 18.3% and assembly type and related with 17.3%. However, for this year, the assembly sector was the recipient of the majority of loans followed by miscellaneous manufacturing and food/drink/tobacco in that order.

The criterion in allocating loans in this year was not necessarily a function of the number of firms in the sector since wood and related activity received the lowest percentage of loans. No firm conclusion can be drawn from loans by industry in the absence of detailed size breakdown by industry for each year, but the data seem to suggest some preference for firms in specific industries.

Evidence of problems with credit access was also brought out by Camejo (1971) who, in a study on race and business, found that racial discrimination contributed to the dominance of some families in the business sector. This process led to what he termed 'market discrimination' against certain racial groups in relation to access to capital. Given the lack of success of particular ethnic groups in business, it is argued that the changed policy environment can only serve to exacerbate the difficulties faced by businesses which do not have the resources to compete with international producers.[57]

Another facet of lending in Trinidad & Tobago is brought out in the experience of the Small Business Development Company (SBDC) in its role as loan guarantor to small businesses. Some of their discoveries were the variation of lending within banks, from one branch to the next, or even in the same bank from one credit officer to another. Credit officers in commercial banks were found to have an orientation to not lending to small enterprises, which were viewed with suspicion. Variation of interest rates by lenders above the prime lending rate, while applied by commercial banks, can be lowered if the guarantor can eliminate some of the risks and the administrative costs involved in lending to small businesses.

It was also found that commercial banks tended to split loans between overdraft and fixed assets even though the latter might be recommended. This is because of the higher interest rates of overdraft (Allahar & Browne 1995). Clearly, there are still difficulties in this arrangement relative to small firms obtaining loans despite guaranteeing of commercial loans by SBDC.

Financial deregulation and trade liberalization is likely to pose barriers to new entrants and may destroy the viability of those businesses that already face problems with respect to credit access. Hence, the context in which the policy of financial liberalization is applied may lead to results which deviate from what is expected to benefit all firms in the private sector, regardless of size, ownership and other such considerations.

Bank-firm relationships[58]

Despite the crisis of 1970 and the subsequent nationalization of most banks, the main complaint against banks was that a prejudice in favour of specific businesses relative to credit access still existed. In the pre-1970 period, before the Black Power uprising mentioned earlier, the banks in Trinidad & Tobago were foreign-owned since they were subsidiaries of banks from the UK, USA and Canada. Until the immediate post-1970s, therefore, credit officers and bank managers were mainly of European descent or at least exceeded other ethnic groups.

There was inequality with respect to collateral requirements, which made it difficult for business owners of non-European descent to obtain start-up capital and overdraft facilities. Loans were on a short-term basis and for fixed investments rather than for working capital, with severe impact due to high interest rates. The severity of the high interest rates was the complaint of the small business community in general.

The reasons ascribed by the bank for this loan policy was the lack of a track record in business management, particularly for persons of African descent and/ or smaller businesses. Therefore many businesses, particularly the smaller ones, were at a disadvantage relative to accessing loans since they were seen as a greater credit risk. The refusal to grant bank loans was without regard to the presence of savings accounts in these same banks that exceeded overdraft requirements. It was alleged that a 'no loans policy' to persons of African descent was a means of protecting the interests of other members of the business community.

There was however a lack of uniformity in the treatment meted out to persons of African descent by the banking sector; in some cases, a loan refusal by one bank did not necessarily imply a loan refusal by another. The difference in treatment was attributed to the sensitivity of the credit manager to the prevailing conditions and differences in the assessment of risk. Often it was the case that the indigenous banks also posed difficulty to persons of African descent relative to loan requests. In general, the complaint was an unevenness in treatment to persons of African descent compared to other members of the community. On the question of collateral, however, one banker differed from the others in expressing the view that business strategy should have priority over collateral requirements in loan assessments, and that banks should play a role in guiding businesses to viability.

Smaller businesses contended that the attitude of the financial institutions was not justified on the grounds that these businesses were first-generation and therefore did not have any track record. They complained that stricter criteria were used in accessing loans for start-up capital as well as in assistance during the economic downturn. Some businesses were able to secure lower interest rates in order to keep the loans performing, while loans were called in more readily for others.

On the other hand, persons in support of the banks as well as banking personnel indicated that banks have an obligation to their depositors and shareholders. Therefore banks should be more concerned with the ability of the person to repay the loan than with the subsidizing 'profligacy'. The collapse of indigenous banks such as the Workers' Bank was cited as an example of a bank that made irresponsible loans to persons of African descent.

On the criteria of the bank's assessment of loan applicants, one banker mentioned: the ability to repay, the stability of the business, the savings pattern of borrowers, and the administrative costs involved in managing the loan. Some loan applicants, he continued, were unable to distinguish between profits and revenue from sales, such that they ended up spending the capital that should be reinvested in the business.[59] He admitted that value judgements are made regarding the ability of some of the loan candidates to repay.

The banker also contended that larger businesses are in a more favourable position than smaller ones and are often given prime lending rates since these involve less administrative costs. Large firms are also given volume discounts, thereby benefiting from lower management costs. In this context, firms that belong to groups are given special consideration with respect to loans since the parent/holding company can act as the guarantor. Even if smaller businesses with collateral are charged higher interest rates, through a neglect of loan payment, these businesses often find themselves with overdraft problems and facing liquidation.

Similar to the cases of firms that belong to groups and favourable bank relationships is the phenomenon of interlocking directorates which typifies a relationship of economic power combined with wealth. Reid (1977) looked at the concentration of economic power by families in Jamaica and found that the presence of interlocking directorates and kinship relations led to a monopolization of the wealth of Jamaica by 21 white or 'near' white families. [60] He did not explore practices with respect to innovation and expansion of capital accumulation by this group. However, there was not much articulation of the processes involved in these arrangements.

Parris (1985) linked interlocking directorates in Trinidad & Tobago with economic power blocs, the majority of whom were of European descent.[61] The existence of this phenomenon, he argued, spanned financial and media companies which served to reinforce the position of power that these blocs held.[62] Therefore, financial policies of the banking sector, and public opinion through the news media were shaped to the advantage of these power blocs and to the disadvantage of their competitors and other individuals in society.

2.5.3 Market orientation

There is a paucity of information in the literature regarding firms' experience with accessing foreign markets, which may, however, be partly due to financial constraints, but also to technical and informational problems. The historical feature of domestic market orientation of indigenous firms was depicted above as well as the policy thrust of the government in different industrialization phases. In addition, the import-substitution phase of government policy highlighted above sought to give protection to manufacturers so they could become competitive. However, the import-substitution industry was noted for few backward linkages and relied heavily on imported raw materials and other intermediates and capital goods. Relative to exports, the strategy of diversification was mainly resource-based industrialization, implying that the country continued to rely on petroleum and energy-based industries such as urea, methanol and fertilizers and in more recent years natural gas.

Small market size together with a domestic market orientation are reasons given for the failure of firms to achieve significant economies of scale in production which can in turn lead to export expansion and international competitiveness (Toney 1995: 19). During the period of adjustment, efforts at trade reforms and financial, monetary and exchange rate policies were implemented to facilitate firms in the private sector, particularly the non-oil manufacturing industry within this sector. The embracing of the changed macroeconomic environment of the adjustment period is highlighted in the following response by a private sector organization: Yip Choy (1995), in his capacity as Chairman of the Trinidad & Tobago Manufacturer's Association (TTMA), saw the performance of the export sector as excellent since the liberalization policies, quoting a figure of 40% increase in output of exports since the devaluation of 1993.[63]

The TTMA actively set about organizing trade missions for its members regionally as well as outside of the region. These missions contributed to the changing focus of businesses relative to production for export markets. For the most part, membership in these organizations comprise large and well-established firms. Problems still exist with market penetration of smaller firms who do not have recourse to these organizations and may not benefit from the ETAF facility described earlier.

Suitcase traders – opportunities or threats

Standing out as a prime example of innovative strategy was the penetration into the main shopping area by persons of mainly African descent through an innovative business practice known as the 'suitcase trade'. As a business activity, its popularity grew during the oil boom period. The 'suitcase trade' entailing business trips to countries such as Curaçao, Panama, Miami and New York for the purchasing of merchandise such as clothing, footwear, watches and so on, gave rise to a thriving business in the 1970s and early 1980s and presently in the commercial areas. The merchandise to be sold was brought into the countries in large suitcases, hence the term 'suitcase trade'. Most of the sales took place on pavements outside established businesses or in 'organized markets' in which individual structures are built of wood or other materials.

While some of the larger store-owners sought to destroy these activities, others found a means of co-operation through the purchase of the merchandise from these small businessmen or through the hiring of these small businessmen as sales agents. A contractual relationship therefore developed between these small entrepreneurs and the larger merchants with some of them acting as importers for the larger businesses. However, there was little penetration relative to manufacturing activities which were seen as involving too much risk, being highly volatile and highly capital intensive.

The expenditure involved in this trade was a return air ticket. Income from employment, casual or permanent work, would often be used to fund this project. In the case of persons going to New York in particular, there was always a base of relatives where they could stay. While some persons who were plying this trade were not otherwise gainfully employed, there were cases where some of them were employed as part-time or casual labourers, or where the spouses or partners were employed; these were sources of funding to start the business.

The profits were often re-invested in the business to fund future trips and purchases. In some cases, relatives who were living abroad were the ones who were providing the capital, and/or the items that were being sold. Some of the businesses were actually owned by relatives living abroad who would travel often bringing the items to stock the business from time to time. In general, these businesses never kept proper accounts and were unable to ascertain how much was operating expenditure, profits and so on. In addition, persons often traveled to the USA to find gainful employment, the proceeds of which were used to finance the goods that were sold on their return home. Nevertheless, these traders were able to penetrate the domestic market setting, providing competition for well-established traders.

2.5.4 Main issues arising from the Caribbean experience relative to the firm

It is argued that Caribbean entrepreneurs have not been able to make fundamental changes in their production strategy due to the historical role of the plantation system. Little or no value added accrues to the local economy which is also responsive to the needs of the industrialized countries and international capital. Caribbean economies are perceived as lacking in a capital goods sector, and the islands are dependent on foreign technology, technical skills and the high income market that is necessary for innovation (Stewart 1994). Consequently, identifiable structural constraints which relate back to the historical processes of the evolution of Caribbean economies are:

- openness;
- dependence on a single staple;
- significant foreign ownership of the staple by multinationals; and
- resource allocation problems relative to unequal access to credit.

Given these considerations, the question therefore arises as to the appropriateness of the policies of the IMF and World Bank relative to economic recovery in the private sector of Trinidad & Tobago. In light of the historical strategies, the following issues arise at the macro level:

- The economy of Trinidad & Tobago is one in which, despite the oil booms of the 1970s and attempts at nationalization, dependency still exists relative to technology, high import content of production – through raw materials and capital equipment; imported taste patterns; and the need to supply a staple to foreign concerns.

- The economic thrust or the internal dynamics have traditionally been and continue to be externally propelled.
- The receipt by government of revenues from taxes, royalties and so forth of foreign multinationals, particularly in the petroleum sector, were the main mechanism by which resources could be made available to develop other sectors.
- The banking system and other institutions are a legacy of the past and are oriented towards the transfer of the surplus to foreign owners and firms or the local elite class. This factor therefore affects the capacity of firms and individuals in their responses to current economic and social problems.

At the level of the firm, the historical features and patterns of production have influenced their responses through the following factors:

- the heavy dependence on imported raw materials, which are subjected to the openness of the economy (through the exchange rates), and which affect the cost of production of firms;
- chain reaction of high wages transmitted from the staple sector to some other sectors of the economy;
- the inaccessibility by many entrepreneurs to available finance from a banking system that is biased against businesses based on ownership, size, and ethnicity considerations. An overriding factor has been the discriminatory lending policies of banks either through credit rationing or cost;
- foreign exchange restrictions during particular periods;
- problems in access to foreign markets;
- land ownership may not lend itself as ready collateral for the purposes of business loans. Multiple ownership also poses a problem relative to its use as collateral;
- property forfeiture through indebtedness brought on by the failure of some groups to obtain direct bank loans has been the experience of some failed entrepreneurs in Trinidad & Tobago;
- family commitment, interlocking directorates including financial, media and so forth, business patronage, all surface as a support base to enterprises.

2.6 Conclusions

Best (1980: 159) argues that the level of generalization of orthodoxy has led to a rising demand for differentiation amongst the economies, societies and so on. He posed the question as to whether the outcome has been a single capitalist world order with a range of different subtype as has been suggested or a number of distinct systems each of its own kind. He contends that although the central hypothesis that developing countries have been subjected to a debilitating domination has been widely expressed, a related hypothesis that these countries have been subjected to intellectual domination is not so explicit. The analysis of the experience of Trinidad & Tobago is applicable to countries with related if not similar experiences of foreign domination or exploitation of resources.

Even where such experience is absent, the presence of segmented or underdeveloped factor markets in many economies leads to situations in which practices such as described in the case of Trinidad & Tobago emerge. The analysis of the historical processes that fashion the features of the firm at the point in time that it needs to restructure can be applied to other countries. Firms have given structures, commitments and behaviour patterns relative to investment, operating costs, technology employed, indebtedness etc. that cannot be easily reversed.

> It is as if the world only started after World War II or even in the 1980s. We seem not to have realized that the phenomena we were dealing with may have had explanations the depths of which we simply had to plumb and explore in the annals of history (Best 1996: 3).

The degree of flexibility that is expected in the market-oriented policies of adjustment is therefore being questioned relative to the historical and structural experiences of firms. These experiences lead to heterogeneity in the private sector based on characteristics such as size, ownership ethnicity and industry; resulting in the differential impact of these policies on firms.

Therefore, it is unrealistic to say that devaluation of the exchange rate will result in expenditure switching into traded sectors, and improvement in the balance of payments, or that financial liberalization will result in increased savings which will increase the volume and efficiency of investment at the level of the firm and the economy. These policies fail to take into consideration the structure, history, and heterogeneity which affect the capacity of economies, private sectors and firms to adjust. The next chapter discusses the theoretical expectations with respect to the policies from macro- and microeconomic perspectives.

Notes

1. The study focuses on the manufacturing sector.
2. Trinidad & Tobago was re-discovered in 1498 and was ruled by Spain until British colonial rule started in 1797.
3. The Marxist political economic tradition was borne out of a rejection of these prior traditions, analysing the problems of backwardness in terms of the metropole and relative to the world capitalist economy (Bernal 1984). This tradition will not be presented here nor the neo-classical tradition some of which was discussed in the last chapter. No attempt is being made to present Lewis' model in its entirety. The focus is on what can be learnt from it relative to the structural features depicted about Caribbean economies.
4. Sources of labour identified included: subsistence agriculture, casual labour, petty trade, wives and daughters in household. He also argued that an unlimited supply of labour existed in those countries with large population relative to capital and natural resources such that there were large sectors of the economy in which the marginal productivity of labour was negligible, zero or negative (Lewis 1954: 402).
5. The basis of its determination was the earnings in the subsistence sector.
6. This is through the re-distributive effect from wages to profit.
7. A supply-led resource-based strategy in activities such as 'sugar-refining, chocolate, utilizing copra and dairy product etc.' was recommended by Lewis (St Cyr 1980: 19).
8. This was until the thriftiness of the people was able to ensure a build-up of capital (St Cyr 1980: 20).
9. The work of Best (1968), Girvan & Jefferson (1971), Girvan (1973) and Beckford (1972) are important pieces in this tradition.
10. These economies were seen as 'hinterlands' or overseas extensions of metropolitan countries, beholden to international firms with goods and services being traded between subsidiaries and parent companies (Best 1968).
11. Initially, in the hinterland of settlement the settlers produced export staples as well as food for domestic consumption.
12. The residentiary sector comprised domestic agriculture, some staple agriculture, own account services, maroons and urban tradesmen (Best 1968).
13. The shift in the staple from agriculture to other minerals in these islands did not alter the relationship of the plantation system. Hence, in the case of Trin-

idad & Tobago with the discovery of oil in 1907, the dominance of sugar shifted to oil as the new staple. Since the process of oil exploration and refining was highly capital-intensive, a mineral-based enclave was created within the economy with negligible labour employed and taxation and royalty revenues being earned by government.

14. From a survey of secondary industries in Trinidad & Tobago by the Secretary of State for the Colonies in 1941 and cited in Best (1980) – manufacturing industries existed, some of which used local inputs such as cocoa, coconut, rum, while others used imported material such as tobacco leaves, soda ash, and provided in most cases for domestic demand. For example a matches company sold 85% of its output locally, Angostura Bitters used local rum and sold 50% of its output locally, as did companies which produced jams and jellies.
15. Essentially, Best (1968) argues that the micro behaviour has been fashioned by this total plantation institution to such an extent that no distinction can be made between the macro and the micro framework – knowing about one is like knowing about the other.
16. Low wages did not lead to investment in labour intensive industry and to unemployment reduction but there was, instead, a shift to more capital-intensive production and further dependence on metropolitan markets and technology etc.
17. See Best & Levitt (1980: 53).
18. For example, net inflow of direct foreign investment was 128.4 million TT$ compared to outflow of 170.6 million TT$ (1973) (St Cyr 1981).
19. See St Cyr (1981) for further insight into this issue. The calls for industrialization were raised amidst a rapidly expanding labour force relative to the rate of growth of employment.
20. First Five-Year Plan (1958–62), Second Five-Year Plan (1964–68) and Third Five-Year Plan (1969–73).
21. The role of the IDC was to act as an agent to execute the industrial policy of government, specifically the promotion of industry through creating an atmosphere to attract industrialists. Other institutions that were set up in later years included a Management Development and Productivity Centre (1965), a Development Finance Corporation (DFC 1970), a Small Business Division of the IDC (1970), a Caribbean Industrial and Study Institute (CARIRI) and the Bureau of Standards with specific aims in business development.
22. Diversification in the Third Five-Year Plan (1969–73) was to be achieved through the promotion of livestock and fishing production in agriculture, increased production of cocoa, citrus, sugar and other traditional crops and

through the development of manufactured exports to serve regional and international markets.

23. The closing down of British Petroleum oil companies in the late 1960s led to the acquisition of these assets by the government under a joint venture arrangement with a US company. The companies that withdrew were compensated handsomely for their assets.
24. These would include the entire public sector, i.e. civil service, local government, state enterprises, daily paid, special projects etc.
25. Not only did the price of oil decline but there was also less crude oil production, which contributed to lower oil revenues.
26. Information was taken from official sources such as: Medium-Term Policy Framework Documents (1993–95 and 1994–96), Draft Medium-Term Planning Framework (1989–95), several reports on the Review of the Economy, World Bank-Trinidad & Tobago Policy Agenda for Sustained Development-Report No. 10417-TR.
27. This is from the Republic of Trinidad & Tobago Ministry of Finance: Trinidad & Tobago government's relationship with the International Monetary Fund and the Paris Club 1990.
28. The target for the Common External Tariff (CET) with the CARICOM region was to be at 0–20% by 1998.
29. The financial sector review of 1991 found that Trinidad & Tobago's financial sector was largely free of market distortions with interest rate being market-determined and the financial system reasonably competitive (Review of the Economy).
30. Source: personal interviews I held with bankers; and Hilaire (1994), Farrell et al. (1986), Thom (1992).
31. Legislation proposed/established included: the adoption of a Free Zone Act in 1988 to establish Export Free Zones (one such free zone was opened in 1998); the establishment of an Anti-Dumping authority under Regulations of the Anti-Dumping and Countervailing Duties Act No. 11, 1992; Foreign Investment Act 1990; Companies Act (re-modelled) 1995;
32. The traded sector includes import-competing and exporting sectors.
33. See Tables A2.1 and A2.2 in Annex I for further details.
34. For 1966–81, the base is 1970 = 100, and for 1982–94, the base is 1985 = 100. Data was linked using a crude method.
35. Public sector accounts showing a more accurate representation of private and public investment were available from 1981. A crude estimate of the ratio for the years in which the breakdown was available was applied to the

earlier years to get a better idea of public and private savings and investment.

36. The fiscal deficit reflects a broad definition of the government accounts as per note 35.
37. These figures are period averages for 1969–73, 1974–81, 1982–87 and 1988–90.
38. Because of data unavailability, the base year of each period differs.
39. Some of this information is from my own knowledge having worked during 1987–90 on the survey of business establishments in the national accounts department of the Central Statistical Office, Trinidad & Tobago.
40. These figures are based on information gathered by the business establishment survey and register of companies and therefore relates to responses received. The estimated percentages are based on my knowledge of the register of establishments and is subject to correction in the absence of actual information. My estimate is that of approximately 23,000 firms on the register of establishment in 1985, roughly 2,300 were in the manufacturing sector.
41. Ryan & Barclay (1992) estimated that approximately 250 businesses went into receivership in the 1986–90 period with retrenchment of approximately 8,000 persons.
42. The breakdown of persons with jobs by sector was not available for 1994 so this year was excluded from the average.
43. These percentages are based on response data.
44. Source: The Central Statistical Office, Trinidad & Tobagor, egister of business establishment.
45. Even though a breakdown of businesses by ethnicity and employment size is not available, it is safe to equate 'small' businesses with 'businesses run mainly by persons of African and Indian descent'. This is not to say however that there are no large businesses owned by these ethnic groups but, particularly for the former, it will be negligible.
46. I do not wish to enter into a discussion about the definition of ethnicity. However, for the purposes of consistency I use 'descent' to qualify the description relative to various groups in Trinidad & Tobago.
47. It is not my personal intention to focus on problems faced by any particular ethnic group, but to deal with businesses in general. However, I am limited by the available literature that identifies constraints relative to particular ethnic groups.
48. Information from other sources includes interviews with private sector personnel, banks, etc. that I conducted, or which were conducted in the media.

49. Cited in Ramsaran (1992).
50. Ramsaran (1992) also argued that, in the colonial period, these persons accumulated large sums of capital so that in the post-colonial era they were the best positioned to use their acquired capital to expand into businesses.
51. Bereton (1972), cited in Ramsaran (1992), argued that persons of African descent were denied land as well as entry into commerce unless they were able to inherit estates from their families or from free coloured planters; but these were few. Ramsaran (1992) also showed in his findings that 75% of persons of African descent surveyed had access to land which compared favourably with the other groups.
52. Ryan & Barclay (1992) argue that this process also occurred with descendants of Indians and French Creoles (persons of mixed European and African descent).
53. William Ryan (1971) argued against this process by which victims are blamed for their misfortune.
54. According to Ramsaran (1992) the feature of multiple land ownership was common among persons of African descent in Trinidad & Tobago.
55. Ramsaran surveyed businesses employing 5 or more persons; however 64% of his respondents were businesses with less than 10 employees. Ryan & Barclay (1992) surveyed mainly micro-entrepreneurs with less than 10 employees so there is a greater representation of larger businesses in Ramsaran's survey.
56. Ryan & Barclay (1992) found in their results a heavier reliance on own savings/ profits to start/continue in business than bank loans.
57. The case of CLICO, an insurance company that is black-owned, is often cited as an example of the problems that black businesses experience.
58. The material used in this section is taken mainly from *Sharks & Sardines* by Selwyn Ryan and Lou Anne Barclay (1992) as well as from interviews I had with members of the banking community in Trinidad & Tobago during 1995/96, and from newspaper clippings, other media interviews and so forth.
59. Often such loan applicants are sent by the SBDC to the commercial banks with well drawn-up business proposals.
60. Cited in Ramsaran (1992).
61. He argued that these interlocking directorates form a mechanism for the concentration of both information and wealth (cited in Ramsaran 1992).
62. As mentioned earlier, before independence and until the early 1970s, the banking system was foreign-owned with banks from Canada, the UK and the USA.

63. The source of this information is the Trade and Industry Supplement of the *Sunday Guardian* newspapers (1 November 1995) as well as a personal interview I conducted with the General Manager of the TTMA in 1995.

Annex I

Table A2.1 Growth rates of selected indicators by period

Variable	1966/73	1974/80	1981/87	1988/94	1995/98
Real GDP growth	3.1	7.0	–3.5	0.1	3.5
Traded growth	6.3	4.0	–2.8	2.1	2.7
Non-traded	3.7	11.4	–4.6	–0.3	4.8
Agriculture	0.8	–3.2	0.9	4.3	–4.5
Manufacturing	9.4	6.2	–3.8	1.3	5.5
– Food	7.7	5.9	–0.7	–0.4	5.2
Textiles	4.7	–0.7	–8.0	–8.6	–6.8
Assembly	17.6	10.7	–8.7	2.1	–1.2
Petroleum	0.2	–2.6	–2.0	–0.3	0.8
Services	3.7	11.4	–4.6	–0.3	4.8
– Construction	12.3	18.6	–12.5	1.1	9.5
Unemployment (%)	13.5	12.6	15.0	20.0	15.2
Export	6.2	1.4	0.9	2.8	–
Import	8.0	16.5	–2.6	–4.0	–

Source: Republic of Trinidad & Tobago-C.S.O. National Income and Annual Statistical Digests Reports, several years.

Table A2.2 GDP growth rates by sector, 1988–94

Sector	1988	1989	1990	1991	1992	1993	1994
Food processing etc.	–3.6	5.4	0.7	3.3	–3.9	–2.4	–1.7
Textiles, garments etc.	–10.2	–4.9	17.0	–7.5	–3.7	–32.9	–11.0
Printing etc.	–12.0	–9.2	8.7	2.4	2.6	21.1	–7.6
Wood & related	–11.6	14.8	19.9	17.3	10.0	–10.2	34.9
Chemicals & related	1.0	0.5	11.3	7.3	1.9	–2.2	16.0
Assembly & related	–4.2	29.2	–12.0	8.8	4.0	–12.6	7.4
Miscellaneous	–3.2	6.0	2.5	4.6	–0.9	–3.0	3.6

Source: Republic of Trinidad & Tobago-C.S.O. National Income and Annual Statistical Digests Reports several years.

Table A2.3 Trade ratio as a percentage of GDP, selected years (constant prices 1977 = 100)

Year	X	M	(X + M)/GDP (%)
1966	36.4	34.8	71.2
1970	42.8	41.7	84.4
1975	36.6	62.1	98.7
1980	30.5	86.6	117.1

Source: Republic of Trinidad & Tobago, Central Statistical Office, National Accounts Report (several years).

Table A2.4 Trade ratio as a percentage of GDP, selected years (constant prices 1985=100)

Year	X	M	(X + M)/GDP (%)
1982	22.5	25.1	47.6
1986	33.2	31.9	65.1
1990	42.6	22.6	65.2
1994	48.4	26.0	74.4
1996	53.3	30.2	83.6

Source: Republic of Trinidad & Tobago, Central Statistical Office, National Accounts Report (several years).

Table A2.5 Imports by economic end-use (percentage of total imports)

Year	Total raw materials	Intermediate goods	Capital goods	Consumer goods	Total
1980	41.3	20.7	22.8	15.2	100.0
1981	41.1	21.4	19.8	17.7	100.0
1982	29.9	22.7	30.1	17.4	100.0
1983	8.1	33.4	31.9	26.7	100.0
1984	8.0	37.0	23.2	31.7	100.0
1985	9.3	34.7	26.6	29.5	100.0
1986	7.3	37.6	32.7	22.4	100.0
1987	12.4	35.1	28.5	23.9	100.0
1988	17.9	34.5	26.9	20.7	100.0
1989	15.7	32.1	30.6	21.6	100.0
1990	22.9	31.1	23.6	22.3	100.0
1991	22.8	31.9	24.7	20.6	100.0
1992	18.8	33.1	26.4	21.8	100.0
1993	23.2	25.6	32.4	18.7	100.0
1994	14.3	33.0	30.2	22.4	100.0
1995	19.6	27.2	35.0	18.2	100.0
1996	28.1	24.8	30.5	16.5	100.0

Source: Republic of Trinidad & Tobago, C. S. O, Annual Statistical Digest (several years).

Table A2.6 Reported retrenchment, manufacturing sector, 1982–94

	1982 to 1986		1987 to 1994	
Industry	No. of persons retrenched	% retrenched out of persons with jobs	No. of persons retrenched	% retrenched out of persons with jobs
Total retrenched (all industries) of which	22064	6.0	13399	3.0
Total manufacturing	7740	17.0	3514	9.3
– Food processing, drink etc	1889	16.5	1018	8.5
– Textiles, garments headwear etc.	2544	31.0	198	5.7
– Printing and paper converters	375	10.1	365	10.1
– Wood and related products	267	10.1	86	2.1
– Chemical and related	450	10.6	650	14.1
– Assembly type and related	2006	29.7	1178	15.8
– Miscellaneous manufacturing	209	2.2	19	0.9
No. retrenched in manufacturing as a percentage of total retrenched	35 %	–	26%	–

Source: Ministry of Labour, Study and Planning Division, Retrenchment Register, and own spreadsheet.

Table A2.7 Loans outstanding to commercial banks (column per cent out of total loans outstanding), manufacturing sector

Industry	1986	1987	1988	1989	1990
Food, drink, tobacco	14.4	19.6	18.8	18.6	20.6
Textiles, garments	8.7	7.2	9.0	9.7	7.4
Printing & paper converters	3.7	3.9	3.0	3.4	4.5
Wood & related	4.1	4.6	4.6	3.4	3.6
Chem. & non-metallic materials	12.9	7.6	9.2	9.2	7.7
Assembly type & related	42.6	40.9	41.2	38.5	38.7
Miscellaneous	13.7	16.2	14.2	17.1	17.6
Total manufacturing	100.0	100.0	100.0	100.0	100.0
	1991	**1992**	**1993**	**1994**	**1995**
Food, drink, tobacco	16.9	22.1	14.7	10.7	9.1
Textiles, garments	9.7	7.8	9.1	10.1	8.4
Printing & paper converters	6.0	5.3	6.7	4.3	5.5
Wood & related	4.7	3.7	4.4	3.2	3.3
Chemical & non-metallic materials	8.3	7.4	8.3	11.1	8.6
Assembly type & related	35.8	40.3	39.2	41.2	51.8
Miscellaneous	18.5	12.8	17.8	14.3	13.3
Total manufacturing	100.0	100.0	100.0	100.0	100.0

Source: Quarterly Statistical Digest Vol X No 1, March 1996; Central Bank of Trinidad & Tobago; and Annual Statistical Digest, 1990, Central Statistical Office.

Annex II

External Arrangements with the IMF and World Bank

1. Compensatory and Contingency Financing Decision (CCFF) No. 8955-(88/126).

2. The document from (1) is contained in a detailed description of the technical parameters and procedures to be used by the Fund for the purpose of applying the provisions of the external contingency mechanism of the CCFF. The duration of the measurement of external deviations from the baseline period projections was from 1 January 1990 to 31 December 1990. The external contingency to be taken into account in the baseline period were the balance of payments effects due to changes in export prices for crude petroleum and other petroleum and energy based products such as methanol, urea, steel; changes in the interest payments (variable rate) on external debt; and net of interest receipts on foreign reserves. The maximum amount of contingency financing permitted for unfavourable/favourable contingent deviations was to be SDR 42.5 million (25% of quota).

3. Letter of Intent re-CCFF was dated 14 March 1990. Earlier Letter of Intent was also done for the 1989 loan in 1988.

4. Initial debt consolidation agreement was from 25 January 1989 to 1992.

5. Debt rescheduling was negotiated again in 27 April 1990 until 2000.

6. A structural adjustment loan of 40 million dollars in January 1990 from the World Bank along with technical assistance loan to help with the implementation of adjustment measures. The structural adjustment loan was aimed at eliminating distortions and increasing efficiency in production, state enterprise reforms and public utilities operations, investment incentives, and financial reform. The technical assistance loan was to assist in the strengthening of the government's social sector policies and programmes including the maintenance of a social safety net.

7. Inter-American Development Bank loans were also accessed during the period of 1990-93 with linkages to the programme of the World Bank in areas such as public utilities reform, tariff reform health, etc.

8. Business Expansion and Industrial Restructuring Project of 27 million dollars. While this project was due to start in 1992, it did not actually start until 1996.

3 The Micro-level Impact of Macroeconomic Policies: The Firm Under Adjustment

3.1 Introduction

In the application of structural adjustment in developing countries, macroeconomic policies are normally recommended by the IMF and the World Bank as part of a package of stabilization and economic restructuring. Emphasis is given in these macro policies to appropriate price signals that ensure the proper functioning of markets. These price incentives ought to lead to the efficient operation of firms, increased profitability and investment - particularly in the traded goods sector. Adjustment policies do not clearly articulate the manner and the processes by which firms adjust to become more efficient. To better understand the impact of the macro policies, it is worthwhile to understand how these policies affect the firm and possibilities for adjustment.

In seeking to analyse the impact of macro-level adjustment policies through looking at the micro-level (firms) effects and responses, a major problem is the absence of an integrated body of theory linking the macro policies and the micro units, with the core of the problem being the separateness of macro and microeconomic theory (Lamberte et al. 1992: 43).[1] While the research provides a backdrop for linking the macro policies of adjustment and the micro theory of the firm, its aim is not to develop an integrated theory to link the macro and micro perspectives. However, the exploratory approach used in this research can contribute to bridging the gap that exists in analysing macro/micro problems of this kind.

Section 3.2 starts with an overview of the rationale for and the theoretical framework of adjustment – which implies both structural adjustment and stabilization. This section also contains a discussion of selected policies. The neo-classical theory of the firm begins the discussion in section 3.3 which includes brief insights into product, labour and capital markets under perfect competition, as well as alternate market forms/models of the firm; drawing out implications for LDCs and adjustment. Section 3.4 summarizes the discussions and a brief conclusion follows in section 3.5.

3.2 The Rationale for Adjustment

3.2.1 An overview of the micro and macro aspects

There is no denying the importance of an adjustment programme in its goal to reposition economies on a path of sustainable growth. Most developing countries in the 1970s and early 1980s experienced a series of shocks - some of which were derived externally from changes in the international economic environment and others from internal sources. These shocks included adverse movements in the terms of trade, increased oil prices, recession in industrialized economies, debt and interest rate problems, and local financial crises that culminated in capital flight in some cases. The effect of these shocks on the national economies led to the implementation of stabilization and structural adjustment programmes from the IMF and the World Bank.

The policies recommended by these international institutions include reduction of the fiscal deficit, domestic market deregulation, import liberalization and the creation of a competitive exchange rate. The overall objective of adjustment is the integration of developing countries into the world economy through a process of economic liberalization, which entails elimination of quantitative restrictions and other international trade barriers, the end of pricing interventions and decreased state intervention.

Getting the prices right is an aspect of the policy thrust that links the macro and the microeconomic levels of adjustment with the hope that individual efficiency attained through micro-level response to relative prices can lead to overall economic efficiency. Hence, macroeconomic policies should enable the microeconomic units to respond rationally to market-determined price incentives leading to recovery at the macro level. These policies are aimed not merely at achieving stabilization of the economy in its own right, but ultimately the thrust is toward private sector recovery, and specifically that of private investment as a cornerstone for overall economic recovery.

Under a series of assumptions (discussed in Chapter 1), the representative firm passively carries out production in a private enterprise system and produces a desired level of output that is socially optimal. Divergence in the objectives as laid out in adjustment programmes and the achievement of sustainable growth in developing economies was discussed relative to private investment recovery. In part, the problem has to do with the differential impact of adjustment policies on different groups of firms given a heterogeneous private sector, which in essence is a key issue in this research. In the adjustment framework, factors such as ownership patterns, the action of interest groups and social organizations do not matter.[2]

Furthermore, in LDCs the conditions of the market in which the firm operates; that is, the origins of technology and intermediate inputs in the production process pose constraints on the optimization problem of the firm, which can affect the outcome of the macro policies and the recovery of private investment. In discussing the framework that underlies adjustment both at the macro and micro levels, the literature as expounded by the World Bank, IMF and Washington consensus in general is largely silent on issues of heterogeneity, and on structural and historical factors that affect economic agents opting instead for the notion of a representative firm and the sameness of developed and developing countries.

Not surprisingly, an adjustment programme can have differential impact on micro units. This can arise out of differences in market conditions, or out of structural differences in firms and their experiences that affect their access to and ownership of resources, their structure of production and their indebtedness. In this context, credit access and market orientation of firms were discussed in the previous chapter relative to the experiences of different types of firms in a developing country.

While there is an abundance of literature on the macro theory of adjustment and on the theory of the firm, the discussion in this chapter will attempt to focus on the monetary, financial and exchange rate policies at the macro level, given that these were some of the main policies applied during the period of adjustment in the country case study.

Lamberte et al. (1992) identify three channels through which adjustment policies can affect firm/households or vulnerable groups: (1) the product or goods market, (2) the factor markets and (3) government expenditure. They also see the following as mechanisms through which policies are felt: (1) relative prices, (2) income or purchasing power and (3) access (or lack thereof) to resources. However, in this approach they do not fully articulate the question of heterogeneity as present in private sectors apart from distinguishing between the formal and informal sectors, the latter of which is viewed as a vulnerable grouping.

In examining these channels and mechanisms, it is important to have an understanding of the macro policies and the neo-classical theory of the firm and its alternatives. These two concerns are discussed in the sections that follow, which will also incorporate, wherever possible, an examination of the macro/micro content and the relevance to the themes of heterogeneity, history and structure. The following section presents an overview of the IMF's stabilization programme.

3.2.2 The framework underlying stabilization policies

The main program objective of the IMF is stabilization of the economy through the achievement of a sustainable balance of payments position in the short to medium term (IMF Occasional Paper No. 55, 1987). Another objective is price stability and a low inflation rate in order to achieve external balance and growth. Demand is therefore adjusted in line with the available resources of the economy using a combination of fiscal, monetary and exchange rate policies with reduction of the fiscal deficit in order to release savings for private investment.

The underlying framework of the IMF has its basis in papers articulated by Polak (1957) and Robichek (1967).[3] The central focus of their analysis is the role of the Central Bank in credit expansion, which is seen as the source of the balance of payments (BOP) crisis. Domestic credit control should eliminate inflation and BOP problems. The basis of this approach is monetarist since it centres on the neutrality of money. Hence, real variables seem not to be affected by money changes in the long run, which therefore affects only prices.[4]

The core relationships in the IMF model are: the budget constraint of the external sector which links the current account balance of the country with its manner of financing – foreign borrowing and changes in reserves; and the monetary system constraint which links changes in the money supply, (ΔM), with changes in reserves, (ΔR), and in domestic credit total (ΔDC) or to both the public (ΔDC_g) and private (ΔDC_p) sectors (equation 3.1).

$$\begin{aligned} &\Delta R = \Delta DC \\ \text{or} \quad &\Delta R = \Delta M - (\Delta DC_p + \Delta DC_g) \\ &\Delta M = \Delta R + \Delta DC_p + \Delta DC_g \\ &\Delta R = X - Z + \Delta FI \end{aligned} \tag{3.1}$$

The interdependence in fiscal and monetary policy comes out in 3.1: the reliance of government on bank credit to finance its fiscal deficit affects changes in the money supply – specifically domestic credit changes. The last line of equation 3.1 reflects the balance of payments position in terms of exports (X), imports (Z) and net external indebtedness (FI) not held by the banking system.

By imposing ceilings on domestic credit as well as on its distribution between public and private components, the IMF aims to improve the BOP position of a country and to avoid the crowding out of private sector credit by the public sector. This credit ceiling of the IMF is made relative to the commercial banking system which assumes a well-developed system of financial intermediation. The need for a strong financial system is to prevent informal financing, outside the regulated banking system, from weakening the effect of the credit ceiling.

Apart from monitoring the balance of payments, the IMF also monitors the inflation rate (Mills & Nallari 1992). In the context of the competitiveness of the economy, domestic inflation can impact the real effective exchange rate causing an appreciation and therefore a decline in competitiveness. In the monetarist approach, inflation is viewed as deriving from a situation in which aggregate demand is excessive relative to the economy's supply capacity.

The relationship between prices and money is expressed through an equation based on the quantity theory of money (see 3.2 below). As shown in Chapter 1, this establishes the relation between the level of nominal income (PY), the money stock (M), and the income velocity of money (V) (P – the price level and Y – real income).

$$P \equiv \frac{MV}{Y} \quad \text{such that} \quad dP = dM - dY \tag{3.2}$$

The equation of exchange implies that the rate of growth of the money supply (dM) less the rate of growth of real income (dY) is equal to the inflation rate (dP) with the velocity of money (V) assumed to be constant. However, it does not necessarily follow that one has to contain inflation to achieve growth since it is the relative growth of inflation to that of money which matters. Relative to the view that the income velocity of money is not constant, it is thought satisfactory in the IMF approach if the demand for money is predictable relative to income (IMF 1987: 14).

The approach of the IMF is criticized on the grounds that there is a lack of articulation of capital markets in LDCs since the option of holding alternative assets such as bonds and access by individuals to foreign capital markets is limited. A more critical assessment of monetary policy is discussed in a later section.

3.2.3 The underlying framework of the World Bank

The programme of the Bank, termed structural adjustment, was aimed at longer-term structural change to enhance economic efficiency; to have greater flexibility in the economy; to expand the stock of human and physical capital; and to improve the standard of living (Thomas et al. 1991). The orientation of its policies is therefore towards the shifting of resources to more efficient uses in the economy. This shift ought to lead to systemic structural changes by use of market incentives. Trade and exchange rate policies, financial reforms and public sector management are some of the methods used to create the market incentives. Privatization and institutional reforms are also recommended to increase efficiency in both the public and private sectors.

The analytical framework that underlies the Bank's programme is purportedly based on the Harrod-Domar two-gap model and its extensions. Known as the RMSM (Revised Minimum Standard Model), the model focuses on the availability of foreign savings to bridge the domestic savings gap. This model is a means of estimating the resource needs of a country relative to a target growth rate. Primarily, the RMSM is a 'planning tool' used in calculating the amount of investment, imports, and external borrowing necessary to sustain an exogenous GDP growth rate (Addison 1989: 25).

This economic framework, however, seems far removed from the emphasis that is placed on relative prices in the actual macroeconomic policies applied. In these policies, the real exchange rate (which depicts the relative prices of global and domestic prices), the real wage rate, and the real interest rate are key relative prices which play an important part in the movement towards market-determined prices. However, these relative prices are not in the RMSM model which is projected as their framework (Mills & Nallari 1992).[5] Hence, this framework is, in reality, a Swan-Salter modelling approach of traded/non-traded sectors (Lal 1984) and textbook microeconomics (White 1996: 792).

The RMSM is also criticized for the assumptions of capital flows that occur between rich and poor countries and the stability of the incremental capital output ratio (ICOR). The counter argument is that the tendency of World Bank programme objectives in the 1980s has been towards emphasizing the increase in exports and domestic savings, higher real interest rates and increased efficiency through a reduction in ICOR.

Despite these objections, the RMSM underpins the analysis of resource requirements in adjusting countries. In fact, in most World Bank projections, higher growth rates are largely based on a lower ICOR. The actual adjustment policies are the subject of a wide body of criticism from various angles.[6] Monetary, financial liberalization, and exchange rate policies are discussed below.

3.2.4 Monetary policy: The transmission effects to firms

Essentially, the transmission mechanism through which monetary policy works is through changes in real balances which lead to a portfolio disequilibrium at the prevailing interest rate and income. In response to changes in real balances, it is assumed that portfolio holders can vary their money and asset holdings thereby changing the prices of assets and the interest rate. The nature of financial markets in developing countries and the degree of integration of domestic and foreign goods in financial markets determine the extent of choices that portfolio holders can have as well as the effectiveness of various instruments of monetary policy.[7]

The change in the interest rate can also have an impact aggregate demand. Starting with an increase in the money supply, there is portfolio adjustment and changes in spending that lead to interest rate changes and affect aggregate demand. The effect of monetary policy depends on the exchange rate regime and on the presence or absence of capital mobility.

In the approach to the balance of payments, the focus is on how changes in the money supply impact economic activity.[8] Specifically, the effects of changes in the nominal money stock vis-à-vis output, domestic prices and the interest rate are evaluated. Making allowances for an open economy, under a fixed exchange rate regime, the supply of money is not exogenous since it can be altered based on balance of payments changes. In the transmission process of monetary policy, the demand for real money balances, M^d/P, (where P is the domestic price level) can be assumed to depend on Y, real domestic income; r, the domestic rate of interest and π, the rate of inflation as shown in equation 3.3:

$$\frac{M^d}{P} = F(Y, r, \pi) \tag{3.3}$$

In the approach to financial programming, changes in the demand for money balances can take the form:

$$\Delta M^d - \Delta P = k_1 \Delta Y + k_2 \Delta r + k_3 \Delta \pi \tag{3.4}$$

The parameters of real income, interest rate and inflation which are all elasticities with respect to real money demand are such that: $k_1>0$, $k_2<0$ and $k_3<0$. Increases in the growth rate of domestic interest and inflation will lower demand for real balances while a similar increase in the growth of real income will increase the demand for real balances. The link with the balance of payment can be shown using equation 3.1 , which can be rewritten as (with the variables having the same meaning as above):

$$M = R + DC \Rightarrow \Delta M = \Delta R + \Delta DC \tag{3.5}$$

Hence by equating changes in money supply and demand the following equation results:

$$\Delta M^d = \Delta M$$
$$\Rightarrow \Delta R + \Delta DC = \Delta P + k_1\Delta Y + k_2\Delta r + k_3\Delta\pi \qquad (3.6)$$
$$\Rightarrow \Delta R = \Delta P + k_1\Delta Y + k_2\Delta r + k_3\Delta\pi - \Delta DC$$

The above relation does not take into consideration the impact of the money multiplier on the money supply and therefore on changes in international reserves and on domestic credit. However, what equation 3.6 further implies is that a loss in international reserves (ΔR) will result in increases in domestic credit (ΔD), in interest rate (Δr) or in the rate of inflation ($\Delta\pi$), while there will be an increase in reserves with increases in the domestic price level and income since $k_1>0$, $k_2<0$ and $k_3<0$ as in equation 3.4. In a small open economy with free mobility of capital and a fixed exchange rate regime, and in which domestic prices and interest rates are equal to international prices, an excess supply of money will be reflected in the balance of payment as a loss in reserves, in a schema such as the following:

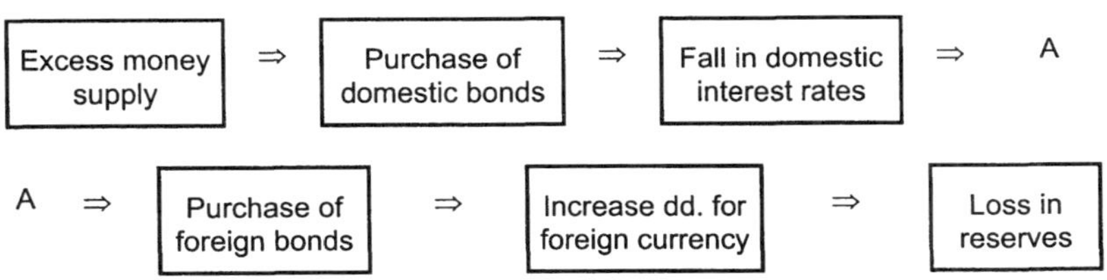

The outflow of reserves implies a loss in the money supply which cancels out the effect of the initial increase in the money supply. While there is a similar result under a system of fixed exchange rate and capital controls, the process entails a reduction in savings and an increase of investment due to the fall in interest rate as a result of the purchase of domestic bonds.

Impact of monetary policy on firms

Often, in the short run, firms cannot automatically make changes in their production structure or activities in response to problems of export instability or terms of trade, which are beyond the control of many developing countries (Killick 1984). Thus, problems with the underlying structures of demand and supply are not tackled in this monetary approach resulting in the reappearance of the deficit once the monetary restraint is eased.

The impact of tight monetary policy on firms is also felt through the inducement of economic contraction which leads to the postponement of investment decisions by firms based on adverse expectations about the duration of the recession (Servén & Solimano, in Corbo 1992). Describing the quantity theory of money as an oversimplification, Lim (1987) argued that tight monetary policy will lead to extreme cuts in incomes, personal consumption expenditure, and possibly, government spending. These factors represent a combination of channels/mechanisms through which the impact of monetary policy is transmitted to firms.

Another link between monetary policy and firms is seen when tight monetary policy increases the interest rates on loans to firms, which in turn leads to increased cost of working capital/investment. Small and medium firms which experience problems in accessing credit may be affected to a greater extent than larger firms.

The response of firms to increased financial costs can in turn cause a fall in economic activity, a transference of costs through mark-up prices by firms that are able to pass on cost, or an overall fall in aggregate supply greater than the fall in demand. This sequence could lead to further inflationary pressures and stagflation (Taylor 1983). Consequently, the possibilities for restructuring vary with the ability of firms to recover the costs of adjustment. Assuming that firms borrow for working capital purposes, the impact of the interest rate is represented in equations 3.7 to 3.10 which is an adaptation of Taylor (1981).

$$W_r = wN + eP_0mQ_i \tag{3.7}$$

where W_r is working capital requirements to pay the total wage bill (wN) and eP_0mQ_i is the cost of imported intermediates (where P_0 is foreign currency price of imported intermediates, e is the nominal exchange rate, Q_i is output, m is the intermediate import-output coefficient, w is the wage rate and N the numbers employed). The supply of working capital from banks to firms is total assets (reserves for deposits) A_t, plus loans to firms (B_f) less deposits from members of the public (D_p):

$$W_s = A_t + B_f - D_p \tag{3.8}$$

Deposits from the public, which are liabilities to commercial banks, is a function of the interest rate and is either loaned to firms for the purchase of physical capital, *PK*, or held as deposits, and can be expressed as:

$$D_p = \phi(i)(A_t + PK) \tag{3.9}$$

Hence the working capital requirements less that which is supplied can be written as (combining and rearranging equations 3.7 to 3.9):

$$\begin{aligned} W_r - W_s &= wN + eP_0mQ_i - (A_t + B_f - D_p) \\ &= wN + eP_0mQ_i - A_t - B_f + \phi(i)A_t + \phi(i)K \end{aligned} \tag{3.10}$$

Based on equation 3.10, an increase in the demand for money by members of the public (D_p) implies that there is less money available to supply working capital to firms. This equation also shows that any variation in money supply that impacts the interest rate, also adversely affects firms for working capital or investment purposes. The process of adjustment through monetary policy therefore affects both the availability and the cost of credit to firms in the private sector as far as investment and working capital is concerned.

In situations where firms face problems in accessing credit or discriminatory practices in the cost of credit based on criteria such as ownership, size, or traditional bank-firm relationships as discussed in Chapter 2, tight monetary policy can have differential effects on the debt structure, profitability and investment of firms. Firms with traditional relationships with banks may continue to receive credit while firms with no traditional linkages/relationship with banks may face increasing difficulty in accessing credit or may be unable to afford the cost of credit that the bank prescribes. The latter group may include small firms or firms that cannot meet the necessary collateral requirements.

3.2.5 Financial policy: Underpinnings and impact

In periods of adjustment, financial liberalization is a policy recommendation that includes the removal of financial restrictions and the implementation of a free market interest rate. These measures ought to lead to an efficient allocation of resources and increased savings and investment which should solve the problems experienced with access to investment credit.

It was stated in Chapter 2 that financial policy in Trinidad & Tobago did not largely entail the direct repression of interest rates but rather the application of indirect measures on the reserve requirement ratio and other restrictions relative to the direction of credit. These policies served indirectly to create a situation of financial repression. These credit directives took the form, for example, of guidelines with respect to the down-payment requirements on consumer loans and were not in the form of directing credit to particular sectors or firms. The financial policy environment was also shown to be one in which credit rationing of different types of firms based on considerations such as ownership was pervasive. Thus relative to instances of financial restrictions and problems of credit access by some firms, the financial liberalization policy which has been recommended for use in LDCs is relevant to the discussion of firm restructuring in Trinidad & Tobago.

An overview of the debate on financial liberalization

Financial liberalization involves freeing up the financial systems in developing countries with the aim of achieving greater financial efficiency. It comprises the dismantling of controls on credit allocation and interest rates, removal of foreign exchange controls and a reduction of the fiscal burden on the private sector.[9] The imposition of financial restrictions is therefore part of the policy of financial repression where the interest rate is also affected though not by a deliberate policy of interest rate repression. The solution to problems of financial repression is liberalization of the financial system which should complement stabilization in stimulating private sector output through targeting higher savings and investment and improving the quality of investment.[10]

The works of McKinnon (1973) and Shaw (1973) have formed the basis for policy recommendations concerning finance in developing countries.[11] They argued that the development process has been hindered by the distortions of financial prices such as interest rates and foreign exchange rates. The result is a reduction in the real rate of growth and the real size of the financial system (Shaw 1973: 3–4).[12]

McKinnon's views are based on the complementarity between money and physical capital in which he argued that the demand for real money balances will be strongly influenced by the propensity to save and invest. The lack of organized finance in developing countries confines economic units to self-financing. The lower the opportunity cost of holding money, the higher is the real deposit rate of interest and the greater the incentive to invest. McKinnon's complementarity between money and physical capital is represented in equation 3.11.

$$\frac{M}{P} = f(Y, \tfrac{I}{Y}, i - \pi^e) \qquad (3.11)$$

where *M* is the demand for money, *P* is the price level, *I*/*Y* is the ratio of gross investment to GNP, *i* is the nominal deposit rate, and π^e is the expected rate of inflation.

Shaw's analysis is based on financial deepening through the expansion of financial intermediation between savers and investors. Liberalization is thought to be able to allocate savings more efficiently through the competition that results, with savers having 'a wider menu of portfolio choices'. He differed from McKinnon in his view that self-financing of investment was symptomatic of a repressed economy (Shaw 1973). Consequently, his debt-intermediation model is one that incorporates allowances for inside money. Shaw's debt-intermediation view is represented in equation 3.12.

$$\frac{M}{P} = f(Y, v, i - \pi^e) \qquad (3.12)$$

where money demand, *M*/*P*, is a function of *Y* (*GNP*), ν, which is the opportunity cost of holding money, and the nominal interest rate minus expected inflation, $i-\pi^e$.

Increased financial intermediation leads to the pooling of risks in financial institutions, the achievement of economies of scale, and the reduction in exposure of the individual saver. Transformation of short-term savings to long-term loans is also made possible.

Financial repression is said to intensify weaknesses inherent in LDCs through the regulation that is placed on increasing interest rates thereby distorting the economy by producing a bias in favour of current consumption and against future consumption. The repression of interest rates, therefore, induces inefficiencies in resource allocation. This effect is reflected in the prevalence of negative real interest rates and disequilibrium in the organized money market. The result is excess demand for loans relative to available funds and excess demand for investment relative to savings.

The aspect of credit selectivity implies that banks allocate a minimum percentage of their asset portfolios for loans to priority sectors at subsidized rates of interest. This policy is seen as resulting in an inefficient allocation of investment.[13] Raising the interest rate is thought to lead to increased saving and investment which could then deter investors from implementing low-yielding investments.

The macroeconomic arguments that support the policy of financial liberalization go back to the Harrod-Domar model and its derivatives, while at the microeconomic level, the framework for the analysis of saving and investment is based on the neo-classical approach in which savings is automatically translated into investment through the interest rate mechanism.

Figure 3.1 illustrates the McKinnon-Shaw hypothesis where the deposit interest rate (r_1) is held below the market rate (r_0), such that the amount of savings at this rate is S_1 and the amount of investable funds available is I_1, with r_i representing the loan rate of interest. Hence, both savings and investment are lowered by I_0–I_1. Normally, the lending rate is fixed close to the borrowing rate therefore the excess demand for investment in this case is I_2–I_1.

This situation leads to the rationing of credit. The liberalization of the interest rate at r_0 is such that the higher rate on deposits leads to increased savings. Additionally, inefficient investment projects that

Figure 3.1 Saving and investment under repressed interest rate

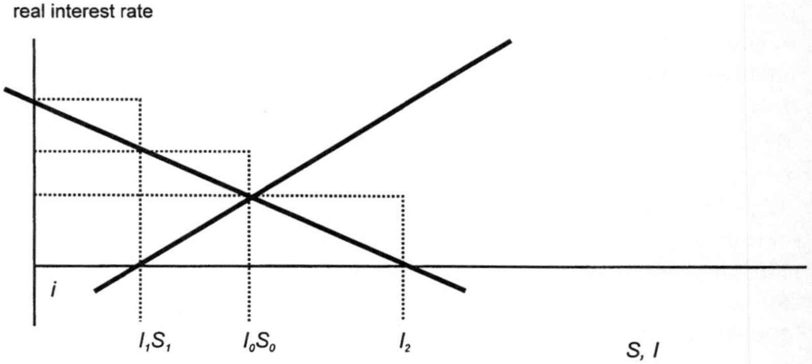

would normally have been funded at the lower interest rate cannot be funded at the higher interest rate.

Hence, while the volume of investment increases, the efficiency of the resulting investment under liberalization also increases. The core of McKinnon and Shaw's arguments can be summarized by stating that savings are positively related to the real interest rate at each rate of economic growth. The practice of institutionally placing a ceiling on the nominal rate of interest holds the real rate of interest below its equilibrium level resulting in low savings and investment and the inefficient allocation of investable funds based on non-price criteria (Fry 1988).

Underpinning the arguments of financial liberalization are assumptions about savings behaviour. The derivation of savings behaviour has its roots in two areas. One, the life-cycle theory of consumption associated with Modigliani (1963),[14] which assumes an inter-temporal pattern of consumption and savings: individuals plan their consumption and saving behaviour so as to optimally allocate consumption over their lifetime. Two, the permanent income hypothesis (Friedman 1957),[15] which views consumption behaviour of individuals as being based on their permanent or long-term income and not on their current income. Therefore, the savings behaviour of the economy is determined by aggregating individual savings over the lifetime of resources available in the future. There is not much attention placed on the internal savings of the firm as a source of savings for investment.[16]

Some effects of financial liberalization on firms

The debate on financial liberalization is centred to a greater extent on the role of the interest rate in stimulating savings and less on the efficiency of allocation of investment through financial deepening. The arguments are many and wide ranging.[17] In this section, the focus of the discussion will be mainly on issues surrounding credit access and the effects of financial liberalization on firms.

Credit access by firms is said to be adversely affected by financial liberalization due to portfolio shifts between assets and also the shifting of funds from the informal financial market to deposits in the formal financial system (Taylor 1983 & 1990). Stricter credit requirements in the formal sector result in a reduction of available funds to firms that do not qualify for formal sector loans. As in the case of monetary contraction and its impact on interest rates, the tendency is for higher interest rates under financial liberalization to lead to increases in the costs of working capital and production at the level of the firm. The interest rate can enter production costs of firms as follows:

$$C = (awN + beP_0mQ_i)(1 + i) \quad (3.13)$$

where the cost of production (*C*) is assumed to be made up of the total wage bill and the intermediate imports bill. The interest factor (*I*) reflects that the costs of the current inputs are used up in production long before the sale of the output (Taylor 1981). The wage rate is *w*, thus *wN* is the total wage bill, and eP_0mQ is the intermediate import bill as described earlier with *a* and *b* being technology coefficients. As an element of production cost, increased interest rates can be reflected in higher mark-up prices by large firms rather than through efficient resource allocation among firms.

An increase in interest rates brought on by financial liberalization may feed back into the working capital and production costs of the firm as well as the costs entailed in the use of the capital stock. Given that the profit of the firm is total revenue minus total cost, then the increased costs of production can reduce profitability leading to bankruptcy and economic contraction.

With respect to portfolio shifts into financial assets, Fry (1988) showed that increased real deposit rate led to higher demand for financial assets both in the short and long term, thereby increasing financial savings. However, he saw this shift as automatically increasing investable funds. The counter argument is that these portfolio shifts do not necessarily lead to real investment.

The presence of segmented markets in developing countries in which saving and investment plans are principally self-financed through non-homogenous household firms also causes a bias in favour of large-scale producers (FitzGerald & Vos 1989). The expectation is that increased financial intermediation under financial liberalization ought to remove the biases in credit allocation that existed in favour of large firms, with small firms being able to benefit from increased access to credit. However, this expectation may not materialize.

FitzGerald (1989: 15) argued that large enterprises generate large retained earnings, have traditional links with banks and other firms, and are often members of 'ownership groups', such that the preferential access to credit by large firms is not the result of a financial repression policy but 'a perfectly rational accumulation strategy'.

Arguing against financial liberalization, Jansen (1990) sees subsidized credit and government intervention as circumventing the behaviour of financial institutions who are either reluctant to lend to agriculture and household firms or charge them higher loan rates with collateral requirements, which lessens their capacity to borrow.

The ineffectiveness of the interest rate relative to the efficient allocation of resources was discussed in Chapter 1. This argument was brought out by Stiglitz & Weiss (1981) in which credit rationing and imperfect information, due to asymmetric information about the borrower, leads the lender to use the interest rate as a device to sift out risky borrowers. As a result, loans are not necessarily allocated to the most efficient project.

Empirical studies on financial liberalization

The interest sensitivity of savings in developing countries has been the focus of various empirical studies. Some of the studies reported in Fry (1988) include:

- Fry (1986) used pooled time-series data on 14 Asian countries in which the ratio of savings to income was positively related to the real deposit rate of interest.
- On the quality and quantity of investment: Fry (1981) on 12 Asian countries in which the ratio of domestic credit to income was positively related to the real deposit rate.
- Fry (1980) showed that the ratio of investment to income was positively related to the availability of domestic credit.

Financial liberalization efforts in Latin America showed that the real cost of borrowing by productive firms for working capital purposes increased. The cost of foreign borrowing was cheaper which resulted in massive external debt for the government, with no atomization of credit suppliers, and with asset concentration in a few conglomerates (Arietta 1988).

In the case of Uruguay, de Melo & Tybout (1986) looked at the effect of domestic savings to GDP on firms for the years 1962-83 and found that there was a structural shift within this period. During the 1960s, savings rates were sensitive to foreign capital inflows and appeared to have been influenced by policies of financial repression. In the period of the 1970s, the real exchange rate played a dominant role, in particular, real appreciation discouraged savings. They concluded that controlling for the effect of the real exchange rate, savings rates shifted upward with financial liberalization. Relative to credit allocation by firm size, they found improvement in credit allocation with small firms increasing their leverage and average financial costs relative to large firms. However, this last conclusion was based on 'size coefficients' which they state were not statistically significant ('mild evidence': 579).

Giovannini (1983) had two main findings on the methodology used to assess the financial liberalization theory. In his paper, he concluded that the real interest elasticity of savings is not easily detected, such that the results obtained in the 1960s data by Fry cannot be reproduced in the 1970s. He further concluded that the models used in the past suffered from defects that made them difficult to interpret. These defects included: quality and homogeneity of the data across countries, aggregation of private and public savings leading to biased results, absence of tax considerations, and the exclusion of other relevant variables.

Another argument surrounding the effects of financial liberalization was made by Foxley (1981), who looked at the combined effects of the policies, arguing that a sharp rise in the cost of borrowing increased the costs of production, pushing up prices in the process.[18] Firms were forced to cut production when faced with declining demand, increases in unsold inventories, and higher costs of borrowing capital.

With the importance given to the role of the private sector in the development process, financial liberalization has also been viewed as the mechanism by which these countries are able to obtain both the savings needed for investment as well as to improve the quality of this investment. The above arguments, however, show some weak points relative to adverse aspects of this policy on credit access and costs considerations of firms. Some of the empirical studies discussed are listed in Table A3.1 in the Annex to this chapter.

The literature on financial policy shows problems that may result in access to credit by firms under financial liberalization with implications for different firms such as those that are able to borrow in formal financial markets versus those that rely on informal borrowing. This problem originates from the attraction of funds from the informal sector with the result that firms that borrow from informal sources are faced with a reduction in funds. The bias with respect to availability of funds was also mentioned as existing against small-scale producers/ household firms and against enterprises in agriculture. Smaller firms may not necessarily benefit from increased financial liberalization, since credit-rationing problems are intrinsically institutionally based rather than the result of financial repression.

Differential conditions experienced by firms under financial liberalization find support in the depiction of the country case study in Chapter 2, based on differences in access to resources of firms. On the question of credit rationing, the formulations of credit access problems by FitzGerald (1993); the view of institutionally-based credit rationing by Worrell (1985) and the evidence in Farrell & Crichton (1986) of credit restrictions by commercial banks based on firm size are relevant for the analysis of firms in Trinidad & Tobago under adjustment as opposed to the conventional view of directed credit ceilings and so forth. Based on these experiences, it is expected that under financial liberalization, the conditions of firms which have difficulty in obtaining credit will be worsened both in terms of profitability and investment, while other firms, particularly large firms with traditional links with banks, may not suffer any negative effects.

3.2.6 Exchange rate policy and firm-level adjustment

The target variable in exchange rate policy is the real exchange rate (RER), while the instrument that is used in policy implementation is the nominal exchange rate. The aim of a devaluation is to improve the international competitiveness of a country and its balance of payments position by changing the relative prices of traded and non-traded goods (Mills & Nallari, 1992).

Exchange rate policy is aimed at a switch in the pattern of expenditure in favour of goods and services of the devaluing country through a reduction in the demand for imports and an increase in the demand for exports. This result is achieved through the raising of the domestic currency price of imports and reducing the foreign currency price of exports, with the net effect of a devaluation on foreign exchange earnings being positive. However, the way in which the devaluation affects exports differs between small and large countries. This will be discussed later in this section.

As part of a stabilization policy, devaluation therefore works together with demand reduction to improve the current account of the balance of payments through expenditure switching. The real exchange rate can be defined in different ways to reflect the varying approaches to analysing the effect of devaluation on an economy. Two versions that are given below are those involving the domestic price index and the price of traded to non-traded goods.[19] The former is defined as:

$$RER = \frac{eP_w}{P_D} \qquad (3.14)$$

where P_W is the world price index (WPI), P_D is the domestic price index and e is the nominal exchange rate. This format is the purchasing power parity version. W_D, the wage index can be used as a proxy to domestic prices, P_D. The targeting of the wage rate in adjustment policies is therefore a mechanism by which the cost of production and domestic prices can be kept down to improve the competitiveness of the industries concerned (Mills & Nallari 1992). The relative price of tradable (P_T) to non-tradable (P_{NT}) version of the exchange rate for small open economies is:[20]

$$RER = \frac{P_T}{P_{NT}} \qquad (3.15)$$

Generating a trade surplus entails the shifting of domestic production from non-traded to traded sectors which should be accomplished through an increase in the price of tradable goods relative to non-tradable goods, in order to achieve a real devaluation.[21] Incentives are therefore given to producers to shift resources into more efficient uses in the private sector. It is possible that the real exchange rate will remain the same despite devaluation. Producers can raise the mark-up on their unit costs or wages can rise by the amount of the devaluation thereby negating the effect:

$$P = (wb + mP_0e)(1 + \alpha) \qquad (3.16)$$

where P is the price of output for a sector, w is the wage rate, b is the labour-output coefficient, m is the intermediate import-output coefficient, P_0 is the foreign currency price of imported intermediates, e is the nominal exchange rate and α is the mark-up rate. Any increases in w or α can feed back into domestic prices, canceling the effect of the devaluation since, from equation 3.14, we can write that:

$$\Delta RER = \Delta P_w - \Delta P_D \tag{3.17}$$

Equation 3.17 shows that a nominal devaluation will be a real devaluation if the changes in the domestic price index are less than the changes in P_w (the world price index). However, if manufacturers are able to pass on costs through mark-up pricing or if wages increase such that the term on the right-hand side in equation 3.17 is equal to zero, then there will be no real devaluation.

Therefore, a crucial issue for an effective devaluation is that the nominal wage rate should remain constant (FitzGerald 1993).[22] Hence combining equations 3.14 and 3.16, the RER can be expressed relative to the cost of production in equation 3.18, which explains more fully the use of wage restraint in achieving increased competitiveness. Assuming that imported costs of intermediates cannot be easily varied to the extent that individual producers are able to suppress wages, then this is a mechanism by which they can improve profitability.

$$RER = \frac{eP_w}{(wb + mP_0e)(1+\alpha)} \tag{3.18}$$

Thus the question of economic adjustment through the lowering of the cost of labour is achievable through wage reduction or reduction of persons with jobs - the latter having implications for the productivity of the firm. If increases in output occur with labour reduction, then devaluation indirectly induces increased efficiency in production. FitzGerald (1989) argued that while the lower import-intensive nature of small-scale enterprises implies a market advantage relative to smaller increases in unit cost as a result of devaluation, the reduction in real wages implies reduced expenditure on the products of small-scale industries.

The expansionary effects of devaluation can be eroded if workers try to recover their real wages or if wages are indexed. If wages increase, not only is the effect of the devaluation cancelled out, but also the profitability and competitiveness of the firm are affected. The Structuralist theory of inflation puts forward the view that wage indexation leads to a sequence of price increases. An upward movement in prices leads to a fall in the real wage and an increase in the nominal wage which are then passed on in mark-ups, causing further price increase and an activation of a wage-price spiral. If money wages do not increase, then the distribution of income tilts towards higher profits for producers at the expense of wage earners leading to a decline in consumption. Devaluation therefore has redistributive income effects which can be contractionary (Krugman & Taylor 1978). The movement of wages is a critical factor in devaluation.

It is argued that the impact of devaluation on supply (since it raises the incentives to produce exports) is more important than the demand switching effect, i.e. away from imports (Killick 1984). However, the offsetting effects of the impact on exports versus that of imports can produce a fall in output. For a devaluation to be effective, the Marshall-Lerner condition is:

$$\eta_m + \eta_x > 1 \tag{3.19}$$

that is, the elasticity of demand for imports (n_m), plus the elasticity of demand for the country's exports (n_x) should be greater than one. In the short run imports and exports are not very responsive to price changes; therefore, it is argued that there is economic contraction. The Marshall-Lerner condition is only a partial condition since income effects are ignored.

Exports may be further inhibited through the impact of inflation which can contribute to the erosion of the exchange rate causing a loss in competitiveness. High import content of production adversely affects the competitiveness of exports as well as the profitability of the firm. In developing countries, the strong dependence on production using imported inputs justifies its inclusion as a cost component in the production structure, along with wages (including income of small proprietors), profits and bank interest.[23] This may lead to income effects as discussed earlier or may affect small firms that are unable to pass on costs (Taylor 1990).[24]

$$P_m = eP^*_m \tag{3.20}$$

where P_m is the overall import price index, and e is the nominal exchange rate multiplied by P_m^*, price of imports;

$$P_D = \delta P + (1 + \delta)P_m \tag{3.21}$$

where the overall domestic price, P_D, is made up of the domestic component, (P), and a proportion from the imported component, P_m, which is the import price index;

$$P = \alpha P + (1 - \alpha)P_N = \alpha(eP^*_T + (1 - \alpha)P_N \tag{3.22}$$

where P_T, is traded price (index) , P_T^*, the price of traded goods, and non-traded price is P_N with P, the domestic price;

$$P_N = \alpha w + \beta P_0 = \alpha w + \beta(EP_0^*) \qquad (3.23)$$

Equations 3.20 to 3.23 above illustrate how devaluation can feed back into prices resulting in increased costs to firms/producers in the private sector and increased inflation. The increases in the price of imported goods (3.20) leads to an increase in the domestic price level in 3.21 (P is domestic prices while P_D is the overall domestic price index). Equation 3.22 is an illustration from the traded/ non-traded definition of the exchange rate. In 3.23, P_0 is the price of imported intermediates which – as seen earlier – feeds into the costs of production of the firm; w is the wage rate, α and β are the technological coefficients. In this equation, shows how devaluation affects non-traded prices P_N.

Given the structural characteristics of developing countries there are non-price constraints which militate against the automatic expansion of firm exports through a devaluation. These constraints include lags in supply due to long gestation periods, the unavailability of local raw materials for production which therefore have to be imported, capacity constraints, problems in accessing external markets, all of which affect the short run response of firms to a devaluation. If many developing countries produce the same products for export, it may not be the case that devaluation will increase exports for all the countries concerned without some measure of trade displacement for some countries.[25]

Exchange rate policy can also affect the demand for firms' domestically produced goods through its impact on the real wealth held by households and the private sector. One channel is through the real cash balance effect in which case the increase in the price level as a result of a devaluation reduces the real stock of money. This in turn leads individuals to restore their real money holdings to the desired level thereby reducing domestic expenditure and having a contractionary effect on demand. A second effect is the shifting of portfolios from assets to money, which leads to an increase in the interest rate in the absence of perfect capital mobility.

In the event that the private sector is able to hold assets which increase with a devaluation, then the real wealth effect may not be contractionary. When foreign or local firms hold assets denominated in foreign currency, devaluation causes the real value of the stock of foreign assets to increase subject to the increase in the domestic price level. Thus, firms with foreign denominated assets can gain by such holdings if the nominal devaluation is in fact a real devaluation. On the other hand, firms with external liabilities are likely to experience a negative wealth effect since a real devaluation increases the real value of interest payments on external debts (Lizondo & Monteil 1989).[26]

For small countries as opposed to larger countries, it was stated that the transmission effects differ relative to the expansion of exports. In the case of a small country, an exchange rate devaluation causes an upward movement in the prices of traded goods, thereby reducing demand. Thus either imports decrease or exports increase. For a large country, the reduction in price due to the devaluation feeds back to producers causing a shift in the supply curve. The essential difference in the response lies in the fact that the small countries are price-takers whereas the large countries are price-setters.

Differential effects of devaluation

The discussion on exchange rate policy has identified possible effects on firms. Not addressed clearly in this discussion are the problems which different types of firms face in response to a devaluation. Small, local firms that are conditioned to a domestic market orientation may experience difficulty in reorienting their production to focus on an export market. In part, this difficulty will be due to lack of finance, lack of information relative to finding markets, lack of prerequisites to enter these markets; as well as to problems of quality of output. While both local and foreign firms may experience adverse effects through the cost of imported raw materials, intermediates and capital goods, it is possible that the effect will be lessened in the case of foreign firms where parent/affiliate companies can offset these costs.

Additionally, local firms with foreign denominated accounts may also be able to offset the costs of a devaluation on imported inputs or capital assets. The question of debt/assets will vary with the extent to which firms possess foreign denominated debt/assets. Some large local and foreign firms may be affected relative to the impact of devaluation on foreign denominated debt/assets.

Small firms with less capital-intensive production may also find it impossible to further reduce wages or labour. This option is possibly more applicable in the case of larger firms that are able to shift to more capital intensive production over time. Hence relative price changes may force labour to be more productive. Though not forming a major part of the discussion, the question of the impact of adjustment on labour relative to conditions of work, such as hours worked and remuneration is paramount.

The effect of a devaluation on firms in the private sector does not automatically lead to increases in exports nor does it automatically induce lower costs of production across the board. There are differentiated outcomes by firms depending on the structural/institutional heterogeneity that exists in the economies of developing countries. Some of these concerns will be taken up in the analytical chapters that follow.

3.2.7 Summary of the effects of macro policies on the firm and private investment

Tables 3.1 and 3.2 below summarize the effects of the macro policies on the private sector/ firms and specifically on private investment. Table 3.1 looks at what ought to happen to private investment under adjustment, the rationale behind these expectations, the transmission mechanisms from the theoretical perspective of adjustment and the counter-claims relative to what happens in reality. Table 3.2 summarizes the overall effect on macroeconomic aggregates and the implications for the private sector/ firm relative to the expectations and criticisms of these policies. Highlights of these summaries are discussed below.

Tight monetary policy

- Restoration of macroeconomic stability to create credibility and necessitate investment response by firms through inflation control and elimination of BOP problems.
- Reduced domestic credit and changes in credit allocation between the public and private sectors can improve the BOP and prevent the crowding out of private investment by public investment.
- Reduced ceiling and changes in allocation can affect the availability of money to firms for investment purposes.
- Increased interest rates that can (a) increase working capital and production costs, (b) result in a fall in investment due to increased cost of

Table 3.1 *Selected adjustment policies as they impact on private investment (I_p)*

Policy	Desired effect on I_p	Transmission to I_p	Rationale for adjustment	Criticism
Monetary Policy Reduced monetary growth/credit direction	$I_p \uparrow$	Credit directed to the private sector, stabilization enables I_p	High inflation which is monetary in nature; distorted credit allocation in favour of public sector	Adverse effect on I_p through high interest rate, high cost of bank credit
Financial policy Interest rate deregulation, dismantling credit controls	$I_p \uparrow$ and improved efficiency	$S_p \uparrow \Rightarrow i \uparrow \Rightarrow I_p$	Increased & positive real interest rates on deposits leads to higher savings; low and negative real lending rates lead to credit distortions and inefficient I_p through financial repression	S_p is not interest elastic; nor does $S_p \Rightarrow I_p$
Fiscal policy reduced government expenditure;	$I_p \uparrow$	$S_p \uparrow$	I_g crowds out I_p to finance deficit;	I_g and I_p complementary Ricardian equivalence
tax policy revision	$I_p \uparrow$	$S_g \uparrow$	less reliance on S_p to finance fiscal deficit, crowding in I_p	
Exchange rate policy devaluation	$I_p \uparrow$	Increased international competitiveness, shift production into tradables	Overvalued exchange rate	Counterproductive, increased cost of production
Trade liberalization	$I_p \uparrow$	Increased allocation of resources in tradables	Greater market access for exports, induces efficiency through increased foreign competition	Infant industry-cannot compete internationally

Table 3.2 Macro policies: Suggested effects and criticisms

Policy	Expected Effect: IMF/Bank	Real Effect: Critics (Macro)	Real Effect on Private Sector
Tight monetary policy-credit ceilings- public private	Improved balance of payments position reduces demand; high interest rate and inflation control	Economic contraction-lower AD, lowers output; stagflation, structural problems remain, indebtedness and bankruptcy	Lower inputs and production, high cost of borrowing for working capital, high cost of production, pass through effect, postponement of investment due to adverse expectations, shorter financial speculation rather than productive investment, bias against small firms, redistribution in favour of profit earners at expense of wage earners
Reduced fiscal expenditure, reduced subsidies, investment, and other public expenditure	To match credit ceiling of public sector in improving BOP, alleviate crowding out of private sector expenditure	'Overkill' domestic demand, public and private expenditure complementary, downward inflexibility of expenditure, and prices	Reduced private sector investment, reduced production
Exchange rate devaluation	Complements demand management through expenditure switching-hence improves BOP, encourages competitiveness through forcing low cost of production, shifting of resources to more efficient uses	Increased cost of imported intermediates, greater pass through effect tilt in favour of profit rather than wage earners,	Higher cost of production, higher prices, deleterious effect on small firms and wage earners

Table 3.2 (Continued)

Policy	Expected Effect: IMF/Bank	Real Effect: Critics (Macro)	Real Effect on Private Sector
Trade liberalization	Improves allocation of resources, within import competing and from non-tradables to tradables, induces lower cost of production, access to foreign technology, capital, DFI, larger markets, and economies of scale, removes anti-export bias	Leads to BOP problems in the short term- through import liberalization, does not open doors to new loans, depends on the ability of structure to adapt, infant industry cannot compete initially internationally, transitional costs, uncertainty	High import content of production, causes shrinking of industries faced with flood of imports, export response modest, cut in economic activity and unemployment, upgrading of plant and structure not immediate, skills and physical input required not immediately available, productive structure takes time to adjust
Financial liberalization-interest rate liberalization	Increased savings for investment, increased efficiency of investment, substitution of capital by labour	Investment determines savings: therefore with high interest rate, reduced investment and savings, or increased savings lead to economic contraction through withdrawal, portfolio shifts among assets, external debt increase, no atomization of credit suppliers	Bias in favour of large firms, increased cost of production via increased cost of borrowing, reduced availability of capital in informal sector affects smaller firms capacity to borrow, does not efficiently allocate funds for investment, pass through effect

loans for investment purposes, (c) increased indebtedness, reduced profitability and increased instances of bankruptcy.

- The impact of tight monetary policy on consumption and government expenditure can result in a fall in domestic demand, affecting output and the postponement of investment decisions of firms.
- Inflationary process can result through the passing on of costs by some firms.

- In light of the above and linking back to the discussion on access to resources in Chapter 2, it is expected that monetary policy will vary in its impact on different types of firms as described below.
- Smaller firms with less articulated bank-firm relationships may suffer more adversely from reduced domestic credit which would affect their ability to meet working capital and investment needs. It is expected that profitability will be negatively affected while the interest payments and indebtedness will increase negatively affecting both the profitability and investment status of these firms.
- Larger firms or foreign firms with more established relationships with banks ought not to be affected by tight monetary policy since interest rates will be prime and credit will be accommodated. Additionally, foreign firms can borrow from their parent/affiliates abroad so that the effect of a credit crunch is lessened.

Financial liberalization

- Increased volume of investable funds available to firms at an interest rate that will lead to more efficient investment and increased economic growth.
- Volume of investment does not necessarily increase since increased savings do not imply increased investment.
- interest rate is an ineffective device to sift out efficient investment.
- Increased interest rates will increase cost of production through increased cost of working capital.
- Increased costs cause a reduction in firm profitability and have a negative effect on investment.
- Firms may invest in financial assets foreign or domestic rather than productive investment.
- Reduced availability of funds for smaller firms due to attraction of informal sector savings into formal financial system with stricter credit requirements.
- Credit access negatively affected through portfolio shifts into financial assets.
- Borrowing capacity of households/firms and sectors such as agriculture is lowered with leverage availability in favour of large-scale firms.
- differential impact on firms under financial liberalization will be therefore similar to that described for large/foreign and small firms.

Exchange rate policy/devaluation

- Increased production in the tradable sectors particularly exports and therefore increased investment in these more efficient uses.
- Increased competitiveness for producers by inducing lower cost of production leading to increased efficiency.
- Increased cost of imported inputs and therefore increased cost of production but if wages do not increase, net effect is ambiguous for exporters.
- Passing on of cost through mark-up pricing may increase to maintain profitability and can result in an increase in the domestic price level.
- Wage/labour reduction as a means of firm adjustment with implications for small firms and for productivity increases.
- Redistributive effect of the above leads to economic contraction that adversely affects the sales of firms.
- Holding of foreign assets by firms can lead to a positive wealth effect while foreign liabilities lead to an adverse effect.
- Real wealth effect on households and reduced remuneration of labour can lead to economic contraction.

In the above discussion on the macro framework implications, the impact of these policies on firms was raised. However, the conceptualization of the firm in the context of the adjustment framework has not yet been established. Therefore, the next section discusses the theory of the firm and the alternative approaches/models of the firm, an understanding of which can lead to further insights into the relationship between the macro policies and firms.

3.3 The Conceptualization of the Firm under Adjustment

The discussion above approached the macro/micro concerns of the study through a review of the macroeconomic literature, bringing out wherever possible the implications for the firm and the differential effects due to firm heterogeneity. This section looks at the conceptualization of the firm which ought to respond to the macro policies. It starts with the neo-classical theory of the firm under perfect competition and also looks at monopoly and oligopoly firms/market conditions. In subsequent sections, alternative models that try to give a better representation of the firm are presented and evaluated relative to their relevance to LDCs.

3.3.1 The neo-classical theory of the firm: The transmission of adjustment through product and factor markets

Due to the mechanisms of relative prices and incomes, product and factor markets have been identified as mechanisms through which the effects of adjustment can be transmitted to the firm. A central issue in neo-classical economics is a market capable of achieving efficiency in resource allocation and economic welfare through the determination of pricing and output decisions by firms. These decisions on prices and output are dependent on the degree of competition existing in the market in which a firm operates and its choice of technology. Perfectly competitive markets are assumed in the neo-classical theory of the firm under the following conditions: [27]

- Product homogeneity of individual commodities;
- Atomistic competition, such that no individual buyer or seller can influence the market price;
- Perfect knowledge or rational expectations exist between buyers and sellers;
- Free entry and exit for firms wanting to enter or leave the industry; free mobility of technology;
- Firms maximize profits or minimize cost and consumers maximize utility.

Under these assumptions, the law of one price exists for a particular commodity and is determined through the interplay of market forces of supply and demand, with the firm being a price-taker. In the presence of perfect competition, the price of a product is equal to the marginal cost and marginal revenue. In Chapter 1 the assumptions of the perfectly competitive market system were discussed relative to the achievement of a socially optimal equilibrium. A social optimum describes a situation in which there is efficiency in consumption, production, product mix and distributional equity. In the following sections, the discussion provides a closer examination of product and factor markets and the processes of price and output determination under perfect competition from which the process of restructuring of the firm can be discussed.

Product and factor markets

In the theory of production, using the cost minimization approach and assuming the simple case of a firm with two inputs: capital (K) and labour (L), the conditions for cost minimization are derived as follows:

$$C = wL + vK \quad (3.24)$$

which is subject to the constraint that a fixed level of output is produced:

$$Q = F(L,K) \quad (3.25)$$

where Q represents fixed output and C represents the cost of producing the fixed level of output with w and v being the wage rate and the price of capital respectively. Using the Lagrangian multiplier the conditions can be derived as follows:

$$C = wL + rK - \lambda[F(L,K) - Q] \quad (3.26)$$

The first order conditions for cost minimization are:

$$\frac{\partial C}{\partial L} = w - \lambda F_L = 0 \quad (3.27)$$

$$\frac{\partial C}{\partial K} = w - \lambda F_K = 0 \quad (3.28)$$

$$\frac{\partial C}{\partial \lambda} = F(L,K) - Q = 0 \quad (3.29)$$

By combining equations 3.27 and 3.28 the following is obtained:

$$F_K / v = F_L / w \quad (3.30)$$

In equation 3.30, the implication is that in minimizing cost a firm will choose its factor inputs such that the ratio of the marginal product of each factor to its price is equal.[28] If this is not the case, then the firm can reduce cost by substitution of factor inputs, using the cheaper factor more intensively. Equations 3.27 and 3.28 can also be used to obtain the following:

$$\lambda = v / F_K = w / F_L \quad (3.31)$$

which can also be rewritten as follows:

$$\lambda = v\frac{\partial K}{\partial Q} = w\frac{\partial L}{\partial Q} \qquad (3.32)$$

Equation 3.31 measures the additional factor input cost of producing an additional unit of output using either capital or labour with λ representing the marginal cost of production. The alternate version in equation 3.32 shows that the cost of a small increase in output is the increase in the wage bill ($w\partial L/\partial Q$) if labour is increased (capital fixed) and an increase in capital costs ($v\partial K/\partial Q$) if capital is increased (labour fixed). The above gives the long-run cost minimization conditions of the firm.

The short-run cost minimization is:

$$Min\ C = wL \qquad \text{s.t. } Q = F(L) \qquad (3.33)$$

In the short run, labour, L, is the only variable factor of production, with the solution to the optimization problem being reduced to minimizing cost relative to labour. Since labour and capital are substitutes then the required level of output is produced in the short run by using the fixed amount of labour more intensively. It can be shown that the short-run marginal cost (SRMC) is:

$$\lambda = w / F_L \quad = w\frac{\partial L}{\partial F} \qquad (3.34)$$

The short-run marginal cost is the ratio of the wage rate to the marginal product of labour or equivalently the increase in the wage bill from producing one extra unit of output. The conditions of equilibrium of a firm as derived from above are:

- that the marginal productivity of the last dollar must be equal;
- that the marginal physical productivity of any factor must be proportional to the price.

Similarly, it can also be shown that the optimal condition for profit maximization is the point where the marginal revenue and marginal cost curves intersect. Relative to the scale of operation, increasing returns to scale exist when output expands by a larger proportion than the increase in inputs; constant returns to scale imply that outputs increase by the same proportion as the increase in inputs; while decreasing returns to scale imply that output expands by a smaller proportion than the increase in inputs.[29]

As in the product market, the forces of supply and demand determine wages and employment in the labour market as well as interest rate and loans in the capital market. Assuming perfectly competitive markets, the interplay of supply and demand of labour determines the equilibrium wage. In the case of labour supply, an individual is seen as dividing her time between leisure and work. The amount of labour to be supplied is derived from the solution to the optimization problem of maximizing leisure, subject to income which represents a foregone purchasing power.

Considering the demand for labour and capital by the firm, the long-run demand conditions for labour and capital can be derived using the profit maximization approach. The revenue function can be taken as $R(Q)=PQ$ where $Q= F(L,K)$ and is subject to the cost constraint $C=wL+vK$:

$$\begin{aligned}
&\max \pi(L,K) = PF(L,K) - wL - vK \\
&PF_L - w = 0 \\
&PF_K - v = 0 \qquad (3.35) \\
&\frac{F_L}{F_K} = \frac{w}{v}
\end{aligned}$$

Hence, as with the previous conditions for the product market, the condition for profit maximization is that a firm uses input of capital or labour to the point at which the marginal value product is equal to its price.

The capital market describes the market for loans in which the price is the interest rate premium paid on loans and deposits.[30] The consumer is seen as exercising preferences with respect to consumption now as against future consumption based on current and future income. Taking into account depreciation, the cost of a unit of capital good at the end of the next period is $(1-\delta)s$ where δ denotes the amount by which the equipment will depreciate and s the current market value of a unit of capital good. As a result, K is chosen such that the present value of the net worth of the firm is maximized giving the condition that:

$$v = (r + \delta)s = PF_k \qquad (3.36)$$

where δs is the value of the capital and, rs is the opportunity cost of using a unit of capital. Thus, the demand for physical capital is a function of the rate of interest (r), the price of output (p), the depreciation rate (δ), and the current market price of a unit of capital. In the previous section, it was shown that as v increases the demand for the capital good will decrease implying an inverse relationship between the demand for physical capital and these parameters with the firm's demand for borrowing also inversely related to the interest rate. The discussion below focuses on the neo-classical theory of product and factor markets within the context of adjustment.

The possibilities for adjustment in product and factor markets

In the neo-classical theory of the firm, disequilibrium is corrected through the adjustment of relative prices which returns the system to a state of equilibrium, however, the theory does not state the process through which the firm adjusts. Monetary policy can affect the firm through the channel of high interest rates which raise the costs of production of the firm since they increase the interest expenses for loans used for investment and working capital purposes..

Since profit is equal to total revenue less total cost then profit will fall with increasing cost of production (all other things being equal) i.e. $i\uparrow \Rightarrow (R - (C)\uparrow \Rightarrow \pi\downarrow$, where i is interest rate, R is total revenue, C is total cost, and π is the level of profit. In the short run, ignoring fixed costs that can be paid in the future, the firm can continue to maximize profit (or minimize loss) at a positive but lower level of output at the point where the price is at least equal to the average cost.

In the long run, since both capital and labour are assumed to be variable, an increase in the rate of interest contributes to increased cost of capital. The flexibility that is assumed in the neo-classical firm implies that it can reduce the capital employed with an increase in the interest rate; or else the firm can choose to cut labour costs. The choice would depend on the relative cost of these factors of production, since the ratio of the marginal productivity of capital and labour must be equal to the ratio of their prices for profit maximization.

Substitution of labour for capital implies that variations in the combination of capital and labour are feasible and carry no costs. This situation may not hold in reality since there are costs for firing workers. There may be resistance by workers or trade unions to wage cuts, specific skills of the workers may imply that they cannot be fired, and fixed assets may not be easily dispensed with because of their use in production or their uselessness in other activities, i.e. the irreversibility of investment discussed previously.

Another option mentioned earlier is for the firm to reduce its output level such that profit is still maximized. The cutback in the level of output (*Q*) can lead to a fall in total revenue (*PQ*). Depending on the demand conditions, the firm can either maintain its profitability at a lower level of output, total revenue and production costs or else it can experience reduced profitability. In the event that the firm can continue to cover it costs at a lower output level without sale of its capital stock, the firm will be operating with excess capacity.

The reduction in profitability implies increased difficulty in paying the total wage bill (*wL*) and in meeting the costs of imported inputs (eP_omQi) and the cost of capital, *vK*. Therefore, in the short run, adjustment can take the form of a reduction in labour or wages to reduce the total wage bill and/or increase productivity. Reduced profitability and economic contraction can therefore lead to a reduction in future investment. Furthermore, since part of the cost of capital must be paid to the bank, then reduced profitability or the absence of profitability may lead to increased indebtedness and bankruptcy.

Apart from the interest rate effect, reduced domestic credit will reduce the amount of money that can be borrowed for new investment or working capital needs, which creates further profitability and investment problems for firms.

interest rate changes as discussed earlier also originate from the policy of financial liberalization. Changes in interest rate due to financial liberalization can lead to increased difficulty in the access to financial and other resources by firms; with differences occurring by type of firms. Large firms with well-established relationships with banks may not be affected due to the prime interest rates that they are charged. As a result, the investment thrust of these firms may continue due to their favourable relationships with banks.

With financial liberalization, it is expected that the increased savings that translate into investable funds will be allocated to firms that are able to achieve the highest rate of return on the capital employed. As a result, the more efficient firms have access to loans for investment while low-yielding investment projects are sifted out of the system via higher interest rates. The application of this policy assumes that firms face equal market conditions at the micro level.

However, it was earlier argued that the policy of financial liberalization while increasing financial intermediation in the formal system lowers the availability of funds to smaller firms in the informal financial markets. These small firms in general have less access to formal credit and often have to rely on informal sources in addition to facing higher interest rates where formal funds are available. Therefore, it is not necessarily the case that only the efficient firms survive. Inefficient firms can survive as long as they are able to obtain loans or lower cost credit . Conversely, efficient firms who do not have access to loans or lower cost credit would not survive due to the inherent biases that exist in the segmented capital markets of LDCs.

Due to credit rationing, small firms are not able to benefit from the increased availability of investment funds during periods of financial liberalization. Furthermore, such policies do not take into account the riskiness of investment of some larger firms. In particular, large firms that have no problems in accessing credit, and invest heavily expecting future increases in sales, are the ones that may face increased indebtedness in the period of adjustment.

Thus financial liberalization can lead to increased costs in working and fixed-capital loans for some firms, which may affect profitability and investment negatively. Possible outcomes due to the channeling of policy changes through capital markets are: increased indebtedness of firms, increased interest expenses, and reduced investment and profitability. These problems can also affect the product market through actions taken by firms such as output/labour reduction to offset problems originating in the capital market which may result in economic contraction. Thus there are possible interactions of the effects of adjustment in factor and product markets.

While the aims of having high-yielding returns and increased volume of investment are good ones, in conditions of segmented capital markets in which credit rationing has been historically applied by financial institutions; the policy of financial liberalization may not produce its intended effect. Thus, unequal conditions faced by some firms in financial markets in LDCs involve cost as well as quantity restrictions with respect to credit based on criteria other than efficiency. The impact of high interest rates under financial liberalization will be therefore more adverse for some firms than for others based on problems with the allocation of credit in LDCs, and biases in favour of firms that have established relationships or interlocking directorates with banks, as described in Chapter 2 in the country case study.

The adverse impact of higher interest rates under financial liberalization is seen in the following scenario. Increased interest rates under financial liberalization may lead to higher interest expenses which can increase the indebtedness of firms through increasing prices and falling demand.

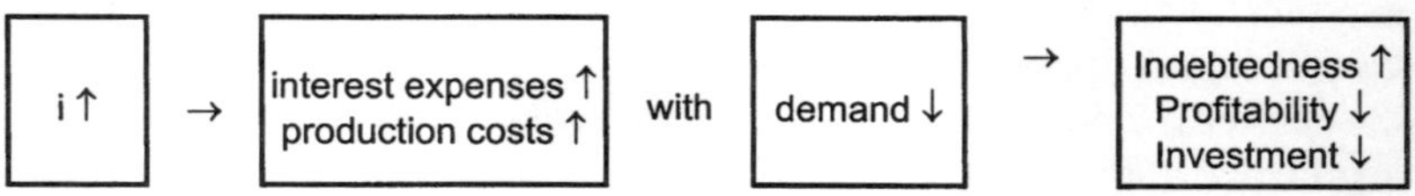

Price changes brought on by a devaluation is another mechanism which acts as a signal leading firms to adjust in product and factor markets. Some of the possible effects discussed earlier are that: (1) a devaluation by leading to reduced cost of labour in foreign currency may make the products of firms more competitive relative to their trading partners; (2) devaluation should result in increased production in the traded sectors.

Theoretically, therefore, firms should experience lower costs of production and by being more internationally competitive should also move into exports. However, penetration of export markets carry costs such as shipping, marketing, and informational prerequisites as well as quality considerations. Getting into export markets is not an easy process particularly for small firms in LDCs that lack financial and other resources or prior export market experience.

The effect of a devaluation is channeled through product markets implying increased costs of inputs of intermediate and raw material goods that are necessary for production. In many LDCs, there is import dependency for raw material inputs into production and for capital equipment, with differences in the degree of dependency by activity. Thus, imported inputs of capital (rKP_0mke) or materials (eP_omQi) would increase while the wage bill as measured in foreign currency would decrease (wL/e). Similarly investment can also be affected due to increased costs of capital goods brought on by the devaluation. Thus even if exports increase, the outcome of a devaluation is ambiguous relative to higher costs of inputs.

Consequently, increased costs of production due to devaluation may force the firm to cut costs by either reducing raw material purchases (in which case output will fall) or by reducing the total wage bill or numbers of people employed. An increase in the costs of imported capital goods can also discourage investment. However, there are limits in the extent to which some firms can further reduce their workforce or wages in response to pressures from the marketplace, without affecting the operations of the firm. To the extent that the firm can suppress its wage bill (wL/e) and/or increase its productivity, then it would be able to maintain its profitability. Downward rigidity in wages in labour markets in LDCs may hamper the process of wage reduction.

Capital market effects of a devaluation are present where firms possess foreign assets/liabilities. Firms that borrow in foreign capital markets and possess foreign liabilities will face increased indebtedness and interest expenses due to the impact of devaluation on their foreign denominated debt and interest payments. Firms with foreign assets will experience gains in financial assets as a result of a real devaluation.

Foreign firms which are linked to foreign capital markets or to parent/ affiliate companies abroad may not be affected adversely. Some large local firms with foreign assets/accounts can also offset the adverse effects of devaluation. However, smaller local firms that are not likely to have foreign assets/accounts or foreign contacts are likely to suffer more severely than the other group of firms mentioned above. Hence, the capital market effects should distinguish different types of firms and asset holdings rather than assume equality of conditions.

The discussion in this section while allowing for heterogeneity among firms does not cater to monopoly and oligopolistic market forms which may yet yield different or additional possible outcomes to those described above. In addition, the relevance of models that attempt to give a more realistic picture of the firm has not been considered. These concerns are explored in the next two sections.

3.3.2 Monopoly and oligopoly in adjustment

Monopoly

In contrast to firms under perfect competition, under a monopoly the firm is the industry. A monopoly is therefore a price-setter with the conditions for profit maximization being derived as described in Annex I. A monopoly firm does not supply up to the point where price is equal to marginal cost and this leads to the possibility of price discrimination. In order to gain extra customers, the monopoly can charge different prices to different customers (e.g. different classes of tickets in train/air fares). This method of price discrimination is such that the market is split into segments with the one in which there is greater elasticity of demand being charged the lower price. Hence, these firms are not governed by market-determined price and output decisions since price and output fixing is the norm. monopoly occurs when there is only one producer and when there are no substitutes for the product.

The monopolist can have control either over price or output but not both simultaneously. The level of output is chosen under the same rules as perfect competition, but the monopolist has the power to engage in price discrimination, that is, different prices in different markets or to obtain higher prices for a lower level of output than would have been possible under perfect competition.

Oligopoly

Unlike the scenarios of perfect competition and monopoly, which are two extreme cases of market forms, oligopoly occurs when a few firms share a large proportion of the industry. These oligopolistic firms take cognizance of its rivals and the industry structure results in differences in firm behaviour from that of perfect competition and monopoly. Since there are few firms in the market, a change in the price or output decision by one firm would affect the profitability of the other firms. Therefore interdependence in pricing and output decisions is a feature that is possible under an oligopolistic market, particularly in the presence of product differentiation. Models which are used to describe oligopolistic firms include (see also Annex I at the end of this chapter):

(a) The Nash Cournot equilibrium, which assumes that there is no collusion among firms and that firms are identical with respect to costs, products, information about the market and objectives. In the Cournot equilibrium, which is a special case, the assumptions are that there is no collusion between firms and that each firm tends to maximize profits under the assumption that the other firms' outputs are fixed or given.

(b) The Stackelberg equilibrium assumes that one firm can be identified as a leader in the market, while the other firms react passively to the initiatives of the leader. The leader firm is aware of the level of output of the followers and of their reaction function.[31] The leader firm is therefore able to use this information to determine its own level of output maximization and its profit relative to the reaction functions of the other firms. It is not clear in this theory how the leader firm is determined or why the other firms arrive at the choice of a passive response.

(c) Equilibria arising from co-operative behaviour such as collusion and cartels.

Oligopolistic firms act by choosing output levels while the price level is determined by supply and demand in the market. The possibility that firms may have an 'output' or 'price' war is also ruled out since it is assumed that each firm is considerate of the impact of output and prices on that of its rivals. However, there are many cases in which a firm is able to set prices in oligopolistic markets while output is determined by market demand or rivalry behaviour.[32]

Hence, price and output decisions are not necessarily market-determined based on supply and demand considerations nor do they necessarily result in the efficient use of resources since oligopolistic firms are able to establish industry equilibrium at higher prices, lower output and higher profits. This framework is described as an 'embarrassment to the explanatory power of orthodox economics' with its concentration on arbitrary assumptions on the response of rivals and its concentration on price and quantity variables. (Kenyon 1979: 36).

Adjustment under conditions of monopoly and oligopoly

The effect of adjustment policies as shown earlier can result in increased cost to firms. A price-setting monopoly can increase its price (depending on the elasticity of demand for its product) by varying the level of output. Thus even though operating inefficiently the monopoly is able to maintain profitability.

Alternatively, any increased costs, at the same level of output, can result in redistribution of income from wages to profit. The argument about market-determined prices and efficiency therefore collapses in this case. While the impact of devaluation will affect the foreign cost component of a monopoly, the response of this firm may be to pass the cost on to the consumer.

While oligopolistic firms are able to pass on cost, if there is interdependence in price-setting then this factor acts as a constraint on these firms. However, it is often the case that the firms independently or in collusion are able to increase their prices. Hence the firm has the ability to maintain profitability in the industry. This is another instance in which the determination of prices and output level is not necessarily based on a criterion of efficiency.

Oligopolies can indulge in non-price competition to try to gain market share, producing at higher unit costs in the process. Thus the effect of increased costs from tight monetary and financial adjustment policies or devaluation can result in a loss of efficiency in order to gain market share.

3.3.3 Other models of the firm and relaxed assumptions of perfect competition

This section contains the alternatives that have been advanced towards a better understanding of the neo-classical theory of the firm as well as the result of relaxing some of the assumptions of perfect competition. The discussion proceeds with a presentation of each model/approach followed by a combined evaluation of their contributions relative to LDCs and adjustment in section 3.3.4.

Structure conduct performance model

The structure conduct performance (SCP) model was developed by Mason & Bain based on the neo-classical theory of the firm. It looks at causal relationships between the structure of an industry, and the conduct and performance of firms within that industry at a particular point in time.[33] Structure describes the environment of the firm and on one level can depict sectoral structure – such as primary, secondary, etc – or on another level can look at market concentration relative to the size distribution of firms. Conduct describes the behaviour of firms in a market – e.g. price determination, advertising, etc. – how these decisions are made and how much expenditure is allocated. Performance reflects issues concerning the enhancement of economic welfare relative to productive and allocative efficiency.

Imperfect information

This approach looks at the violation of the assumption of perfect knowledge under perfect competition. The assumption of perfect knowledge implies that consumers and producers have perfect information with respect to their decisions such that prices are able to fulfil their roles of clearing goods, capital and labour markets. Information asymmetry provided instances of market failure with one focus being in relation to financial constraints and risk behaviour.[34]

The approach of Stiglitz & Weiss (1981) which was previously discussed illustrates how credit rationing and information asymmetry lead to inefficiency of the market rate of interest. The use of credit rationing as a screening device under these conditions is such that it fails to clear the market.[35] Greenwald & Stiglitz (1990) look at information asymmetry relative to the firm and its external environment which consists of external investors of capital and managers of this capital. Focusing on capital market behaviour, they question the neo-classical assumption of the irrelevance of the financial position of the firm and its operating decisions. Their study shows that changes in the financial strength of the firm lead to real consequences. These approaches characterize market failure relative to information imperfections.

Managerial theories

The existence of large firms and the separation of management from shareholders has led to managerial capitalism with targets other than profit being maximized such as sales/revenue or growth, the latter being related to the threats of take-overs.[36] Production is therefore not controlled by the market but by the motives of these managers with their own specific objectives (Marris 1964).[37]

Behavioural theories

The behavioural theories[38] which have been explained by Cyert & March (1992) do not apply any maximization objectives to the firm on decisions of pricing and output but are aimed at 'satisficing' behavior.[39] The aim in 'satisficing' behavior is to achieve satisfactory performance in each of the firm's type of goals, such as production goals, sales goal, profit goal and so on. A core idea in the behavioural theory of the firm is *bounded rationality* which implies that rational actors are constrained significantly by information and calculation limitations which affect the achievement of an optimal decision. The structure of the internal decision-making apparatus is seen as determining price and output decisions. [40]

Transaction costs theories

Transaction costs economics uses a contractual approach to the study of firms.[41] It arose out of the question as to what constitutes the boundary of the firm.[42] The main reason why firms emerged, it is argued, is that some of the transactions that are internal to the firm are less costly than if they took place in the market.[43] The analysis of Williamson centred around concepts of bounded rationality, opportunism and uncertainty.[44] An application of transaction costs in corporate finance is the choice between debt, and equity financing of investment based on the attributes of the asset relative to its deployability. Unlike the MM convention (from the Modigliani-Miller hypothesis), the choice of financing is related to the attributes of the asset. The Modigliani-Miller theory states that the cost of capital is independent of the financial structure of the firm or of the dividend policy (Modigliani and Miller 1958).

Agency theories

Agency theory is seen by Aoki (1984) as bridging the gap between the neo-classical theory of the firm and the managerial theories. While the neo-classical model views the entrepreneur as both risk-bearer and manager, the agency theory makes a distinction between the two. Described by Jensen & Meckling (1976) as a contract in which the principal(s) engage(s) an agent to perform a service which entails decision-making authority, it is possible for the agent to have his own goals which do not coincide with the principals. Thus the problem is how to bring the interests of the principal and that of the agent into accordance. The relevance of this theory hinges on its exposition of the discretionary behaviour of agents.

3.3.4 The alternate models: Their relevance to LDCs and adjustment

This section deals with the relevance of the alternate approaches to LDCs and to adjustment. It is argued that the debates on the theory of the firm are not 'proper critiques of existing theory' but are developments of a theory suited to a different set of questions (Cyert & March 1992: 15). Therefore, it is arguable how much latitude we are able to derive from the alternative approaches relative to the issue of adjustment.

As stated earlier, the SCP model was based exclusively on the neo-classical theory of the firm and was used as the basis for formulating competition policy to promote economic welfare. The SCP model, while giving consideration to market structures and sectoral contribution in the context of industrial policy, has as its main recommendation the advancement of competition. According to this recommendation, the SCP model in the strictest sense would have little tolerance for a monopoly. In practice however a monopoly that has earned its position as a result of superior positioning is not condemned (Ferguson et al. 1988).

Limitations of the SCP model include its definition of structure which is based on the industry-level showing only firm concentration ratios.[45] Thus, by focusing on the structure of the industry, little attention is paid to the inherent structure of the firm that can influence conduct and performance (Ferguson et al. 1988). The underlying motivation on the conduct of firms in the industry assumes that short-run profit maximization is the objective, which may not be the case for all firms. The SCP model is also criticized for its short-run, static nature which does not allow for the current industrial structure to be affected by changes that have occurred in the past. Since this model is based on the neo-classical approach, rivalry and competition among firms are not considered. In this respect, the firm resembles the passive economic units of the neo-classical model (Sawyer 1991).

The SCP approach does not provide an explanation of structure based on the historical processes and experiences of firms that can then be used in a more plausible explanation of the performance of firms under adjustment. Therefore, in the case of LDCs the notion of structure-conduct-performance can be extended to include ownership patterns of firms such as foreign versus domestic as well as a distinction based on size of firm (small, medium and large), relative to their behaviour patterns and the specific experiences of these categories in product and factor markets. This depiction as discussed elsewhere in this research is linked to the access of firms to resources such as land and capital which are historically and institutionally determined.

Hence, the nature and structure of the financial sector and the capital market – including bank-firm relationships as they affect access to credit; the patterns of trade; the nature of the dominant sector; the degree of import dependency for raw material inputs, etc – are important omissions from the SCP model which ought to be included in the conceptualization of the firm under adjustment.[47]

Like the SCP, the information asymmetry approach does not consider the impact of historical factors on market imperfections. Traditional customer relationships between the owners of larger firms and the banks reduce the level of information asymmetry. These bank-firm relationships which may also be discriminatory based on class, gender ethnicity, or size of firm, act as a means of distinguishing high and low-risk customers. For example, bank firm relationships in LDCs may not be as well articulated for small firms as for larger ones. This lack of articulation may be a source of information asymmetry. The same is probably true for foreign versus domestic firms relative to national and international financial markets. Additionally, the monitoring costs for smaller firms are thought to be higher than for larger firms, which contributes to greater capital market segmentation and lowers the availability of loans from formal financial sources. As a result, many small firms are either self-financed to a larger extent or else face higher interest rates from banks and informal sources, as compared to larger firms.

Thus the theory of information asymmetry, while being relevant to the analysis of segmented capital markets as often is the case in LDCs, should also focus on the criteria of ownership and bank-firm links and the impact on credit rationing which contribute to such asymmetry. Incorporation of these features can in turn lead to a more realistic assessment of the impact of adjustment policies on firms.

One general criticism of the theories of managerial capitalism, behavioural theories, agency theory and transaction costs is that these theories are not adequately articulated to be of much practical worth even in the case of developed countries. Managerial capitalism and behavioural theories are directed mainly at organizational problems and processes occurring in large corporations and largely focusing on firms that are not 'owner-managed'. The principal agent approach looks at decision-making processes involving the conflicting interests of managers, shareholders, creditors. Even though there are firms that fit the depiction of a separation between owner and manager, the extent of owner control may still remain significant based either on a family basis or through the shareholding of a single interest group (Hay & Morris 1991).

Managerial capitalism and principal-agent problems focus more on the organizational aspects of the firm relative to the separation of ownership from control. They do not focus on the context of ownership as is relevant to developing countries such as access to financial resources in a segmented market situation and credit rationing behaviour. Relative to the neo-classical theory, managerial capitalism considers that firms maximize targets other than profit. While factors have been identified which managers will want to maximize such as salaries, sales etc, there are no well-developed rules as to what are the conditions for the maximization of these other targets as is the case in profit maximization.

The concept of 'satisficing' behaviour – which has to do with specific aims and objectives within a firm and are constrained on a department level and by different groups of workers, shareholders etc. – does not lay down clear-cut rules as to how these conflicts are resolved. Criticisms relative to problems of defining transaction costs also limit the effectiveness of this approach in analysing adjustment.

Thus relative to LDCs, where one would expect the presence of family-owned and controlled firms even amongst larger enterprises, the applicability of approaches regarding the discretionary behaviour of managers is restricted (Tenjo 1995).[48] Furthermore, the emphasis that is placed on the internal decision-making processes of the managerial and behavioural approach, though relevant to the overall understanding of the firm, limits the analyses of the firm relative to its environment. In addition, the managerial approach is restricted in its application to a small number of large firms.

Criticisms of transaction costs theory include the failure to have a clear definition of transaction costs. The existence of uncertainty as a central element in the consideration of contracts is seen as an alternative perspective that can be taken into account in transaction costs (Hodgson

1988). As a theoretical device, transaction costs is said to have a 'well-deserved bad name because there is a suspicion that anything can be rationalized by invoking suitably specified transaction costs'.[49]

To the extent that these theories can be construed as being applicable to large multinational corporations, the operations of these enterprises in developing countries are such that the decision-making with respect to investment and raw material procurement is often made in the head office, while the day-to-day operating decisions are made in the developing country itself. Hence, these large corporations have a limited scope for discretionary behaviour in the context of investment decisions in developing countries.

As a result, the alternative approaches suffer from limitations that affect their ability to provide us with useful tools to analyse the impact of macroeconomic change on firms in LDCs. However, the transaction costs approach does offer some interesting insights into the issues of contractual arrangements, the financial structure of the firm, and the choice of investment instrument. Hence, there is potential for the use of this theory in analysing the financial behaviour of firms in LDCs under changing macroeconomic conditions, such as adjustment. But in the current study, which is not so much preoccupied with contractual arrangements between firms, the transaction cost approach is not further explored.

3.4 The Microeconomic Impact of Macroeconomic Policies: Summary

This section is a synthesis of the earlier discussions in this chapter on the macro and microeconomic aspects of adjustment. One of the aims in adjustment policies is to achieve greater efficiency in resource utilization. For the producer this implies increased efficiency in production, which means the allocation of factors of production (such that the marginal rate of substitution between factors) are the same for all (firms) industries. According to the neo-classical theory of the firm, all firms face similar demand curves and are price-takers, with market entry and exit occurring at no cost. Under these conditions, firms that are not efficient will simply go out of business while the more efficient ones will survive.

The aim of 'getting the prices right' is therefore designed to increase the efficiency of firms. In reality, there are costs attached to entry and exit such that investment, once committed, is not easily reversed. Alteration in the structure of production and in market focus carry costs. The macro policies assume, implicitly or otherwise, that economies of developing countries are flexible relative to adjustment to macroeconomic changes. More specifically, the firms within the private sectors are assumed to be able to adjust flexibly without consideration of the differences in market conditions that they face. However, firms do not face similar demand curves and market conditions. Thus the investigation of the impact of macroeconomic policies requires a more realistic framework than that provided by the neo-classical approach.

The manner of integration of a developing economy into the world economy determines to some extent how the economies are able to respond to adjustment. An economy that has traditionally been a producer of, and is heavily dependent on, a primary commodity can experience difficulties in adjusting flexibly to relative prices. These commodities may take the form of an enclave sector (such as the petroleum sector in the case of Trinidad & Tobago) with the spending effect being felt through government revenue or through the earnings of the workers employed. The traditional dependency of an economy on one sector, an inward-looking strategy, and a structure of production dependent on imports, pose real constraints to economic restructuring of the manufacturing sector. On the other hand, spillover effects due to revenue from favourable oil prices or investment in the enclave sector may be beneficial to the non-oil sectors in the economy.

Thus, inherent patterns in the structure of supply and demand in developing countries produce situations of inflexibility such that a BOP disequilibrium is not as easily eliminated or changed by tight monetary policy, devaluation or financial liberalization. The extreme openness and heavy dependence on imported inputs would cancel any competitiveness that can be gained by devaluation because of increasing production costs. On the other hand, import liberalization, which may encourage imports of more competitively priced goods, will also have its casualties among domestic enterprises.

With regard to the availability of credit, inherent discriminatory policies in the lending practices of banks - based on criteria of size and ownership of firms - imply that financial liberalization policy will exacerbate problems of credit access faced by small/local firms. In addition, stricter credit requirements imposed on firms in formal financial markets based on this same criteria result in differential effects on, and responses to, adjustment of small firms in contrast to medium/large firms, and of some local firms as opposed to foreign. These occurrences of credit access are largely institutionally entrenched and do not necessarily incorporate efficiency considerations.

Furthermore, under normal circumstances, there is the application of differential rates of interests based on traditional relationships between banks and firms which leads to credit rationing, with some firms not being able to obtain loans from the formal system, or being charged higher interest rates. As a result, tight monetary policy and financial liberalization can have adverse cost effects. Financial liberalization therefore may not necessarily imply higher investment or greater efficiency in investment or financial intermediation as is shown in Tables 3.1 and 3.2.

The pattern of production of the manufacturing sectors, such as assembly type, sometimes requires high import content of intermediates, and is entrenched in a general strategy of import-substitution. During adjustment, a devaluation, which increases the cost of production, can result in the loss of competitiveness rather than in the gain which is theoretically expected (see Tables 3.1 and 3.2). Stimulation of exports may not therefore be achievable in the short to medium term since slow movement into exports implies delays in quality improvement, and the acquisition of technology that might be attained with increased competitiveness.

Taking into consideration that a relatively high percentage of the cost of production goes to raw materials and wages, then there is a likelihood that firms may opt to reduce employment or wages, as well as cutback on production through decreased purchasing of raw material. It is debatable whether this form of adjustment necessarily implies improved efficiency in production or whether it is in reality a mechanism wherein the real wage/labour is used to achieve the goal of reduced production costs.

While adjustment policies ought to lead to economic recovery of the private sector through increasing the efficiency and volume of funds available for investment and the shifting of investment into tradable activities, the criticisms in Tables 3.1 and 3.2, some of which are derived from the Structuralist/Post-Keynesian traditions, are in some respects consistent with the discussion on the possibilities for restructuring of the firm. It is no surprise that the performance of private investment in LDCs was disappointing as discussed earlier.

Thus, the issues concerning heterogeneity of firms in the private sector as well as the historical and institutional functioning of markets as depicted in the Structuralist/Post-Keynesian framework seem to provide a more realistic framework to answer the following questions:

- What has happened to firms during adjustment?
- How have firms responded to policies given the historical and structural constraints which they face, and what were the processes involved?
- Do historical and structural constraints contribute to differential effects/ responses relative to the ability of firms to restructure?

3.5 Conclusion

At the macroeconomic level, the effects of tight monetary policy and financial liberalization are questionable in countries faced with fledging and/or segmented capital markets and institutionalized restrictions and biases relative to credit access as well as interest rates based on criteria such as ownership and size. Furthermore, the domination of the production structure in manufacturing by activities that depend on high imports of intermediates implies that devaluation will be detrimental to some firms even though it may be advantageous to foreign firms with parent/affiliates abroad, to local firms with foreign assets, and to those firms that are already entrenched in export markets. The homogeneity that these policies assume about firms in the private sector may not hold in reality. The historical experience of the firm and the economy is also not addressed in these policies.

At the micro level, starting with the neo-classical theory of the firm, the conditions that are necessary for profit maximization were derived showing that the possibilities of adjustment to the macroeconomic policies may be contrary to what is suggested in the concern with relative prices and efficiency. In other words, given the neo-classical theory and starting with its concept of the firm, it was shown that the macro policies of adjustment can have adverse effects similar to those indicated by the critics of adjustment policies. These effects can lead to increased costs of production, reduction in labour, fall in output through reduced purchases of raw material, reduced demand brought on by unemployment and increased prices or increased indebtedness. These results beg the question as to why are these policies used.

With problems in the availability and the cost of credit in LDCs' financial markets, not only does the cost of production increase but also the effects of the increase are accentuated, based on the conditions faced by different firms. The question of substitution of capital for labour while not possible in the short term can result in the loss of competitiveness for some firms in contrast to those that have advantages of capital intensive operations, such as large local and foreign-owned firms in LDCs. Since capital is not variable in the short-term, the option that is opened to the firm is restructuring through reduction in the quantity of labour or in the wage rate. In the long run, variation in the capital employed might be feasible. However, adjustment assumes that there are no costs of entry and exit and that fixed assets can be put to other uses.

The alternative approaches to studying the firms are not necessarily relevant to LDCs nor do they enhance the analysis of restructuring within firms. However, the models of asymmetric information and transaction costs can provide some useful guides if further modified to suit situations that exist in LDCs. Changes in macroeconomic policies find the firm with an existing structure of production relative to capital assets, raw materials, labour, debt structure, and a given market focus which are not easily reversible or easily changeable when adjustment is required.

Under the existing conditions in developing countries it is uncertain whether relative prices are sufficient for ensuring that the market equilibrium is a social optimum as earlier defined. Thus a theory useful for analysing the impact of adjustment should consider both the history and structural heterogeneity of the firm, its institutional environment as it contributes to this heterogeneity and the processes involved in adjustment. The next chapter will include a summary of the argumentation of the research, information about the available data and the hypotheses that are to be investigated.

Notes

1. It is stated that while economic theory provides a framework for analysing the links between micro units and adjustment policies, the number of such links and the complexity of their interactions are such that the policy impact is impossible to predict a priori (Behram & Deolalikar 1991: 292, cited in

Lamberte et al. 1992: 21). FitzGerald (1989) also comments on the lack of a clearly defined theoretical link between macroeconomic adjustment policy and small-scale enterprises.

2. See FitzGerald & Vos (1989).
3. These papers have been cited in IMF Occasional Paper No. 55, 1987: Khan, Monteil & Haque (1990), Mills & Nallari (1992) and reprinted in IMF Staff Paper, 1977.
4. In the short run, real variables are affected because of misperception and money illusion.
5. In the earlier set of these Revised Minimum Standard Models (RMSM), domestic savings and capital output ratios were linked to the real growth rate.
6. See Nowzad (1981) for a review of some of these criticisms.
7. In closed economies or in those that are not closely integrated there is not much leverage for domestic residents to obtain net credit from abroad. In closely integrated settings there is also the possibility that there can be an expansion of money through foreign exchange conversion brought on by a BOP imbalance.
8. Even though money and monetary variables play an important role in IMF adjustment, it is argued that this does not make these programmes monetarist (IMF 1987: 2).
9. See Thomas et al. (1991) for a review of financial liberalization.
10. See Killick et al. (1984) for financial sector reform and stabilization, and Khan & Knight (1982) for a review of supply-side policies relative to economic stabilization.
11. Early work with regard to the role of finance in development can be found in Schumpeter (1934).
12. Repression was not seen as being intentional, but through financial restrictions it led to seignorage.
13. Some of the arguments for inefficiency are high delinquency in repayment, less than optimal savings and low-yielding investment.
14. This reference includes the work of Albert Ando, cited in Dornbusch (1990).
15. Cited in Dornbusch et al. (1990).
16. A survey of the literature on savings is found in Gersovitz (1988).
17. The literature on this topic is quite extensive and its contributors are too numerous to mention individually.
18. Cited in Killick (1984).

19. As a measure of a country's overall competitiveness in international markets, an increase in the RER implies that foreign goods are more expensive than domestically produced goods – a real exchange rate depreciation with a decrease implying an appreciation.
20. Tradable goods refer to goods or services that can be traded while non-tradables cannot be traded. A trade-weighted RER can also be constructed using the trading partner's share of trade as weights. This is known as the real multilateral exchange rate.
21. By reducing the foreign currency price of exports and increasing the domestic currency price of imports, devaluation should serve to stimulate the traded goods sector.
22. See also Kaldor (1983).
23. Pointing to Polak's model as a 'theoretically incomplete description of the economy', Taylor (1987, 1990) sees the value of production as containing the elements listed herein.
24. See also Krugman & Taylor (1978).
25. Lewis (1980: 560) argued that given resources and flexibility, LDCs can increase their trade with MDCs (More Developed Countries) but at the risk of displacing other LDCs' trade. He argued 'what one can do cannot be done by all'. Along similar lines, Eshag (1983: 35) argued that if all countries were to increase production they cannot all increase export at the same time.
26. See Van Wijnbergen (1986) for a discussion of exchange rate management and the external debt of the private sector.
27. Several microeconomics texts exist with these assumptions.
28. The conditions for profit maximization which is similarly derived show that the price of output, P, which is the marginal revenue (MR), must be equal to the marginal cost of each factor of production, i.e. P = MR = MCL = MCK.
29. The appeal of a firm with constant returns to scale is that if scale does not matter, then factor proportions are the crucial determinants of welfare (Layard & Walters 1978: 65). It is thought however that the constant returns-to-scale firm does not project a convincing model since it may not hold true if the scale is halved; all factors of production cannot be varied in the short run. It is possible that the technology is such that increasing returns to scale may be a more probable outcome (Varian 1978).
30. The capital market is being simplified in this discussion.
31. The reaction function determines the level of output of the follower firms.
32. This model is attributed to J. Bertrand in which a firm lowers prices with the hope that no price reaction from its competitors will occur and with the expectation of getting the entire share of the market (Hay & Morris 1991).

33. Cited in Ferguson & Ferguson (1988).
34. See Greenwald & Stiglitz (1990).
35. Greenwald & Stiglitz (1990) defined credit rationing as occurring when: (a) among loan applicants who appear to be identical, some receive a loan and others do not, and the rejected applicants would not receive a loan even if they offered to pay a higher interest rate, or (b) there are identifiable groups of individuals in the population who, with a given supply of credit are unable to obtain loans at any interest rate, even though with a larger supply of credit they would. Cosci (1993) defined credit rationing in terms of equilibrium rationing which occurs in the long run when the loan rate is set at its equilibrium level while dynamic credit rationing occurs in the short run when the loan rate is not fully adjusted to its optimal level.
36. See Penrose (1959) on the theory of the growth of firms, Baumol (1962) on the theory of the expansion of the firm, and Marris (1964) on the theory of managerial capitalism.
37. See Marris (1964).
38. See a collection of literature on this topic in the volumes on behavioural economics edited by Earl (1988) which includes the work of Simon who has contributed to this topic.
39. Marris (1964) states this 'satisficing' (sic) level is without regard to the solution being optimal.
40. Other core concepts are: imperfect environmental matching which shows that the match between the environment and the rules followed by organizations may be slow to evolve, necessitating the specification of a process for organizational adaptation. Secondly, there is unresolved conflict which assumes that organizations comprise multiple actors with conflicting interests that are not resolved by the employment contract. Behavioural theories assume that these conflicting interests are continually being negotiated (Cyert & March 1992).
41. This approach has its origins in the work of Coase (1937) cited in sources such as Aoki (1984), Williamson & Winter (1991), Cyert & March (1992), and Aoki, Gustafsson & Williamson (1990). John R. Commons is also credited with pioneering work in this area. Cyert & March (1992) are credited for literature on the theory of economic organization including: the firm as a governance structure which defines the boundary of the firm (from the market) and its capacity relative to its organizational functions; asset specificity which leads to long-term contractual arrangements because of the non-trivial nature of the investment.
42. This issue was raised by Coase (1937) as cited in Williamson (1990: 10 in Aoki et al. 1990). He also questioned why there was not one big firm. He

concluded that there were differentials in transaction costs between the firm and the market.

43. The firm is regarded as a 'governance structure in which the internal structure, the incentives and the controls matter' (Williamson 1990: 13 in Aoki et al. 1990). It is the presence of these factors affecting long-term contracting that make the firm possible.
44. Explained by Simon (1957, cited in Ferguson et al. 1988) as the capacity of the human mind to solve complex problems compared to the size of the problem whose solution requires objectively rational behaviour. The solution is made using limited information. Opportunism refers to a conflict of interest that exists within as well as between organizations.
45. See Sawyer (1991 reprint) for a critique of the SCP approach.
46. Tenjo (1995) argued that the empirical nature of this model has led to oversimplification in its application to the industrialization processes in developing countries. He recommends that the SCP should include a study of the strategic behaviour of firms in developing countries and its impact on market structure.
47. Tenjo (1995) also argues that the managerial theories are based on a perception of the evolution of developed economies and the multi-divisional format of the modern corporation with a hierarchical managerial approach
48. Stanley Fischer (1977) cited in Hodgson (1988: 200).

Annex

Conditions for Profit Maximization in a Monopoly

Let q be the output of the firm with cost function $C(q)$. The price of the firm's output is a function of q, $p(q)$ and revenue is therefore equal to $p(q)q$. A monopoly faces a downward sloping demand curve such that $p'(q)<0$. The solution to the optimization problem is:

$$\max\ p(q)q - C(q) \tag{A3.1}$$

The first order condition is:

$$p(q) + p'(q)q - C'(q) = 0 \tag{A3.2}$$

The second order condition is:

$$2p'(q) + p''(q)q - C''(q) < 0 \tag{A3.3}$$

From A3.2 the necessary condition for profit maximization is that marginal cost, while still equal to marginal revenue, is no longer equal to price:

$$MC = p(q) + p'(q)q = MR \tag{A3.4}$$

Marginal revenue can also be expressed as:

$$MR = p\left(1 + \frac{q/dq}{p/dp}\right) = p\left(1 + \frac{1}{e_{xp}}\right) \tag{A3.5}$$

The factor $(1+1/e_{xp})$ is called the degree of monopoly where e is the elasticity of demand and is <0. Therefore, if e is less than -1 then MR is positive while $e_{xp} = -1$ means that MR = 0 and $e > -1$ but <0 implies that MR is <0. By restricting output the monopoly can therefore increase price and profit. While marginal revenue is equal to marginal cost, the level of output is inefficient such that price exceeds marginal cost.

Oligopoly

The market demand curve for a product can be represented by:

$$p = a - bx \tag{A3.7}$$

where p is the price and x is the total quantity demanded. The linear cost function of n firms is given by:

$$c_f = cq_f \tag{A3.8}$$

where $f = 1 \ldots$n are the firm numbers and q_f is the output of firm f. The total quantity demanded or consumed is equal to the sum of the firms' outputs:

$$x = \sum_{f=1}^{n} q_f \tag{A3.9}$$

The profit function of an oligopolistic firm is:

$$\pi_f(q_f, x) = (a - bx)q_f - cq_f \tag{A3.10}$$

In maximizing profits, the assumption is that all the other firms' outputs are fixed, that is $dx/dq_f = 1$. The first order condition as derived from equation A3.9 is:

$$a - c - bx - bq_f = 0 \tag{A3.11}$$

If we sum over all the n firms we get:

$$n(a - c - bx) = 0 \tag{A3.12}$$

where

$$x = \frac{n}{n+1}\frac{a-c}{b} \tag{A3.13}$$

The individual output of each firm is:

$$q_f = \frac{1}{n+1}\frac{a-c}{b} \qquad \text{(A3.14)}$$

From A3.13 as the number of firms (n) increases, the output of each firm falls though total supply increases.

Table A3.1 Financial liberalization, selected empirical studies

Study	Content	Findings
Fry (1981c)	On the quality and quantity of investment in 12 developing Asian countries.	The ratio of domestic credit to income (the channel through which the investment rate is affected) was positively related to the real deposit rate.
Fry (1986a)	Using pooled time-series on 14 developing Asian economies.	A statistically significant result relative to the increase in the savings rate for a given increase in the real deposit rate of interest – but small magnitude to warrant policy significance.
Warman & Thirlwall (1994)	Tested the hypothesis that raising real interest rates will induce more saving and investment – on Mexico 1960-90 – distinguishing between financial saving and total saving.	Financial saving was positively related to real interest rates through capital flows and domestic asset substitution; total saving is invariant to real interest rates; investment is positively related to the supply of credit from the banking system; the net effect of interest rates on investment is negative.
Giovanni (1985)	Using the implications of the neo-classical theory of consumption, the interest elasticity of savings is explored using annual data for 18 countries and quarterly and monthly data for Korea and Argentina respectively.	A positive and significant impact of interest rate on domestic savings to GNP – but the empirical success depended crucially on the presence in the sample of influential points (years of post-financial reforms in Korea). Inter-temporal substitution in consumption in per capita terms – only in 5 of 18 countries does the path of consumption change with changes in the real interest rate, in the majority of cases the response of consumption growth to the real interest rate is insignificant.

Giovanni (1983)	A review of the empirical analysis on the interest elasticity of savings in developing countries.	The real interest elasticity of savings is not easily detected. The models in the past suffered from defects that made them difficult to interpret – these included: quality and homogeneity of the data across countries, aggregation of private and public savings; absence of tax considerations, exclusion of other relevant variables.
Tybout & de Melo (1986)	Looked at the experience of financial liberalization in Uruguay for the period 1962-83, focusing on the ratio of domestic savings to GDP as affected by real income growth, lagged savings, foreign savings, and the real interest rate.	A structural shift with the 1960s showing savings rates sensitive to foreign capital inflows. During the 1970s the real exchange rate (RER) was important with a real appreciation discouraging savings. Controlling for this effect, savings rates shifted upward with financial liberalization. They found improvement in credit allocation with small firms increasing their leverage and average financial costs relative to large firms. This last conclusion was made based on size coefficients which- they state- were not statistically significant ('mild evidence': 579).

Notes to tables: Fry (1981, 1986) cited in Fry (1988).

4 The Framework for Analysing the Firm Under Adjustment

4.1 Introduction

This chapter sums up the argument of the study, presents the hypotheses, and provides information about the data such as: the sources of data/coverage, the method of collection, sampling design, the strengths and weaknesses of the data. It therefore sets the foundation for the formulation and investigation of the study hypotheses, in addition to providing information about the technical aspects of the study, the quality of the data, and the limitations relative to the interpretation of the results.

Section 4.2 describes the sources of the data, the method of collection, the sampling design and related issues. Section 4.3 contains a profile of the sample of firms in the major data set. Section 4.4 provides a brief recap of the argumentation and the hypotheses of the study.

4.2 Sources of Data, Sampling Design and Method of Data Collection

The data for the study were derived from different sources. In order to make the study feasible, the focus was on the manufacturing sector of Trinidad & Tobago. The two main sources of data used in the analysis are the following:[1] *The Annual Survey of Business Establishments, 1983–1994* – Republic of Trinidad & Tobago Central Statistical Office (CSO)[2] and *A Survey of Businesses in 1995–96*.[3]

4.2.1 The Annual Survey of Business Establishments[4]

The survey objective

The annual survey of business establishments is a yearly enquiry into the operations of business units in Trinidad & Tobago. The primary objective of this survey is to collect most of the data needed from establishments in order to compile the National Accounts of Trinidad & Tobago. For a few years in the 1970s and 1980s, the data were also used to compile reports on business activity. Since the survey is mainly preoccupied with the compilation of the national accounts, firms employing 10+ paid employees are more frequently represented than those with <10 employment.

Essentially, the national accounts are aimed at providing the accounts of the nation over a period of time. Various tables are produced to inform economic planners on industrial activity such as production, expenditures, changes in fixed capital, stocks, financial transactions, assets and liabilities. Supporting data for these accounts are also compiled in various other sources such as trade statistics, government records (e.g. income tax), as well as household budgetary surveys and *ad hoc* small business surveys.

The initial purpose of the establishment survey was to collect data in four distinct areas: wages and employment data for firms employing 10+ persons, the index of production on sales and purchases in physical units, national accounts estimates and balance of payments estimates. There were changes in the administrative aspects of these areas but a relatively close association remained with respect to the units selected for the different purposes in so far that they were all being used to monitor industrial activity. The indices from wages and employment and from production contribute significantly to the derivation of national accounts preliminary and constant price estimates based on the collected sample data.

Although responsibility of the balance of payments was handed over to the Central Bank in 1989, the Central Statistical Office (CSO) continued to have input into its compilation during the final stages. These events represent briefly the background of the design of the annual survey. The actual sampling design is discussed below, referring to the original design and presenting – wherever possible – changes that occurred over time.

Description of survey methodology, original survey design: 1966–1970s

In the original survey design in 1966, the establishment was the unit of enquiry with data being collected for approximately 11 sectors or industrial activities. Details on some of the definitions and sectors covered are given in Annex I at the end of this chapter. The sampling frame comprised a register of establishments, which is an up-to-date (as is feasible) listing of firms compiled from various sources. These sources include: the population census – visitation records, the continuous sample survey of population – (household labour force survey) listing records, the value-added tax (VAT) establishment listing register, telephone directory, register of companies' records, business associations and many other sources. The sampling procedure was applied separately for each industry, for example, in the case of the manufacturing sector, a sample was separately selected for each of the seven industries comprising manufacturing. This approach represented a first level of stratification.[5] The stratification of the data was aimed at reducing total sampling variance.

Within each sector the firms ('population') were ranked in descending order of employment size, using the register of establishments described above. The set of establishments that accounted for 70% of employment within each sector was designated 'ES1' and was surveyed with certainty every year, subject to their being in operation. The assumption was that there was close correlation between output and employment. Since information on employment is in most cases more universally available for firms than information on output, the former was used largely as a criterion for selection. The remaining firms of 10+ employed by sector were designated 'ES2' and a random sample was systematically selected from these. Although a rotating sample was recommended, the sample once selected was not changed. Another problem at that time was the lack of a consistent method of adding new firms to the register.

Developments of the sampling design: 1970s–1987

As noted, problems of coverage existed relative to the inclusion of new firms based on the way the actual implementation of the design was done. Thus, one of the first steps taken towards revising the design was the establishment of procedures to compile and maintain a sufficiently comprehensive register of business establishments, which would take into consideration the births and deaths of firms.The next phase of the sampling design, from the 1970s and extending to the late 1980s, saw the setting up of a unit to monitor the register of establishments, keeping it as up-to-date as possible to improve the coverage of firms. From this register a judgement sample was selected of the most important firms by sector, usually this was interpreted as all firms with 10+ employment since these were assumed to contribute significantly to output. These firms were subjected to an interview-type survey of data collection, which was done by a permanent field staff.

The remaining firms on the register (which would have been firms with <10 employees) were surveyed by mail; but the response rate was usually very low. The records for the <10 firms were, however, not well maintained relative to births and deaths of firms. Nevertheless, as a qualification of this statement, the industrial sectors that are noted for a proliferation of firms with <10 employees are retail distribution and personal services. The manufacturing sectors therefore contain a relatively small percentage of small firms compared to these sectors; but within the manufacturing sectors the number of <10 firms will generally be larger than the 10+ category (see Tables A4.6 to A4.8 in the Annex to this chapter).

Changes in the late 1980s

In the late 1980s, efforts were made to revive elements of the original design to eliminate as far as possible the value judgement that had entered into the selection procedure. The starting point was ensuring that the register was as complete a listing as possible of firms of all sizes from various sources, with procedures put in place for adding new firms and so forth. Thus, the selection of an ES1 to be selected within each sector based on stratification of employment size and a 70% cut-off was re-instituted. However, for the manufacturing sectors, firms with 10+ employment continued to be chosen with certainty since there was little or no difference between the 10+ cut-off and this new procedure, but there were differences in the cut-off for the services sector.

The ES2 also by sector was then selected using a random sampling procedure and reflected firms of <10 employment size for the manufacturing sectors and <15 employment for the services sectors. The entire survey was structured in the form of an interview. Thus efforts were also made to improve the coverage and response rate of this part of the sample.

Essentially, the survey is a continuous enquiry of establishments with a new sample selected annually. However, there is an element of panel in so far as firms in the ES1, who continue to fall in that part of the sample, remain in existence and respond to the survey. Comparison of a panel over time implies that identical firms can be obtained for the entire period of analysis. To the extent that there have been problems with the registration of firms and the lack of response in different years, the ability to capture such a panel element is limited. Observation of the data set showed that there was inconsistency in the response of some firms such that the missing data for specific years excluded some firms from the panel. In the case of this research, only a small panel was possible and it was thought not to be very useful in analysing the hypotheses of the study.

Method of data collection, editing procedures

The method of data collection utilized a permanent survey staff (all trained and with some knowledge of accounting procedures), but initially the smaller firms were surveyed by mail. By the late 1980s, the survey was done as an interview, with a postal survey being utilized only to assist in updating of the register. Editing procedures were put in place at the field and office levels with built-in checks on the questionnaires being used to check the quality of the data. Efforts were also made to implement a procedure whereby the editing checks were subjected to a computer edit along with a manual edit.

Questionnaire amendments

The basic format of the questionnaire remained the same. Changes were made because of duplication or the lack of utility of some items, for example, items on wages and employment at a detailed level which were never used. Relative to items of expenditure, the changes made would have been a reflection of any changes in the conceptual changes in the national accounts and would have been done mainly to obtain a greater level of disaggregation.

For example, while in the past the item "interest and bank charges" had been collected as one item, the need to obtain interest payments apart from bank charges for the purposes of compilation of special accounts led to the separation of this item in the questionnaire. Thus, in effect the item remained but the questionnaire codes that were used and the level of disaggregation changed. Inclusion of items occurred as a special supplement to collect data relative to the compilation of input – output accounts. In general, therefore while there were changes in the questionnaire, they were minimal if any, with the conceptual changes being more at the level of the national accounts compilation relative to the use of the data at that stage.

Data limitations

The limitations of the data are largely derived from three sources: coverage relative to the different phases of the sampling methodology and overall survey objective, response rate and biases due to incomplete information/missing data, editing, coding and interviewer biases at each stage. No assessment is available as to the extent of these biases.

The quality of the data is fairly reliable in so far as there were effective quality control procedures implemented by experienced officers who were responsible for the built-in questionnaire checks. Other measures that ensured reliability of the data were the handling of queries based on the knowledge of the establishment, the comparison from one year to the next of the data at various stages in the processing, and the use of computer editing.[6]

For the years 1988–93, the response rates for the manufacturing sector, firms selected with certainty, were normally between 56% and 70% out of the total sample selected. No response rates are available for the earlier years. Information on entry/exit rates of firms from the register is not available, but this could have been a contributory factor for the small panel element that was obtained.

Relative to coverage and sampling methodology, one main limitation is that particularly for the early years there is little representation of very small firms such as those with less than five employees or even under ten employed. While this feature was addressed to some extent, since the main objective of the survey was to compile data for the national accounts, emphasis relative to collection of returns from these firms is not as strong as for larger firms with 10+ employees. Thus, there may be limitations with respect to the sample size particularly for the <10 firms, making it difficult to perform analysis by specific categories within this group. As will be shown later, the foreign firms are a small group relative to the local firms, which may limit analysis by specific characteristics within this group (of foreign firms).

Coverage of data set and strategy for data analysis

This data set covers a period of 11 years: 1983, 1984 and 1986-94, and was arranged as a pooled time-series, cross-sectional set to perform econometric work relative to the effects of the policies on firms. While a new sample is being collected in each year, there is some consistency in the units that occur and a higher degree of consistency in the questions that are asked. Relevant tests of pooling across selected characteristics were performed and will be reported with the econometric results in Chapter 8. This data set contains information on private firms of varied sizes relative to employment, activities (manufacturing), ownership, and so forth. Surveys of this kind can be used effectively to monitor variation in trends over time for different types of firms (Dale & Davies 1994). The pooling of the data also increases the sample size; and, the assumption is that the structural parameters of the equations are the same over time/categories, with the inability to pool representing differences over time/categories.

As mentioned above it was not possible to get a particularly large and useful panel of identical firms throughout the years. Thus categories of firms with selected characteristics are used to analyse temporal variation of structural features relative to the variables of interest to the study.

The survey data therefore represents repeated cross-sectional data over time for different firms, but with some element of identical firms limited by firm non-response in specific years. Dale & Davies (1994) state two ways of organizing this data: (1) as micro data at the individual level or (2) as macro data with the aggregation of cases across categories. For the 10+ firms, the empirical tests on the pooling of the data will be used to suggest employment size groups for analysis. As far as the sampling design is concerned, the stratification prior to firm selection improves the precision of estimates by sector/industry.

Provided there is consistency in the variables used as well as in its definition; it is possible to perform pooled cross-section analysis over time at the individual level. Individual level data can also be grouped in multilevel tables with time as a factor (Dale & Davies 1994).

As a first phase of data analysis, categories of firms were analysed over time based on groupings suggested by the theoretical discussions and sampling design. Categories of firms by size, ownership (foreign/local) and industry were used to compare changes over time in variables of interest such as leverage, interest expenses, raw material expenses, profitability and investment. This approach is similar but not identical to the use of pseudo panels described by Dale & Davies (1994). Panel data enable the analysis of identical sampling units over time. On the other hand, while repeated cross-sectional data allows for the analysis of temporal variation, the sampling units differ. The advantage of the use of pseudo panels or repeated cross-sectional data is that they do not suffer as severely from problems of attrition as is the case with genuine panel data and may therefore be available over a longer period than panel data. The population of firms bears a measure of similarity to a human population to the extent that births and deaths of firms occur. Heterogeneity is expected to exist between firms of different sizes, ownership, and industry. These factors will be used as a basis for deriving homogeneous categories, for comparison over time of repeated cross-sectional data. The stratification procedure by sector (industry) with the view of improving the precision of estimates of each sector's contribution to GDP also implies the presence of heterogeneity by industry. Hence, categorization of the data by industry was also performed.

While the firms with 10+ employment were subjected to a census, the sampling design dictates that firms with <10 employees should also be appropriately weighted by industrial sector to provide unbiased point estimates. Due to the unavailability of information on the sampling fractions by year and sector, estimated weights were used for the individual manufacturing sector to take into consideration the stratification procedure. This method of raising the data for the <10 employment size firms is an unavoidably crude estimate of weights due to the absence of detailed information by year on the population of firms. Yet, this is somewhat attenuated by some available data for 1992 and 1993 as well as my own knowledge of the register as it was compiled in 1985, incorporating information received from the 1990 Population Census. Based on information for these years regarding the number of firms on the register by industry, individual industry weights or sampling fractions were worked out for the <10 (employment size) firms by comparing the number of firms selected with the number on register.

4.2.2 Survey of businesses, 1995–96

The second data set is a narrow survey comprising mainly qualitative data focusing on the response and the effects of the policies of adjustment on firms. The basis used to select this data was the register of establishments described above. Thus, no further details relative to the sampling frame are necessary. While it was a much smaller data set, there was an in-depth inquiry relative to the processes of firm-level restructuring that was not available from the data set of the annual survey of establishment.

The selection of this sample was based on prior exploratory analysis of the annual survey data in which patterns relative to the movements of establishments across time were evaluated for selected variables such as sales, expenses, profit, assets, and so forth. Thus, a few firms were subjectively selected using the criteria of the positioning of the firms in the distributions of variables across time. Out of 77 firms selected, a total of 30 responded.

4.3 Profile of Responding Firms: Annual Survey of Business Establishments

The data in this section relates to the annual survey data described in section 4.2.1, with the description of characteristics based on response data for the years 1983–94. Since the objective is to present a profile of the responding firms, no effort is therefore made in these tables to obtain population estimates for firms in the <10 employment size group. Differences in totals may be due to missing data on specific characteristics. A breakdown of the sample for each year is shown in Table 4.1 with the percentages for each year out of the total for the 11 years ranging between 6.5 to 11% . Thus, the number of firms represented in the pooled data is relatively consistent by year.

By industrial activity, food processing/drink and tobacco, assembly and related, as well as chemicals and related are the sectors with the highest representation. This feature suggests that firms in these sectors probably contribute more to GDP than the ones in the other manufactur-

Table 4.1 Profile of firms by year of data

Year	No. of firms	%
1983	235	8.0
1984	267	9.1
1986	264	9.0
1987	279	9.5
1988	271	9.2
1989	279	9.5
1990	285	9.7
1991	323	11.0
1992	269	9.1
1993	280	9.5
1994	192	6.5
Total	2,944	100.0

Note: Percentages are out of total for 1983–94.

ing sectors which is also reflected in Table 2.5 (Chapter 2). Thus, there is consistency in the sample design relative to significant representation of firms/ sectors based on contribution to output when using the proxy of employment size of firms as a selection criteria.

Approximately 87% of the firms are locally-owned while13% have some degree of foreign ownership.[8] There were lower percentages of foreign firms in 1991–93, but the values for the other years were approx-

Figure 4.1 Profile of firms by year (each year as a percentage of pooled data)

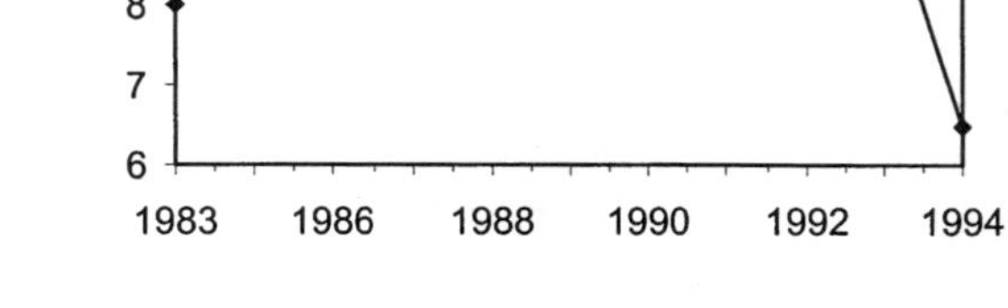

Table 4.2 Profile of firms by industry

Industry	No. of firms	% frequency
Food processing, drink, tobacco	595	20.2
Textiles, garments, footwear, headwear	402	13.7
Printing & paper converters	393	13.3
Wood & related	237	8.1
Chemicals & related	445	15.1
Assembly & related	612	20.8
Miscellaneous manufacturing	260	8.8
Total	2,944	100.0

imately 12.5 to 17%, with 1986 being exceptionally high at 20% (Tables 4.3 and 4.4). The foreign firms are mainly large firms with about 80–87% of them falling in the 25+ employment category for most years. Table 4.9 provides further details of ownership by employment size.

By employment size (Table 4.5), the pooled sample reflects a fairly good representation of small/medium and medium/large firms where these descriptions are used to depict the 10–24 and 25–49 size groups respectively. Like many of the other variables analysed in this study, employment is positively skewed, there are a large number of smaller firms and fewer extremely large firms. Available data from the register of establishments for 1993 are shown in Tables A4.6 and A4.7 in the Annex to this chapter and show the small numbers and percentage of 10+ firms,

Figure 4.2 Number of firms by industry

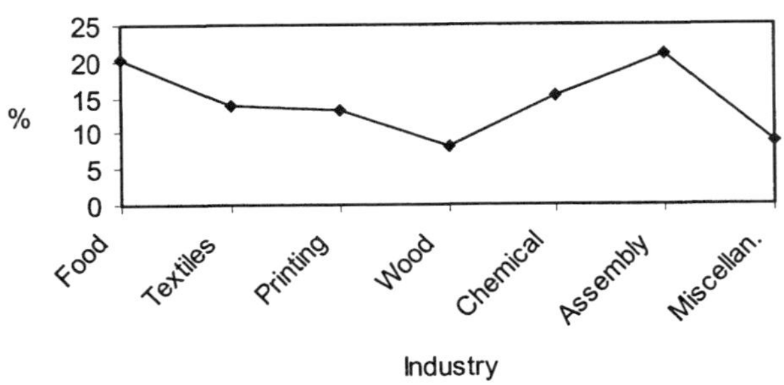

Table 4.3 Profile of firms by foreign/local ownership

Ownership	No. of firms	% frequency
Locally owned	2,546	86.5
Foreign owned	397	13.5
Total	2,943	100.0

Table 4.4 Profile of firms by foreign/local ownership by year (row percentages)

Year	Local	Foreign	Total
1983	85.1	14.9	100
1984	84.4	15.4	100
1986	80.3	19.7	100
1987	84.9	15.1	100
1988	84.1	15.9	100
1989	83.3	16.5	100
1990	88.1	11.9	100
1991	90.4	9.6	100
1992	89.9	10.1	100
1993	92.1	7.9	100
1994	87.4	12.6	100
Total	86.5	13.5	100

with the larger percentage of <10 group comprising mainly firms with no paid employees.

The profile of firms by use of leverage is represented in two ways. Table 4.6 shows leverage inclusive of foreign and local liabilities (denoted as foreign and local, and local alone in Figure 4.5) while Table 4.7 is limited to the local liabilities position (ratio to total assets). While the former shows the total debt structure of the firm, the latter shows the extent to which the firms are locally liable, i.e., their ability to use the local financial market.[9] This latter format is useful in analysing changes in the firm's debt structure, relative to the application of monetary and financial policies of adjustment in the domestic economy. Table 4.6 shows that the majority of the firms in the survey had liability ranging from

Figure 4.3 Profile of firms by foreign/local ownership and year

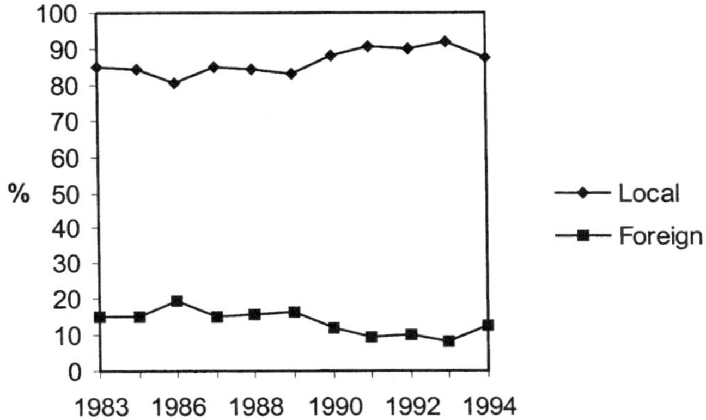

Figure 4.4 Profile of firms by employment size group

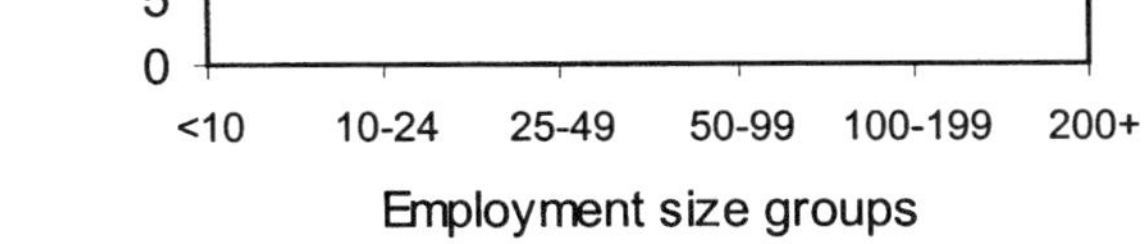

Table 4.5 Profile of firms by employment size

Employment size	No. of firms	% frequency
<10	477	16.2
10–24	824	28.0
25–49	598	20.3
50–99	476	16.2
100–199	378	12.8
200 +	189	6.4
Total	2,944	100.0

50–70% of total assets, and is followed by the 25–50% and the 75–100% groups, in that order.

Comparing local liabilities to assets, there are approximately 7% more of the firms in the lowest leverage group, less than 25%, (lower use of leverage controlling for foreign liabilities) and about 2 to 3% less firms in the higher leverage groups. Except for these changes, the two distributions are fairly comparable.

Thus, the sample appears to be fairly consistent by year and, with the exception of the very small firms, reflects the distribution by activity and employment size of firms in the private sector.

Table 4.8 compares two measures of size of firms: asset size and number of employees. Firms seemed to be fairly well correlated by asset size, with the larger percentage of smaller firms associated with smaller size total assets, and the converse for the larger firms, and the medium-

Figure 4.5 Profile of firms by use of leverage

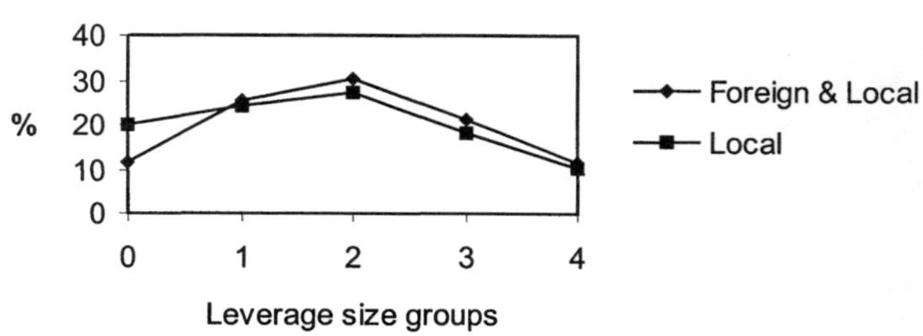

Table 4.6 Profile of firms by use of leverage (foreign and local liabilities)

Leverage	Code	No. of firms	% frequency
Less than 0.25	0	303	11.6
0.25–0.50	1	660	25.3
0.50–0.75	2	783	30.1
0.75–1.00	3	551	21.2
1.00 & over	4	307	11.8
Total		2,604	100.0

Table 4.7 Profile of firms by use of leverage (local liabilities only)

Leverage	Code	No. of firms	% frequency
Less than 0.25	0	515	19.8
0.25–0.50	1	631	24.2
0.50–0.75	2	710	27.3
0.75–1 .00	3	477	18.3
1.00 & over	4	271	10.4
Total		2,604	100.0

Table 4.8 Employment by asset size (row percentage)

Employment	Asset size (TT million $)				
	< 0.5	0.5–1.0	1.0–5.0	5.0+	Total
< 10	*68.8*	16.1	13.6	1.4	100
10–24	*32.2*	20.9	42.6	5.6	100
25–49	9.9	12.7	53.1	23.3	100
50–99	7.4	2.1	32.8	56.7	100
100–199	7.1	–	5.3	*87.6*	100
200+	14.3	0.5	2.1	*83.1*	100
Total	25.2	11.4	31.0	32.4	100

Table 4.9a Employment by ownership (row percentage)

Ownership	Employment size groups						
	<10	10–24	25–49	50–99	100–199	200+	Total
Local	17.6	30.2	21.2	15.0	11.6	4.4	100
Foreign	7.3	13.9	14.6	23.7	21.2	13.5	100
Total	16.2	28.0	20.3	16.2	12.8	6.4	100

Table 4.9b Employment by ownership (column percentage)

Ownership	Employment size groups						
	<10	10–24	25–49	50–99	100–199	200+	Total
Local	93.9	93.3	90.3	80.3	77.8	59.3	86.5
Foreign	6.1	6.7	9.7	19.7	22.2	40.7	13.5
Total	100.0	100.0	100.0	100.0	100.0	100.0	100.0

sized firms also being consistent with asset size. Table 4.9a looks further at ownership by employment size (row percentage); in which overall approximately 80% of the foreign firms are in the 25+ employment size group, implying that the foreign firms are mainly large firms. The local firms are approximately evenly distributed between 25+ and <25 size categories. The column percentage shown in Table 4.9b shows that as the employment size group increases beyond the 10–24 group, the percentage of foreign firms increases.

Table 4.10 gives an idea of employment size over time. The years 1986–91 showed a dip of the number of firms in the 200+ employment size group, ranging from 3.9 to 6.1%. These percentages compare with figures of as high as 8.9% in 1983 and 7.9% in both 1984 and 1994.[10]

Finally, from the sample data, employment size by sector shows that in most sectors there are more small firms than large, and the data is positively skewed. Among the responding firms, within sector distribution by firm size shows that wood and related activity, miscellaneous manufacturing and assembly have the largest proportion of smaller firms, in that order. Food processing, assembly and chemicals are the industries with the highest percentage of large firms.

Table 4.10 Employment size groups by year (row percentage)

Year	Employment size groups						
	<10	10–24	25–49	50–99	100–199	200+	Total
1983	8.1	26.8	23.8	16.6	15.7	8.9	100
1984	15.0	22.8	20.6	18.7	15.0	7.9	100
1986	22.3	25.4	14.8	19.3	12.5	5.7	100
1987	27.2	21.5	18.3	14.3	13.3	5.4	100
1988	11.1	34.3	22.9	12.9	13.3	5.5	100
1989	10.4	31.2	23.3	16.1	12.9	6.1	100
1990	15.8	30.2	21.1	17.2	11.9	3.9	100
1991	23.5	27.9	17.3	15.5	9.6	6.2	100
1992	13.8	29.4	21.9	16.7	11.2	7.1	100
1993	14.3	32.5	17.1	16.1	12.9	7.1	100
1994	13.7	24.7	24.7	14.2	14.7	7.9	100
Total	16.2	28.0	20.3	16.2	12.8	6.4	100

Table 4.11 Employment size by leverage (total, row percentage)

Year	Leverage size groups					
	<0.25	0.25–0.49	0.50–0.75	0.75–1.00	1.00+	Total
<10	24.3	18.2	18.2	20.4	19.0	100
10–24	15.6	21.4	30.3	19.0	13.8	100
25–49	9.5	26.4	27.6	23.5	13.1	100
50–99	5.6	25.2	37.2	24.8	7.2	100
100–199	4.8	31.1	35.3	20.7	8.1	100
200+	4.9	43.2	32.7	16.0	3.1	100
Total	11.6	25.3	30.1	21.2	11.8	100

Table 4.12 Sector by employment size

Employment	Food	Textiles	Printing	Wood	Chemicals	Assembly	Miscellaneous
< 25	32.0	41.8	42.9	71.2	42.0	45.5	53.3
25–49	17.4	28.4	27.2	13.9	19.1	17.4	18.8
50–99	14.1	20.4	18.3	6.3	19.3	17.1	12.3
100+	36.4	9.4	11.4	8.5	19.5	19.7	15.8
Total	100.0	100.0	100.0	100.0	100.0	100.0	100.0

Additional tables are given in Annex 4.1, which show further breakdown of respondents by year of data, and ownership including some cross-tabulations. Section 4.4 below summarizes the argument of the study.

4.4 The Approach to Analysing the Private Sector under Adjustment

4.4.1 Summary of the argument

The study looked at the role of the private sector in adjustment in Chapter 1, addressing the prominence given to this sector in adjustment policies. Private enterprise development has its roots in the early writings of the classical school. The chapter looked at the dynamics of the role assigned to the private sector by moving through the neo-classical era, the early development economists, and the currently influential neo-liberalist tradition. The argument for the role of the private sector relied on the state/market dichotomy and was primarily ideologically based. Hence, the chapter looked closer at the functioning of markets, the assumptions on the achievement of a social optimum as well as the competing approaches. The historical and institutional basis of markets are central to these competing approaches, which provide a more realistic explanation of market functioning, and help to explain adjustment in LDCs.

Concerns of the Structuralist and post-Keynesian tradition were therefore discussed, looking at the factors which gave rise to specific structural features in developing countries that obstruct the smooth functioning of markets and affect the allocation of resources for the financing of investment and working capital. Thus problems surfaced with access to credit, due to the presence of segmented markets, ownership patterns, and traditional relationships between economic agents and institutions. Economic dualism due to uneven growth and reflected in market segmentation, inequitable access to technology, and in general uneven development within and between sectors underpins the structure of many LDCs. Special emphasis was placed on private investment relative to the capacity of the private sector to fulfil its role in economic recovery.

This led, in Chapter 2, to a discussion of the private sector in a developing country context (Trinidad & Tobago), in which some main themes relative to ownership and credit access, openness, import dependency of manufacturing production, etc. were identified as being pervasive and rooted in the historical origins of Trinidad & Tobago. The argument therefore traced the historical origins of the development of the private sector based on the experience of Caribbean economies, to its impact today in a changed policy environment.

Of vital importance to this study is the effect of the macro policies of adjustment, through the analysis at the micro level of firms in the private sector of a developing country. Theoretically, there is a gap in economic theory relative to these two levels of analysis. This gap is to some extent bridged in the post-Keynesian and Structuralist literature though not necessarily in a well integrated form. Hence, Chapter 3, in an attempt to bridge the macro-micro gap, discussed the macro policies of adjustment and their impact on firms as well as the neo-classical theory of the firm, which is arguably really about markets.

The transmission mechanisms in the study are primarily relative prices, the real exchange rate and the real interest rates, with the channels of transmission being markets, particularly product and factor markets.[11] To the extent that there are problems with the functioning of markets as illustrated in the review of the Structuralist/post-Keynesian literature and the country case study, changes in the macro policy environment may not achieve the results that ought to occur relative to the attainment of a social optimum and private investment recovery. Therefore, features such as ownership, size, and import-dependent production also surfaced in this chapter as structural, heterogeneous factors that ought to be considered relative to explaining the situation faced by firms in a developing country during adjustment.

The current chapter has so far dealt with the question of the data used in the analyses – its coverage, limitations and advantages. The dynamic aspect of adjustment relative to temporal variation in the data was also discussed in this chapter. The use of pooled cross-sectional data over a number of years, while increasing the sample size, enables to some extent comparison of categories of firms over time. Limitations of the data rest in the unreliability of firms with <10 employment originating from the survey objective and design, which gave priority to firms with 10+ employed persons. This factor was further aggravated by coverage relative to firm registration and, of course, problems of non-response.

The study strategy in exploiting this feature of heterogeneity and structure uses a framework that caters to the historical and institutional features that fashion the firm and markets, and can give an idea of the process of change over time. The framework may also help to explain the macroeconomic aspect of policy changes through an understanding of the nature of the changes at the micro level, without the assumption that the micro changes necessarily add up to reflect the macro foundations through aggregation and optimization. In this context, identification of the channels and transmission mechanisms are two steps towards bridging the gap in the macro and micro theory of adjustment. With this in mind, the main themes and hypotheses of the study are outlined below.

4.4.2 The main themes of the study

The main issues of the study surround the need to incorporate and integrate the inherent structural aspect of the firm and the economy with the historical processes and experiences in analysing the impact of macroeconomic policies of adjustment. In this context, themes previously identified will be modified in order to narrow the focus of the analysis. In the case of the economy of Trinidad & Tobago, some of these features were: a heavy reliance on imported intermediates, lack of access to external markets for manufactured goods, openness of the economy to imports of manufactured goods, and institutionalized problems with credit access. The modified themes are:

- credit access/ rationing
- structure of production
- inherited debt/asset structure
- openness
- heterogeneity
- the use of price relatives.

Credit access/rationing

Problems with credit access by firms have been identified as an inherent characteristic of the private sector in Trinidad & Tobago. Its manifestation has taken the form of subjective assessment of credit with concerns such as ownership, size of firm and bank-firm relationships being paramount. Small and medium-sized firms are among those that experience this subjective criteria of credit access.[12] The transmission mechanism is the real interest rate and the channel is the capital market.

Structure of production/historical experience

The inherent structural characteristics of the country's development meant that a distinctive feature of the firm's production pattern was the dependency on imported intermediates. Raw materials and labour costs are important factors in the operating expenditure of the firm. When a high percentage of the cost structure of the firm is fixed and there is a decline in demand, these aspects of operating costs do not automatically decline. The structural features of production limit the flexibility of firms to adjust to changes in relative prices. This structure exists at the initial point of adjustment and cannot be easily reversed. In this case, the effect of macro policies is transmitted through product markets and through the mechanism of the real exchange rate, which increases raw material expenses. An offsetting effect is the cheapening of labour in foreign currency.

Inherited asset/debt structure

Ownership of assets, fixed and financial, places firms in a position to facilitate production through meeting working capital needs, and to enable future investment in real or financial assets. Acquisition of assets can be done through borrowing. It was argued that firms have different debt histories, which are explained through traditional experiences in being able to access credit from banks. Worrell (1985) saw credit rationing as being guided by institutional norms. The traditional lack of access by some firms and/or the availability of credit at discriminatory prices are institutional features that some firms face, argued partly on size/ownership criteria. The experience with respect to leverage use by these firms might have led to bankruptcy or problems of indebtedness during the period of adjustment.

On the other hand, expectations of profit might have led some firms into heavy borrowing for investment, which were not sustainable during the adjustment period. With changes in the macroeconomic environment, the composition of the asset/liability structure relative to the extent of financial leverage could lead to adverse effects on some firms due to continued lack of access/cost of credit or the need to continue heavy borrowing. Similar to the cost structure of production at the initial point of adjustment, this asset/liability structure is given, affecting the flexibility and direction that adjustment can take in the face of changes in the real interest rate and the real exchange rate. The channel through which adjustment is felt based on this theme is the capital market with both the real interest rate and the real exchange rate being transmission mechanisms.

Openness

The openness of the country is manifested through the dependency on export earnings from a major staple, on imported intermediates and capital goods for production, on foreign investment, and on imports of consumer goods. This pattern which goes back to the historical demand for foreign manufactures by the 'plantation' economy has been pervasive over time. The exchange rate and differentials between the world and domestic interest rates are the mechanisms that transmit the impact of adjustment to an economy with an inherent pattern of openness and dependency. Essentially, both the capital and product markets are channels through which adjustment effects are felt. The petroleum (including energy-based) sector has been the one that has benefited largely from direct foreign investment.

Heterogeneity

The feature of heterogeneity depicted the private sector as not being in line with a representative firm that can respond flexibly to relative price incentives. Instead, inherent structural features fashioned through history and by institutions and differentiated by ownership, size of firm, and activity have implications for the allocation of resources, lead to a differential impact, and affect the response of different types of firms to adjustment. These groups of firms are identifiable by specific patterns of behaviour.

Key price relatives

The key relative prices of interest are the real exchange rate, the real lending rate of interest and the real wage rate. The exchange rate affects 1) firms through the channel of the cost of imported raw materials purchased for production, 2) the wage rate through the impact on labour costs, and 3) the interest rate through interest expenses - with all the relative prices having an impact on the liability and asset position of firms, which need to meet production expenses through debt.

In light of the above considerations, the hypotheses of the study are presented in the next section.

4.4.3 Transmission mechanisms of macroeconomic shocks to firms

Macroeconomic shocks are transmitted to firms through changes in relative prices. In the context of this study, the relevant prices that are being analysed are the real exchange rate and the real interest rate. The channels through which these mechanisms work are the product and factor markets. The earlier discussions suggested that expectations of adjustment might not be realized because of structural features of markets and production in developing countries. These features lead to differential results of the micro-units within private sectors, which comprise structurally heterogeneous groups.

This section seeks to further clarify the transmission effects of macro economic policies on firms as they can inform the hypotheses to follow.

Transmission of changes in the exchange rate to firms

Exchange rate devaluation or liberalization can impact directly on the cost structure of firms if it purchases its materials directly from abroad or through indirect purchases from a wholesaler/manufacturer who imports. The effects of the exchange rate are explained in equations 3.14 to 3.23 in Chapter 3, as it impacts on costs/wages, prices, and output of firms.

Whether the effect is direct or indirect, it is expected that the cost of raw materials will increase. The effect of the increases in the raw materials can also work its way through the firm to affect other aspects of the cost of production, output and the asset structure depending on how the firm responds to the increase. These transmission mechanisms of changes in the exchange rate are discussed below.

Quantity versus price adjustments to changes in the exchange rate: reduction in purchases of imported raw materials

The increased price of imported inputs can lead to quantity adjustments through a reduction in the quantity purchased. The transmission effect of reduced purchases of raw materials will impact on the firm through a reduction in output leading to reduced sales, profitability, investment and employment (all things being equal). The result is economic contraction of the firm and the economy, and a firm that is no longer competitive. The firm can therefore make quantity adjustments when faced with increased relative price effects.

For exporters, there is a trade-off between the price competitiveness and the production costs brought on by the devaluation. There are no guarantees that exports will automatically increase from a devaluation, if the import content of manufacturing increases significantly. However, where the devaluation brings about significant price competitiveness in the domestic economy relative to that of the economy of the trading partners, market penetration is possible.

Firms whose market focus is largely domestic face the additional demands of export market penetration with the result that quantity adjustment may imply a reduction in domestic sales and production.

Quality adjustments to changes in the exchange rate: purchasing of cheaper raw materials abroad or locally

The effect of this measure on the firm may prevent any increase in the cost of raw materials as a result of exchange rate devaluation. The savings on raw material costs may affect the quality of the material inputs and also the quality of the resulting output. While these savings may allow the firm to cut or maintain costs; changes in quality may affect the demand for the firm's products. This effect can be positive where persons faced with lower incomes or increased prices are willing to purchase a product of lower quality rather than an expensive substitute. On the other hand, the impact can be a fall in demand where quality differences are not cost-effective for the customer – i.e., the inferiority of the product causes a switch to a more superior but costly product.

Transmission effect of changes in the exchange rate through labour, productivity and wages

Increased costs brought on by devaluation can force the firm to cut other aspects of its costs in the process of adjustment. The issue of quantity adjustment arises if the devaluation leads to a cut in employment in order to cut the wage bill to offset the impact of the increase in imported material inputs.

Possible transmission of the above measure can lead to a reduction in output concomitant with reduced employment or, alternatively, productivity increases. In the former case, reduced output and employment will result in a fall off in sales, adversely affecting profitability and investment, and resulting in excess capacity which is also a cost to the firm. If productivity can increase, then this will lead to more efficient production, profitability and possibly to increased investment.

The relationship between changes in wages and exchange rate devaluation was discussed earlier. Devaluation may lead to increased wages where workers try to offset the effect of increased costs. There can therefore be a dual transmission effect of the real exchange rate on the cost structure – on the imported inputs and on wages. The transmission effect of increased wages results in increases in operating costs, reduction in profitability and dim possibilities for investment.

It may be possible however for some firms to suppress wages; in which case, the transmission effect of devaluation is felt through the absence of changes in the wage bill, which allows firms to be cost effective and price competitive.

Transmission effect of changes in the exchange rate through the asset structure

The resulting price effects above, after impacting on the cost structure of the firm and output, can also be transmitted to the asset structure. Firms may be forced to borrow to offset the increased costs of raw materials and wages. Reduction in output and demand and falling profitability may imply that those firms that resort to distress borrowing to meet their financial commitments are faced with increased indebtedness which feeds back through principal and interest repayments to affect their profitability and capacity to invest.

It may however be the case that firms may decide as a result of the devaluation to engage in investment in financial assets denominated in foreign currency rather than in productive assets. The differentials between foreign and local currencies and interest rates (discussed below) may lead the exchange rate changes to cause firms to shift their portfolio into foreign currency, affecting the composition of the asset structure of the firm as well as the financial versus real asset structure.

These are some of the major mechanisms of transmission of the exchange rate on firms. Below the discussion focuses on the transmission mechanisms of interest rate changes.

Transmission mechanisms of changes in the interest rate

In Chapter 3 the impact of the interest rate in adjustment was discussed through looking at financial liberalization and its impact on firms. This section tries to give a more precise picture of the mechanisms of transmission of the interest rate as it can inform the hypotheses that follow.

Transmission of the interest rate effect through increased interest payments on the existing debt

While interest income is considered property income, it forms the major revenue of the banking system and is included as part of the value added of that industry. The reverse side of interest received is that of interest paid by those firms who receive these indirect services (financial intermediaries) from the banking sector.

The use of short-term debt such as overdraft payments can result in fluctuations in interest payments if interest rates were to increase and can lead to bankruptcy. Apart from the impact on current production, the interest rate can also impact the cost of long term debt – the current maturity aspect.

Hence, increases in payments for loans are one of the major ways that interest rate increases can be transmitted to firms.

Transmission of changes in the interest rate on working capital

Taylor (1981) argued that the interest rate factor should be reflected in the cost of production. Interest paid by firms, while not linked directly to the goods and services produced, is an aspect of current expenditure and enables production.

The transmission effect of increases in interest rate can affect the availability or accessibility of working capital requirements of the firm. Reduction in working capital affects the firm's ability to finance production – labour expenditure, the cost of raw materials, and other supplies and services in the face of macroeconomic changes.

The initial conditions of firms, particularly the cost and asset structure, the market focus, size of the workforce, industry and ownership patterns are critical issues in the determination of how macroeconomic shocks impact firms. These conditions will be articulated in the hypotheses that follow.

4.4.4 The hypotheses of the study

(a) Characteristic features of firms and their historical production and asset structures are directly linked to their ability to circumvent the effects of relative price changes arising from macroeconomic policies – specifically, from monetary and exchange rate policies which affect the interest rate and the exchange rate.

(b) Furthermore, structural features in production and debt structures that have been historically determined such as a heavy dependence on imported raw materials, differentials in credit access and cost pose constraints to profitability and investment of firms under adjustment.

(c) The above effects are experienced in general through the following relative price changes:
- exchange rate devaluation which results in increased costs of imported inputs of raw materials, and imported capital equipment; this increased cost of production and liabilities negatively affects the profitability and investment capacity of firms;
- interest rate increases through the interest expenses account contribute negatively to profitability and increase the cost of investment which is thus negatively affected.

(d) The heterogeneous nature of firms in the private sector, manifested by differences due to size, foreign/local ownership and industry, is one of the factors that has bearing on the allocation of resources.

Thus, firms do not face equal conditions or identical market prices resulting in differences in the results of (c) above.

(e) Relative to (a) and (d), the application of tight monetary policy, credit ceilings and financial liberalization in a scenario that contains inequalities in access/cost of credit in financial markets, and is based on an allocation of credit that is institutionally and historically determined, is likely to have differential effects on the profitability and investment position of different categories of firms through changes in their cost structure of production and their asset/debt structures. These effects may include the following:
- the interest rate effect on profitability of smaller firms acting through interest expenses is likely to be negative due to higher biases faced in financial markets that result in high interest rates and collateral requirements;
- the continued ability of some large local firms to invest because of traditional relationships with banks may result in positive effect of interest expenses on investment;
- foreign firms that do not borrow in the domestic economy because of other options relative to parent/affiliate or international banks, will remain unaffected by these policies, while those that borrow domestically are likely to suffer some negative effects, though not as extreme as local firms;
- generally, the debt structure of all categories of firms may limit their capacity to invest or be profitable because of its irreversibility and inherent inflexibility in substitution of factors of production;
- particularly high users of leverage, which may normally be large firms, may experience adverse effects of liabilities to total assets on profit and investment during the period of adjustment;
- low users of leverage (which maybe as a result of inherent problems with access to credit for investment/working capital purposes) may experience negative effects relative to their use of leverage on investment and profitability.

(f) While the local asset situation of the firm may act as a buffer to induce profitability and investment, the cost of holding stocks and the accumulation of debt can result in a negative effect of local assets on profitability and investment.

Table 4.13 Summary of main themes to be explored in the hypotheses

Main themes of hypotheses	Policy being questioned	Transmission/effects/argumentation
Historical/structural aspects of firm and economy, and firm heterogeneity affect capacity to restructure (a), (b), (c), (d)	Exchange rate, financial and monetary policies	Relative price changes through factors in the production/asset structures lead to changes in profitability and in the volume and efficiency of investment by firm size, ownership, industry
Openness, domestic market focus (g)	Exchange rate policy, tight monetary policy	Real exchange rate on production structure increases cost of production with offsetting positive effect on export market penetration for some firms-which may imply positive net effect in these cases; but in general net effect is negative particularly for smaller local firms with greater domestic market focus. Tight monetary policy affects domestic demand and therefore the sales of the firm, as well as the interest rate. Wage constraint may offset the effect of increasing costs.
Credit rationing, cost, size/ownership differences, general (e)	Financial liberalization/ monetary policy	Relative price changes affect access to resources of smaller firms leading to problems in the capacity to adjust, while larger firms have greater access to resources. There is also greater inflexibility in adjusting the structure of larger firms, due to higher expenses, larger labour force, larger wage bill, larger liability and so on. Foreign firms are largely unaffected since they can get credit from abroad.
Asset/debt structure-use of leverage differences (e) & (f)	All policies but specifically financial liberalization	Relative price changes through production and asset structure leverage can magnify or lever up the capital base while it may also inhibit through severe indebtedness
Productivity/financial efficiency changes (h)	All policies	Through cuts in labour, wages, or increases in output productivity can be affected, relative price can lead to gains in profitability, discouragement of financially inefficient activities/ investment

(g) Relative to the differential effects of exchange rate policy, the following may result:
- activities that are rigidly dependent on foreign raw materials cojointly with a domestic market focus can at worse disappear or change from traded to non-traded, unlike the expectations of adjustment policies of increased investment response in traded sectors through a shifting of relative prices against non-traded activities.

- to the extent that firms are able to limit wage increases, the effect of the devaluation may be lessened.
- smaller firms and specific industrial activities may not have the capacity to lower their wages or limit wage increases due to already existing low wage levels.
- larger firms with already existing high wages may be able to limit their wage increases or impose a wage freeze.

(h) It follows therefore that in the period of adjustment expected gains in financial efficiency and productivity gains may not automatically improve private investment and profitability.

In the next three chapters the assessment of these hypotheses will be carried out using a combination of econometric modelling, exploratory data analysis and qualitative data.

Notes

1. Informal interviews, the media and other sources were also used.
2. Data for 1985 was not available.
3. Survey compiled by the author.
4. The information is partly based on my own knowledge of the survey, having worked on it in the late 1980s, and on some documentation available from the published reports.
5. The initial survey design benefited from consultants provided by the Canadian Bureau of Statistics.
6. Of course editing of data is never a complete task because of its copious nature. It should also be noted that the computer editing measure was never fully implemented, thus decreasing data quality. The detailed manual checks at every stage still left items that needed adjustment, e.g. figures with incorrect decimal points. Thus additional checking of totals and other such tasks were carried out prior to use of the data. Some cases of incorrect data were thrown out or corrected wherever possible during the exploratory stage of the study. As the analysis progressed there were fewer errors.
7. The sources of data unless otherwise noted are from the Annual Survey described in this chapter.

8. There was no cut-off point for classification of foreign/local ownership; thus, once a firm had a percentage of foreign ownership it was classified as such.
9. Actually local and total liabilities are probably equal or approximately equal for close to 90% of the firms.
10. The lower representation of the smaller firms with <10 employed (relative to the overall survey objective of compilation for the national accounts) as well as the response rates will affect to some extent the reliability of the data in this group.
11. The study does not delve into the intricacies of labour markets under re-structuring of enterprises; but, in so far as data on employment and average wages and salaries of firms are useful in gaining insights into movements in productivity and the real exchange rate these variables are used.
12. Traditionally, small firms are defined as those with less than 10 employees. While there are no definitions of medium and large firms, groupings used for the remaining firms are: 10–24, 25–49, 50–99, 100+. These groupings are an adaptation of frequency groups used to analyse firms at the Central Statistical Office–Annual Survey of Business Establishment. To some extent, the groups also reflect other size variables such as total assets and output.

Annex

Table A4.1 Number of local firms by employment size group and year of data (with column percentage)

Year	Employment size group									
	< 10		10–24		25–49		50–99		100+	
	No.	%	No.	%	No.	%	No.	%	No.	%
1983	17	3.8	60	7.8	49	9.1	32	8.4	42	10.3
1984	39	8.7	56	7.3	48	8.9	43	11.3	40	9.9
1986	53	11.9	60	7.8	34	6.3	39	10.2	26	6.4
1987	73	16.3	55	7.2	45	8.3	29	7.6	35	8.6
1988	27	6.0	86	11.2	56	10.4	24	6.3	35	8.6
1989	27	6.0	79	10.3	57	10.6	32	8.4	38	9.4
1990	44	9.8	80	10.4	53	9.8	43	11.3	31	7.6
1991	71	15.9	85	11.1	52	9.6	42	11.0	42	10.3
1992	35	7.8	74	9.6	55	10.2	37	9.7	40	9.9
1993	38	8.5	88	11.4	47	8.7	39	10.2	46	11.3
1994	23	5.1	46	6.0	44	8.1	22	5.8	31	7.6
Total	447	100.0	769	100.0	540	100.0	382	100.0	406	100.0

Table A4.2 *Number of local firms by industry group and year of data*

Year	Food	Textiles	Printing	Wood	Chemicals	Assembly	Miscel-laneous
1983	44	36	24	23	23	43	7
1984	44	36	29	28	27	42	20
1986	40	34	34	25	21	41	17
1987	49	33	40	29	28	38	20
1988	53	40	27	20	37	34	17
1989	54	49	32	12	29	43	14
1990	38	44	36	24	35	50	24
1991	48	42	38	30	42	62	30
1992	38	14	35	18	44	68	24
1993	37	33	42	19	42	65	20
1994	31	18	25	8	32	39	15
Total	476	379	362	236	360	525	208

Table A4.3 *Number of local firms by employment size group and industry*

Ownership	Employment size groups				
	<10	10–24	25–49	50–99	100+
Food	53	111	96	64	150
Textiles	41	117	111	75	35
Printing	53	115	101	63	30
Wood	91	78	32	15	20
Chemicals	38	144	67	44	67
Assembly	102	153	93	95	82
Miscellaneous	69	51	40	26	22
Total	447	769	540	382	406

Table A4.4 Number of firms by employment size group and ownership

Ownership	Employment size groups						
	<10	10–24	25–49	50–99	100–199	200+	Total
Local	447	769	540	382	294	112	2544
Foreign	29	55	58	94	84	77	397
Total	476	824	598	476	378	189	2941

Table A4.5 Distribution of firms by foreign/local ownership and industry

Year	Food	Textiles	Printing	Wood	Chemicals	Assembly	Miscel-laneous
Local	476	379	362	236	360	525	208
Row %	18.7	14.9	14.2	9.3	14.1	20.6	8.2
Col. %	(80.0)	(94.3)	(92.1)	(99.6)	(80.9)	(85.9)	(80.0)
Foreign	119	23	31	1	85	86	52
Row %	30.0	5.8	7.8	0.3	21.4	21.7	13.1
Col. %	(20.0)	(5.7)	(7.9)	(0.4)	(19.1)	(14.1)	(20.0)

Selected Definitions and Concepts

1. An *establishment* is defined as that unit of an enterprise operating at a single location and under the control of one management, which can be recognised as being engaged in a clearly identifiable form of economic activity (i.e. producing one or more major or similar goods and/or services normally associated as the output of a specific industry). It should also function as an independent accounting unit with separate records of its operating expenditure, receipts, employees and other activities ancillary to production, not necessarily on the same site but under the control of one management.

2. The *enterprise* is that business unit that independently exercises the highest degree of financial and managerial authority over its own activities and that of its branches and subsidiaries. It can be identified as the legal entity in the case of incorporated enterprises, for example, corporation, joint stock company, co-operative, limited liability, partnership, or the unit for which consolidated balance sheets and profit and loss statements are available.
3. Employment figures are total employment for the last full pay-week in May and November of each year to account for seasonality. The employment figure is an average of these two values for May and November.
4. *Raw materials* include the value of materials purchased during the accounting year to be used as inputs into the manufacturing process. Materials purchased for works of a capital nature were excluded. Valuation of imported material was at c.i.f. and duty paid recorded separately, while local raw materials exclude delivery costs, which are also separately recorded.
5. *Total sales* refers to the amounts received (receivable) for goods and services sold during that year, even if not produced in that year. Taxes collected on behalf of government are excluded.
6. *Receipts from production* is the value of goods and services produced/assembled by the establishment and sold during the year.
7. *Output* is valued at the price at which it is sold, adjusted for changes in stocks.
8. *Investment* is total capital expenditure for the year: new assets, alterations and renovations on construction of buildings etc., plant machinery and transport equipment, furniture and office equipment.
9. *Total assets* comprises external assets and investments, local assets and investments, fixed assets, and all other assets. *Total liabilities* consist of external liabilities and local liabilities. *Local assets* consists of T&T currency cash on hand or on deposit, accounts receivable less bad-debt allowances, inventories and other current assets. *Local liabilities* consists of bank overdraft and short-term loans, accounts payable including notes payable, current maturities of long-term debt, taxation and dividends payable, long-term bank loan (>1 year), other long-term loans, debentures and all other local liabilities.
10. *Wages and salaries* comprises payments received by employees before deductions for contributions to social security, personal income tax, etc., and includes bonuses, tips, commissions etc.

List of Manufacturing Activities: Trinidad & Tobago System of National Accounts (T&TSNA)

4 Food processors drink and tobacco
- Meat processors
- Poultry processors
- Diary processors
- Fruit and vegetable processors
- Fish processors
- Grain and feed mills
- Vegetable oils and animal fats
- Bakeries
- Miscellaneous food processors
- Tobacco factories
- Breweries (including wine factories)
- Non-alcoholic beverages

5 Textiles, garments, footwear, headwear
- Spinning, weaving and finishing of textiles
- Manufacture of wearing apparel
- Manufacture of footwear
- Manufacture of head-wear

6 Printing and paper converters
- Newspapers
- Printing and other paper products

7 Wood and related products
- Sawmills
- Furniture and related products

8 Chemicals and non-metallic minerals
- Industrial gases and paints
- Pharmaceuticals and other chemicals
- Clay products – bricks , blocks and tiles
- Glass and glass products
- Cement
- Concrete products – blocks, tile, ready-mix concrete

- Plastic products for construction

9 Assembly type and related industries
- Motor vehicle assembly
- Batteries, mufflers and radiators,
- Tires and tubes
- Assembly of appliances
- Assembly of electronic items
- Boat building and ship repair
- Manufacture of metal building materials
- Manufacture of metal containers
- Manufacture of metal furniture
- Manufacture of all other metal products

10 Miscellaneous manufacturing
- Leather products
- Pottery and china
- Straw and crafts
- Jewellery
- Plastic products (excluding. construction materials)
- Miscellaneous manufacturing

Note: The number preceding each activity is an identifying sector number.

Number of Firms (approx.): Register of Establishments

Table A4.6 *No. of firms from the Register of Establishments by firm size, estimate up to 1993, manufacturing sectors*

Activity	No. of firms per employment size group					
	0	1–4	5–9	10–24	25 +	Total
Food etc.	317	43	48	43	67	518
Textiles	109	18	10	47	39	223
Printing	163	35	26	12	14	250
Wood	227	72	54	26	17	396
Chemicals	96	17	16	31	31	191
Assembly	212	63	33	37	30	375
Miscellaneous	131	15	24	19	20	209
Total	1,255	263	211	215	218	2,162

Table A4.7 *Percentage distribution of firms in Table A4.6 showing <10 and 10+ employment size (row percentage)*

Activity	% distribution per employment size group		
	0–9	10+	Total
Food etc.	78.8	21.2	100
Textiles	61.4	38.6	100
Printing	89.6	10.4	100
Wood	89.1	10.9	100
Chemicals	67.5	32.5	100
Assembly	82.1	17.9	100
Miscellaneous	81.3	18.7	100
Total	80.0	20.0	100

Table A4.8 Percentage distribution of firms in Table A4.6 showing <10 and 10+ employment size (column percentage)

Activity	% distribution per employment size group		
	0–9	10+	Total
Food etc.	23.6	25.4	23.9
Textiles	7.9	19.9	10.3
Printing	13.0	6.0	11.6
Wood	20.4	9.9	18.3
Chemicals	7.5	14.3	8.8
Assembly	17.8	15.5	17.3
Miscellaneous	8.7	9.0	13.4
Total	100.0	100.0	100.0

5 Structural Changes During Adjustment: Heterogeneity Based on Size of Firm

5.1 Introduction

In this chapter, the analysis of the performance of firms during adjustment begins with the evaluation of selected variables in the production and asset structures of firms over the period 1983–94 relative to firm size. Following the presentation of the theoretical aspects and hypotheses in the previous chapters, this analysis attempts to bridge the gap between the macro and micro aspects of the study by looking at factors in the structure of the firm that are likely to be affected by relative price changes. These factors can in turn affect the profitability and investment outcomes of firms. This analysis addresses some of the main themes highlighted in the formulation of the hypotheses in Chapter 4, such as heterogeneity based on size/access to resources, the inherited production/asset structures of firms and changes in relative prices brought on by the need for economic adjustment.

Thus, the main aims of this chapter are two: (i) to analyse trends in selected structural factors of firms aimed at identifying temporal variation if present, and (ii) to bring out the context under which different categories of firms were adjusting based on the assumption of a heterogeneous private sector. Patterns with respect to ownership and industry are discussed in Chapters 6 and 7, with the same aims as above.

This chapter is therefore concerned with the analysis of patterns in key factors around which the hypotheses of the study are concerned.

The underlying rationale of this analysis is that the historical experiences of firms/economies give rise to structural features in the production/asset base of firms and in the capital/product markets. These structural features lead to a heterogeneous private sector specifically with regard to access to resources and differential impact of/response to adjustment policies. These differences relative to the access to resources/markets, patterns of production, use of credit, and market focus lead to differences in options when dealing with the effects of adjustment. Section 5.2 opens with a discussion of the structural features in the firms to be analysed in this and the next two chapters, including the selection of the relevant groupings used in the analyses. Section 5.3 contains analyses of employment size groups based on selected variables. Firm size and heterogeneity is discussed in section 5.4. Conclusions follow in section 5.5.

5.2 Approach to Analysing Structural Changes: Variables and Groupings

There are many firm-level characteristics that can provide useful insights into the restructuring processes of firms over time. The analysis in this chapter and the following two are limited to the choice of *size, ownership* and *industry* which are viewed as three key characteristics that contribute to differences among firms. These characteristics were mentioned earlier in this research in arguments surrounding the historical experiences of firms in Trinidad & Tobago relative to access to and cost of credit, the need for imported raw materials and market access.

Industry, size and type of ownership are also related to differences in other characteristics such as capital/labour intensity, export/import orientation and so forth.[1] The analysis uses repeated cross-section data.[2] While these groupings are not panels that allow us to evaluate change over time in a strict sense, temporal variation of categories of firms almost equivalent to that of genuine panels can be evaluated.

This chapter uses five employment size groups: <10, 10–24, 25–49, 50–99 and 100+ employed. The idea behind these groupings is to attempt to get as homogeneous size groups as possible to explore differences over time between and within these groups. The data for the <10 employment size category is weighted to take into consideration the selection of a random sample of firms with <10 employment size by industry. As explained in the previous chapter, in the absence of detailed information on the sampling fractions, a crude but hopefully reasonable method was used to take into consideration the weighting of these firms by industry.[3]

The following are the variables used in the analysis with variable names in capital letters where necessary:[4]

- *Leverage* (LEVER) is represented by total liabilities (local and foreign) to total assets. Local leverage is related to financial claims on the domestic economy and is defined as local liabilities to total assets. In most cases these two ratios are quite close so only one is used.
- The *local assets ratio* (LOC) to total assets comprises current assets such as accounts receivable, cash/ currency on hand or in bank, inventories and other local current assets.
- The *interest expenses ratio (INTER) is the ratio of total interest payments to total expenses.*
- *Raw materials* purchases to total expenses (RAW) is the ratio of the cost of materials purchased for the year to the total current expenses.
- *Profitability* (NEW2) is represented by net profit after tax to total sales.
- The *investment to assets ratio* (INV1) comprises the total of new construction, plant machinery, equipment, furniture and office equipment, and major alterations and/or renovations of these groups, as a ratio to total assets.
- The *average wage* (AVGWAGE) is the total wages and salaries paid to employees divided by the numbers employed.
- *Output* (OUTPUT) is the value of production adjusted for stocks of finished goods and work in progress.
- *Capital to employment ratio* (CAPEMP) is total fixed assets at original cost to total employment.
- *Output to employment ratio* (OUTEMP) is total output to total employment.
- The key price relatives that are used are the real exchange rate (RER), which is the bilateral RER with the USA, the major trading partner and the real lending rate (RLEND) which is the median interest rate adjusted for inflation.
- The weighting variable for the <10 firms is W1.

The analysis starts below using categories of employment in which the years prior to official structural adjustment will be depicted as 1983–88 and the adjustment years as 1989–94. In carrying out the investigation, *median values* were used for all the variables from the survey data and are set at current prices. However, total output is at *constant prices, 1985=100*. The ratio average wage/salary was found by dividing total wages and salaries *at constant price (1985=100)* by total employed. The definition of wages was previously explained in the Annex to Chapter 4. Therefore with the exception of total output (OUTPUT), average wages (AVGWAGE) and capital to employment (CAPEMP), the conversion of the other variables to constant prices using the same GDP implicit price deflator was not necessary.[5]

Of the variables listed above, the main variables analysed were leverage, highlighting the firms' use of debt, patterns with respect to raw material and interest expenses, average wage/salary, output to employment, profitability and investment ratios. These variables are among the major ones to be affected by relative price changes in goods and factor markets. Output to employment and average wage/salary reflect mechanisms by which firms can respond to relative price changes by wage suppression, employment reduction or output expansion. The real exchange rate (RER) and the real lending rate of interest (median) are key transmission mechanisms of adjustment policies used to analyse trends in the firm level variables and to assess whether there are any possible links between the macroeconomic policies and the performance of profitability and investment.

5.3 Changes Across Employment Size Groups

5.3.1 Leverage use

The policy changes discussed in Box 2.2 of Chapter 2 show that financial/monetary policy led to positive real lending rates of interest (RLEND) from 1984, with some fluctuations throughout the years, following a period of negative real lending rates during the oil boom and early 1980s. The real deposit rate, however, remained negative due mainly to wide differentials between nominal lending and deposit rates charged by banks. One effect of this policy change is the impact on use of leverage among firms.

Firms with < 10 and 10–24 employment sizes

Generally, there was little variation within and across years in leverage use over the entire period 1983–94 for firms with <10 employment size. However, minor changes around the period 1988–90 suggest changes in leverage use in this period. Figure 5.1 shows, however, that the median value decreased between 1983 and 1984 for the <10 group. For the post-1984 period, the tendency was for increased median values until 1990, when there was a declining pattern in leverage use, and fluctuating leverage use for the remaining years.

The decrease in leverage use in the initial period for the <10 firms may have been due to the increased cost of credit which discouraged new loans. Another factor which may have affected leverage use is the increased indebtedness resulting from existing loans and liabilities, which came out of the post-oil boom economic contraction. The 10–24 group showed an increase in leverage use for the 1983/84 period, reflecting the increased cost of credit due to an increase in the real lending rate of interest. Leverage use, however, remained more or less the same throughout the period of the data, which reflects little effect on this group by adjustment relative to increased indebtedness/use of credit. As argued earlier smaller firms receive less credit than larger firms. The 10–24 group showed even less variation in leverage over time than firms with <10 employed. For both groups of firms, there were firms with very high extreme values for some years but no noticeable pattern among these outliers.

Figure 5.1 *Total leverage use (medians): Firms with <10 and 10–24 employed*

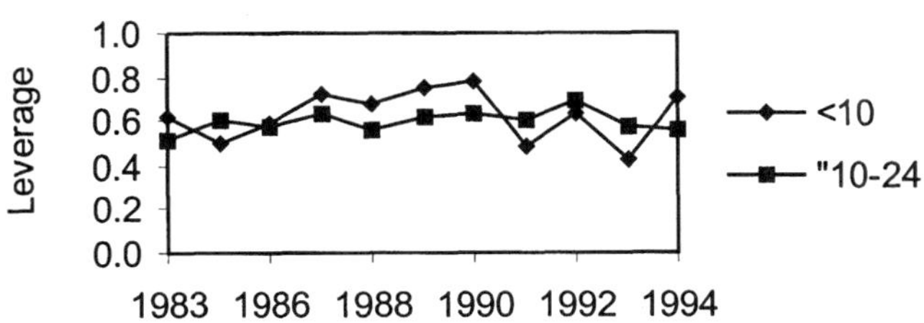

Firms with 25–49, 50–99 and 100+ employment sizes

Figure 5.2 shows leverage use for the three larger groups of firms. The median values of leverage use for the 25–49 and 50–99 groups increased from 1983 through to the post adjustment year, 1986, with a more pronounced increase for the 25–49 group. The 50–99 group showed less change between 1984 and 1986. The adjustment years 1990–94 saw almost similar patterns in leverage use for both size groups, with no clear pattern of increase or decrease during this period.

The data show variation over time for these larger groups. For the 25–49 group, fluctuations around the period 1986–89 reflect changes in leverage use over time consistent with the description above of a more pronounced increase in leverage use for this group. There was less variability in leverage use before and during adjustment for the firms in the 50–99 group which reflects a lesser effect of macroeconomic changes on the use of debt by these firms.

Similar to the <10 group, the 100+ group – the largest firms – experienced an initial fall in leverage extending up to 1986. For the pre/early adjustment period, leverage increased for this group, declining in 1990 and following a similar trend as that of the 25–49 and 50–99 groups for the remaining period of adjustment. However, there was a more noticeable drop in leverage use for the 100+ group, coinciding with the devaluation/floating of the dollar policy change in 1993.

For the 100+ group, 1986/87, 1989/90, 1992 and 1994 show greater spread around the respective median values. More concentrated variability around the median reflects less differences in leverage use among the firms for those years, with the reverse being the case for increased variability. This suggests that in the years of greater spread in the 100+ category, leverage use differed more than in other years. These were years that preceded or fell within the period of macroeconomic changes brought on by adjustment policies.

There was some similarity in the initial response of leverage use by the <10 and 100+ groups but with a more prolonged decrease in this period for the larger group. The question of differential access to credit therefore arises. Increased interest rates adversely affect credit accessibility and cost for the smaller firms; while ease of availability leads large firms to diminish their use of credit or to go out of operation. As expected there is more variation in leverage in the larger size groups due to greater access to credit.

Figure 5.2 *Total leverage: Firms with 25–49, 50–99 and 100+ employed*

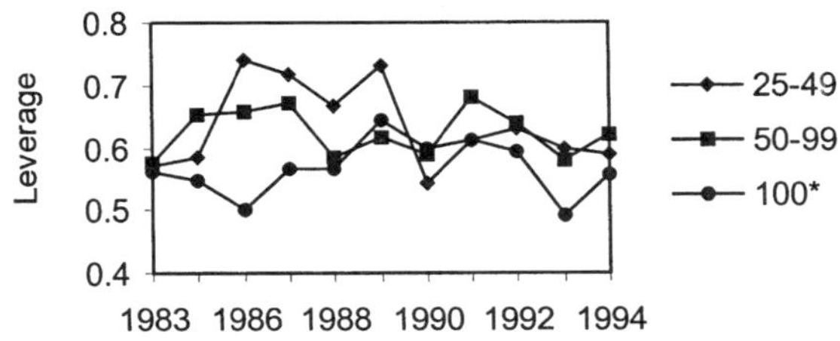

5.3.2 Interest expenses and the real lending rate of interest

Macroeconomic policy changes resulting in interest rate increases affect the interest expenses of firms. The distinction of this phenomenon by group is also the differential access and cost of credit by firm size. Smaller firms, it was argued, face greater difficulties in accessing credit from commercial banks; and normally face higher costs of credit when they are able to obtain credit from banks and other financial institutions. Below, trends in interest expenses (as a ratio of total expenses) are discussed by firm size.

Firms with < 10 and 10–24 employment sizes

The <10 group – the smallest firms – experienced no change in the interest expenses ratio for the initial period 1983–86 (Figure 5.3). One would expect the interest expense ratio to increase in this period if these firms were able to access loans. The steadiness in the ratio for this period suggests some fall-off in the size and volume of loans for some firms balanced by increased interest expenses for others. For the 1986/87 period, the ratio increased and remained constant up to 1989, after which there were some fluctuations for the rest of the period. For the smaller firms, there were periods of little change in the median values particularly before 1990. In addition, the data show differences in variability around the mean for some years such as 1987 and 1992–94.

Figure 5.3 Interest expense as percentage of total expenses and real lending rate: Firms with <10 and 10–24 employed

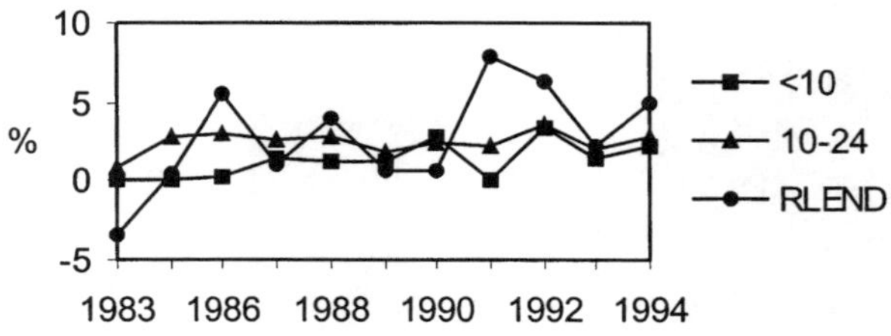

In Figure 5.3, the 10–24 group shows an increasing interest expense ratio from 1983 to 1984, which remains at this increased rate with minor fluctuation during the rest of the period. This movement seems to be in keeping with the initial rise in RLEND, placing this group of firms at a higher rate of interest expenses.

Firms with 25–49, 50–99 and 100+ employment sizes

Figure 5.4 shows the interest expenses ratio for the 25–49, 50–99 and 100+ groups. All three groups show increasing interest expenses ratio during 1983–86, in keeping with increasing RLEND during that period. In 1987, with falling RLEND, interest expenses fell for all three groups. However, in 1988, with increasing interest rates, interest expenses increased for the 25–49 group, but decreased for the larger firms in the 50–99 and 100+ groups reflecting differences in effect of/response to interest rates, maybe due to reduced use of overdraft.

Following 1988, there was a declining trend in the interest expenses ratio for the 25–49 group until 1991, notwithstanding declining interest rates for some of those years suggesting either smaller loans, a fall-off in loans or possibly lower interest rates on loans or a combination of all three factors. Increasing variability occurred from 1983 to 1987 and 1992/93 in the 25–49 group, with the variability among firms decreasing for the years 1988–91 and 1994 (Figure 5.4).

For the 50–99 group, the period 1988–94 saw some fluctuation in the interest expenses ratio but with little change during 1989–91. This

Figure 5.4 *Interest expenses as percentage of total expenses and the real lending rate: Firms with 25–49, 50–99 and 100+ employed*

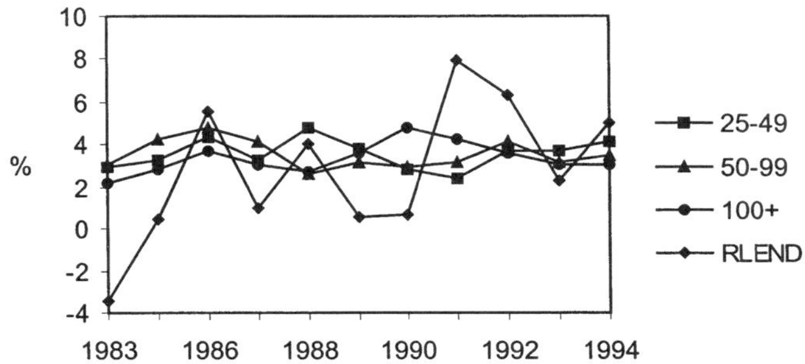

lack of variability is consistent with the pattern of leverage use for this group.

For the 100+ firms, there was an increase in interest expenses during 1987–90, but a decline in 1990–94. These changes reflect adjustment in interest expenses perhaps due to larger loan commitments for this group. Leverage use for this group as discussed in the previous section increased from 1986 to 1989, which must have affected interest expenses. Variations over time for this group point to changes in the interest expense ratio.

From 1988 to 1991, the interest expense ratios appear to be inversely associated with RLEND for the 100+ group, with this same feature apparent in 1988/89 for the 50–99 group and in 1991 for the 25–49 group, suggesting a negative effect of RLEND on use of credit for these years. Thus, even among the larger firms, there are similarities/differences relative to changes in interest expenses, which possibly reflect both differences in the interest rate effect and in the amount of indebtedness, overdraft and longer term loans that the firms can sustain.

5.3.3 Raw material purchases and the real exchange rate

Firms with < 10 and 10–24 employment sizes

For the <10 employment group, the raw material expense ratio declined from 1983 to 1984 in keeping with the post-oil boom economic contraction, and showed increases for the years 1988, 1989 and 1992 (Figure 5.5). From 1992 to 1994, this ratio decreased. Thus, for the year coinciding with the 1988 devaluation there was a corresponding increase in raw material expenses; while in 1993, the year of a larger devaluation, there was a decrease in this ratio for this size group. These movements suggest that the smaller devaluation in 1988 was sustainable in 1988/89 (see Table 5.6) for these smaller firms as reflected in the increased raw material costs; but the 1993 devaluation may have led to a reduction in purchases of raw materials or to the use of cheaper sources, as reflected in the reduction of costs for that year. Figure 5.6 shows the differences in the ratio across years expressed in the variability of the positions of the boxplots over time, with the boxes for most of the years obviously showing different variability as reflected in their positioning, size and median bands.

Figure 5.5 Raw material expenses as a ratio of total expenses and the RER: Firms with <10 and 10–24 employed

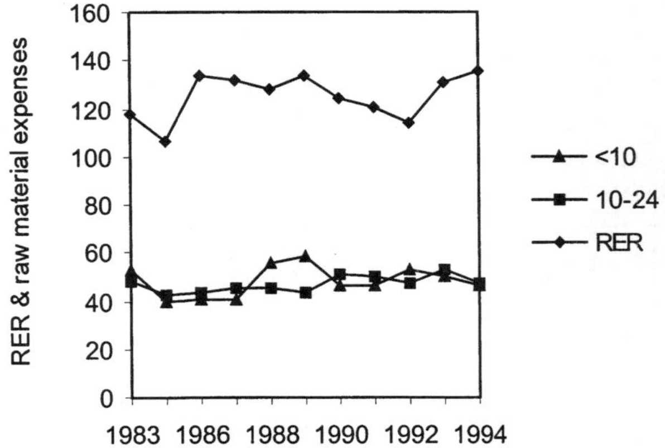

Figure 5.6 *Boxplots of raw material expenses ratio: Firms with <10 employed*

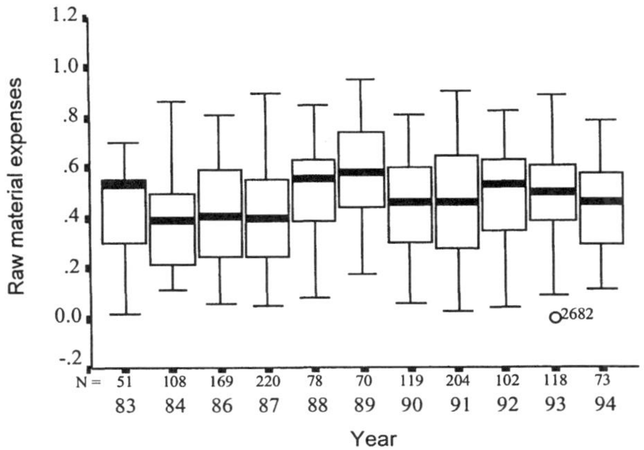

Notes: 1. The boxplots display simultaneously the *median* as the band across the width of the box, the *interquartile range* (IQR) as the height of the box, and the smallest and largest values outside the box but within 1.5 IQR as the lines drawn from either end (whiskers). Outliers, cases within 1.5 and 3 times the IQR, are designated by a small circle (o) outside the upper and lower edges. Very high outliers known as extreme values are cases occurring beyond 3 times the IQR at either end and are designated by asterisks (*). The box gives an idea of the spread or variability of the data. The closer the median is to the centre, the more symmetric the data. On the other hand, if the median is closer to the upper or lower edge, it indicates negative and positive skewness, respectively.

The boxplots can therefore bring out differences from one period to the next or across categories, based on the heights/positioning of the boxes, as well as tracking changes in the average value over time through looking at differences in the median values drawn through the width of the boxplots. *In effect, if the boxplots are not identical in size, positioning, and so forth, there is evidence of variation.* The identifying numbers for outliers/high extreme values are simply case numbers, therefore it is not possible visually to assess from this number whether there are repeated cases of outliers/high extreme values.

2. Analysis weighted by W1.

Initially during 1983/84, raw material expenses also decreased for the 10–24 group. There was a small increase in the raw materials ratio in 1988 with a more noticeable increase in 1993. These differences are also shown in the positions of the boxplots in Figure 5.7, with boxes 1988 and 1993 reflecting higher median values. There was greater concentration of values around the mean in 1993 for the <10 group, reflecting perhaps a narrowing of the gap in raw material costs among firms for that year. This pattern suggests that the increased costs due to the 1993 devaluation affected firms in the 10–24 group in a very similar fashion.

Firms with 25–49, 50–99 and 100+ employment sizes

Raw material expenses fluctuated in these three size groups. The years 1986, 1988 and 1992 showed increases in raw material expenses for all three groups, with only 1988 coinciding with a nominal devaluation. In 1993, another nominal devaluation year, there was a decrease in the ratio of raw materials to total expenses, which suggests decreased purchasing or the use of cheaper sources for raw materials by firms in the 25–49 group (Figures 5.8 and 5.9). In the initial period of the data, the raw material expense ratio increased.

Figure 5.7 Boxplots of raw material expenses ratio: Firms 10–24 employed

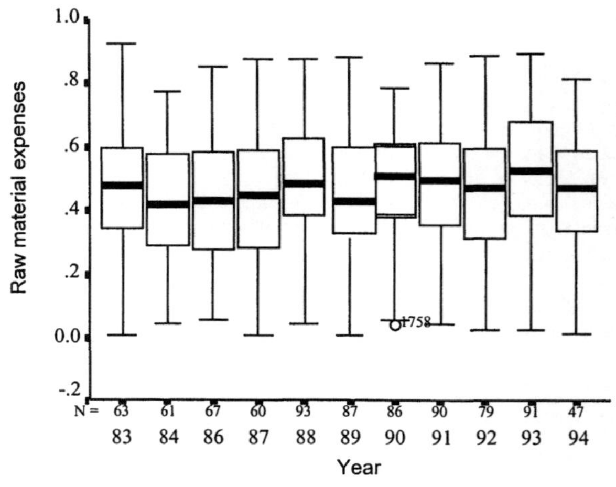

In the 50–99 category, the raw material ratio increased during 1983–87. For the years of the devaluation, this ratio fell in 1988 and increased in 1993. It is possible that the restructuring process in 1988 led to a decrease in purchasing of raw materials or that this devaluation, which was not a real devaluation, had no effect on the firms in this group through their ability to find cheaper alternative sources.

Movement in the raw material to total expenses ratio showed a decrease during 1983–86 for the 100+ firms, which probably represents early restructuring measures reflecting the post-oil boom crisis (Figure 5.8). For these large firms, the raw material expense ratio decreased in 1988, increased in 1993, and showed little or no changes from 1988 to 1992. The boxplots show marked changes in variability for the adjustment period 1988–94, unlike the changes in the positions of the boxes for the years 1983–86 (Figure 5.10).

5.3.4 Profitability and the real lending rate

The general pattern for the profitability variable (represented by net profit after tax to total sales) showed *declining* profitability during the pre-adjustment period in all size groups. This decline, which followed the post oil boom crisis, spanned the period 1983–87 (approximately)

Figure 5.8 *Raw material expenses as a ratio of total expenses and the RER: Firms with 25–49, 50–99 and 100+ employed*

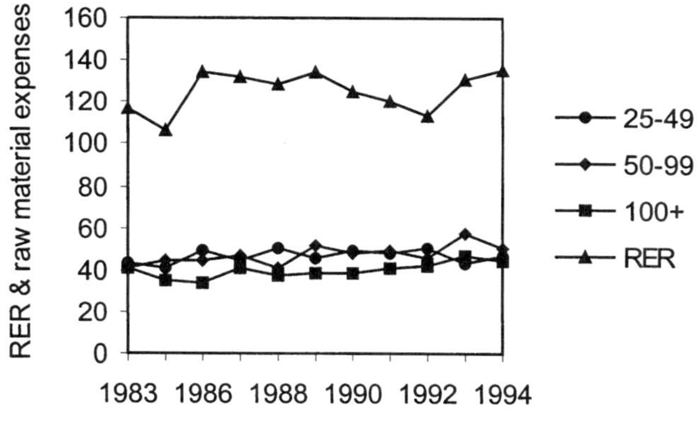

Figure 5.9 *Boxplots of raw material expenses ratio: Firms with 25–49 employed*

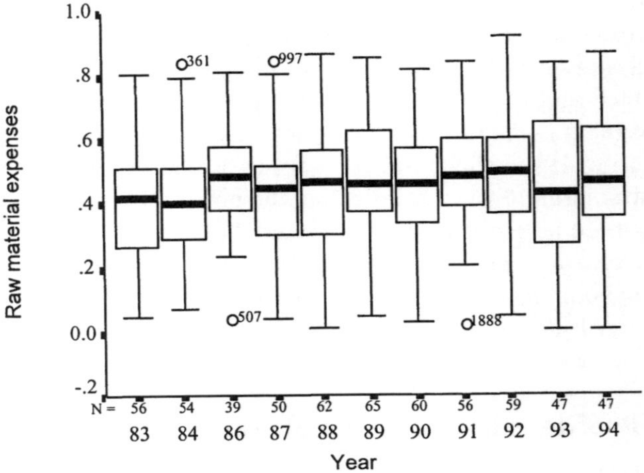

Figure 5.10 *Boxplots of raw material expenses ratio: Firms with 100+ employed*

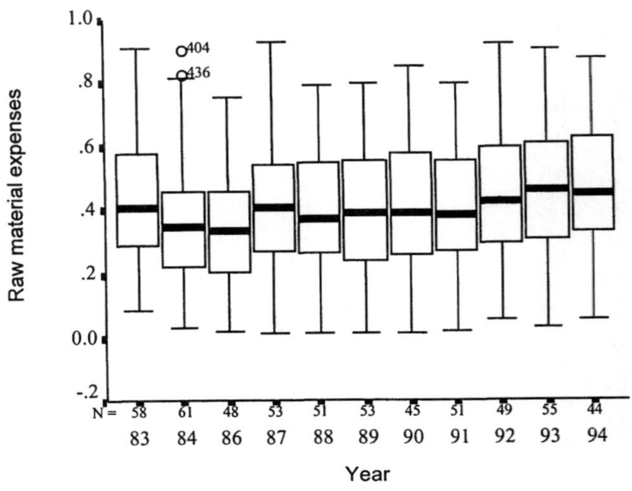

and was consistent with *increasing and positive interest rates,* among other macroeconomic adjustment changes (Figures 5.11 and 5.12).

Firms with < 10 and 10–24 employment sizes

In the adjustment period following the decline in profitability for all size groups described above, apart from an increase in profitability in 1988 in the <10 size group, the years 1988–92 showed little change in profitability. In fact the trend between 1988 and 1992 showed a slight decrease in profitability, declining for the remaining period of the data.

The data also give an idea of changes over time in profitability for the <10 group with the number of low outliers (extremely low profitability) exceeding the number of high outlier (extremely high profitability) (boxplots not shown). The differences, although minor, perhaps reflect the lack of change from the pre-adjustment to the adjustment period relative to the recovery of profitability for both groups. The sector that seemed to be most represented by loss-making outliers among these smaller firms was assembly and related manufacturing, the sector that is most heavily dependent on imported raw materials. While there were firms with differing degrees of leverage use, firms with leverage ratio close to or equal to 1 (high indebtedness) seemed to dominate among the loss making outliers.

The trend in the 10–24 group almost mirrored that of the <10 group. Major differences were that profitability fell from a lower rate in 1983 and tended to be at a slightly higher rate throughout the period for the 10–24 group. There was a proliferation of extreme values/low outliers of the profitability variable, particularly for the adjustment period 1988–93.

Figure 5.11 Profit to total sales and the real lending rate: Firms with <10 and 10–24 employed

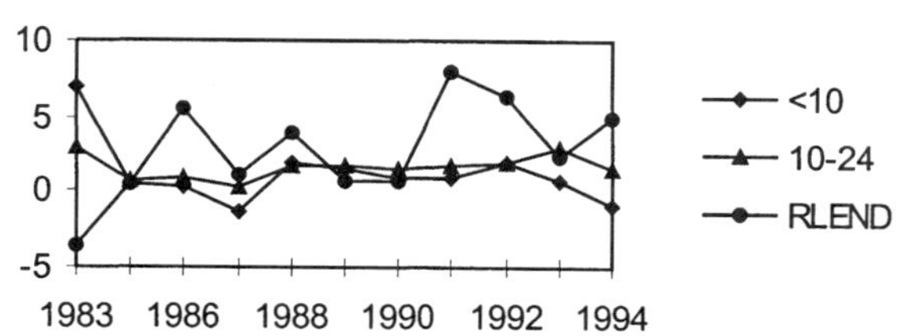

Firms with 25–49, 50–99 and 100+ employment size

Figure 5.12 shows the patterns in profitability and RLEND for the larger size groups. For the 25–49 group, profitability after the initial years of decline increased until 1989, declining again until 1992, after which there was a small amount of fluctuation at this lower rate through to 1994. For the 50–99 group, after the decline with increasing RLEND for the period 1983–87 profitability showed little change except for an increase in 1991, declining again from 1991 to 1993, with a small increase in 1994.

The 100+ group showed some recovery in profitability after the initial decline in the 1983–86 period with an increase in 1987; but it fell again in 1988 until 1990, fluctuating in 1991 and 1992. Profitability was on the rise for the remainder of the period for this size group.

Regarding profit to total sales, for the 50–99 size group there are noticeable differences in variability across years compared to the other two groups. Boxplots (not shown) reveal a concentration of outliers at either end of the distribution, highlighting the existence of firms that were highly profitable in spite of adjustment as well as firms that had heavy losses.

Figure 5.12 *Profit to total sales and the real lending rate: Firms with 25–49, 50–99 and 100+ employed*

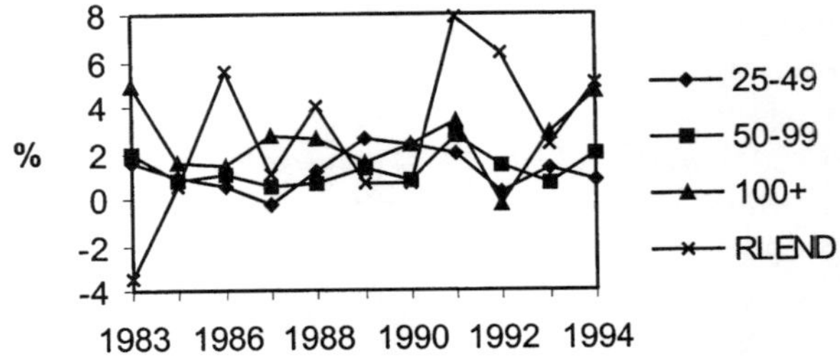

Box 5.1 *Cases of firms that stood out as repeated outliers for some/all years: 10–24 size group*

While differences noted cannot be generalized, insights can be gained relative to what caused firms to be high (low) repeated outliers evident from the data (boxplots not shown). Following two of the outliers in this group, the first case is that of a high outlier, which maintains this position in all but one year of the data. This firm was a foreign owned company that changed to local ownership in 1994, still maintaining its status as a highly profitable firm in this year. The firm seldom borrowed locally on a long-term basis from banks and other financial institutions, with its liabilities being external or short term such as overdraft, accounts payable. Interest payment was normally 1 per cent or less of total expenses and except for the year it changed ownership, leverage was normally <25% of total assets. This firm belongs to the food processing, drink and tobacco industry.

The second case is that of a firm that was a low outlier for four years. The firm appeared as a low outlier in 1984, 1988, 1992 and 1993, recording profits in 1987 and 1994. The remaining four years, the firm had losses, though not extremely heavy, relative to the other firms. This firm was locally-owned and operated in the assembly and related industry, with leverage use ranging from 57 to 93% (liabilities to total assets) over the years. In the initial years, the overdraft and short-term loans formed a major part of liabilities; but in subsequent years long-term loans contributed significantly. Interest payments for this firm ranged from about 9–14% of total expenses. Thus, the lower use of leverage, the difference in the type of leverage of the high outlier, and the differences in interest payment ratios related to ownership are factors that contributed to differences in the performance of these firms.

5.3.5 Investment and the real lending rate

Firms < 10 and 10–24 employment sizes

Investment to total assets fluctuated throughout the period of the data with high percentages of investment to total assets for some years in the <10 group particularly for 1984, 1987 and 1990 (Figure 5.13). The real lending rate of interest (RLEND) was positive but low in 1987 and 1990, which would have facilitated the investment thrust of the smaller firms that were traditionally able to access credit. There is, however, an inverse association between RLEND and investment for some years. Partly responsible for the high investment to total assets ratio is the low valuation of assets for firms in this group. In absolute terms, investment was low relative to other size groups.

For the 10–24 group investment, which was apparently at a high level in 1983, declined through 1992 and showed an increase in 1994, which was close to the median value of 1983. Thus, while investment

Box 5.2 Cases of firms that stood out as outliers for some/all years: 100+ size group

Among the outliers that appeared repeatedly in some years (boxplots not shown) was the case of a foreign firm in the 100+ group, with similar behavioural patterns to the case highlighted in the 10–24 group – external liabilities, no overdraft or short-term loans in short-term liabilities, no local loans from banks or other financial institutions, leverage usually close to 30%, interest expenses ratio that were normally close to 0%, and with falling employment levels from 1983 through to 1994. The industry was food processing, drink and tobacco. While there were cases of local firms as high outliers, they did not appear as repeated high outliers among the highly profitable firms in all size groups. Local firms were more consistent as low outliers (loss-making) in each size group for some/all years. There was one case of a firm that happened to be a local firm changing from a high outlier to a low outlier and vice versa as well as not appearing as an extreme value. This firm is highlighted below.

This local firm in the 100+ size group was in the assembly and related industry and had external liabilities from 1983 to 1986. In 1986, the firm changed from profit- to loss-making The firm did not appear as an outlier for the period 1983–86, then it was located among the low outliers in 1987. In 1988, it also did not appear as an outlier but appeared again from 1989 to 1993 as high and low outliers. For one of these years, a drastic fall in employment changed this firm from an extremely large 100+ size to a 50–99 employment size company. This firm was normally highly leveraged with its debt comprising both short and long-term bank loans and as stated above there were external liabilities in the early period of the data.

Around the start of adjustment 1987/88, the firm did not appear to have overdraft/ long-term loans but continued to receive large long-term bank loans. Thus, it would appear that the firm engaged in distress borrowing around the start of adjustment. Of note also was the higher interest expenses ratio usually ranging from 12–26%. It appears that moves towards import liberalization

Figure 5.13 Investment to total assets and RLEND: Firms with <10 and 10–24 employed

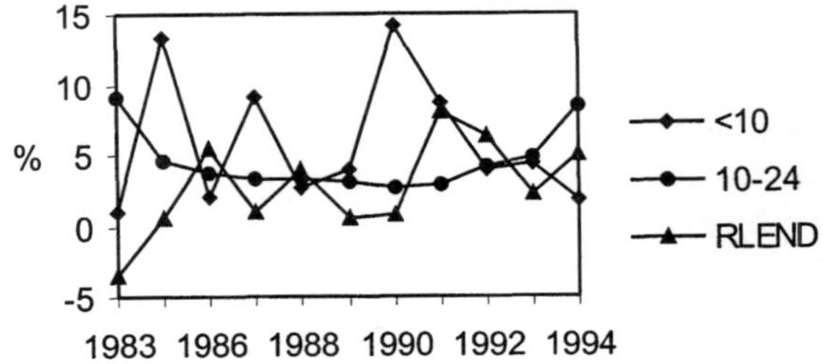

stagnated for this size group throughout most of the adjustment years, there was an improvement in its performance by 1994 (see Figure 5.13).

These two employment size groups show some difference in the variability of investment about the median for the <10 firms. Greater variability can be seen in the years of high investment, 1984, 1987/88, 1990 and 1993. The 10–24 group shows little variability for most of the years from 1986 to 1992.

Firms 25–49, 50–99 and 100+ employment sizes

Investment trends for the 25–49, 50–99 and 100+ employment size groups are shown in Figure 5.14. The general trend for the 25–49 group was one of decline from 1983 to 1988 despite fluctuations in the real lending rate. Evidence of an inverse association between investment and the real lending rate was found in the years 1983, 1984, 1988–90 and 1991–93, indicating a possible negative effect of RLEND in this group.

For the 50–99 group, there was declining investment in the period 1983–86 reflecting the effect perhaps of increasing real lending rates on this size group. Similarity in the direction of movement of investment and RLEND occurred in the pre-adjustment period 1987/88 followed by an *inverse association* throughout the rest of the period, *including the adjustment period.* Thus the adjustment thrust of this size group appeared to be adversely affected by high real lending rates, with some increases for the years 1988/90 and 1992/93 when interest rates were low.

Figure 5.14 Investment to total assets and RLEND: Firms with 25–49, 50–99 and 100+ employed

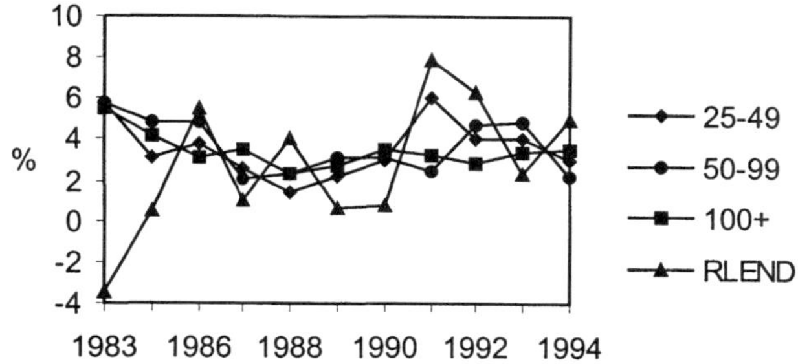

The 100+ group showed an almost consistent inverse relationship with RLEND similar to that of the <10 group. Generally, investment declined from the oil boom rate for this size group. While the smaller firms might have been affected by a lack of finance to invest due to high interest rates and difficulty in accessing funds, the larger firms could have been affected by high interest rates given the scale of investment required. Additionally, the option not to invest could have been exercised by the larger firms.

The data show variability over time of investment to total assets for the 25–49, 50–99 and 100+ size groups. For the 25–49 group, 1988 saw decreased variability in investment among these firms. This was the initial year of adjustment. Increased variation among the firms occurred in 1987, 1989, 1991 and 1993, showing differences in the performance of investment in these years among the firms of the 25–49 size group. For the 50–99 group, there were also differences across years in investment performance though not as large as in the 25–49 group. The variability for the 50–99 group decreased in the years after 1984 showing that the pattern with respect to investment was similar for most years, particularly from 1986 to 1992. The 100+ size group showed less variability about the median values across years as compared to the other size groups.

5.3.6 Changes in the real exchange rate and the average wage

Firms < 10 and 10–24 employment sizes

Figure 5.15 shows the rate of change in average wage/salary relative to changes in the real exchange rate. Assessment of this variable is linked to the policy of devaluation in which control of the domestic wage rate is a mechanism by which competitiveness of domestic industries can be increased, recalling equation 3.14 in Chapter 3.

The rate of change of average wage/salary declined from the years 1984 to 1987 for the <10 group. For the remaining years, the rate of change in this variable fluctuated, culminating in a large increase in 1994. To some extent there is an inverse association between changes in the RER for 1983, 1984 and 1988 to 1994. In the 10–24 group, the declining rate of change of the average wage/salary continued into 1988 from 1984 with very small increases, if any, for the remaining years. The

Figure 5.15 Changes in average wage/salary and the RER: Firms with <10 and 10–24 employed

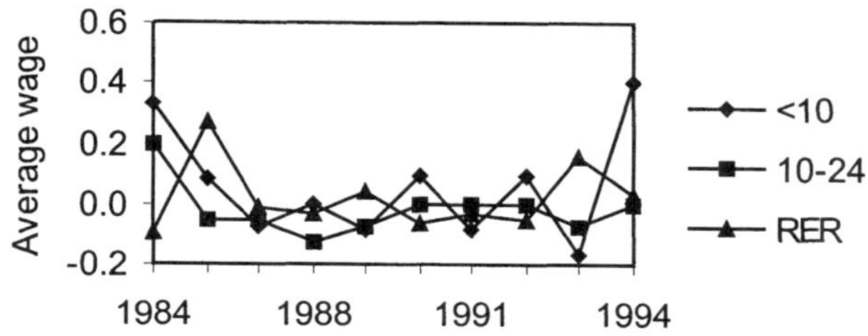

years 1990–92 saw no change in the average wage while for some years the change was in the opposite direction to the change in RER. This suggests that the average wage was used to counteract changes in the RER for both size groups.

Data for the <10 group hint at some differences over the years based on the size and positioning as is shown in the decrease in variability for 1988. There is no consistent pattern of declining or increasing average wage/ salary for the <10 group, while the 10–24 group shows a consistent pattern of declining average wage. Thus for the <10 group, the suppression of the average wage/salary as a means of offsetting changes in the exchange rate was not as obvious as for the 10–24 size group.

Firms 25–49, 50–99 and 100+ employment sizes

For the 25–49, 50–99 and 100+ size groups, there were years/periods in which changes in the real exchange rate were in the opposite direction to changes in the average wage rate during some of the years of adjustment. This trend signals the use of wages/salaries to counteract the effects of adjustment on the cost structure of firms (Figures 5.16 to 5.17). In the 25–49 size group, an inverse association between the two variables occurred from 1992 to 1994. For the remaining years, the changes were in the same direction, whether declining or increasing with a larger decline in wages than in RER for 1988/90 and a greater increase in wages than in RER for the years 1983 and 1991. The pre-adjustment

Figure 5.16 Changes in average wage/salary and the RER: Firms with 25–49, 50–99 and 100+ employed

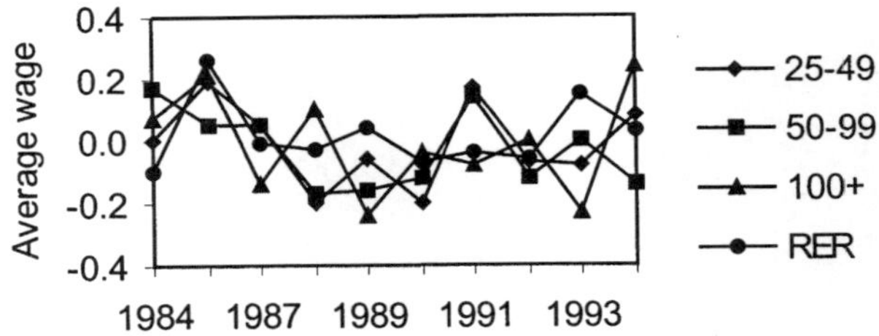

years, 1984, 1986 and 1987 saw the decline in RER greater than the decline in average wages.

For the 50–99 group, the pre-adjustment years 1983 and 1984 and the adjustment period 1989–94 (with the exclusion of 1991) saw the change in the average wage moving in the opposite direction to the change in RER. In 1991 (during the Gulf War, which implied favourable oil prices), both variables changed in the same direction (increasing) with the change in the average wage being greater than the change in RER. These movements suggest the use of average wage in this size group to cope with the effects of the devaluation.

For the 100+ group, changes in average wage/salary moved in the opposite direction to RER during the adjustment period (1988–94). This inverse pattern for the adjustment years was the most consistent of all the size groups, comparable to that of the <10 group in which the inverse association between changes in both variables lasted throughout the adjustment period. *Thus, all groups used the average wage as a means of cutting costs relative to changes in the RER with more consistent use throughout adjustment years by the <10 and 100+ groups.*

The boxplots of average wage/salary (rates, not changes) for the 100+ size group is shown in Figure 5.17. Declining real wage can be seen in the period 1988 and beyond.

Figure 5.17 Boxplots of average wage/salary: Firms with 100+ employed

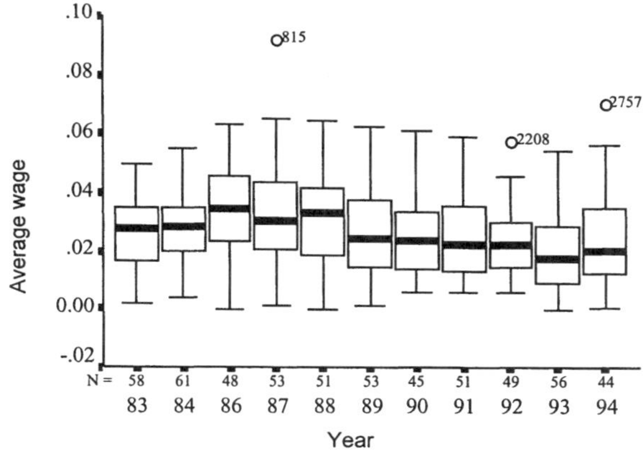

Note: Analysis weighted by W1.

5.3.7 Output to employment

Firms < 10 and 10–24 employment sizes

Some evidence of increasing output to employment is shown in Figure 5.18 for firms in the <10 group, with an increase in this ratio from 1983 to 1989. However, in 1990 output to employment decreased, increasing again from 1991 to 1994 though not up to the level of 1990. Boxplots (not shown) for this employment size group showed some changes over time such as greater variation in 1989, when there was a peak in output to employment. Declining output to employment seemed to have occurred in general for the period 1984–92. Increasing output was mainly responsible for the increase in output to employment in the period 1983–86, but decreased output and employment was reflected in 1987. Both output and employment increased in 1988 and 1989; but the fall in output in 1990 was not accompanied by any change in employment.

For the 10–24 group, there was an increase in output to employment from 1983 to 1984 with little change from 1986 to 1990 and followed by a marked increase in 1993 during the adjustment period (Figure 5.18). There was little change in output to employment for this size group for the period 1986–90 coinciding with the description given above.

Figure 5.18 Output to employment: Firms with <10 and 10–24 employed

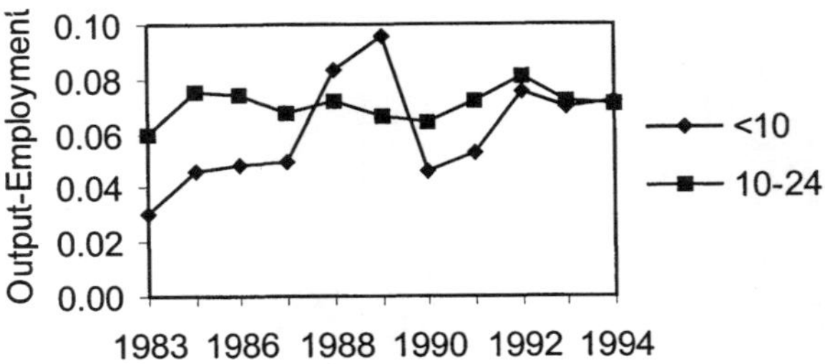

Firms 25–49, 50–99 and 100+ employment sizes

For the 25–49 and 50–99 groups, there is no clear pattern of increase or decrease of the output to employment ratio even though an increasing pattern in output to employment is apparent for the period 1983–86, with a declining pattern for 1991–93 (Figure 5.19). There was some variation over the years for the 25–49 size group but little change for the 50–99 group.

The output to employment ratio was always higher for the 100+ employment size firms and it increased from 1984 to 1988 before declining from this year until 1993. There is little variability obvious in this ratio for the period of the data.

5.3.8 Summary of findings by size group

Leverage use

- Increasing leverage ratios for the 10–24, 25–49 and 50–99 size groups in the immediate post-oil boom period 1983–84, particularly for the 25–49 group, coincide with increasing real lending rates to positive values. The exceptions were the <10 group, which showed an initial decrease, and the 100+ size group in which the decline in leverage use was for a longer period than for the <10 size firms. While the 100+ firms were possibly able to survive with lower leverage given their preferential access to credit, the 10+ firms were probably forced

Figure 5.19 Output to employment: Firms with 25–49, 50–99 and 100+ employed

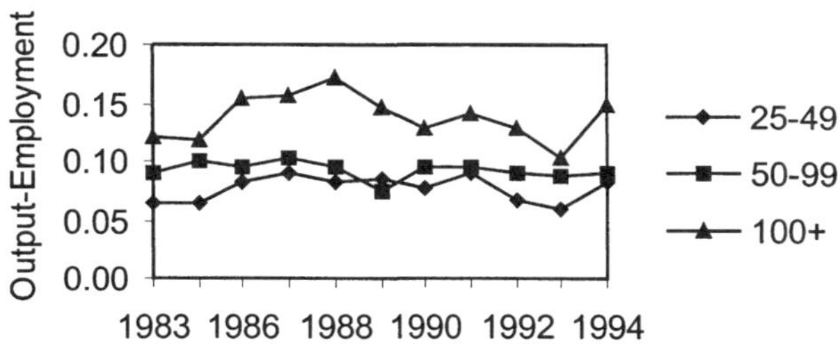

to survive on lower leverage in this initial period since problems of credit access/cost may have been intensified by the initial increase in interest rates. Another explanation for the fall in leverage use in the 100+ category in the 1983–86 period could have been prior excessive borrowing during the oil boom period which led to a decrease in borrowing given increased interest rates.

- During the adjustment period, the general pattern in the <10 size group was an increasing trend in the pre and early adjustment period signalling that the pre-adjustment economic crisis led to increased use of leverage by the firms in this group who were able to obtain such leverage. There was declining but fluctuating leverage in the latter part of the adjustment period.
- Leverage use for the 10–24, 25–49 and 50–99 size groups displayed minor fluctuations during the adjustment period but little change over the years.
- Leverage use for the 100+ group, which increased during the pre- and early period of adjustment, 1987–89 (showing the greatest variability), reflects economic contraction and other macro policy changes. This group of firms, with easy access to credit, may have indulged in over-borrowing during the period of the oil boom as mentioned above, leading to problems of indebtedness during this period.
- Thus the smallest and the largest (100+) firms seemed to have experienced declining use of leverage in the early pre-adjustment period possibly due to changes in RLEND but for different reasons. There

was increased use of leverage during the early part of adjustment, possibly due to the need of larger firms to undertake borrowing to offset past indebtedness, while the smaller firms borrowed as the only means of survival given the economic crisis. For the other size groups, apart from increasing leverage use at the onset of the post-oil boom crisis coinciding with increases in RLEND, the pattern remained largely unchanged.

Interest expenses

- With the exception of the <10 size group, firms of all sizes appeared to have experienced some negative effects due to increased real lending rates in the initial post-oil boom period. For firms with 10+ employment size, interest expenses increased with the appearance of positive real lending rates in the pre-adjustment period.
- During the initial period of increasing interest rates, interest expenses appeared to be unresponsive to these changes in the pre-adjustment period with minor fluctuations in the adjustment period for the <10 group.
- The data showed little variation in interest expenses for the 10–24 group during adjustment; but some firms apparently had high extreme values particularly during the years 1991–93 (boxplots not shown).
- While interest expenses increased at the start of adjustment (1988) for the 25–49 group, the ratio declined from 1988–91. This may be due to lower interest payments for these firms or a decrease in the value/quantity of loans.
- The 50–99 group showed little change in interest expenses during the adjustment years suggesting that they were unaffected by changes in RLEND during this period.
- The 100+ group exhibited more pronounced increases in interest expenses than the 25–49 and 50–99 groups in the period 1988 to 1990, with the interest expenses moving in opposite direction to RLEND. While loans for this group are easily accessible, the increased indebtedness suggested above may have led to increases in interest repayments during the early part of adjustment.
- Variability over time and between groups is present in the data (boxplots not shown).

Raw material expenses

- There were mixed responses of variability in raw material expenses for the <10 firms. This ratio declined in the initial period (1983–84) and in the adjustment years of 1993/94, increased in 1988/89 and 1992, and showed little change in the pre-adjustment period (1984–87 and 1990/91). There is some evidence of both increasing costs as well as reduction in purchases of raw material expenses.
- The 10–24 group showed little change in raw material expenses throughout the period of the data.
- Some variability in raw material expenses appeared for firms in the 25–49, 50–99 and 100+ size groups, with minor fluctuations for the first two size groups and periods of declining costs (1983–86) and of little change (1988–92) for the 100+ size group. Early restructuring after the post-oil boom period was possibly the rationale behind the decline in raw material expenses during the initial period for the 100+ size group.
- The data show temporal variation as well as differences between groups.

Profitability

- There was declining profitability during the pre-adjustment period (approximately 1983–87) for all size groups consistent with increasing and positive real interest rates.
- During the adjustment period, many extreme values/outliers appeared at either end for all size groups. There were problems with profitability for some firms, while other firms in all size groups were able to remain profitable – with variability for the 50–99 group being the most visible probably due to the positioning of the outliers in this group.
- Use of leverage in terms of foreign/local or short versus long-term featured as differences within size groups with respect to patterns in profitability of some firms that showed high extreme values.
- Evidence of variation was most visible in the 50–99 group (boxplots not shown).

Investment

- Investment, which was at a high level during the oil boom period of the 1970s, declined from its ratio at the beginning of the period 1983

for all size groups with the exception of the smallest firms, the <10 size group.
- In the <10 group, investment was at a relatively low level compared to the other groups and major fluctuations occurred throughout the period of the data.
- The pattern of investment for the 25–49 and 50–99 showed some evidence of a possible inverse association with the real lending rate of interest for some years during the adjustment period.
- The 100+ size group showed an almost consistent inverse relationship between investment and the real lending rate of interest during the adjustment period.

Average wage
- Average wage/salary was one component of firms' cost structure used as a means of countering the effect of the devaluations during adjustment. Differences in terms of its use are evident by size group.
- Inverse patterns between changes in RER and changes in average wage/salary were present in all size groups and were most consistently so in the period 1988–94 for the <10 and 100+ groups.

Output to employment
- Productivity as measured by output to employment seemed to have increased amongst the smaller firms (<10). This increase was due mainly to increases in output, since there was little change in employment particularly during the adjustment period.
- For the 10–24, 25–49 and 50–99 and 100+ groups, output to employment showed little change overall, but fluctuated over the period of adjustment.

5.4 Firm Size and Heterogeneity

In the earlier theoretical chapters, differences based on size have been related to structural features that influence the behaviour of the firm with regard to labour dynamics, production, consumption, savings and investment, as well as access to credit and sources of financing for working capital needs.

The very high and low outliers shown by the data for all groups masks variation over time and points to significant variation within groups. The patterns of some of the repeated very high/low outliers were described above for a small and large size group and point to characteristics or features that cut across size groups.

A significant factor that should be taken into consideration in this notion of heterogeneity is that there are other characteristics of the firm which cut across this divide such as ownership and activity which will be discussed in later chapters. These other features have affected the performances of the variables discussed in this chapter (as illustrated in the pattern of behaviour of the outliers).

A small foreign-owned firm will be in a better position say with regard to financing its investment or working capital needs from its parent company or investors from abroad than a small local firm without that financial support and facing restrictions in the domestic financial market. Similarly, a large local firm with a domestic market focus that is reliant on imported intermediates may be worse off than a large foreign firm which acts as a regional export centre, whose intermediates can be paid for in foreign currency and who can receive loans from its parent company.

Despite this aspect of dualism (size and ownership) that cuts across firm size, the exploratory data analysis has attempted to identify why firm size matters in adjustment and how it portrays true heterogeneity in the private sector. The following key issues can be said to contribute to firm heterogeneity based on size:

- As firm size increases *access to credit increases and the cost of credit decreases*. Small as opposed to medium and large firms face greater restrictions in financial markets. Collateral requirements of small firms are larger and the cost of credit is higher as compared to larger firms, who have established, traditional relationships with financial sector institutions. This phenomenon was shown in the leverage decline of the smallest firms due to these circumstances with regard to borrowing. At the other end, unrestricted availability of credit proved to be detrimental for the very large firms.
- Although all size groups and the manufacturing sector reflect a high percentage of imported inputs in production flexibility; *price adjustment of imported inputs increases with firm size*. A larger firm is able to search worldwide and procure more competitive prices for its raw materials; but a small firm does not have the resources to perform such a search.

- *Quantity adjustments* in raw material purchases are likely to be more severe for both the very small and very large firms who have a greater degree of domestic market focus. In this case, small size denotes less capacity to afford the price increases of imported inputs, which are brought on by exchange rate devaluation. For very large firms, the combination of a drop in domestic demand and the inability to switch to exports brings about quantity adjustments as the only response.
- Very large firms are likely to reduce the size of their labour as a mechanism of adjustment. This behavior decreases with firm size. However, very small and very large firms are characterized by wage suppression.

Fundamentally, the question of size and heterogeneity in firm behaviour is linked to the historical and institutional norms discussed in earlier chapters, particularly in terms of the financing criteria to which small firms are subjected.

5.5 Conclusions

This chapter explored structural changes in firms based on size, looking at firms' cost and asset variables considered to be affected by adjustment policies. It also looked directly at the effects on profitability and investment based on firm size. The analysis rested on the belief that firms of different sizes have different experiences with respect to access to and cost of credit which in turn leads to differential experiences and responses to indebtedness, payments of interest expenses and costs of raw materials, with implications for wages, labour force and output. Variability present in the data over time was also explored and showed temporal differences for some variables and size groups.

The results summarized above show problems of varying extents based on the analysis of the firms by size group. These problems include indebtedness of very small/large firms, high interest rates and its impact on access to loans for all firms on the one hand; and the lack of responsiveness to interest expenses by the smallest firms on the other hand. Furthermore, average wage was used to circumvent the effects of adjustment brought on by changes in the real exchange rate, with most consistent use of this mechanism by the smallest and largest firms during the adjustment period. There was also an apparent increase in productivity for the very small firms. Problems with profitability in all size groups become evident given the proliferation of outliers as well as some measure of decline. Investment began to decline in the pre-adjustment period and did not show any sustained or marked recovery during the adjustment period. The next chapter follows a similar method of analysis and looks at structural changes based on ownership, which emerged as an important factor in distinguishing the performance of profitability within groups.

Table 5.1 Selected indicators (medians): Firms with <10 employed, by year

Year	Output (mln TT$)	Employment (no.)	Output to Employment	Average Wage	Capital to Employment
1983	0.206	7.0	0.030	0.009	0.000
1984	0.253	6.0	0.046	0.012	0.000
1986	0.287	5.0	0.048	0.013	0.006
1987	0.214	5.0	0.050	0.012	0.007
1988	0.490	7.0	0.083	0.012	0.006
1989	0.570	7.5	0.095	0.011	0.006
1990	0.406	7.0	0.046	0.012	0.007
1991	0.250	5.0	0.053	0.011	0.004
1992	0.363	6.0	0.075	0.012	0.018
1993	0.452	5.0	0.070	0.010	0.012
1994	0.392	6.0	0.072	0.014	0.024
All years	0.332	6.0	0.059	0.012	0.008

Table 5.2 Selected indicators (medians): Firms with 10–24 employed, by year

Year	Output (mln TT$)	Employment (no.)	Output to Employment	Average Wage	Capital to Employment
1983	0.894	15.0	0.059	0.015	0.010
1984	1.239	15.0	0.075	0.018	0.015
1986	1.088	15.0	0.074	0.017	0.019
1987	0.858	16.0	0.067	0.016	0.014
1988	1.129	14.0	0.072	0.014	0.009
1989	0.965	16.0	0.066	0.013	0.016
1990	0.865	15.0	0.064	0.013	0.012
1991	1.090	15.0	0.072	0.013	0.013
1992	1.250	15.0	0.081	0.013	0.015
1993	1.158	16.0	0.072	0.012	0.017
1994	1.281	15.0	0.071	0.012	0.020
All years	1.081	15.0	0.071	0.013	0.014

Table 5.3 Selected indicators (medians): Firms with 25–49 employed, by year

Year	Output (mln TT$)	Employment (no.)	Output to Employment	Average Wage	Capital to Employment
1983	2.58	37.0	0.065	0.016	0.015
1984	2.44	37.0	0.064	0.016	0.024
1986	2.75	34.0	0.082	0.019	0.022
1987	2.93	33.0	0.091	0.020	0.031
1988	3.10	36.0	0.083	0.016	0.028
1989	3.02	35.0	0.084	0.015	0.026
1990	3.01	35.0	0.076	0.012	0.018
1991	3.28	35.0	0.090	0.014	0.033
1992	2.06	36.0	0.067	0.013	0.023
1993	1.72	36.0	0.058	0.012	0.022
1994	2.26	35.0	0.082	0.013	0.025
All years	2.75	35.0	0.078	0.015	0.027

Table 5.4 Selected indicators (medians): Firms with 50–99 employed, by year

Year	Output (mln TT$)	Employment (no.)	Output to Employment	Average Wage	Capital to Employment
1983	6.01	69.0	0.091	0.018	0.036
1984	8.61	73.5	0.100	0.021	0.041
1986	6.01	70.0	0.096	0.022	0.025
1987	7.51	64.0	0.103	0.023	0.041
1988	6.67	66.0	0.095	0.019	0.039
1989	5.57	68.0	0.075	0.016	0.030
1990	6.21	75.0	0.095	0.014	0.025
1991	6.51	74.5	0.096	0.016	0.026
1992	6.75	70.0	0.091	0.014	0.035
1993	5.59	75.0	0.087	0.014	0.025
1994	5.23	72.0	0.090	0.012	0.037
All years	6.62	71.0	0.091	0.018	0.032

Table 5.5 Selected indicators (medians): Firms with 100+ employed, by year

Year	Output (mln TT$)	Employment (no.)	Output to Employment	Average Wage	Capital to Employment
1983	23.6	170.5	0.121	0.027	0.043
1984	23.7	170.0	0.119	0.029	0.059
1986	25.5	162.0	0.153	0.035	0.070
1987	27.0	159.0	0.156	0.030	0.066
1988	24.8	140.0	0.173	0.033	0.063
1989	21.8	143.9	0.147	0.025	0.062
1990	19.8	141.0	0.129	0.024	0.050
1991	22.9	162.0	0.141	0.022	0.045
1992	20.4	167.0	0.129	0.022	0.036
1993	19.2	162.0	0.102	0.017	0.032
1994	21.7	136.0	0.150	0.021	0.035
All years	22.8	159.0	0.134	0.026	0.054

Table 5.6 Selected indicators (medians): Firms with <10 employed, by year

Year	Leverage	Local Levarage	Local assets	Raw materials	Interest expenses	Profit to sales	Invest. to total assets
1983	0.619	0.326	0.203	0.528	0.000	0.069	0.010
1984	0.501	0.490	0.280	0.393	0.000	0.004	0.134
1986	0.587	0.585	0.370	0.403	0.003	0.002	0.021
1987	0.722	0.646	0.378	0.402	0.014	–0.014	0.090
1988	0.671	0.669	0.158	0.553	0.013	0.019	0.027
1989	0.756	0.624	0.648	0.581	0.013	0.014	0.040
1990	0.775	0.530	0.569	0.458	0.027	0.008	0.142
1991	0.478	0.289	0.219	0.458	0.001	0.008	0.087
1992	0.632	0.618	0.463	0.530	0.033	0.019	0.039
1993	0.432	0.397	0.642	0.498	0.015	0.007	0.043
1994	0.710	0.710	0.566	0.458	0.023	–0.010	0.019
All years	0.630	0.563	0.400	0.462	0.022	0.005	0.055

Table 5.7 Selected indicators (medians): Firms with 10–24 employed, by year

Year	Leverage	Local leverage	Local assets	Raw materials	Interest expenses	Profit to sales	Invest. to total sales
1983	0.521	0.363	0.439	0.479	0.008	0.029	0.090
1984	0.596	0.595	0.517	0.420	0.028	0.007	0.046
1986	0.580	0.563	0.521	0.432	0.030	0.008	0.037
1987	0.638	0.605	0.626	0.449	0.026	0.002	0.032
1988	0.554	0.486	0.401	0.4485	0.028	0.016	0.033
1989	0.625	0.582	0.575	0.436	0.018	0.017	0.031
1990	0.636	0.623	0.567	0.509	0.025	0.014	0.027
1991	0.610	0.592	0.562	0.502	0.022	0.017	0.028
1992	0.690	0.660	0.604	0.475	0.036	0.019	0.041
1993	0.575	0.557	0.562	0.528	0.020	0.030	0.048
1994	0.557	0.542	0.540	0.475	0.027	0.014	0.084
All years	0.605	0.571	0.529	0.471	0.027	0.013	0.037

Table 5.8 Selected indicators (medians): Firms with 25 –49 employed, by year

Year	Leverage	Local leverage	Local assets	Raw materials	Interest expenses	Profit to sales	Invest. to total assets
1983	0.571	0.404	0.558	0.431	0.030	0.015	0.058
1984	0.584	0.545	0.447	0.404	0.033	0.009	0.031
1986	0.742	0.737	0.568	0.493	0.044	0.005	0.038
1987	0.716	0.632	0.532	0.449	0.033	–0.002	0.026
1988	0.667	0.547	0.544	0.498	0.048	0.011	0.014
1989	0.733	0.698	0.569	0.461	0.038	0.026	0.022
1990	0.544	0.414	0.583	0.487	0.028	0.023	0.030
1991	0.613	0.535	0.536	0.476	0.024	0.020	0.061
1992	0.631	0.624	0.531	0.501	0.037	0.002	0.040
1993	0.600	0.553	0.546	0.432	0.037	0.013	0.040
1994	0.590	0.590	0.554	0.468	0.041	0.008	0.030
All years	0.647	0.599	0.548	0.458	0.036	0.012	0.035

Table 5.9 Selected indicators (medians): Firms with 50–99 employed, by year

Year	Leverage	Local leverage	Local assets	Raw materials	Interest expenses	Profit to sales	Invest. to total sales
1983	0.576	0.433	0.449	0.414	0.031	0.019	0.058
1984	0.654	0.584	0.516	0.444	0.042	0.008	0.048
1986	0.656	0.590	0.528	0.454	0.048	0.010	0.048
1987	0.671	0.597	0.518	0.465	0.041	0.005	0.021
1988	0.584	0.540	0.550	0.409	0.026	0.007	0.024
1989	0.618	0.491	0.504	0.512	0.032	0.013	0.031
1990	0.590	0.565	0.566	0.483	0.030	0.008	0.031
1991	0.679	0.614	0.587	0.493	0.032	0.027	0.025
1992	0.637	0.636	0.549	0.454	0.041	0.014	0.047
1993	0.580	0.555	0.609	0.572	0.032	0.006	0.048
1994	0.622	0.576	0.561	0.501	0.035	0.020	0.022
All years	0.625	0.576	0.548	0.467	0.036	0.012	0.034

Table 5.10 Selected Indicators (medians): Firms with 100+ employed, by year

Year	Leverage	Local leverage	Local assets	Raw materials	Interest expenses	Profit to sales	Invest. to total sales
1983	0.559	0.412	0.427	0.407	0.022	0.049	0.055
1984	0.546	0.480	0.446	0.346	0.028	0.015	0.042
1986	0.501	0.463	0.356	0.339	0.037	0.014	0.031
1987	0.565	0.500	0.412	0.412	0.031	0.027	0.035
1988	0.564	0.524	0.416	0.375	0.027	0.026	0.024
1989	0.643	0.557	0.421	0.391	0.036	0.015	0.027
1990	0.598	0.501	0.477	0.384	0.048	0.023	0.035
1991	0.611	0.577	0.480	0.410	0.043	0.034	0.032
1992	0.591	0.535	0.446	0.419	0.036	–0.002	0.029
1993	0.491	0.424	0.413	0.465	0.031	0.028	0.034
1994	0.557	0.512	0.525	0.440	0.031	0.046	0.035
All years	0.512	0.474	0.433	0.388	0.034	0.025	0.035

Notes

1. Ultimately, the choice of characteristics or rather the exclusion of some characteristics rests with the availability of information and the length of the research.
2. The use of time-series/cross-section data was discussed in Chapter 4.
3. The estimated weights were also discussed in Chapter 4.
4. To cope with the length of the chapter not all variables shown in the tables are analysed and in a few instances some diagrams are omitted.
5. All variables have been adjusted using the GDP deflator 1985=100 wherever this was necessary. For the ratios of two variables this step was not necessary.

6 Structural Changes During Adjustment: Heterogeneity Based on Firm Ownership

6.1 Introduction

The previous chapter explored selected variables in the cost and asset structures of firms based on differences with respect to size of firm. Another area of distinction is firm ownership (foreign/local), which, like firm size, has relevance in the access to and cost of credit to finance investment and working capital. It is argued that foreign firms, as a subgroup of actors in the private sector, are part of a global network that relies on intra-group sales, can have favoured access to banks both local and international, and can borrow internally from parents and affiliate companies (FitzGerald 1993).

The nature of the firm in developing countries, specifically in the Caribbean region, was addressed through looking at the early development of plantation-type economies in which the dual economy feature of foreign/residentiary sectors was identified. This distinction typified the foreign firm as having easier access to markets and modern technologies through their relationship with parents/affiliates abroad, as well as cheaper access to imported raw materials and intermediates. Foreign firms were characterized as operating solely for profit.

The local firms that emerged were viewed as having difficulty in access to cheap raw materials, capital and foreign markets and the foreign exchange necessary to facilitate imported investment and intermediate goods. In Chapter 2, evidence of credit-rationing in the Caribbean was viewed as being institutionally based with some firms never being able to qualify for credit (Worrell 1985: 120). Farrell & Crichton (1986) saw that credit allocation among firms were biased against small and medium firms. In the analysis of firm size in the previous chapter the possibility of a distinction based on foreign/local ownership surfaced when tracking outliers over time.

Consequently, it is expected that the impact of and response to adjustment will differ based on foreign and local ownership of firms. As in the previous chapter, the aim of this chapter is to look at structural features such as leverage use, interest expenses and raw material expenses as well as profitability and investment, in order to analyse the impact of adjustment. The variable definitions are the same as described in the previous chapter. The chapter therefore continues below in section 6.2 with an exploration of changes in structural factors based on ownership. Section 6.2 also compares the impact of adjustment on the two groups through looking at trends in relative prices. Section 6.3 contains a brief summary of the results. Conclusions follow in section 6.4.

6.2 Structural Changes in Variables Based on Firm Ownership

6.2.1 Leverage use

On average, foreign firms had lower median leverage use ratios than the local firms, and their initial response to increasing real lending rates of interest was different. Leverage use dipped for the foreign firms in 1983/84, and after a small increase in 1984/86, it declined until 1988, when there was a sharp increase. Leverage increased initially for the local firms representing possibly increased indebtedness with declining leverage in 1988. During the adjustment period the tendency was a decreased use of leverage for the foreign firms (1990–92); but little deviation for the local firms (1989–92).

Both groups of firms showed increases in this ratio in 1989 with the peak being more prominent for the foreign firms. In 1989, there was greater liquidity in the economy due to money supply growth of about 10% following two years of declining growth rate at the onset of adjustment. On average, there appears to be a higher ratio of debt to assets and more inflexibility in the debt structure of local firms as opposed to foreign-owned firms. Figure 6.1a shows leverage use by ownership. Figure 6.1b shows the medians with respect to local liabilities, with the foreign firms displaying an initial lower use of local liabilities, which increases over time, at least up to 1989. The period 1987–90 showed a bit of decline in local liabilities for local firms, but increasing use of local leverage between 1987–89 for foreign firms with a peak in 1989.

Regarding variation over time for leverage use by local firms, the presence of several high outliers points to problems of very high use of debt relative to total assets by many local firms, which occurred throughout the years. Variation of leverage for the local firms is evident, for example, in 1986/87, 1989 and 1992 as compared to the other years.

Figure 6.1a Leverage use by foreign/local ownership

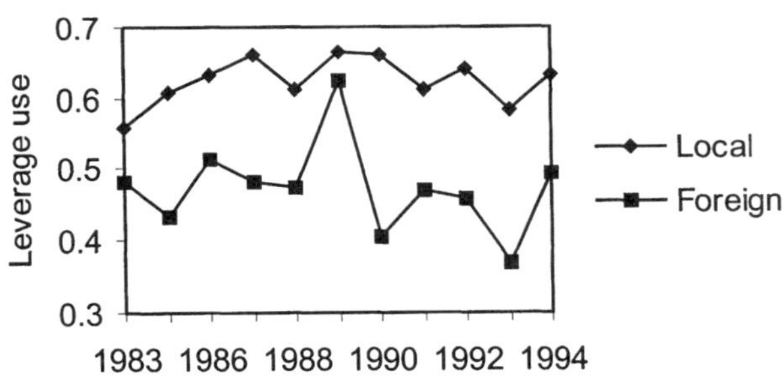

Figure 6.1b Leverage use (local liabilities) by foreign/local ownership

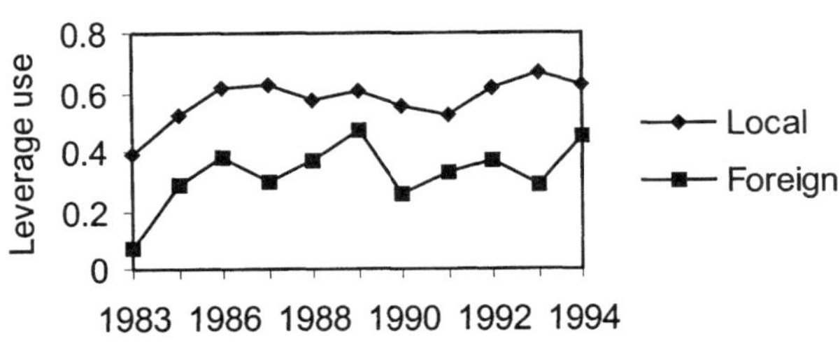

A comparison of selected years before and after the start of adjustment shows differences between the two groups in leverage use for 1983, 1988 and 1993 with wider variation among the local firms (boxplots not shown). In 1983 and 1988, while the distribution of local firms appears to be similar, there was a change in the use of leverage for foreign firms, with the tail moving from being negatively skewed in 1983 to being positively skewed in 1988. In other words, in 1983 there were some foreign firms with extremely low leverage use, but by 1988 there were few foreign firms with high leverage use. A comparison of 1988 and 1993 shows a reduction of the differences both within and between groups relative to ownership. Thus it would appear that adjustment had the within group effect of reducing the gap in leverage use among the local firms with a similar within group effect for the foreign firms. On either side of 1989, on average there was still a gap in the use of leverage between the two groups.

6.2.2 Interest expenses and the real lending rate of interest

Differences in the relationship between interest expenses for foreign and local firms are seen in the pre-adjustment year of 1984, when interest expenses fell for the foreign firms with increasing real interest rate but increased moderately for the local firms (Figure 6.2). From 1987–90, the interest expenses increased mildly for foreign firms but decreased for local firms. Other than these two points there is marked similarity in the movement of this ratio for both types of firms relative to the real lending rate. While in general interest expenses are lower for foreign than for local firms, the adjustment year of 1990 shows closer median values of interest expenses to total expenses for foreign and local firms. This pattern reflects the increased use of leverage by foreign firms during the course of adjustment. However, the tendency for foreign firms was towards the use of short-term rather than longer-term liabilities such as overdraft/short-term loans, accounts payable, taxation payable, etc, in contrast to both short and long-term liabilities by local firms.

Thus at the onset of adjustment, interest expense ratios are lower for foreign firms than for local firms. The differences and changes of the interest expense ratios of these two groups of firms relative to increasing

Figure 6.2 Interest expenses, foreign/local ownership and the real lending rate of interest

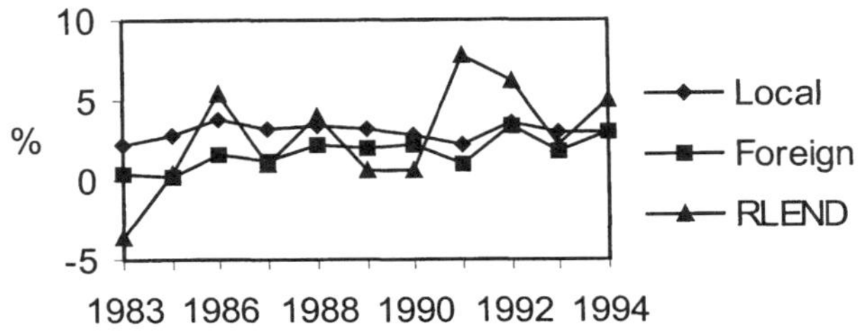

interest rates imply either lower borrowing of some local firms in the early adjustment period or increased borrowing (short-term) of foreign firms which, as it is argued, have easier access to credit.

For both foreign and local firms there was variation over the years 1983–94. Many outliers existed in the case of local firms; but during some of the adjustment years there were no outliers among the foreign firms pointing to a moderate effect of interest rate changes on interest payments.

6.2.3 Raw materials and the real exchange rate

Patterns in the cost structure of raw materials differed for some critical years based on ownership. In the initial period of the data, raw material expenses decreased from 1983 to 1986 for foreign firms but showed no consistent pattern (decreasing and then increasing) during these years for local firms (Figure 6.3). This change in the cost structure of raw materials for local and foreign firms, coming after the oil boom, reflects the economic downturn which led to the 'fallout' of firms (closures) and reduced purchasing of raw material. Output for local firms fell from 1984 to 1987 (Table 6.1). The devaluation of 1988 saw an increase in the raw material expenses ratio for local firms but a decrease for foreign firms. The 1993 devaluation with the floating of the dollar, which was a larger percentage devaluation, resulted in increasing raw material expenses ratio for both foreign and local firms.

Figure 6.3 Raw material expenses, foreign/local ownership and the real exchange rate

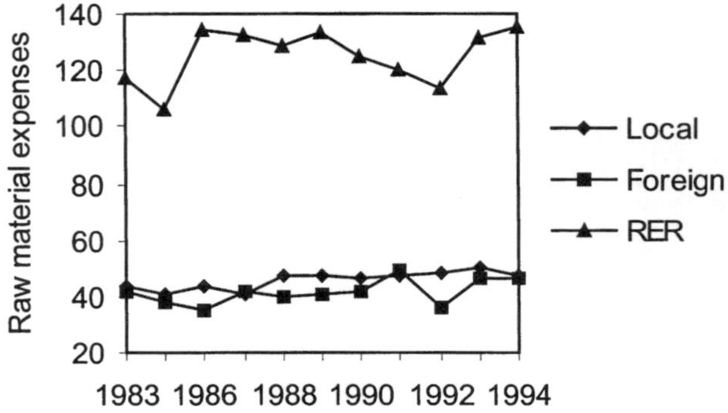

While the increase in raw material expenses for the local firms can be explained by the devaluation, the increase in the ratio for the foreign firms is not so easily explained since sources of raw materials for these firms were cheaper. This indicates that in 1993 foreign firms were similarly affected as a result of the policy change. Interviews I held with foreign firms indicated that raw material expenses increased as a result of the devaluations.

It appears that the lower percentage devaluation of 1988 had little effect on foreign firms in comparison to the 1993 devaluation. The differences in the effects on foreign firms for both devaluations possibly imply that the response of firms may have been to buy cheaper raw materials or to reduce purchases of raw materials as cost-cutting measures in 1988 as compared to 1993. The boxplots in Figures 6.4 to 6.8 contrast the changes over time and between both groups of firms in which the variability and the median changed from 1983 to 1988 for foreign and local firms. In 1983 there is greater variability in raw material expenses among local firms than among foreign firms. In 1988, this situation is reversed with foreign firms showing greater variability. By 1993 there is little difference shown between both groups of firms with respect to the cost of raw materials. Thus, relative price changes due to adjustment ap-

Figure 6.4 *Boxplots of raw material expenses by local ownership*

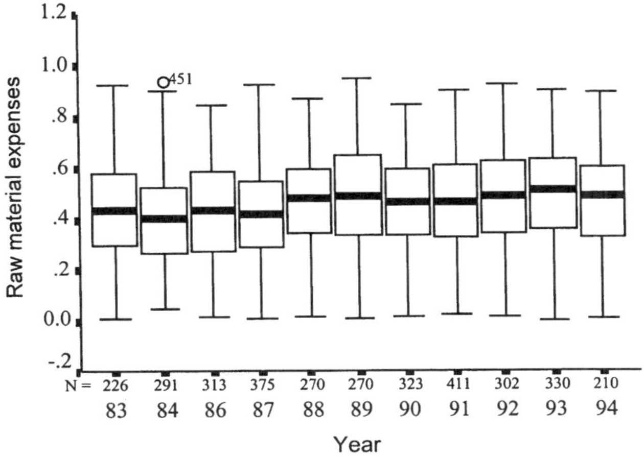

Note: Analysis weighted by W1.

Figure 6.5 *Boxplots of raw material expenses by foreign ownership*

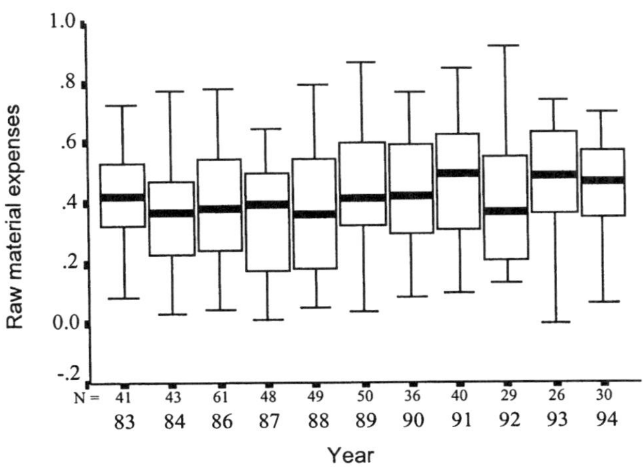

Note: Analysis weighted by W1.

Figure 6.6 *Boxplots of raw material expenses by foreign/local ownership, 1983*

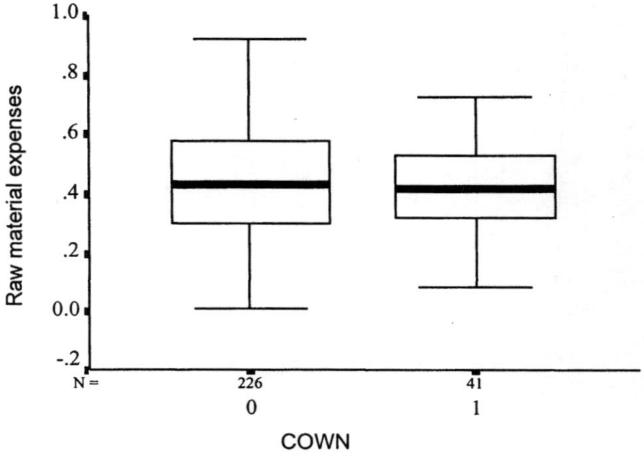

Note: Analysis weighted by W1.

Figure 6.7 *Boxplots of raw material expenses by foreign/local ownership, 1988*

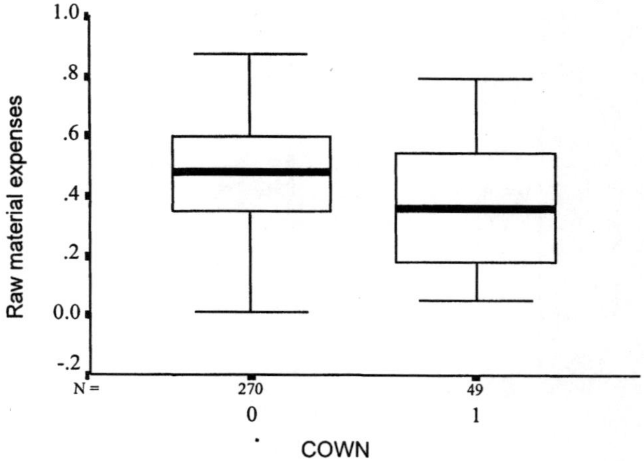

Note: Analysis weighted by W1.

Figure 6.8 *Boxplots of raw material expenses by foreign/local ownership, 1993*

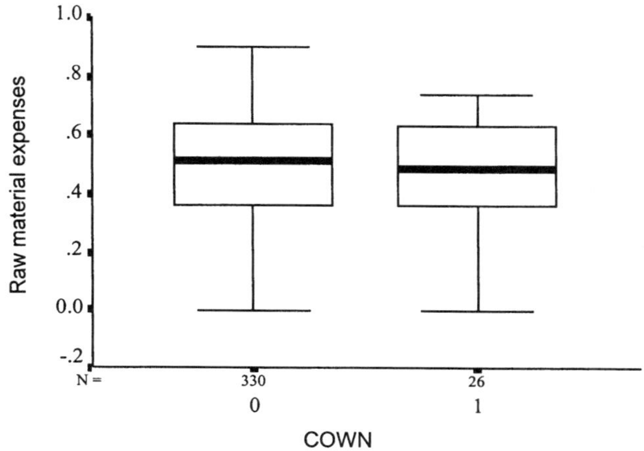

Note: Analysis weighted by W1.

pear to have had some impact in bringing this aspect of the cost structure closer together by 1993 for both groups of firms. Boxplots 6.6 to 6.8 also show differences in within group effects particularly as concerns the foreign firms.

6.2.4 Profitability and the real lending rate of interest

The profitability rate for foreign firms on average exceeds that of local firms for most of the period 1983–94 (Figure 6.9). The downward trend in profitability is identical during the 1983–87 period for both groups of firms. Recovery for both foreign and local firms occurred in 1988. However, in 1989 the profitability of foreign firms declined while that of local firms increased, showing that early adjustment measures must have had some negative effect on both groups. In this year, leverage use for foreign firms also increased sharply.

For the remaining adjustment period (1990 onwards), profitability increased in general for foreign firms except in 1994, but there was little change in the profitability of local firms.

Figure 6.9 Profit to total sales and the real lending rate of interest, foreign and local firms

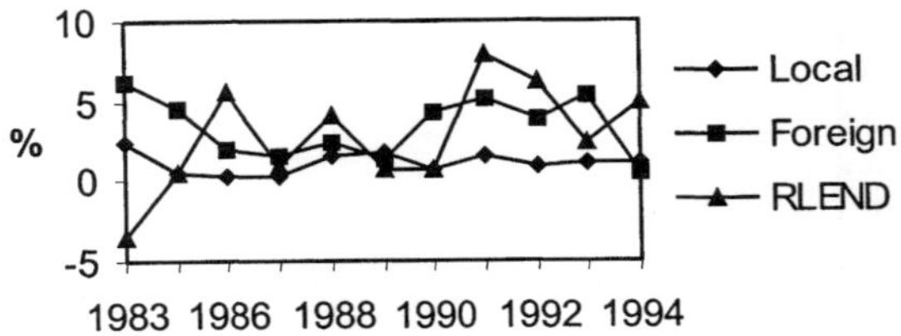

Thus, for local firms profitability remained relatively low with intermittent increases but with no signs of sustained recovery during the adjustment period. Foreign firms performed better during adjustment with a tendency towards increasing profitability despite fluctuations throughout. Both foreign and local firms tended to show an adverse effect of increasing real lending rates in the early period of 1983–87. There was little or no effect for local firms throughout the adjustment; but to some extent there was a positive effect on foreign firms during part of the adjustment period. The data show outliers for very profitable local firms as well as many more firms with large losses signalling a problem with lack of profitability for this groups. While there were also low outliers among the foreign firms, these were mainly concentrated in the early adjustment years of 1988–90. Among the foreign firms there was greater within group variability in 1989, which was the year that the median profitability value approximately coincided for both groups.

6.2.5 Investment and the real lending rate of interest

Unlike profitability, the rate of investment for foreign firms was lower on average than for local firms (Figure 6.10). The trend was similar for both groups from 1984–88 with falling investment in the pre-adjustment period. Investment exhibited an increasing trend for both groups in the period 1988–91.

Figure 6.10 Investment to total assets, foreign/local firms and the real lending rate of interest

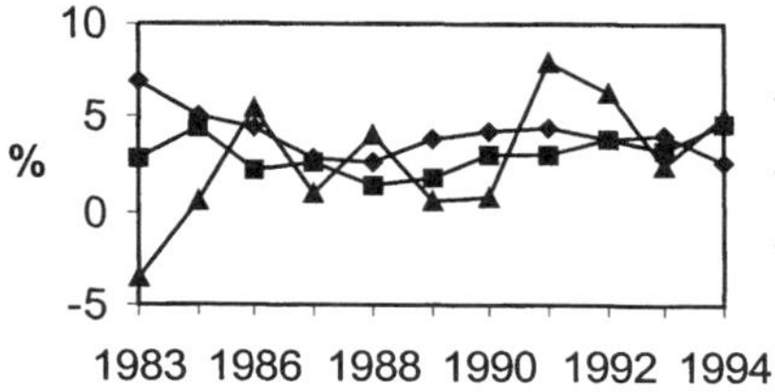

6.2.6 Changes in real exchange rate and the average wage rate

Changes in the RER and the average wage for foreign and local firms were similar for the period 1984–88. In 1989, increasing RER was accompanied by a marked decrease in the average wage for foreign firms but an increase for the local firms which had declined sharply in the previous year, 1988 (Figures 6.11 and 6.12). The period of 1990–93 saw a freeze in the average wage for the local firms but a dramatic rise for that of foreign firms in 1991 followed by an equally dramatic decline in 1992. The real devaluations of 1988/1993 were accompanied by falling wages for both years with that for foreign firms falling to a lower rate.

Figure 6.11 Changes in the bilateral RER and average wages, foreign/local firms

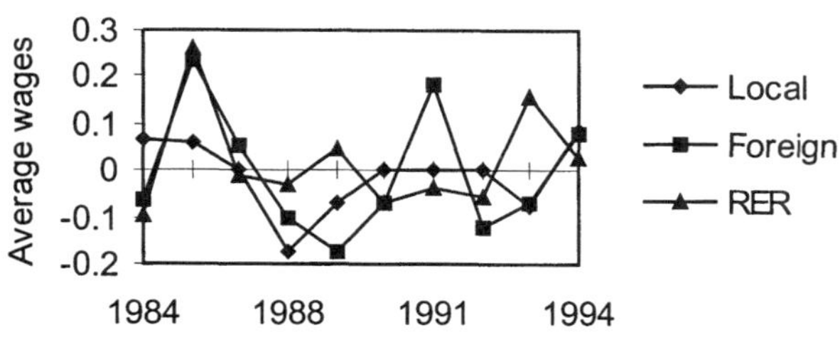

Figure 6.12. Boxplots of average wage/salary levels, foreign firms

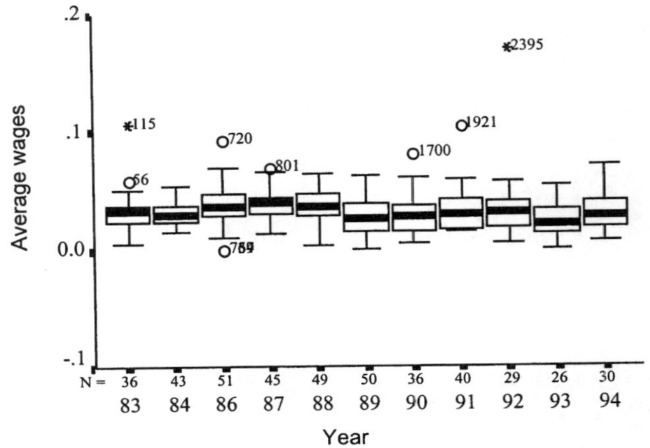

Note: Analysis weighted by W1.

While both groups of firms responded to adjustment by varying average wages, the foreign firms were able to adjust this variable to a greater extent relative to increases/decreases in the movement of the RER. One reason is that the average wage rate was higher for the foreign firms and therefore there was room for varying this rate through limiting increases or cutting back employment in specific years. There was a concentration of very high outliers showing the ability of some local firms to maintain high average wages. In the case of foreign firms too some variation was apparent in average wages throughout the period.

6.2.7 Output to employment

As seen in Figure 6.13, foreign firms operated at a higher level of output to employment than local firms. Productivity increased markedly for the foreign firms in 1991 after falling in the early adjustment period. This increasing trend continued for the remainder of the adjustment period. Significant movements in the pattern of productivity were not easily discernible among the local firms but there appeared to be a fall in output to employment around the pre-adjustment period followed by a decline

Figure 6.13 Output to employment by foreign and local ownership

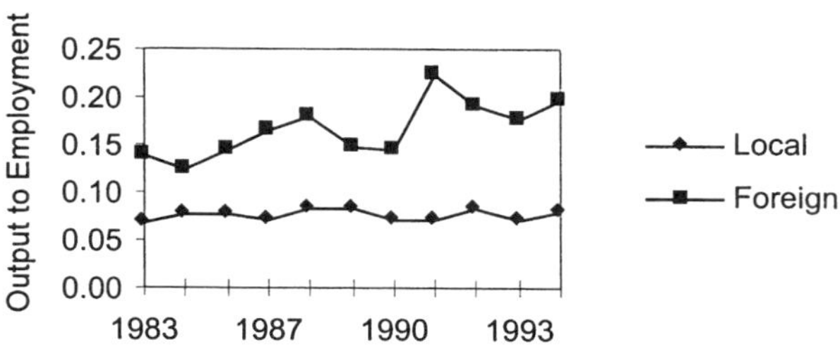

for about three of the adjustment years (1989–91). In addition, there was falling employment from 1983 until 1988 and generally lower employment for the local firms in the adjustment period compared to the early post-oil boom period.

As was the case for average wages, some local firms were able to maintain very high output to employment ratios as evident by the presence of outliers throughout the period. There was some variation over time in output to employment in the case of foreign firms.

6.3 Summary of Results

6.3.1 Leverage use

- In general, foreign firms use lower leverage than local firms and the composition of leverage for foreign firms comprises lower local leverage relative to foreign leverage.
- In addition, the local liabilities of foreign firms tended to be more short-term, which differed from local firms whose debt structure was more evenly distributed between long- and short-term local liabilities.
- The initial response coming out of the oil boom period showed that leverage use for local firms increased during the adjustment period showing little variation within group at this increased level.
- The initial post-oil boom response of foreign firms showed declining leverage use; however, this was followed by increasing leverage use in 1986. Then, in response to increased liquidity in 1989, foreign

firms increased their use of leverage but this was mainly in overdraft and accounts payable rather than long-term loans.
- Thus, the adjustment period saw a narrowing of the within group variability in leverage use among foreign firms as well as a narrowing of the gap between foreign and local firms.

6.3.2 Interest expenses

- The initial effect of increased real interest rate in 1983/84 differed between foreign and local firms, with interest expenses falling for foreign firms until an increase in 1986 similar to their pattern of leverage use. For local firms, interest expenses increased from 1983 to 1986. Local firms therefore experienced automatic increases in interest expenses with increasing real lending rates while foreign firms did not.
- In the early adjustment period, interest expenses declined for local firms but increased for foreign firms reflecting increased difficulty in access to or the cost of credit for local firms but increased borrowing for overdraft and other short-term purposes by foreign firms.
- During 1990–94, differences between these two groups relative to interest expenses seemed to have disappeared.

6.3.3 Raw material expenses

- Initial response by foreign and local firms differed with foreign firms showing consistent decline in raw material expenses and fluctuations occurring in the case of local firms.
- As for the devaluation years, the devaluation of 1988 did not seem to affect foreign firms as much as local firms, but both groups of firms appear to have been similarly affected by the devaluation of 1993.

6.3.4 Profitability

- Initially profitability declined for both groups of firms during 1983–87.
- Profitability was generally higher for foreign firms than for local firms except for declining profitability in 1989 for the former, which coincided with profitability of local firms and with a sharp increase in leverage use for foreign firms. Within group variability increased for

the foreign firms in 1989, making the variability decidedly more than it was for the local firms in this same year.
- Local firms showed little change in profitability during the adjustment period.
- Declining profitability of foreign firms reduced the gap with local firms by the start of adjustment, but increased profitability beyond 1989 led to a reappearance of the gap in profitability between the two groups.

6.3.5 Investment

- In general, there was a decline in investment after the oil boom, which continued until 1988.
- Initially the foreign firms increased their investment rate, which was at a lower rate than the local firms' in 1983, showing that the investment thrust of foreign firms was not adversely affected by the appearance of positive real lending rates in 1983.
- Investment fell from a high oil boom rate (in the pre-1983 period) for the local firms.
- From a very low rate in 1988, there was an increase in investment for both groups during the adjustment period until 1992, when a fall in investment occurred for both groups. The pattern in this period is similar for both groups of firms.

6.3.6 Average wage

- Both groups of firms appeared to have used the average wage to counteract the effects of changes in the RER.
- To some extent, the foreign firms were able to vary the average wage more than the local firms during the adjustment years of 1990–92, in which there was no change in the average wage of local firms.

6.3.7 Output to employment

- Output to employment was generally at a higher level for foreign firms.
- For foreign firms, the tendency was for this ratio to show an increasing pattern from 1984 through the adjustment period, despite an initial decrease in 1983/84 and a slump in 1989/90.

– Local firms showed little change in this ratio throughout the period of the data.

6.4 Conclusions

Structural changes in the selected variables analysed in this chapter have shown differences in patterns over time and within and between ownership groups. During the adjustment period, there was similarity in the patterns of investment and reduced variability within groups for leverage use or between groups for interest expenses.

The results summarized in this chapter point to similarities as well as differences in the effects of adjustment policy variables based on the distinction of ownership. Thus initial conditions, differential access to and cost of resources faced by different categories of firms, as well as inherent differences with respect to debt and production may lead to differences in the effect of the key price variables of adjustment on the private sector as a whole. The results suggest that while there are some grounds for similarity, no one single statement can always be made relative to the performance of private investment and its profitability without recognizing the differences among firms.

Table 6.1 Selected indicators (medians), locally-owned firms, by year

Year	Output	Employment	Output to Employment	Average Wage	Capital to Employment
1983	2.08	32.0	0.067	0.015	0.022
1984	1.76	24.0	0.077	0.016	0.025
1986	1.09	15.0	0.076	0.017	0.023
1987	0.82	12.0	0.071	0.017	0.020
1988	1.60	20.0	0.083	0.014	0.020
1989	1.86	25.0	0.083	0.013	0.030
1990	1.31	19.0	0.072	0.013	0.019
1991	1.00	12.5	0.071	0.013	0.022
1992	1.55	21.0	0.081	0.013	0.029
1993	1.23	18.0	0.070	0.012	0.026
1994	1.64	20.0	0.078	0.013	0.027
All years	1.42	19.0	0.075	0.014	0.024

Table 6.2 *Selected indicators (medians), foreign-owned firms, by year*

Year	Output	Employment	Output to Employment	Average Wage	Capital to Employment
1983	9.04	85.0	0.137	0.032	0.034
1984	11.71	100.0	0.125	0.030	0.033
1986	9.03	70.0	0.144	0.037	0.063
1987	8.24	61.0	0.166	0.039	0.061
1988	8.03	62.0	0.180	0.035	0.061
1989	10.45	76.0	0.147	0.029	0.051
1990	7.84	65.0	0.145	0.027	0.034
1991	6.21	31.0	0.224	0.032	0.054
1992	10.40	73.0	0.191	0.028	0.063
1993	10.32	85.0	0.177	0.026	0.070
1994	9.93	64.0	0.197	0.028	0.077
All years	8.94	68.0	0.158	0.033	0.053

Table 6.3 *Selected indicators (medians), locally-owned firms, by year*

Year	Leverage	Local leverage	Local assets	Raw materials	Interest expenses	Profit to sales	Invest. to total sales
1983	0.559	0.386	0.419	0.439	0.023	0.023	0.069
1984	0.609	0.527	0.375	0.411	0.028	0.005	0.050
1986	0.632	0.614	0.432	0.437	0.038	0.002	0.044
1987	0.660	0.630	0.457	0.404	0.033	0.002	0.028
1988	0.611	0.576	0.403	0.478	0.034	0.015	0.026
1989	0.664	0.609	0.507	0.472	0.032	0.018	0.038
1990	0.659	0.555	0.562	0.468	0.029	0.008	0.043
1991	0.613	0.523	0.439	0.471	0.023	0.015	0.044
1992	0.640	0.618	0.510	0.486	0.037	0.009	0.039
1993	0.582	0.664	0.562	0.498	0.031	0.011	0.040
1994	0.631	0.630	0.555	0.475	0.030	0.011	0.027
All years	0.627	0.581	0.476	0.461	0.030	0.010	0.041

Table 6.4 Selected indicators (medians), foreign-owned firms, by year

Year	Leverage	Local leverage	Local assets	Raw materials	Interest expenses	Profit to sales	Invest. to total sales
1983	0.483	0.073	0.642	0.413	0.005	0.062	0.029
1984	0.432	0.285	0.511	0.375	0.003	0.045	0.044
1986	0.516	0.381	0.461	0.351	0.016	0.019	0.022
1987	0.482	0.302	0.469	0.417	0.013	0.016	0.027
1988	0.472	0.367	0.448	0.398	0.022	0.025	0.013
1989	0.625	0.467	0.543	0.404	0.020	0.014	0.017
1990	0.404	0.258	0.519	0.418	0.023	0.043	0.030
1991	0.468	0.326	0.464	0.491	0.011	0.051	0.030
1992	0.458	0.374	0.511	0.365	0.035	0.039	0.039
1993	0.369	0.285	0.445	0.468	0.018	0.054	0.032
1994	0.492	0.455	0.495	0.465	0.031	0.005	0.046
All years	0.477	0.314	0.494	0.408	0.027	0.035	0.027

7 Structural Changes During Adjustment: Heterogeneity Based on Industry

7.1 Introduction

In Chapters 5 and 6, the themes of heterogeneity and structure were explored from the perspective of firm size and ownership. Examination of these themes continues in this chapter with an evaluation of the effect of policy changes over time looking at variation based on industry. This evaluation is discussed in section 7.2. Section 7.3 presents a summary of the results, and conclusions follow in section 7.4.

7.2 Variation of Structural Factors by Industry

Based on type of industry, this analysis explores differences between firms by looking at structural factors such as the degree of indebtedness, raw material and interest expenses, and so forth. The aim is to see if there are any implications for the impact of adjustment based on the industry to which a firm belongs. Features contributing to differences on an industry basis include export orientation/market focus, capital/labour intensity and dependence on imported raw materials. The institutional bias in lending by commercial banks against small/medium firms is a feature that cuts across industries contributing to the dualistic nature of these industries relative to the mode of production, use of credit and so forth.

The inward orientation of the industrialization thrust and the high dependence on imported raw materials can lead to differences in the impact of adjustment. An added significance of the examination of heterogeneity by industry is that this characteristic also embodies differences relative to technology/capital intensity and scale of operation. Thus, the distinction based on industrial activity is fundamental to understanding the dynamics of adjustment. This chapter is specifically concerned with the analysis of the patterns of structural changes during adjustment in three manufacturing sector industries: food processing/ drink/tobacco, assembly and related, and textiles/garments.

7.2.1 Leverage use

All three industries displayed different responses to macroeconomic changes as shown by the data on the use of leverage during the initial period, which followed the oil boom (Figures 7.1 and 7.2). Assembly increased its use of leverage until 1987. Textiles initially decreased its leverage between 1983 and 1984, followed by an increase from 1984 to the pre-adjustment year of 1987. In the food processing sector, leverage use declined from 1983 to 1987.

There was little change over time in leverage use for the food processing/drink activity throughout the entire period of the data, except for a decline in the pre-adjustment period. The fluctuations in leverage use in this industry were within a relatively small range. Assembly and related also showed minor fluctuations apart from the increase in leverage use in the early period. The fluctuations in leverage use for the assembly industry were at this higher rate for the rest of the period in comparison to 1983: from about 58% liabilities to total assets in 1983 to approximately 64–73% for the years after 1983. In the textile/garments sector, there are more obvious differences in leverage use over time as shown in Figures 7.1 and 7.2.

The positioning of the high outliers, firms with high leverage use, shows that these are concentrated between the years 1984–90 for the food processing sector and between the years 1988–92 in the assembly sector. The greater variation over time for the textile/garments sector reflects problems that this sector has traditionally experienced (even before the adjustment period) relative to its ability to compete with im-

Figure 7.1 *Leverage use over time: All industries*

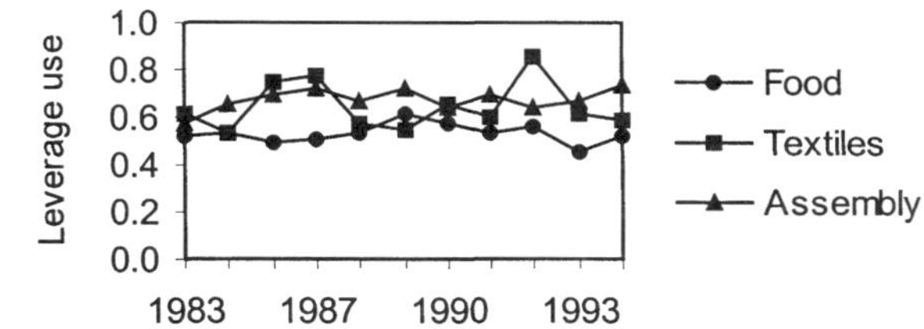

Figure 7.2 *Boxplots of leverage use over time: Textiles/garments industry*

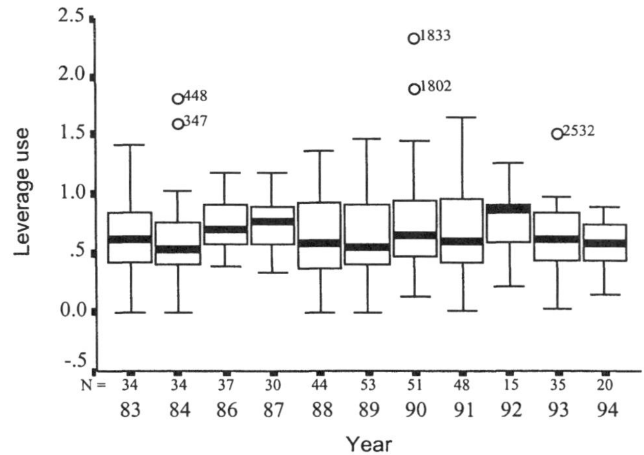

Note: Analysis weighted by W1.

ports. These problems were exacerbated during the oil boom period when increased incomes prevailed.

Hence, while the initial decline in leverage use was a response to increasing real lending rate to a positive value from 1983 to 1984, the increase and fluctuations in leverage use reflect the low growth rate of the textile sector in the post-oil boom and adjustment periods. The fact that the assembly sector showed little change after the initial increase in leverage suggests that the survival method for this sector entailed high use of leverage. The assembly sector is inward-oriented, with some exceptions. The textile/garments activity reflects the problems experienced by firms in this sector in accessing credit. Of the three industries, food processing appears to be the one with the least problem in leverage use, being able to survive with lower use of leverage.

7.2.2 Interest expenses and the real lending rate

In all three activities, interest expenses increased with increasing and positive real interest rates during the early period of the data (Figure 7.3). As was the case in leverage use, there are some differences by activity in the period of 1983–86, with textiles showing a sharp increase compared to food processing. The assembly sector showed a decrease in interest expenses between 1984 and 1986, reflecting a measure of uncertainty in light of the higher interest rates during these years.

While the trends for food and assembly are somewhat similar throughout the period, there is a gap between the two, indicating that the interest expenses ratio for food processing was always lower than that for assembly. This factor may be a reflection of the larger use of leverage discussed above. During the adjustment period, interest expenses for the assembly sector declined from 1988 to 1990 (increasing during 1990–92); the same was true for the food processing sector for which interest expenses declined during 1988–91 (increasing during 1991–93). Similar to the use of leverage, the trend in interest expenses showed wider fluctuations in the textile activity than in the other two sectors, with a tendency for persistent increase during 1989–92. The median values of interest

Figure 7.3 Interest expenses and the real lending rate: All industries

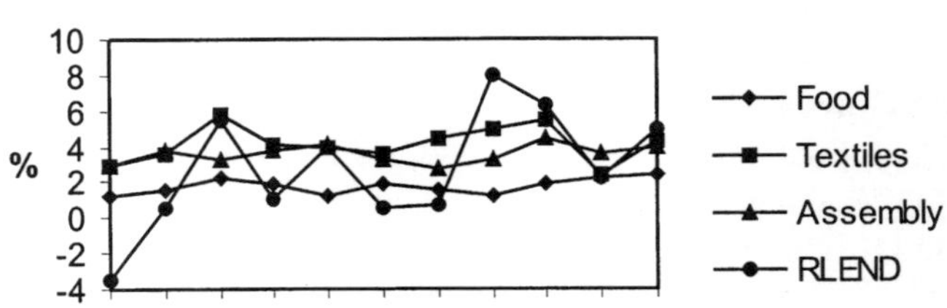

expenses in the textile industry were higher than those in the food processing sector, and either similar to or higher than those in the assembly sector.

Interest expenses in food processing moved in a similar direction with RLEND for the period 1983–87 and exhibited an inverse relationship from 1988–94. This pattern suggests a negative relationship with the real interest rate in the adjustment period.

The textiles/garment industry showed little flexibility in being able to avoid increases in interest payments since the interest expenses ratio closely followed the direction of the real lending rates. It is possible that the firms in this sector that were able to borrow had to continue doing so in order to survive during the adjustment period and were subjected to the going rate of interest.

In the case of assembly, there was in general a similar pattern to food processing. However, it occurred at a higher rate of interest expenses. While it may be evident that the interest expenses increased for assembly in 1991 – at a higher interest rate than in 1986 – it should be noted that the experience with liquidity in this year was favourable due to a mini boom in oil prices related to the Gulf War, from which the economy as a whole benefited.

Assembly and related activity showed an inverse relationship with RLEND for the period of 1986–88, indicating that, like food processing, there was a choice with respect to borrowing for this period, which is consistent with the fluctuations in leverage around 1983–87. However, during 1988–90 interest expenses declined despite low interest rates for 1989/90; this was followed by increasing interest expenses with increasing or high real lending rates. This pattern may imply that there was debt accumulation on which interest had to be paid, suggesting a bit of inflexibility caused by the debt structure reflected in the movement in the interest payments. From 1989 to 1994, the movements in both variables are similar suggesting that credit allocation continued for this sector despite problems with indebtedness.

Thus there was, to some extent, inflexibility in the direction of movement of interest expenses in the textiles/garment industry throughout the period, while the food processing/drink industry was able to vary its pattern of interest payments relative to changes in RLEND. The assembly industry displayed a mixed scenario, with inflexibility in interest payments in some years. Changes in interest expenses were, however, evident, suggesting variation in payments on loans over time for each activity. The textiles and assembly industries show greater variability and changes over time as compared to the food processing industry, reinforcing the points above.

7.2.3 Raw materials and the real exchange rate

There were three nominal devaluations in 1985, 1988 and 1993. Our concern in this section will centre on changes in raw material expenses during these years. While in 1993, the nominal devaluation turned out to be a real devaluation, the 1988 devaluation was not reflected as a real devaluation. The 1985 devaluation occurred in December of that year, and its impact in 1986 showed that this was also a real devaluation.

Figures 7.4 to 7.7 show changes in the growth rate of the ratio of raw material expenses over time as compared to the change in RER for all three industries. In the food processing sector, changes in the median values of raw material purchases appear to be negligible during the pre-adjustment period, but variation around the median values is evidenced by the varying sizes of the boxplots in Figure 7.5 for the period 1983–87. In the food processing sector, the change in raw material expenses in 1993 shows a decline in the growth rate, while no change is observed in 1986 and 1988, the years in which nominal devaluation occurred. The adjustment period 1988–94 shows much more variation in raw material expenses than the pre-adjustment phase.

In the textile/garment industry there was an increasing rate of change between 1984 and 1986, which then remained constant between 1986 and 1987. This increase in 1986 reflects the end of the year devaluation of 1985 shown in the rising real exchange rate and raw material expenses (Figure 7.4b). The lower rate of change of raw material expenses than in RER signalled that there was still something to be gained by these firms relative to the real devaluation of 1986. There was a slight increase in the raw material expenses ratio in 1988, but at a declining rate when compared to the rate of change for the previous year. Throughout the period of the data on raw material expenses there were fluctuations in the rate of growth from one year to the next as reflected in Figures 7.4b and 7.6. Also noticeable in Figure 7.4b is an inverse association between the changes in RER and the changes in raw material expenses ratios during the period of 1988–93. This reflects

Figure 7.4a *Changes in RER and raw materials to total expenses: Food processing/drink/tobacco industry*

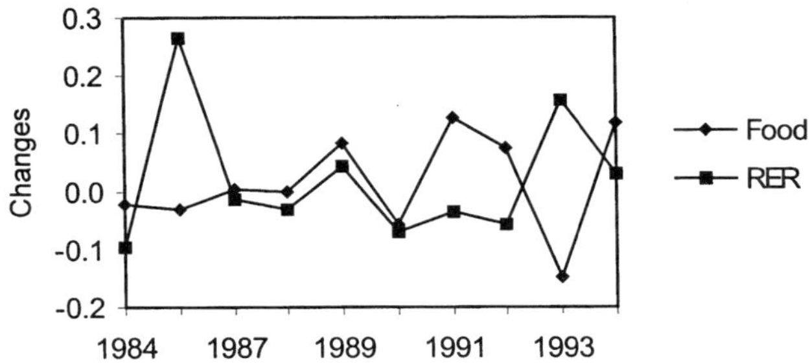

Figure 7.4b *Changes in RER and raw materials to total expenses: Textile/garments industry*

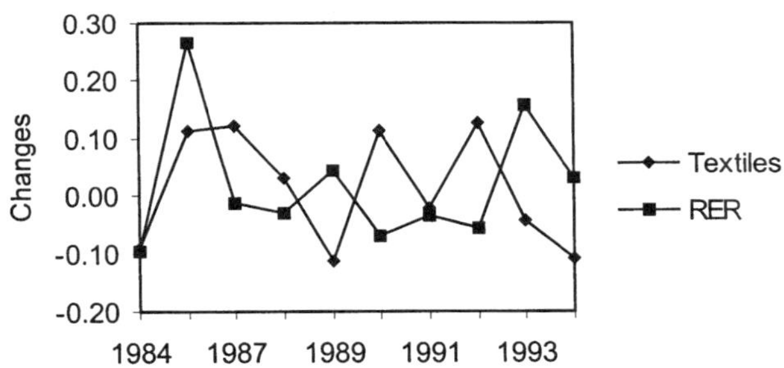

the negative impact of RER on the purchasing of raw materials, which as was argued earlier is largely imported.

Figures 7.4c and 7.7 highlight changes in raw material expenses in the assembly industry. There are wide fluctuations in raw material expenses in this industry as compared to food processing, similar to that of the textile industry. During the pre-adjustment period, the increase in 1986 in this ratio almost matches that of the real devaluation, with the increasing real exchange rate being accompanied by an almost identical increase in the raw material expenses ratio. The years 1988 and 1993

Figure 7.4c *Changes in RER and raw materials to total expenses: Assembly and related industry*

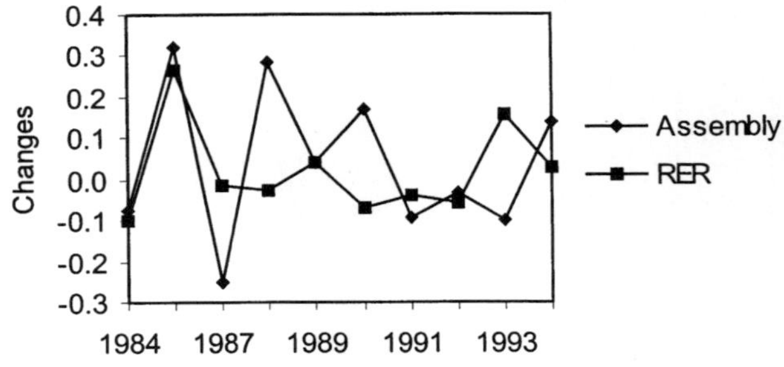

Figure 7.5 *Boxplots of raw material expenses: Food processing/drink/tobacco industry*

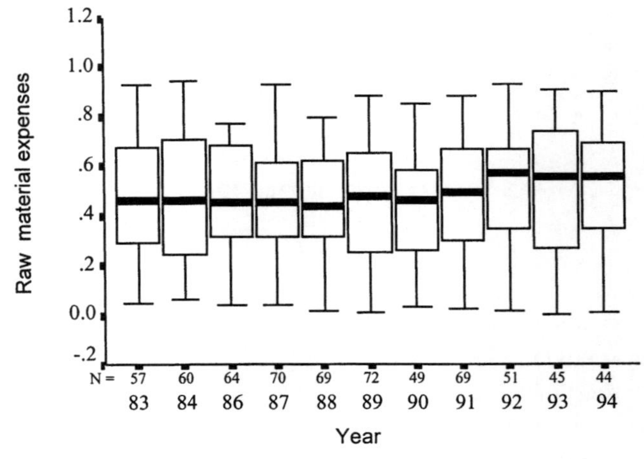

Note: Analysis weighted by W1.

Figure 7.6 *Boxplots of raw material expenses: Textiles/garments industry*

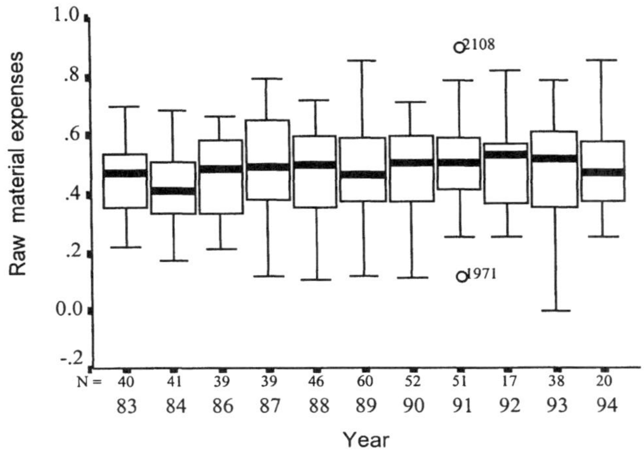

Note: Analysis weighted by W1.

Figure 7.7 *Boxplots of raw material expenses: Assembly and related industry*

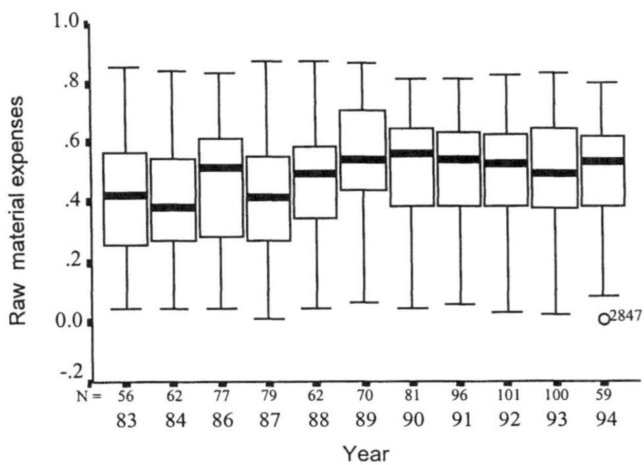

Note: Analysis weighted by W1.

saw decreases in this ratio, coinciding with real exchange rate devaluation in those years. The adjustment period, 1988–94, reflected an inverse relationship between the changes in RER and changes in the raw material expenses ratio.

The assembly and the textile industries stand out in that order as those that probably experienced the most noticeable changes in the raw material cost structure in response to changes in the RER. Their greater domestic market focus probably contributed to the difference in the effect of the RER since an offsetting positive effect might have been gained through export sales if these industries were more outward-oriented. The decline in all three sectors during the 1993 devaluation possibly reflects a period of uncertainty since the devaluation was accompanied by a policy of managed floatation of the dollar.

7.2.4 Profitability and the real lending rate of interest

Declining profitability was common in all three activities during the pre-adjustment period, though it was not necessarily the same for all. This decline could have been a result of the effects of 'Dutch' disease in the 1970s. In general, all three industries follow similar trends during the pre-adjustment and part of the adjustment period with some exceptional years (Figure 7.8). In the case of textiles, 1987 and 1989 showed better median profitability than the other sectors. While the performance of this sector in 1987 may be due to a ban on imported garments imposed

Figure 7.8 Profitability to sales and the real lending rate: All industries

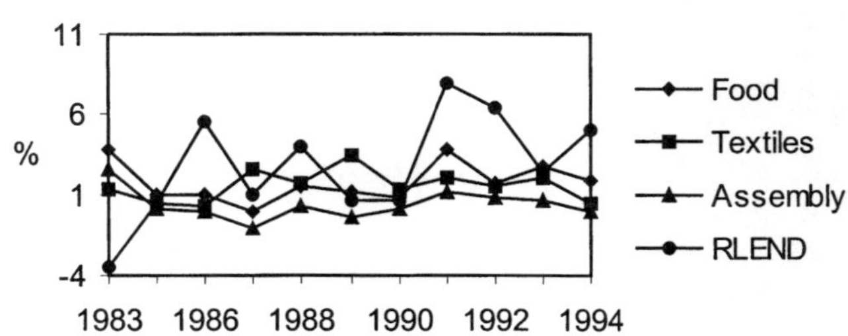

by the government, no explanation can be found for the performance of profitability in 1989.

There was also a tendency towards fluctuating profitability in food processing in the post-1987 period at a higher level than the 1987 decline, which reflected continued expenditure on food in contrast to assembly products. The assembly industry, while showing increased profitability in the early part of adjustment (1990–91), showed declining profitability for the remaining years (1992–94). The textile industry exhibited fluctuating profitability in the post-1987 period. Thus, in all three industries the performance of profitability does not show signs of sustainable recovery during the adjustment period.

Traditionally, the textile sector has been very outspoken about the effects of imported garments and the impact of devaluation and high interest rates on its operations. In the adjustment years of 1990–92, there was not a pronounced increase in profitability yet neither did profitability seem to decline for this sector. Links between the interest rate and profitability are not quite clear since for some years high interest rates occurred with low or high profitability. The positioning of the outliers shows obvious differences between the three industries. While food processing has a fair amount of both high and low outliers, profit- and loss-making firms, the other two sectors show a greater proportion of low (loss-making) outliers.

7.2.5 Investment and the real lending rate of interest

In the initial period of the data, there was declining investment for both the assembly and food processing industries from about 1983 to about 1986 (Figure 7.9). The remaining period saw fluctuations in investment in both sectors. There was increasing investment in textiles initially in 1983/84, followed by fluctuating investment for the remainder of the years. Largely, the relationship between investment and the real lending rate of interest suggests that the real interest rate and investment were negatively related for all three sectors, with the exception of a couple of years such as 1993. During this year, investment declined along with the real lending rate of interest possibly reflecting the uncertainty of other macroeconomic changes, such as the floatation of the exchange rate in that year.

Figure 7.9 *Investment to total assets and the real lending rate of interest: All industries*

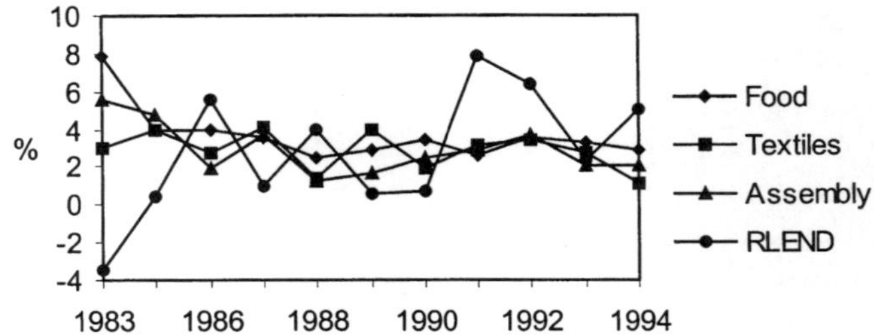

The food processing industry showed a dramatic decline from 1983 to 1988, remaining almost at the 1988 rate despite some fluctuations. Thus there was no recovery of investment for this sector. Investment in the assembly industry showed some increase after 1988 through 1992, but much below the pre-adjustment rate of investment. Beyond 1992, investment appeared to decline in this industry.

All three sectors showed variation over the years in the investment rate, with a decline very apparent for the years 1983–88 in the food processing industry.

7.2.6 Average wage and the real exchange rate

Declining average wage or inverse movements in wages with changes in the RER seemed to have been used as a mechanism by which firms were able to offset the costs of devaluation and interest rate increases. This method appeared across all sectors with a difference only in extent (Figure 7.10). For food processing, average wage declined during the period 1984–88, which preceded the official adjustment programs. While this variable fluctuated for the remaining period, it was clear that there were significant decreases in average wages in both years of the devaluation, 1988 and 1993.

In the textiles/garments sector, with the exception of 1991 and 1987, there was an inverse relation between RER and the average wage

Figure 7.10 Changes in RER and average wage: All industries

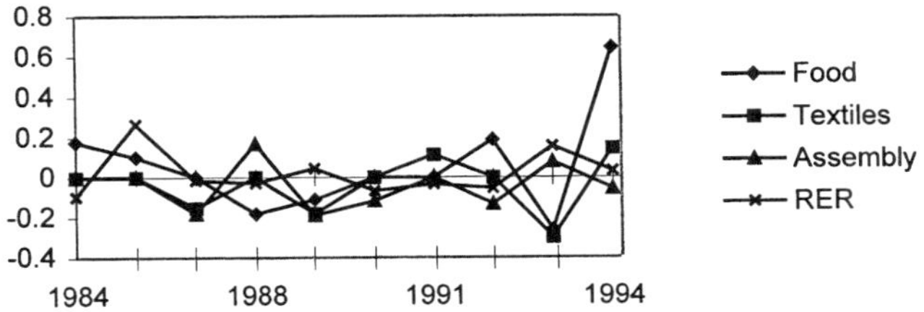

with marked decline in 1993. A decrease in average wage would have assisted this sector to cope with the effects of the devaluation on costs.

While the assembly industry showed a similar pattern of movement with the RER during the period of adjustment, the increase in the average wage was always less than the increase in RER. On the other hand, in other years there was an inverse association between changes in average wage/salary in this sector and the RER. Again, it is clear that wage control was a mechanism used across sectors to maintain competitiveness.

The declining pattern in average wages is more obvious in the textiles/garments and the assembly industry if actual averages and not changes in the median values are shown.

7.2.7 Output to employment

The food processing and assembly industries had higher ratios of output to employment than the textile industry, with the highest ratios occurring in food processing (Figure 7.11). While output to employment increased in the food processing industry from 1983 to 1984, there was a declining trend from 1984 to 1989. With the exception of 1987, output declined while employment also declined in general. After 1989, output to employment fluctuated in this sector.

There was little change in output to employment for the textiles/garments sector during the entire period. There was declining output as well as employment in the period 1987–91 with fluctuating movements in both variables through the remaining period.

After an initial increase from 1983, assembly showed a declining trend in output to employment from 1984 to 1988, after which the ratio

Figure 7.11 Output to employment: All industries

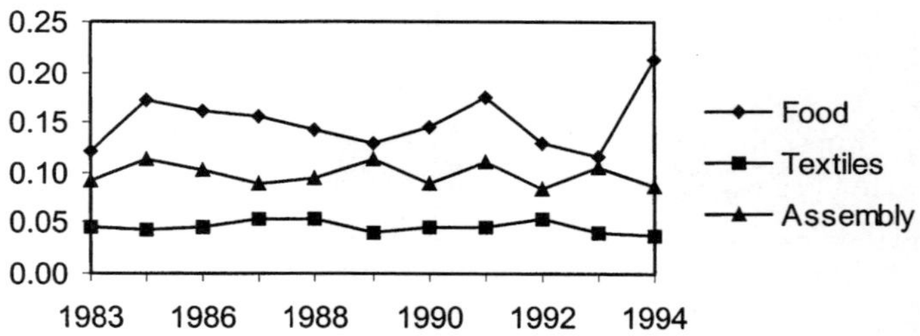

fluctuated. As for the textiles sector, both output and employment declined with the exception of 1988/89 when both output and employment increased.

For all three industries, changes in output seemed to bear some association to changes in employment such that reduction in the latter implied reduction in the former. Variability in this ratio is visible in the food processing and assembly industries over time, but not as evident in the textiles sector possibly due to the presence of a very high outlier. This firm had very low employment and obviously very large output. It is possible that the activity of this firm is distribution rather than manufacturing. Dropping the outlier reveals greater variation in output to employment over time.

7.3 Summary of Industry Results

7.3.1 Leverage use

- Differing responses to macroeconomic changes were shown for all three industries in the initial period of adjustment. Leverage use increased in assembly and decreased in food processing; while in textiles, it initially increased then decreased.
- At these new rates, food processing and assembly used leverage consistently. This implies that the assembly industry needed to increase its use of leverage in order to remain viable; while the firms in the food processing sector were able to survive at a lower rate of leverage

use. The textile/garment industry seemed continuously susceptible to macroeconomic changes exhibiting continuous fluctuation in leverage use.

- Food processing and assembly tended to have extremely high users of leverage as compared to textiles (taking into consideration the number of firms), though these outliers were concentrated in different periods. In the case of the food industry, the high users of leverage were concentrated closer to the pre and early period of adjustment, while for the assembly industry the outliers spanned from the beginning of the adjustment period to the middle.

7.3.2 Interest expenses

- All three industries showed increased interest expenses along with the increase in the real lending rate to positive values in the initial period of the data. There was a sharper increase in the case of textiles between 1984 and 1986. Assembly showed an increase in interest expenses and then a decrease in this same period, while food processing increased throughout this entire period.
- There was a consistent gap in interest expenses (median values) between assembly and food processing as well as textiles and food processing for almost the entire period, with assembly and textiles showing consistently higher ratios than food processing. Differences in variability within and across industry groups were also present throughout the period of the data
- For the period of 1989–92, the gap in interest expenses between food processing and textiles tended to increase with increasing interest expenses. In 1993, interest expenses in textiles declined such that the median value coincided with that of food processing. This movement seems to suggest a decline in loans for the textile industry.
- To some extent there was an inverse association between interest expenses and the real lending rate for the food processing industry during the adjustment period, 1988–94. This association shows the sector's ability to lower its borrowing or its inability to borrow at higher interest rates.
- The option to reduce borrowing with increases in interest rates is apparent to a lesser extent in the textiles and assembly sectors. For the pre-adjustment period, 1983–87, the trend in interest expenses for the

textile industry seems to follow the direction of the real lending rate, the same is true for the 1993/94 period. In the period 1988–92, interest expenses increased regardless of the movement in interest rates. Interest expenses largely increased in general with increases in the real lending rate. Even at lower interest rates, the textile sector seemed to have higher interest expenses suggesting some differences in the interest rate charged to firms in this sector.

- Overall, there appeared to be more variation in interest expenses in the assembly and textiles sectors than in food processing.
- Based on the above observations, the reaction of firms to the interest rate is reflected accordingly in the patterns of their interest payments.

7.3.3 Raw material costs

- Variation in raw material costs over time was present in all three industries, with assembly and textiles showing more variation in cost structure than food processing throughout the entire period.
- There was little or no change in raw material expenses for the food processing industry as a result of the 1986 and 1988 devaluations, but its expense ratio decreased during the devaluation of 1993.
- Raw material expenses in the textile industry showed increases during both the 1986 and 1988 (slight) devaluations; but decreased during the 1993 devaluation.
- In the assembly sector, the increase in the raw material expenses ratio matched that of the real devaluation in 1986, but showed a decline during the 1988 and 1993 devaluations.
- Changes in raw material expenses in the food processing sector appeared to move in the same direction as changes in RER for the period 1987–92, with an inverse association occurring in 1993/94. An inverse association was also evident for the assembly sector during 1988–94 and for the textile sector in the 1988–93 period. The textile sector experienced a decline in raw material expenses in 1994.
- From the above, it appears that the assembly sector, with decreases in both 1988 and 1993 and a longer inverse relationship, was the sector most adversely affected by changes in RER, followed by textiles and food processing in that order.
- Interestingly, the response to the 1993 devaluation in all three activities appears to have been a reduction in either purchases of raw mate-

rials or cheaper sourcing of these materials as reflected in the cost decline in that year. In the case of assembly, the decline also occurred in 1988, suggesting reduced purchasing in response to the devaluation. For the other two sectors, in the face of uncertainty relative to the floatation of the exchange rate, it is also possible that producers tended to reduce their purchases of raw materials.

7.3.4 Profitability

- Profitability declined in general for all three industries during the pre-adjustment period.
- The textile sector had a profitable year in 1987 as a result of a special government policy relative to restrictions on imported garments. During the period of adjustment there were no clear signs of recovery in this sector.
- In the food processing sector, the tendency during the adjustment period shows fluctuating profitability at a higher rate than the 1987 decline. There was, however, no clear indication that this sector had recovered during the adjustment period.
- While the assembly sector showed an increase in profitability in the early part of adjustment, the post-1991 period showed declining profitability.
- The assembly sector seemed to be the least profitable, showing a more definite declining trend during the latter part of adjustment.
- Profitability varied across sector during the pre-adjustment/adjustment period, including within sector differences over time.
- Positioning of firms with high extreme values shows that food processing tended to have a concentration of both high (with very high profits) and low (loss-making) outliers. The tendency for the other two sectors, textiles and assembly, was for firms with extreme values to be concentrated mainly as loss-making firms at the lower end of the distribution.

7.3.5 Investment

- Food (1983–88) and assembly (1983–86) showed declining investment in the initial pre-adjustment period. On the other hand, textiles, which was at a lower rate of investment in 1983 as compared to the other activities, initially showed an increase in 1984, but this rate was still lower than that of the other two sectors.

- For the remaining years, investment in all three sectors fluctuated, declining in the textiles industry in 1993 and 1994, and showing decline or no change in food processing and assembly during these same years.
- Overall, there was an inverse association between investment and the real lending rate of interest in all three sectors.

7.3.6 Average wage

- Variation of the average wage was a mechanism by which firms responded to adjustment to offset the effects of relative price increases due to devaluation. There was evidence of declining average wages or no changes for some years, as was the case in the textile and assembly industries in 1983/84.
- In the nominal devaluation year of 1986, the increase in RER was associated with decreases in average wages in all three industries. In 1988, declining RER saw a decline for food processing but increasing average wages for textiles and assembly. In 1993, increasing RER was associated with a smaller increase in average wage for food processing and decreasing average wages for textiles and assembly.
- It should be noted that there were some differences between sectors in the use of average wage as a mechanism for survival or as a means of remaining competitive.
- In 1994, the food processing sector showed an increase in wages bringing it back up to the levels of the 1986 and 1987 pre-adjustment years.

7.3.7 Output to employment

- Output to employment was at a higher ratio in the food processing sector almost throughout the period in comparison to the other industries. In turn, textiles had lower output to employment ratios than the assembly sector.
- There was little variation in output to employment for textiles and assembly, while more variation was shown in the food processing sector. This sector experienced declining output to employment from 1984 to 1989, during the pre and early adjustment period. This was

followed by increasing ratios from 1990/91 and decreasing ratios in 1992/93, with a very high increase in 1994 during the adjustment period.

- The decline in output to employment in the food processing sector during the 1984–89 period was mainly due to falling output (1984–89) and also to declining employment to some extent. The fluctuating patterns in all three industries, as well as the absence of variation in assembly and textiles, imply that there is no clear indication that adjustment led to increased productivity in these industries.

7.4 Conclusions

Continuing the investigation of the research, this chapter explored aspects of the cost and asset structure of the firm relative to differences based on industrial activity. Differences surfaced with respect to patterns in leverage use, raw material purchases and interest payments.

Declining profitability and investment in the pre-adjustment period and a lack of recovery in both of these variables, as well as the use of the average wage as an offsetting mechanism in response to devaluation seemed to be common in all three sectors but with some subtle differences relative to the prolongation of the effects/uses. For example, the assembly sector seemed to be the hardest hit relative to profitability, while the food processing sector was able, at the end of the period, to get its average wage back up to the level of the initial period of the data. Productivity increases did not seem to materialize in any of these three industries.

Thus, the evaluation of the private sector based on industry as an aspect of heterogeneity can bring out differences in the response of firms to changes in relative price as they affect firms' asset and cost structure. In the next chapter, issues relative to structure and heterogeneity are explored more formally using econometric modelling supported by available qualitative and quantitative data.

Table 7.1 Selected indicators (medians): Food processing/drink/tobacco industry, by year

Year	Leverage	Local leverage	Local assets	Raw materials	Interest expenses	Profit to sales	Invest. to total sales
1983	0.520	0.325	0.395	0.455	0.013	0.038	0.079
1984	0.528	0.499	0.422	0.445	0.016	0.010	0.040
1986	0.494	0.490	0.380	0.431	0.023	0.010	0.039
1987	0.512	0.500	0.358	0.433	0.019	0.000	0.035
1988	0.538	0.489	0.343	0.433	0.013	0.015	0.025
1989	0.616	0.562	0.431	0.468	0.019	0.012	0.028
1990	0.568	0.532	0.565	0.441	0.015	0.009	0.034
1991	0.538	0.514	0.514	0.497	0.012	0.037	0.026
1992	0.562	0.543	0.505	0.533	0.019	0.017	0.036
1993	0.456	0.446	0.488	0.455	0.023	0.028	0.033
1994	0.516	0.494	0.567	0.508	0.024	0.019	0.028
All years	0.522	0.495	0.434	0.453	0.017	0.015	0.035

Table 7.2 Selected indicators (medians): Textiles, garments and related industry, by year

Year	Leverage	Local leverage	Local assets	Raw materials	Interest expenses	Profit to sales	Invest. to total sales
1983	0.612	0.464	0.621	0.435	0.030	0.014	0.030
1984	0.530	0.528	0.494	0.395	0.036	0.005	0.040
1986	0.741	0.633	0.713	0.440	0.058	0.003	0.027
1987	0.767	0.755	0.765	0.494	0.041	0.026	0.041
1988	0.574	0.574	0.618	0.509	0.039	0.017	0.014
1989	0.541	0.537	0.589	0.451	0.036	0.035	0.039
1990	0.650	0.645	0.719	0.502	0.044	0.013	0.019
1991	0.599	0.618	0.562	0.490	0.049	0.021	0.032
1992	0.860	0.752	0.764	0.552	0.054	0.016	0.034
1993	0.613	0.613	0.734	0.528	0.024	0.020	0.027
1994	0.581	0.606	0.757	0.471	0.043	0.004	0.011
All years	0.620	0.595	0.658	0.478	0.042	0.014	0.031

Table 7.3 Selected indicators (medians): Assembly and related industry, by year

Year	Leverage	Local leverage	Local assets	Raw materials	Interest expenses	Profit to sales	Invest. to total sales
1983	0.579	0.393	0.498	0.419	0.029	0.025	0.056
1984	0.651	0.576	0.511	0.387	0.037	0.001	0.047
1986	0.696	0.645	0.446	0.510	0.033	0.000	0.019
1987	0.722	0.628	0.498	0.381	0.037	–0.010	0.037
1988	0.672	0.669	0.416	0.489	0.041	0.003	0.012
1989	0.717	0.653	0.534	0.509	0.033	–0.004	0.016
1990	0.641	0.616	0.557	0.596	0.027	0.002	0.025
1991	0.696	0.665	0.497	0.541	0.032	0.012	0.028
1992	0.641	0.586	0.467	0.523	0.045	0.009	0.037
1993	0.668	0.641	0.635	0.471	0.036	0.006	0.021
1994	0.734	0.600	0.591	0.535	0.040	0.000	0.021
All years	0.669	0.621	0.498	0.479	0.035	0.006	0.026

Table 7.4 Selected indicators (medians): Food processing/drink/tobacco industry, by year

Year	Output	Employment	Output to Employment	Average Wage	Capital to Employment
1983	8.43	55.0	0.120	0.017	0.036
1984	8.91	67.0	0.173	0.020	0.046
1986	7.65	55.0	0.161	0.022	0.060
1987	9.21	55.5	0.156	0.022	0.056
1988	5.30	40.0	0.142	0.018	0.046
1989	5.58	38.0	0.128	0.016	0.042
1990	7.76	48.0	0.146	0.016	0.035
1991	5.55	38.5	0.176	0.016	0.027
1992	8.41	45.0	0.130	0.019	0.031
1993	8.84	98.5	0.116	0.014	0.034
1994	8.00	43.0	0.212	0.023	0.036
All years	7.72	47.0	0.145	0.019	0.041

Table 7.5 Selected indicators (medians): Textile/garments and related industry, by year

Year	Output	Employment	Output to Employment	Average Wage	Capital to Employment
1983	1.53	37.5	0.046	0.013	0.005
1984	1.46	38.0	0.042	0.013	0.010
1986	1.52	35.0	0.047	0.013	0.011
1987	1.48	25.0	0.053	0.011	0.010
1988	1.33	25.5	0.054	0.011	0.007
1989	1.01	25.0	0.041	0.009	0.007
1990	1.06	22.0	0.045	0.009	0.011
1991	1.23	18.5	0.047	0.010	0.012
1992	2.29	45.0	0.053	0.010	0.011
1993	1.36	36.0	0.039	0.007	0.009
1994	1.47	39.0	0.037	0.008	0.009
All years	1.41	29.0	0.046	0.010	0.009

Table 7.6 Selected indicators (medians): Assembly and related industry, by year

Year	Output	Employment	Output to Employment	Average Wage	Capital to Employment
1983	3.12	38.0	0.091	0.022	0.030
1984	2.52	25.0	0.113	0.022	0.037
1986	0.96	12.0	0.102	0.022	0.037
1987	1.43	11.0	0.089	0.018	0.025
1988	1.80	13.5	0.094	0.021	0.047
1989	1.85	22.5	0.113	0.017	0.046
1990	1.32	15.0	0.090	0.015	0.048
1991	1.44	11.0	0.109	0.015	0.045
1992	1.07	13.5	0.083	0.013	0.041
1993	0.93	9.0	0.105	0.014	0.046
1994	1.34	10.0	0.085	0.0132	0.031
All years	1.43	14.0	0.094	0.159	0.039

8 The Private Sector During Adjustment: The Interaction of Price Incentives and Structural Factors

8.1 Introduction

This chapter is an empirical investigation of the hypotheses presented in Chapter 4. Chapters 5, 6 and 7 analysed adjustment of firms through structural changes over time assuming a heterogeneous private sector. The analysis models the impact of relative prices on firms using variables in the cost and asset structures, which act as the medium through which the effects of adjustment are felt. The availability of a survey with qualitative responses related to the stated effects and responses of a small sample of firms will support the analyses.[1] By combining both quantitative and qualitative survey data the aim is to obtain the most plausible explanations relative to the regression results.

The key features of this chapter are (i) an econometric analysis of the impact of adjustment on profitability and investment of firms, and (ii) an exploration of the manner in which firms have responded to the effects of adjustment using qualitative data. Section 8.2 formally presents the models used to analyse the impact of adjustment. Section 8.3 gives the results of the analysis on profit, investment, and – for selected categories – liabilities and interest expenses. Section 8.4 combines the quantitative data results with the qualitative survey data looking at patterns of adjustment in firms. Conclusions follow in section 8.5

8.2 Modelling of the Impact of Adjustment on Firms

In the modelling of the firm under adjustment, this research centres on the importance of structure, heterogeneity and history relative to the experience of firms in the private sector. The approach to the modelling analyses selected factors in the cost/asset structures of the firm. It is assumed that relative prices work their way in affecting profitability and investment through these factors. A direct investigation of the impact of key price relatives (the real exchange rate and the real lending rate) on two key structural factors (leverage and interest payments) will be carried out for the 10+ employment size firms for selected sectors. These sectors are chosen to coincide with the ones which were investigated in Chapter 7.

The data is tested for pooling across years and across characteristics such as ownership, size and activity wherever this is feasible.[2] The next subsection presents the definitions of the variables and the model used to evaluate the hypotheses.

8.2.1 Presentation of models and definition of variables

In analysing profitability and investment of the firm, the models which incorporate variables in the cost and asset structures are outlined below.

$$LNEW2A = a_0 + a_1LRAW + a_2LINTER + a_3LLIB + a_4LLOC + a_5LRECPROD \quad (8.1)$$

$$LINV1 = b_0 + b_1LRAW + b_2LINTER + b_3LLIB + b_4LLOC + b_5LNEW1A + b_6LBFIXASC \quad (8.2)$$

$$LLIBB = c_0 + c_1LRER + c_2LRLEND + c_3LNEW2A + c_4LINV1 \quad (8.3)$$

$$LINTER = d_0 + d_1LLIBB + d_2LRER + d_3LRLEND \quad (8.4)$$

The variables (logarithms of) used in the above models are as follows:

Dependent variables:

LNEW2A
: the ratio of net profit after tax to total sales which, apart from looking at the rate of return to total sales, is also a reflection of the ability of the firm to be efficient relative to its operating expenses.

*LINV*1
: the ratio of investment to total assets where investment is equal to purchase of new buildings, plants, machinery, equipment and major improvements.

Explanatory variables:

LRAW
: the ratio of raw materials purchased to total expenditure is used to evaluate the effect of policies that may affect the cost of raw materials, given a specific exchange rate policy.

LINTER
: the ratio of total interest payments to total expenditure. The effect of increases in interest rates on the structure of the firm's interest expenses is analysed through this variable.

LLIBB
: the ratio of total local liabilities to total assets. The ratio of liabilities to total assets is an approximate measure of leverage. The liabilities consist of bank overdraft, short-term loans, accounts payable, current portion of long-term debt, taxation payable, dividends payable, long-term bank loans, long-term loans (other than bank), and other liabilities. The impact of the debt structure on profitability and investment is analysed via this variable. The choice of local liabilities over foreign and local combined is meant to show the impact of changes in the local financial markets on firms during adjustment.

LLOC
: the ratio of current local assets to total assets. This variable is used to assess the impact of changes in the asset structure of the firm relative to investment and profitability. Total local assets comprised currency/cash on hand and on deposit, accounts receivable, inventories, and other current assets.

LNEW1A
: the ratio of net profit after tax to total assets which is used in the investment equation reflecting the efficiency of the asset base.

LRECPROD
: value of output (sales) is a variable used to analyse differences due to scale in the profitability equation.

LBFIXASC
: total fixed assets is used to analyse differences due to scale in the investment equation. These assets are valued at original cost – net of depreciation.

8.2.2 Expected signs of explanatory variables

In equations 8.1 and 8.2, it is expected that *LRAW* will be negative due to the impact of the devaluation on the cost of the imported component of raw materials. However, there are offsetting positive effects which include: the passing on of cost, benefits from sale of goods produced or stocks of raw materials purchased prior to the devaluation, and wage management. While *LINTER* should show a negative effect on both profitability and investment, differentials in the cost of credit charged by banks may cause reversals of this effect.

Use of leverage, *LLIBB*, is expected to have a negative effect on profitability. Firms may borrow to offset cash flow problems; possibly leading to a positive relationship between *LLIBB* and *LNEW2A*. While increasing debt is likely to adversely affect investment, the use of leverage may also primarily facilitate investment resulting in a positive effect in some cases. In addition, differential access to credit implies that some firms are able to borrow from banks at prime rates for investment purposes, while others are denied loans or are given loans only for overdraft at higher costs. Of interest will be the question of how the liability structure of the firm can offset (or enable) the capacity to invest in the various categories.

The *LLOC* variable should be positive for the profitability equation. However, the composition of local assets may lead to cash flow problems, while the presence of these assets may also imply withdrawal of funds for investment. Consequently, it is possible that *LLOC* may show negative effects on profitability and investment.

Adjustment is expected to have a more positive impact on the profitability and investment of larger firms as opposed to smaller firms as reflected by *LRECPROD* and *LBFIXASC*. However, the lack of flexibility of larger firms in adjusting when faced with massive debts may lead to a reversal of these results.

In the investment equation, *LNEW1A,* it is expected that profitability will enhance investment, although it is possible that increased profits may be invested in financial assets (speculation) and therefore not lead to an increase in productive investment. Hence, the sign of the profitability variable may be negative. The expected signs for the regressions of equations 8.3 and 8.4 will follow after the analysis and presentation of the results of the main variables, profitability and investment. The *GDP* deflator was used to create *constant price estimates, with constant price 1985=100* where this was necessary.[3] Table 8.1 summarizes the expected signs of the variables on profitability and investment.

Table 8.1 Summary of expected signs of variables

Independent variables	Dependent variables		Remarks
	LNEW2A	LINV1	
LRAW	–	–	May be positive depending on reasons given above
LINTER	–	–	May be positive for larger firms or specific sectors containing these large firms
LIBB	–	–	May be positive for cases in which borrowing is used to offset loss-making and investment
LLOC	+	–	The composition of local assets related to accounts receivable and which may turn into bad debt or inventories that cannot be readily converted to cash can affect profitability and investment negatively
LNEW1A	n/a	+	Sign of profitability may be negative.
LRECPROD	+	n/a	Expected to be positive for larger firms.
LBFIXASC	n/a	+	Expected to be positive for larger firms.

8.2.3 Results of the analysis on the pooling of the data

The results on the pooling of the data are summarized in Tables 8.7 and 8.8 at the end of this chapter. For both *LNEW2A* and *LINV*1, foreign and local firms cannot be pooled.

For *LNEW2A,* results for the following categories will be presented:

(i) Local firms with <10 employment size – individual years from 1984–94. No further analysis of seven industrial activities was performed within years due to the small frequencies of firms in these years.

(ii) Local firms with 10+ employment size – seven industrial activities to be analysed separately pooling all years except 1986. No further subdivision of size is required within the 10+ category.

(iii) Foreign firms – five size groups to be analysed separately: <10, 10–24, 25–49, 50–99, 100+. The small number of firms implies that no further testing relative to activity or time period was possible.

For *LINV*1, the results will be presented in the following categories:

(i) Local firms employing <10 – data to be analysed separately for each year (1984–94), regressions for 1983 and 1988 were not possible.

(ii) Local firms employing 10–24 – seven activities to be analysed separately.

(iii) Local firms employing 25–49 – one equation.

(iv) Local firms employing 50–99 – seven separate manufacturing activities.

(v) Local firms employing 100+ – one equation.

(vi) Foreign firms – five size groups to be analysed separately: <10, 10–24, 25–49, 50–99 and 100+.

The above categories on the pooling of the data clearly bring out the importance of the theme of heterogeneity based on size and ownership and will feature in the analysis of profitability and investment below. As discussed in Chapter 4, the small number of <10 firms imposes less reliability on these results, affecting for instance the feasibility of carrying further tests of pooling within years for activity. For foreign firms, the small number of these firms in contrast to local firms implies that further tests of pooling within size groups were not feasible. As for the previous exploratory analysis in Chapters 5 to 7, the <10 firms were also weighted as described in Chapter 4.

8.3 Profitability and Investment: The Effect of Adjustment and the Response of Firms to Adjustment

The data analysis involved the systematic examination of regression residuals, which are the difference between the observed value of the dependent variable and the value predicted by the regression line (Norusis 1994). In the previous chapters, copious exploratory data analysis was carried out to study patterns in the relationships between the variables and to eventually arrive at a workable strategy for the empirical analyses in this chapter. This approach culminated in the use of exploratory analysis in Chapters 5 to 7.

The diagnostics incorporated production of studentized residuals plotted against the predicted and the dependent variables, partial regression plots, boxplots of *DFBETAS,* and other measures of leverage and influence. [4] Consistent and careful study of these diagnostics were done, taking influential values into account. In some cases, dummy variables based on the clustering of specific values of explanatory variables were introduced. Double log ordinary least squares *OLS* specification was used to reduce obvious skewness in the data. It was also necessary to run regressions for subgroups of firms such as foreign/local. Despite these measures, it was also necessary to use one's discretion in order to arrive at the seemingly line of 'best fit'.

Graphical presentation of some of the regression results showing scatters of predicted versus actual values of the dependent variable and some boxplots of studentized residuals are presented in Figures 8.1 to 8.11. In the regressions of *LNEW2A* (10+ firms by industries) for some industries like food processing, the removal of values which were some distance away from the others did not lead to any drastic change in the significance of the coefficients but led instead to the appearance of more such cases. Thus, the removal of these values (or the omission of data) while improving the fit did not change the significance of the coefficients.

The next sub-sections discuss the results in relation to profitability and investment. These results are formally presented at the end of the chapter in Tables 8.7 to 8.19, while a summary is presented in Tables 8.3 and 8.4 within this section.

8.3.1 Regression results on the profitability of firms

LNEW2A: The impact on the ratio of net profit after tax to total sales

The results on the pooling of the data provide *initial support* to the hypotheses relative to differential effects based on firm size, ownership and activity during adjustment. Below, further results are presented, categorized according to the test results from Tables 8.7 and 8.8. The <10 employment size firms were subjected to a different sampling procedure than the 10+ firms. The latter category of firms is analysed separately.

Firms with < 10 employed (results by year)

The regression results on profitability for the group which comprises the smallest firms, the <10 employment size category, are described in this section with 1983–88 being taken as the years preceding the formal implementation of adjustment policies. No results were possible for 1983 because of the small sample size, even after allowance was made for missing data.

Raw material expenses

The ratio of raw material to total expenses (*LRAW*) was significant and negative in 1984, 1988 and 1994. The year 1984 fell during the early crisis period following the oil boom period of 1974–81, while 1988 and 1994 were within the adjustment period. The year 1988 was a devaluation year, while 1994 followed the devaluation/managed flotation of the dollar in 1993. Hence, among the smallest firms there was an initial negative effect of changes in the cost structure of raw material expenses on firm profitability as early as 1984 and also in two years of the adjustment period close to or during the exchange rate devaluation.

Interest payments

Interest payments to total expenses (*LINTER*) had a negative effect on profitability in 1984 and 1987 but a positive effect in 1988 and 1994. Tight monetary policy featured highly among the policies that were implemented prior to the need for official adjustment in the period 1982–87 (Box 2.2 Chapter 2). The year 1988 was the starting point of official adjustment. The changes occurring during this time were expected to negatively affect firm profitability, particularly for the smaller firms. The year 1994 fell in a period of mixed policy including the tightening of liquidity along with the removal of directives to commercial banks on credit policy. It also appears that for the small firms that were able to borrow, the positive results in 1988 and 1994 reflect the following scenario: increasing profitability was associated with increasing interest payments due to short-term loans/overdraft used to offset losses by small firms that could borrow.

Liabilities to total assets

The poor showing of the interest rate variable could have been due to the prominence of the variable representing the debt position of the firm. The liabilities to total assets ratio (*LLIBB*) was significant and negative in all years excluding 1988 and 1993. The largely negative results on profitability are not surprising in light of the expected debt accumulation and bankruptcy by firms across size groups relative to both the post-oil boom and adjustment periods. The positive results in 1988 and 1993 were in the years of devaluation of the exchange rate suggesting perhaps increased use of leverage during those years to offset existing problems with profitability among small firms.

Hence, the use of leverage in general exerted a negative impact on the profitability of small firms but with some measure of positive assistance on profitability in at least two years of adjustment. These results support the argumentat relative to the importance of the debt situation of the firm at the point in time when adjustment is occurring.

Local assets ratio

The local assets ratio had no impact on the profitability of small firms, suggesting the possibility of cash flow problems which would have militated against profitability.

Receipts from production

This variable (*LRECPROD*), as an indicator of size differentials within size groups, showed a positive effect on profitability in 1984, 1986 and 1994 and a negative impact in 1988. Thus, in these years within this group of smaller firms, the larger the firm the greater the profitability for the years mentioned with a reverse result at the start of adjustment in 1988.

Local firms with 10+ employed (by industry)

The results of the pooling of *LNEW2A* (net profit after tax to sales) showed that it was possible to pool the local firms of all 10+ size groups. This may reflect the similarity in the experiences of these firms with respect to the impact of macroeconomic changes on profitability, as it cut across size groups. This observation is consistent with the discussion in Chapter 5 relative to the exploration of profitability by size groups in which similar aspects of profitability were identified across size groups. However, differences surfaced by industry and will be incorporated in the discussion of the results.

Food processing, drink and tobacco

In this industry significant results were obtained as follows:

- raw material to total expenses (*LRAW*) – negative
- interest expenses (*LINTER*) – positive
- dummy variable representing highly leveraged firms with leverage greater than or equal to 1 (*D*11*LLIBB*) – negative
- dummy variable of firms with leverage less than 0.20 (*D*12*LLIBB*) – negative
- dummy variable for firms with interest expenses greater than 5% of total expenses (*D*21*LINTER*) – positive.

The negative result on raw material expenses supports the argument that macroeconomic policy changes (specifically in the case of devaluation of the exchange rate) affect the cost of raw materials, which are largely imported in most of the manufacturing sectors. While it is possible for some of the larger firms in this sector to pass on the costs of imported raw materials as well as to benefit from increased exports as a result of the devaluation of the exchange rate, it appears that these offsetting positive effects were insufficient to bring about a positive impact on profitability.

The favourable result on interest payments as well as on firms with higher ratios of interest payments suggests that this industry contains firms that have access to loans and benefit from preferential interest rates given by commercial banks. Alternatively, as in the case above, the positive result on *LINTER* may reflect the positive association between profitability and interest payments for firms that have access to loans. The results on leverage are interesting in that both firms with very high leverage use and those with lower leverage use had profitability problems.

For the food processing sector, GDP growth rates described earlier showed that the pre-adjustment years (1983–85) had negative growth rates which were followed by some recovery in 1986/87. Negative growth started in 1988 when the government had put into place measures leading up to the economic reforms programme of the IMF/World Bank. During the years of official adjustment, there was positive growth in this sector from 1989–91 followed by negative growth rates from 1992–94. Overall during the period of adjustment this sector had a low and negative rate of growth (–0.4).

Hence, this sector had a mixed performance before and during adjustment at the macro level. The micro-level results showed that firms that received too much credit or too little credit were adversely affected relative to the performance of profitability. Interest payment increases signaled increased profitability – which suggest that either increasing profitability is associated with the ability to borrow or borrowing of funds aided the profitability of the firms. Changes in the raw material cost structure negatively affected profitability. Figure 8.1 at the end of this chapter shows a scatter of the predicted values from the regression against the actual values.

Textiles, garments, footwear etc.

In the textiles/garments sector, the three variables showing significant coefficients were purchases of raw materials to total expenses ratio (*LRAW*) (with a positive effect on profitability), interest expenses ratio (*LINTER*) (with a negative effect on profitability), and very highly leveraged firms (*D11LLIBB*) (with a negative impact on profitability). Unlike the food processing sector, interest expenses exhibited a negative impact in this industry with highly leveraged firms showing a negative effect similar to firms in food processing. These results are in keeping with the argument that differential access to credit as well as cost of credit is affected by macro-level changes. As far as the qualitative data, the firms interviewed in this sector reported mixed responses regarding access to and cost of funds, with the relationship between the owner and the banks being an important factor relative to the terms and conditions of credit.

The result on *LRAW* was a bit surprising and somewhat against the hypothesis of the research relative to an expected negative effect of devaluation on raw material expenses, which in turn was expected to exert a negative impact on profitability. In the qualitative survey data, firms interviewed in this sector and in general indicated a negative effect of devaluation of the exchange rate through the effect on imported raw materials. From the qualitative data, 6 out of 7 manufacturers interviewed from the textile/garment industry indicated that imported raw materials amounted to 90% and over of all raw materials used. The decline in this sector started during the oil boom with approximately 12% reduction in GDP during the period 1982–87. This was caused by the flooding of imported garments into the economy by travelers, particularly via the 'suitcase traders' discussed in Chapter 2.[5]

Nevertheless, a clue to this positive result of raw materials cost on profitability seems to lie in the movement of wages among these firms. To the extent that the garment industry employs a low-waged, largely female labour force, the negative effect of the devaluation on the cost structure could have been offset by positive effects due to the wage structure, and its ability to suppress wage increases during the period of adjustment. The average weekly earnings decreased by 20% in this sector between 1982–88, with a larger decline of 36% from 1988 to 1994 (Central Statistical Office, Economic Indicators Report, several years).

Table 8.2 gives selected indicators (median values) for 10+ size firms in the textile/garments industry looking at the pre-adjustment (1983–87) and adjustment years (1988–94). Although raw material to total expenses increased; the average wage per employee, wages to total expenses, employment, and output to employment decreased from the pre-adjustment period to the adjustment period.[6]

Thus, the figures in Table 8.2 and the trend in the average weekly earnings tend to suggest that a positive result of devaluation on profitability among these firms in the garment industry, acting through the cost of imported raw materials, could have been due to savings in the wage bill of these firms, and not necessarily due to productivity gains. Referring back to the analyses in the previous chapter, declining wages were identified as a factor used by some activities/size groups to maintain competitiveness in the face of devaluation and other macroeconomic changes.

As seen in Chapter 7, the industry trend in this sector for output to employment showed some measure of decline during the earlier adjustment period, with fluctuations for the remaining adjustment period. In general, there was the tendency towards an inverse association between changes in RER and raw material expenses ratio as well as with the average wage.

The (qualitative) survey conducted in 1995/96 showed that while most of the garment manufacturers complained about the negatives effects of trade liberalization and devaluation, as well as about 'suitcase traders', one garment manufacturer had the contrasting view that the industry gained through a devaluation relative to the price competitiveness of its labour. He pointed out that as a result of the devaluations, there was increase in price competitiveness without necessarily increases in quality or efficiency of production. The predicted versus actual values for this regression are given in Figure 8.2 which shows a more even distribution of the points compared to the plot for the food processing industry.

Table 8.2 Comparison of selected indicators for firms 10+ employed: Textile/garments and related activity (median values)

Indicator	Pre-adjustment period 1983–87	Adjustment period 1988–94
Average wage	0.0111	0.0088
Wages to total expenditure	0.2618	0.2148
Raw material to total expenses	0.450	0.5087
Employment figures	36.0	35.0
Output to employment	0.0410	0.0405
No. of firms	127	211

Source: Survey of business establishments and own worksheets.

Printing and paper converters

For the printing and paper converters, the local asset ratio (*LLOCC*) had a positive effect on profitability. The ratio of debt to total assets (*LIBB*) was a significant and negative factor. However, highly leveraged firms (*D*11*LLIBB*), low leveraged firms (*D*12*LLIBB*), and those with relatively high interest expenses ratio (*D*21*LINTER*) displayed a positive impact on profitability. Hence, unlike the case of the food processing sector, users of very high/low leverage saw their profitability enhanced. In the case of highly leveraged firms, it is presumed that these firms have easy and preferential access to credit in this sector; while the low leverage firms rely mainly on their own funds for working capital and investment purposes.

Wood and related products

For wood and related products, changes in raw material expenses (*LRAW*) had a positive impact on profitability. Interest payments (*LINTER*) and very high leverage (*D*11*LLIBB*) also returned positive results on profitability, while local assets had a negative impact on profitability. The positive raw material result for firms in this industry is not surprising since this sector is partly dependent on local raw materials (local wood) as a major part of its inputs. In addition, the reversal of the results for firms with high leverage use made it similar to the high leveraged firms in the printing and packaging sector.

Firms that use very high leverage seemed to have increased profitability in the process, with associated increases in interest payments moving in the same direction as profitability. The high users of leverage actually comprised 7 firms, 5 of which were very large firms with 100+ employment. In addition, only 2 of these firms obtained long-term loans from banks as part of their liability portfolio. Five out of the 7 firms relied on sources other than commercial banks for long-term loans, with accounts payable, short-term loans, and overdraft being present among the liabilities in all cases.

Chemicals and related

In the chemical and related sector, the raw material expenses (*LRAW*) ratio was significant and positive: the lower the ratio of raw material to total expenses (*D*31*LRAW*), the less positive the impact on profitability.

The liabilities to total assets (*LLIBB*) variable was a significant and negative factor in explaining profitability, though low leveraged firms (*D*12*LLIBB*) experienced a less negative impact with this variable being significant and positive.

Unlike the textiles industry, the rationale for the positive impact of LRAW on profitability is not just the use of the wage rate. Based on interviews conducted, the positive impact appears to also originate from the passing on of cost to the consumer as well as the export thrust of firms in these sectors. Thus, the offsetting positive effects of increases in raw material expenses exceeded its negative effects.

Assembly and related

The assembly and related sector results showed a negative effect of interest expenses (*LINTER*), of liabilities to total assets (*LLIBB*), with a more negative impact on the profitability of firms with very high leverage (*D*11*LLIBB*). Firms with relatively low raw material expenses (*D*31*LRAW*) had a more positive impact on profitability than those with a high ratio of raw material to total expenses.

This sector experienced high negative growth in the post-oil boom period. Noted also for high import content of raw materials in the manufacturing process, it was expected that the raw material to total expenses ratio would have shown significant in the model. However, the significance of the dummy variable reflecting differences of firms relative to the ratio of raw material to total expenses compensates for the lack of significance of the raw material variable.

The impact of high interest expenses and increased indebtedness seemed to have overshadowed the effect of raw materials increases in this sector.

Miscellaneous manufacturing

For miscellaneous manufacturing, the coefficient of *LLIBB*, *LRAW* and *LRECPROD* were significant and negative. As explained for the other industries *LRAW* reflects the impact of the increase in raw material expenses, due to the exchange rate policy, on profitability, with this variable (*LRAW*) being consistently negative across all industries. Similarly the variable *LLIBB* reflects the impact of indebtedness also on profitability with a significant negative result reflecting that profitability decreased as size of firm increased in this industry.

Foreign firms: The effect on LNEW2A (by size group)

For the foreign firms, an analysis based on *size group* was necessary. These results are discussed below.

< 10 employment size group

For the foreign firms with <10 employed, a significant and positive result was obtained for the impact of the raw material expenses (*LRAW*) variable on profitability (*LNEW2A*), with a negative impact being shown in the interest expenses variable (*LINTER*). The positive result supports the view that foreign firms tend to be in a more favourable position than local firms relative to the purchase of raw materials, since they can be assisted by parent-affiliates abroad and they have less problems with acquisition of foreign exchange to purchase imported materials. Although having a smaller scale of operation, these foreign firms experienced a positive impact based on changes in raw material expenses.

10–24 and 25–49 size groups

For firms in the 10–24 and 25–49 size groups, *LLIBB* assets to total assets had a significant and negative impact on profitability. Thus, these two groups of firms did not escape the effect of problems with indebtedness during adjustment. Despite the notion that some of the foreign firms do not borrow locally, firms in these groups showed an inclination towards local borrowing from banks and other sources. This was reflected in the composition of local liabilities of these firms, which showed a preference for short-term loans and overdraft.

50–99 firm size

In the 50–99 size group, *LLOC* had a positive effect on profitability. Some of these foreign firms invested in financial assets and benefited from increased interest rates.

100+ firm size

For the largest size group of foreign firms (100+), *LLIBB*, *LINTER* and *LLOCC* had negative effects on profitability. Size of firm also mattered within this size group. The large foreign firms seemed therefore to be adversely affected during the period of adjustment.

8.3.2 Regression results on investment of firms

Local firms (by size group)

< 10 firm size (by year)

The regression results reported by years on investment to total assets for the smaller local firms employing <10 persons showed a mix of positive and negative results over time. The only positive result on *LRAW* to total expenses was recorded in 1989, following the 1988 devaluation.

The interest expenses variable (*LINTER*) had a negative impact on investment in 1986, a pre-adjustment year of crisis, as well as in the adjustment years of 1989 and 1994. Changes in interest payments had a positive effect on investment in the adjustment years of 1990/91 and 1993. The liabilities ratio (*LLIBB*) was significant and negative relative to investment in 1986 and 1987 and positive in 1984 and 1989, showing that there was some positive effect on investment by use of leverage in the immediate post-oil boom period and in an early adjustment year.

The other asset structure variable, the local assets ratio, had a positive effect on investment in the pre-adjustment years of 1984 and 1986; but negative effects in the adjustment years of 1989 and 1992. This may reflect greater problems with the asset base of the firm during adjustment such that it could not support investment. Size of firm (*LBFIXASC*) – fixed assets – mattered relative to the investment thrust even within this group of small firms, with larger firms having a more adverse investment impact in 1989, 1990 and 1991, i.e. the larger the firm the lower the investment thrust during these years. A reversal of this pattern, however, occurred in 1986 and 1994, with larger firms being able to have a greater investment drive than smaller firms

Thus, the importance of local assets during the adjustment years suggested that the tight cash flow situation brought on by tight monetary and fiscal policy led to the accumulation of stocks as well as accounts receivable which could have hampered the capacity of firms to invest.

Profitability had a negative impact on investment during the adjustment years of 1990 and 1993, but a positive effect in 1992. Uncertainty in the economic polices of 1993 as well as both political and economical policies in 1990 could have also been responsible for the failure of profitability to have a significant impact on investment in those years. The year 1990 was politically turbulent in Trinidad & Tobago with labour unrest and an attempted insurrection against the government.

10–24 size group (by industry)

For printing and paper converters, the cost structure of raw materials was a significant factor, with a positive impact on investment. Interest payments showed a positive result in food processing, suggesting that this industry was a positive beneficiary of preferential interest rates for investment purposes. The debt structure of the firm was, however, a negative factor on investment despite the positive result for interest payments. Profitability was able to enhance investment in the food processing sector.

Positive effects on investment in the chemical industry were obtained from the debt/asset structure variable through the effect of the liabilities ratio. However, size of firm mattered in this industry with larger firms tending to have larger investment (*LBFIXASC*).

Miscellaneous manufacturing also showed that size of firm was important with a positive result on *LBFIXASC*, while the local asset ratio had a negative effect on investment. In the textiles industry, the only significant result in this size group was the negative effect of the local asset ratio on investment.

25–49 size group

In the 25–49 category, which contained more medium-sized local firms, the results showed that the ratio of raw materials to total expenses (*LRAW*) and *LIBB* – liabilities to total assets – had no effect on investment. There were negative effects due to the interest expenses (*LINTER*) and local assets (*LLOC*). Firm size was a significant factor (*LBFIXASC*) with investment decreasing with increasing firm size. Firms with lower interest payments to total expenses (*D21LINTER*) were able to have a less negative impact on investment relative to interest rate changes.

The profitability (*LNEW2A*) of the firm also had a positive impact on investment. Thus, for these larger firms, increases in the interest rate played a negative role in investment and a less negative role for firms with lower interest expenses. Expected gains in efficiency as a result of relative price movements therefore did not materialize among these firms since the exchange rate was not a significant factor. Among the liabilities of these firms were accounts payable and other local liabilities.

50–99 size group

The results for the 50–99 size group, which represents some of the medium to larger local firms, had to be analysed by activity. In the food processing/ drink sector, the profitability (*LNEW1A*) of the firm was a significant and positive factor in determining investment as well as the use of leverage (*LIBB*), which had a negative effect on investment. In textile/garments, none of the explanatory variables were significant. In printing and paper products, the local assets ratio (*LLOC*) had a significant and negative effect on investment, while firm profitability (*LNEW1A*) was significant and positive. The asset/ debt structure of the firm was significant in the chemical and related activity with the use of leverage enabling investment while local assets had a significant and negative impact.

Raw materials to total expenses (*LRAW*) and interest expenses (*LINTER*) had significant and negative effects on investment in the assembly industry. There were differences in the effect by firm size, with the smaller firms within this group being able to invest less than the larger ones. Firm profitability was also a significant and positive factor affecting the assembly sector. Thus, among these medium to large firms, relative price signals as reflected through factors in the cost structure were either not important in the investment response of firms, or where they were, the effect was negative. Use of leverage differed by activity, while profitability was a positive factor in some firms as discussed in Chapter 7.

100+ size group

The results for the 100+ size category of local firms showed that interest expenses had a negative effect on investment, with firms with lower interest expenses being in a more favourable position relative to the investment response as shown in the result of *D22LINTER*. While the use of leverage enabled investment through the significant and positive result of *LLIBB*, for firms with very high leverage use (*D11LLIBB*), the effect of liability was reversed, so that *D11LLIBB* had a negative effect on the investment response.

Local assets also had a negative effect on these firms' investment response, with profitability contributing positively. Within this group, there were differences of investment based on size of firm (*LBFIXASC*), with larger firms having a larger investment response. Thus, while there were differences between firms of different size groups, there were also within group differences such that the investment thrust was positive the larger the firm.

Investment in the qualitative data occurred amongst 70% of the firms. The main reasons given for investment were the replacement of obsolete equipment, retooling, wear and tear and general plant upgrading which together accounted for 33% of the responses. Activity diversification in response to export demand accounted for 18% of the responses. The installation of modern equipment was done with the expectations of future profitability of the firm and also to increase efficiency relative to capacity, speed and functions. Investment also implied reduced need for labour, particularly unskilled labour. This was despite increases in costs of imported inputs, which was also indicated as affecting investment in the qualitative survey. Thus, for some firms investment was influenced by a shift from labour intensive to capital intensive production.

Foreign firms and investment response (by size groups)

<10 and 10–24 size groups

For the smallest size group of foreign firms (<10), the only significant factor affecting investment was the negative impact of raw material expenses, in contrast to its effect on profitability. Thus, it would seem that any gains from raw material purchases are favourable for profitability but do not lead to increased investment. In the 10–24 category, interest payments had a negative impact on investment.

25–49, 50–99 and 100+ firm size groups

Raw material expenses and profitability showed positive effects on investment for the 25–49 size group. In the 50–99 size group, liabilities to total asset and profitability were significant and positive relative to investment. Similar to the 25–49 size group, the 100+ group of firms showed that raw material expenses and profitability had positive effects on investment. However, the liability situation of the firm was a negative factor on investment in this size group, which was a reversal of the result for local firms in the same size group.

Table 8.3 Summary of results obtained in regression on LNEW2A (net profit after tax to sales)

Variable *LNEW2A* (profit to sales)	Cost structure		Debt/asset structure		Size of firm
	Raw materials purchases	Interest expenses	Liabilities	Current local assets	(value of production)
Local firms					
<10 by years	Neg. effect in 1984, 1988 and 1994	Neg. effect in 1984, 1987 Pos. effect in 1994	Neg. effect in all years excld.1988 & 1993	No effect	Negative effect in 1988 pos. effect in 1984, 1986 & 1994
10+ (by industry)	Neg. effect in food process. & misc. Pos. effect in textiles	Neg. effect in textiles & assembly, Pos. effect in food & chemical	Neg. effect in assembly, printing, chemical & misc. Pos. effect in wood	Pos. effect in printing	Neg. effect in miscellaneous Pos. effect in printing & chemical
Foreign firms					
<10	Pos. effect	Neg. effect	No effect	No effect	No effect
10–24	No effect	No effect	Neg. effect	No effect	No effect
25–49	No effect	No effect	Neg. effect	No effect	No effect
50–99	No effect	No effect	No effect	Pos. effect	No effect
100+	No effect	Neg. effect	Neg. effect	Neg. effect	Pos. effect

8.3.3 Regressions of structural factors incorporating relative prices

In this section, regressions are reported for two of the variables in the cost/asset structure of the 10+ firms in assembly, food processing, and textiles/garments, in which key price relatives are included among the dependent variables. The results on total local liabilities to total assets (*LLIBB*) and total interest payments (*LINTER*) are given in Tables 8.18 and 8.19 at the end of the chapter and refer to the models in equations 8.3 and 8.4 given previously in this chapter.

The sectors were chosen in order to maintain consistency with those analysed in Chapter 7. The choice of size groups 10+ is due to the inability to pool data over time for the <10 firms. The significance of this feature is that the price relatives (the real exchange rate and the real lending rate) are yearly indicators rather than firm-specific indicators which ren-

Table 8.4 *Summary of regression results: Investment of firms*

Variable *LINV*1 (investment to assets)	Cost structure		Asset structure		Size variable (fixed assets)	Profitability ratio
	Raw materials purchases	Interest expenses	Local liabilities ratio	Curr. local assets ratio		
Local firms						
<10 (by year)	Pos. in 1989	Neg. effect in 1986, 1989, 1994 Pos. in 1990, 1991, 1993	Neg. effect in 1986, 1987 Pos. in 1984 & 1989	Neg. effect in 1989,1992. Pos. effect in 1984, 1986	Neg. effect in 1989,1990 & 1991 Pos. in 1986 & 1994	Neg. effect in 1990, 1993 Pos. in 1992
10-24 (by industry)	Pos. in printing	Pos. in food processing	Neg. in food processing Pos. in chemical	Neg. effect in textiles, misc.	Pos. in chemical, miscellaneous	Pos. in food processing
25-49 size (all years & activities)	No effect	Neg. effect	No effect	Neg. effect	Neg. effect	Pos. effect
50-99 size (by activity)	Neg. effect in assembly & related	Neg. effect in assembly & related	Neg. effect in food processing, pos. in chemical	Neg. effects in printing & packaging & chemicals & related activities	Pos. effect in assembly & related	Pos. effect in food process., printing/ paper converters, & assembly and related
100 + size (all years & activities)	No effect	Neg. effect	Pos. effect. Firms with high leverage significantly different neg. impact	Neg. effect Firms with low current asset significantly different pos. effect	No effect	Pos. effect Firms with higher profitability significantly different neg. effect on investment
Foreign firms						
<10	neg. effect	No effect	No effect	No effect	No effect	No effect
10-24	No effect	Neg. effect	No effect	No effect	No effect	No effect
25-49	Pos. effect	No effect	No effect	No effect	No effect	Pos. effect
50-99	No effect	No effect	Pos. effect	No effect	No effect	Pos. effect
100+	Pos. effect	No effect	Neg. effect	No effect	No effect	Pos. effect

ders it impossible to use them where data is being analysed for individual years.

While the real exchange rate is a macroeconomic indicator that affects all firms, the real lending rate as an indicator of interest rates faced by firms is not so accurate. As pointed out in this research, this is due to the existence of differentials in the rates charged by banks and other financial institutions to firms based on size, traditional links, and so on. In so far as the median interest rates are used, this is the best available point estimate that can be used to assess the effect on some of the intermediate structural variables such as liabilities and interest payments. However, these limitations reinforce the research strategy to use *actual variables in the cost and asset structure that truly reflect changes in costs (such as interest payments and total liabilities) when evaluating the impact of macroeconomic changes*. Thus, these additional results are used to demonstrate that these structural factors are in fact affected by relative price changes, a theme that was already explored when linking RER and RLEND to these factors in Chapters 5 to 7.

In the case of local liabilities (*LLIB*), the real lending rate was significant and positive in the assembly industry, implying that liabilities increase in this industry with increases in the real rate of interest. Increasing profitability led to decreasing liabilities in food processing which seems to support the view that in firm-level studies it is often shown that leverage decreases as firm profitability increases (Tenjo 1995).

There was also a negative relationship between increases in investment and leverage for the textile/garment industry suggesting that firms in this sector do not enter into debt for the express purpose of increasing investment.

The real lending rate was shown to be a significant factor relative to changes in interest payments in the case of the textiles/garment sector with increases in the lending rate leading to increasing liabilities in this sector. In all three sectors, liabilities led to increases in interest payments, which was not an unexpected result.

Based on the above results, the following section delves a little deeper into the issue of firm response during adjustment.

8.4 Adjustment Patterns of Firms

In light of the empirical results obtained and using qualitative information from other sources, a further evaluation is made of the response of firms to adjustment. Since one of the aims of this research is to assess the impact of adjustment policies on firms, the discussion will centre around the policy issues that are reflected in the results and will also incorporate other adjustment policies relevant to explaining the adjustment process of firms.

8.4.1 Exchange rate policy: Responses by firms to changes in costs of raw materials

The results of the regression showed that for small firms, raw material expense changes had a negative impact on profitability, while the effects on investment were mixed. Among the larger firms, the industry results from raw material changes differed relative to the direction of the impact.

Based on the qualitative survey, some firms which were already in export markets indicated that they were able to benefit by being more price competitive relative to their CARICOM (Caribbean Community) neighbours as a result of the 1993 devaluation. Out of 30 firms in this qualitative survey, 47% indicated that the effect of devaluation was negative, 23% felt it was positive, and 23% thought that the overall effect was mixed: both positive and negative. Furthermore, approximately 93% of the firms recorded increased costs of imported inputs, with 26% of firms also experiencing increased cost of capital equipment and 20% experiencing increased debt service burden.[7]

Table 8.5 Perceived effects of the devaluation: Qualitative survey, 1995/96

Effect of devaluation	Percentage
Positive	47
Negative	23
Mixed	23
No effect	7

Source: 1995/96 survey of establishments – own survey.

Thus, an explanation for the differences in the results relative to raw material expenses is also reflected in these responses: despite increases in raw material costs, the perceptions were almost evenly distributed between negative and mixed/ positive effects.

As far as the positive effects of the devaluations: about 33% of the firms stated that they stepped up production for exports; 23% had more profitable exports; while 20% had a mix of positive and negative effects such as more profitable exports (without volume increase), increased competitiveness, reduced labour costs, loss on foreign payments, etc. Thus, it would appear that devaluation facilitated the export thrust of some of the larger firms.[8]

According to some of the larger firms, speculation through the accumulation of foreign currency with the expectation of a devaluation was also used as a mechanism to enhance profitability. Most of the larger firms were allowed to keep US accounts even prior to the 1993 floating-of-the-dollar policy that made this feature more universal in the economy. Thus, there were offsetting activities that might have balanced the negative effects of the devaluation.

Firms exercised cost reduction and export-oriented responsesin order to minimize the negative effects of the 1998 and 1993 devaluations. Among some of the popular responses/strategies that were indicated by firms in the qualitative survey were the search/purchase of cheaper raw materials (23%), the move into new export markets (37%), and increased production in existing export markets (27%).[9]

While some firms reacted to the exchange rate policy only after it occurred, the larger firms and foreign firms were more proactive in their approach. In addition, the larger and the foreign-owned firms were able to hold US$ accounts and did not suffer as a result of the devaluation and floating of the dollar. On the contrary, these firms recorded gains on foreign exchange transactions.

Consequently, the search for new export markets, quality improvements in their products, and so on were not in some cases a response to the devaluation but rather a response to the reduced domestic demand brought on by the general economic downturn of the 1980s. This period that followed the decline in oil prices was marked by a fall in government expenditure and public sector wages as well as increasing unemployment. In some cases, the search for export markets was therefore part of a pre-emptive strategy by firms to survive in the face of declining demand.

Other responses mentioned from the qualitative survey to counteract the effect of increasing raw materials costs involved reduction in the purchasing and the holding of stocks of raw materials (demand-purchasing) and evaluation and adjustment of the production process in order to reduce cost. The evaluation of the production process was done in response to both trade liberalization and devaluation. However, rigidity of the production structure might have rendered the reduction of employment and wages as the only viable options open to the firms.

There were also indications that firms passed on the cost of imported materials to customers. While firms might have initially refrained from adopting this approach, eventually prices had to be increased by the amount of the devaluation in order to maintain profitability. Available export programmes arranged through foreign governments were another mechanism by which exports were facilitated. One such programme came from the Caribbean Basin Initiative (CBI) under the auspices of the American government and comprised the assembly of garments, with components (completely knocked down units – CKDs) that were produced in the United States and the sale of the assembled garment to a buyer in that country. This response was seen as a mechanism by which the firm was able to survive in the face of declining domestic production.[10]

The question of reduced purchasing of raw material leads to the feature of excess capacity of firms. From the qualitative survey, capacity utilization rates for 1994 showed that approximately 34% of the firms indicated that they operated at full or near full capacity, 59% indicated between 50–75% capacity, 7% 25–49% capacity, and 3% almost no production at all. Capacity utilization was closer to 50% or under for the relatively smaller firms in this survey, with a couple of these firms having high rates and taking part in special programmes under the CBI, which involved garment assembly.

Reduction in labour was also explained from the perspective that firms took advantage of the economic decline of the 1980s to reduce their permanent labour force in favour of contract labour, thus reducing their total wage bill and weakening and restricting the activities of trade unions in the process. Firms evaluating their production structures found that the rigidity reflected in the asset specificity of the capital investment rendered the reduction of employment as the only viable alternative. Consequently, the flexibility assumed by the neo-classical theory of the firm was not easily realizable.

Some offsetting responses to the devaluation, at least among the medium to larger firms, were already put in place as a result of contraction in the domestic economy at the onset of the application of adjustment. For the smaller firms, responses to the devaluations included borrowing more money due to increased debt, selling assets, evaluating production to reduce cost, purchasing less raw materials, updating technology and retooling.

As expected, these firms complained about high interest rates, tighter overdraft by banks, and problems with access to credit. Their responses were to restructure their loans, cut down on the collection days for sales, adjust their cash flow to eliminate the need for overdraft, freeze investment, and so forth. In cases where there was no problem with access, there were complaints about the cost of credit. The negative effect of *LLIBB* in the assembly and related industry relative to profitability and the differential effect of firms with large liability (*D*11*LLIBB*) in the 100+ group with respect to investment (negative) are reflected in the following information obtained on large firms in the motor vehicle assembly industry.

From traded to non-traded: The motor vehicle assembly activity – experiences of firms

The assembly of motor vehicles was one activity that disappeared with the 1993 devaluation of the local currency as well as the movements of the Japanese yen against the US dollar. It was cheaper to import completely built-up units (CBUs) rather than import parts as completely knocked down units (CKDs) and assemble them. This activity was therefore converted from a traded to a non-traded one with the firms changing from assembly to trading and new dealerships being created. The massive capital equipment which was asset-specific therefore became 'white elephants' and the firms as well as the groups to which some of them belonged were affected adversely to varying degrees.

Mergers and sale of some of the firms in the motor vehicle industry did not achieve the turnaround that was desired. As a result, adjustment through activity diversification and the consolidation of buildings to house various activities under one roof were strategies that were attempted prior to the creation of car dealerships. Questions were raised as to the suitability of this industry for a small country like Trinidad & Tobago in which the activity served the domestic market. This industry had begun in 1966/67 under the import-substitution industrial strategy in which incentives were given to industries that were able to create jobs.

At that time, all the local retailers turned to assembly following the establishment of the Neal & Massy assembly plant (The Neal & Massy Industries Ltd). This company closed its assembly operation in 1994 and was able to fully depreciate its equipment to zero.[11] Efforts were also made to sell machinery and equipment from the assembly plant but they were to no avail. The adversity which befell this firm was also channeled to the entire group of companies to which it belonged necessitating a group response.

As a group this firm disposed of approximately $TT16 million worth of assets in its Jamaican operations in 1994 and continued to do so through 1995 (TG, 20 December 1995). Sale of the Jamaican assets in 1994 along with sale of assets in Trinidad & Tobago through the consolidation of its local operations was expected to realize $TT100 million. The selling of assets was part of a debt-reduction programme which would have reduced interests costs described as too high. With respect to the assembly plant – a massive structure (350,000 sq. feet) on a 50-acre site – a great deal of its debt had to be written off by its commercial bankers, placing these banks in a precarious position at that time. This outcome highlights the issue of irreversible investment and the question of uncertainty about the future. This group continued to sell its subsidiary companies in Trinidad & Tobago and the Caribbean.

Another main producer in this industry ventured into attempts at producing rather than assembling cars for export with the aid of technology acquired from countries in East Asia. This company also had to give up its franchise to import and sell Toyota cars (after 30 years of ownership), selling its operations in this activity to Toyota Motor Corporation of Japan, which is now entirely handling the importation and distribution of motor vehicles in Trinidad.[12]

Thus, the impact of adjustment policies was not the same for all firms relative to size, activity and ownership. In the case of motor vehicle assembly, this activity moved from being a traded to a non-traded one, in contrast to the expectations of adjustment policies. These policies were intended to lead to increased profitability and investment in the traded sector by creating price signals in favour of traded prices. Firms belonging to 'groups' such as conglomerates with holding companies and subsidiaries experienced adjustment that bore a closer relationship to the mode of survival of the group as an entity rather than the survival of the individual firms. Sales of assets of subsidiary companies were commonplace in this respect, as was reduction in employment due mainly to massive losses and indebtedness.

Options of foreign firms

One major foreign firm is currently graded as 'a wait and see'. This means that decisions may be made by its parent company to close its local operations and relocate in another country depending on the state of the economy and the profitability of the firm. This foreign firm has changed part of its manufacturing activity to a non-traded one and has performed some labour-related cost-cutting exercises along with subcontracting of special activities.

The key point here is that there are differences in alternatives that are available to foreign firms in contrast to their local counterparts, and to foreign firms in contrast to local, family-owned firms whose concern is not just profit but maintaining a family tradition.

Phrased differently, the loci of decision-making of the foreign firms are lodged in the multinational head office or parent companies abroad. When the branches in foreign countries cease to be profitable or once tax concessions that were granted in the initial stages expire, the available alternatives are the closure of the plant or its relocation to another country, where it can be more profitable.

8.4.2 Responses to monetary and financial policy during adjustment

Though it was mentioned earlier that controls on interest rates were not a prominent feature of monetary and financial policy in Trinidad & Tobago, restrictions on capital transactions and selective credit controls as a part of a long-term policy implied that local interest rates were not a true reflection of world interest rates. Indirectly, therefore, there was a form of repression of interest rates.

The variables in the regression that are linked closely to the interest rate are *LINTER*, *LLIBB* and *LLOCC*. The impact on profitability and investment of these variables as seen in the previous section varied across firm characteristics. These variables all showed mixed results, with liabilities producing largely negative results on the profitability of small firms and with negative results by industry of the larger firms. There were mixed results for both small (over time) and large firms (by industry) relative to interest payments and profitability. The local assets variable was not significant relative to the profitability of smaller firms and was significant in two of the manufacturing sectors among the larger firms. These variables also produced varying results relative to investment based on firm size/activity over time.

In the overall results for the qualitative survey data, 60% of the firms thought that the interest rate had a moderate to very high and negative effect on their firms, with 40% of these indicating a very high effect. Thirty percent indicated that there were little or no effects of the interest rate policy. Ten percent indicated that the effect was positive with some firms highlighting the fact that they were able to benefit from substantial financial investments. Also from this data set, the effect of increased interest rates showed up in increased costs of overdraft, with firms experiencing cash flow problems and decreased profitability (50% of responding firms).

Smaller firms in general have greater difficulty in accessing credit because of greater collateral requirements, higher interest rates, and other bank charges. In the qualitative survey, out of 30 interviewed firms, there were only five small ones. The responses regarding access to credit before and after the start of adjustment were mixed; some firms said it was more problematic after adjustment, while others saw no change. One of the reasons given by the small firms that said that there was greater difficulty in accessing credit was the tightening of overdraft facilities by commercial banks. The ones that indicated no change in access before or after adjustment complained about discriminatory interest rates charged as well as collateral requirements which they were unable to meet.

As pointed out in Chapter 2, the perception of the banks is that these small firms are credit risks, that it is more costly to monitor their loans, and that they have difficulty in repaying loans. Thus, their traditional customers, who are usually larger (or foreign) businesses and have established relationships, are the ones favoured relative to loan access and lower interest rates. Hence in safeguarding their depositors' funds, the banks viewed smaller firms with suspicion relative to their ability to repay loans while well-established customers were able to benefit since they were seen as less of a credit risk. The mixed results on the interest rate in the <10 category in various years possibly reflect differences in the sample of firms selected in those years.

In the qualitative survey, indications were that the foreign-owned firms rarely borrowed from the local financial market, relying mainly on funds from their parent company abroad. However, in cases where the firms are joint ventures between a local and foreign partner or there is reasonably significant local ownership (partly foreign-owned), local borrowing occurred also at prime interest rates.

The sources of finance prior to the start of adjustment showed that 47% of the firms in the qualitative survey depended entirely on retained earnings for their long-term capital needs. Twenty-three percent depended solely on bank loans and approximately another 23% relied on a mixed portfolio of retained earnings and bank loans. About 7% of the firms used sources of finance such as share capital issue, depreciation, head office loans, and so on.

For the period after adjustment, 23% of the sample indicated that they relied on retained earnings for long-term financing, 20% highlighted bank loans as their main source of funding, and 50% stated that they relied on a combination of retained earnings and bank loans. In the period before 1988, the practice was to use retained earnings for long-term investment, but the post-1988 period saw the firms shifting to a mixed portfolio of retained earnings and bank loans as a source of funding.

Sixty percent of the firms thought that there was no problem with access to finance either before or after 1988, while 17% thought access to finance has been easier since 1988. Thirteen percent found that access to finance was more difficult, with 7% stating that they do not borrow locally.

These results are not completely surprising due to the heavier representation of the larger firms that normally have long-standing relationships with banks. Those firms who responded that access to credit was more difficult since 1988 thought that the indebtedness of the firm was so high that it rendered access to more funds very difficult. This would

Table 8.6 *Sources of funding for selected manufacturing firms, 1988 & 1994 (percentages)*

Source of credit	1988	1994
Retained earnings	47	23
Loans	23	20
Mixture of retained earnings & loans	23	50
Other	7	7

Source: Qualitative survey data, selected manufacturing, 1995/96.

have made it difficult for firms to invest. Greater liquidity in the system and access to shareholders' funds were some of the reasons given by those who thought that access to finance was easier since 1988. Included in this group would have been some persons complaining about the cost of credit and collateral requirements, i.e. access was possible but with constraints.

Financial speculation relative to the interest rate and exchange rate described earlier was another response that led to profitable outcomes for some of the large firms contributing to differences in the effects of adjustment within this group. Other responses for the larger foreign as well as local firms to increased interest rate charges included operating on a no-overdraft situation, the setting up of a debt collections department, and reducing collection days to increase the recovery of debt.

Problems with respect to the liability situation of the firms could have been the result of borrowing during the oil boom period and the ease with which the borrowing was obtainable particularly for the larger firms. On the other hand, smaller firms might have faced higher interest rates if they had been able to gain access to credit. In addition, the economic contraction following the end of the oil boom left firms with heavy liabilities and excess capacity. This situation was further aggravated by the devaluation of 1985. Thus, the implementation of adjustment policies found many firms in a position of indebtedness and unable to withstand further costs increases.

Furthermore, it appears that for some of the larger firms, ease of access to credit led to a situation of indebtedness which posed problems during the period of adjustment. This situation is reflected in the results of the investment equation for the 100+ firms, wherein the high use of leverage among these large firms was detrimental to the investment thrust. The larger well-established local firms boasted of generous interest rates charged by banks with which they had long-standing relationships. These preferential rates facilitated investment and should have insulated these firms from the severe negative effects of increasing interest rates caused by financial liberalization.

Moreover, the imposition of credit ceilings under tight monetary policy at the start of adjustment would have exacerbated the loss in profitability and investment by leading to economic contraction and fall in sales. Hence, ease of access to credit is not necessarily a good factor relative to its effect on the liability position of firms needing to restructure.

8.5 Conclusions

The effects of adjustment policies on profitability and investment acting through the cost and asset structure of firms clearly show that there are differences due to firm size, ownership and activity. This was reflected in the empirical results and supported by the responses of the qualitative survey data.

For the larger firms without much difficulty in accessing credit as well as for smaller firms with more limited access, the debt structure plays a significant role with respect to the effect of changes in the macroeconomic environment on profitability and investment. While there were positive results in two years of changes in the debt structure on profitability among the <10 size group, the results for the remaining years were negative. The results of the 10+ size group was consistently negative in every industry where the debt structure variable was significant but with some differences by industry with respect to firms that use very high or very low leverage.

There were mixed results on investment by size/industry. However, to the extent that firms are able to access funds without using extremely high leverage, investment can be facilitated as was brought out in the positive impact of *LLIBB* for the large local firms (100+) and the significant but negative results for the high leverage (*D*11*LLIBB*) local, large firms. Thus, from considerations of scale of operation, while one would expect a small firm to be able to adjust more flexibly than larger firms (as larger firms face higher hurdles relative to constraints of costs), rigidities in the production process, asset structure, and labour force of small firms pose problems in restructuring.

However, the options faced by smaller firms relative to their capacity to adjust may be fewer when faced with problems of credit access and may imply a faster transition to extinction. Thus, tight monetary policy, financial liberalization and import liberalization as prominent aspects of adjustment were policies that on average adversely affected firms in the private sector in Trinidad & Tobago, notwithstanding individual cases of successes among larger firms. Despite a high dependency on imported raw materials, these larger firms had traditionally been able to access export markets which also enabled a pro-active approach.

One of the main reasons why foreign firms will continue to produce appears to be that continued profitability must be assured. To the extent that they too utilize the domestic financial markets and have been affected by economic contraction, there were negative effects on profitability due to variables such as interest payments and the debt structure. However, among the foreign firms, there were differences based on firm size. For example, changes in raw material costs had a negative effect on investment for the <10 size group but positively affected the 25–49 and 100+ size groups. Profitability positively affected investment in the 25+ size groups of foreign firms and seems to support the point on the profit motive of these firms to continue operations and to invest.

For the local firms, the reason for remaining in operation appeared to be more that of survival with future expectations of profitability. Invariably, the local firms seem to have more at stake than just making a profit. Local firms literally have nowhere to go; they cannot be easily uprooted and transferred to another site. Staying in operation is a source of livelihood for the owners of these firms, some of which are family-owned. Thus, for them there is the desire to maintain the family tradition of being involved in a particular business activity. Despite reduced profitability there is a greater chance that the local firm will stay in operation with the hope of future expectations of increased profit

Incorporation of the real exchange rate and the real lending rates in regression equations of the debt structure and interest payments showed that increases in interest payments in the assembly industry and in the debt structure of textiles/garments firms were positively related to increases in the real lending rate of interest. Thus, in these two industries direct links between the price relatives and structural factors of cost and asset were observed.

In the context of adjustment, one must distinguish between three types of firms. First of all, there are the larger firms with advantages of capital, access to cheaper credit, and the necessary resources to aggressively penetrate lucrative export markets. These firms emit responses that make them better able to circumvent any adverse effects of adjustment and to make better use of any advantages that can be derived. Secondly, there are the foreign firms, with the resources and the support of their parent companies or affiliates; and thirdly, there are the local small to medium firms (some of which are family-owned), which are generally disadvantaged relative to access to resources and external markets.

In the regression results, the veracity of the hypothesis on heterogeneity of the private sector is reflected in the results with the distinctions by size, ownership and industry, implying that the private sector cannot be taken as a homogeneous group. Given the cost and asset structures of firms, flexible and successful economic restructuring is not an automatic outcome to relative price changes.

Based on the above analysis, the general picture which seems to emerge is that structural adjustment has led to some measure of fallout in the private sector. This is reflected in lower investment and profitability in response to the impact of relative prices on the cost/asset structure as well as the existing indebtedness of the firm at the point in time of adjustment. While there were instances of recovery among some firms and industries, there were simultaneous adverse effects on other firms/ industries. Ultimately, the point cannot be made that adjustment is good or bad for the private sector without further analysis of the kind illustrated in this chapter.

Table 8.7 Results of pooling tests for (LNEW2A) profitability variables

Variable	F-statistic	Critical F value	Results of pooling tests
Foreign/local	10.26	F6,2083=2.1	Cannot pool foreign and local firms
Local firms <10	4.44	F60, 423=1.32	Cannot pool years[1]
Local firms greater & equal to 10	1.3	F18, 1543=1.61	Can pool all firms as one size group.
	0.112	F54, 1195=1.34	Can pool all years excluding 1986.
	2.47	F36, 1221=1.439	Cannot pool activities
Foreign firms <10 (separately) to 10+ size	12.28	F18, 279=1.61	Cannot pool size groups[2]

Notes: 1. Local firms in the <10 categories; there are too few firms in the 1983 group.
2. Cells too small for further testing of activities within years for foreign firms.

Table 8.8 Results of pooling tests for investment variables

Variable	F-statistic	Critical F value	Results of pooling tests
Local firms	2.82	F7, 2016=2.01	Cannot pool foreign and local firms
<10	4.97	F56, 25=1.30	Cannot pool across years-1983, 1988 too few firms
greater than 10	2.58	F21,1320=1.57	Cannot pool across size groups
10–24	1.05	F70, 306=1.30	Can pool data across years
	2.28	F42,333=1.38	Cannot pool across activities
25–49 size group	1.307	F70, 281=1.3033	Can pool data across years
	1.299	F42,239=1.383	Can pool data across activities
50–99 size group	0.810	F70, 205=1.32	Can pool data across years
	2.16	F42, 261=1.38	Cannot pool across activities
100+ size group	0.939	F70, 234=1.30	Can pool data across years
	1.28	F42, 261=1.484	Can pool data across activities
Foreign firms <10 separate 10+	2.58	F21, 281=1,57	Cannot pool across size groups

Note: Subgroups of activities within year too small (<25 employed).

General notes to the tables that follow:

1. T-statistics are given in parentheses, with *–10%, **–5% and *** –1% indicating the level of significance of coefficients in all tables.

2. *D11LLIBB* = 1 if total liabilities to assets (*LIB*) was greater than or equal to 1, else 0. *D12LLIBB* =1 if *LIB* <0.5, else 0.

3. D21*LINTER* = 1 if the ratio of interest expenses to total expenses (*INTER*) was greater than or equal to 0.05, else 0. *D22LINTER*=1 if *INTER* <.01, else 0.

4. D41*LLOCC* = 1 if ratio of local assets to total assets (*LOC*) was less than 0.15, else 0.

5. D31*LRAW* = 1, if *RAW* (raw material to total expenses) was less than 0.20, else 0

6. D51*LNEW*1*A* = 1 if *NEW*1 (profit to total assets) <–0.10, else 0,

7. D52*LNEW*1*A* = 1 if *NEW*1 >=0.10, else 0,

8. D41*LLOC*, *D*12*LLIBB* = 1 if *LOC* <0.20, else 0.

9. Generally the linear model appeared to be suitable, however, individual partial plots of the residuals showed up individual or clusters of values that tended to be influential, changing the results relative to the significance of the explanatory variables. The use of dummy variables helped with the model specification, in some cases pre-empting the exclusion of influential points of leverage and outliers.

10. Other specific notes follow the tables to which they refer.

Table 8.9 *Results of regression on profit to total sales (LNEW2A): Local firms with <10 employed*

Variable	1984	1986	1987	1988	1989
LRAW	–0.148***	–0.007	0.01	–0.032***	0.0
	(–13.3)	(0.48)	(0.76)	(–3.6)	(0.3)
LINTER	–0.018***	–0.003	–0.019***	0.014***	–0.01
	(–6.67)	(–0.33)	(–3.5)	(4.07)	(–0.97)
LLIBB	–0.069***	–0.062***	–0.028***	0.021***	–0.026**
	(–2.8)	(–9.4)	(–4.5)	(4.24)	(–2.25)
LLOC	–0.004	0.0	–0.008	0.03	0.009
	(–0.827)	(–0.01)	(–1.1)	(0.48)	(0.71)
LRECPROD	0.146***	0.042***	0.006	–0.011***	–0.018
	(15.0)	(5.0)	(0.96)	(–2.68)	(1.3)
D11LLIBB					
D12LLIBB					
D21LINTER		–0.002			
		(–0.28)			
D22LINTER		0.004			
		(0.78)			
Constant	0.76***	0.91***	0.87***	0.97***	0.91***
	(39.3)	(24.1)	(31.2)	(62.7)	(26.6)
ht N	34	61	102	25	25
Adj-R Sq.	0.92	0.80	0.33	0.88	0.31
F	68.8	30.8	9.32	28.4	1.68

	1990	1991	1992	1993	1994
LRAW	0.033	–0.023	–0.027	–0.001	–0.19***
	(1.51)	(–1.05)	(–1.09)	(–0.13)	(–11.8)
LINTER	0.005	0.013	–0.001	–0.001	0.015**
	(1.3)	(1.27)	(–0.34)	(–0..55)	(2.34)
LLIBB	–0.056**	–0.048**	–0.016**	0.008**	–0.17***
	(–2.4)	(–2.54)	(–2.04)	(2.20)	(–16.5)
LLOCC	0.006	0.01	–0.013	0.0	0.012
	(0.25)	(0.38)	(–0.91)	(–0.06)	(0.71)
LRECPROD	–0.007	0.045	0.015	0.005	0.11***
	(–0.6)	(3.58)	(1.03)	(1.22)	(14.6)
Constant	0.90***	0.97***	0.92***	0.95***	0.61***
	(29.6)	(19.9)	(43.7.)	(61.1)	(13.4)
N	36	52	49	36	26
Adj-R Sq.	0.20	0.27	0.30	0.24	0.97
F	2.8	3.32	3.74	1.86	137.3

Table 8.10 Results of regression on profit to total sales (LNEW2A): Local firms with 10+ employed, by industry

Variable	Food, drink, tobacco	Textiles garments etc.	Printing, paper converters	Wood & related	Chemicals & related	Assembly & related	Miscel-laneous
LRAW	–0.09**	0.008**	–0.005	0.036***	0.057***	–0.006	–0.01*
	(–2.2)	(2.2)	(–0.80)	(4.47)	(4.19)	(–0.72)	(–1.68)
LINTER	0.004**	–0.003**	0.002	0.01**	0.003	–0.005**	0.001
	(2.0)	(–1.96)	(0.39)	(2.16)	(0.7)	(–2.0)	(0.29)
LLIBB	0.0	–0.004	–0.026***	0.0	–0.047***	–0.013**	–0.16**
	(–0.66)	(–1.5)	(–4.5)	(0.2)	(–3.7)	(–2.3)	(–2.2)
LLOCC	0.001	–0.005	0.008**	–0.012**	0.005	0.004	0.002
	(0.65)	(–1.64)	(2.0)	(–2.4)	(0.6)	(0.89)	(0.6)
LRECPROD	0.0	–0.001	0.007***	–0.002	0.006**	0.002	–0.005**
	(0.83)	(–1.13)	(4.1)	(–0.6)	(2.0)	(0.98)	(–2.3)
D11LLIB	–0.196***	–0.047**	0.096***	0.135***	0.01	–0.075***	0.044
	(–14.4)	(–2.2)	(4.7)	(2.65)	(0.2)	(–4.2)	(1.3)
D12LLIBB	–.007**	–0.002	0.024***		0.028)		0.003
	(–2.14)	(–1.46)	(4.5)		(2.7)		(0.36)
D21LINTER	0.003**	0.0	0.004*	0.0	0.001	0.0	–0.003
	(2.01)	(–0.48)	(1.9)	(0.095)	(0.3)	(0.2)	(–1.1)
D22LINTER	–0.002		0.0	–	–		–0.003
	(–1.45)		(–0.14)				(–1.1)
D31LRAW	0.0	–0.003	0.003	–	–0.06***	0.013**	
	(.020)	(–0.95)	(0.55)		(–4.6)	(2.1)	
D41LLOCC							
Constant	0.94***	0.94***	0.93***	0.99***	0.91***	0.91***	0.93***
	(96.4)	(146.8)	(57.3)	(50.5)	(50.5)	(69.3)	(45.7)
N	198	156	148	87	204	233	57
Adj-R Sq	0..66	0.17	0.27	0.22	0.21	0.26	0.34
F	37.1	3.78	5.12	4.48	5.87	9.93	2.66

Table 8.11 *Results of regression of LNEW2A: Foreign-owned firms by size groups*

Variable	Size group				
	<10	10–24	25–49	50–99	100+
LRAW	0.091***	0.016	–0.013	–0.004	–0.006
	(3.88)	(0.68)	(–0.57)	(–1.2)	(1.56)
LINTER	–0.022***	0.0	–0.002	0.002	–0.004***
	(–3.3395)	(0.21)	(–0.49)	(1.48)	(–2.7)
LLIBB	–0.006	–0.033***	–0.025***	–0.001	–0.014***
	(–0.295)	(–3.1)	(–2.47)	(–0.34)	(–6.05)
LLOCC	0.008	–0.004	–0.005	0.03***	–0.014**
	(0.575)	(–0.27)	(–0.24)	(5.18)	(–2.31)
LRECPROD	0.009	0.013	0.01	0.0	0.005*
	(0.689)	(1.2)	(0.87)	(0.14)	(1.86)
Constant	0.90***	0.92***	0.89***	0.97***	0.88***
	(38.9)	(33.9)	(26.6)	(64.51)	(87.1)
N	37	45	39	69	127
Adj-R Sq.	0.56	0.26	0.25	0.26	0.43
F	10.0	4.14	3.08	5.73	18.0

Table 8.12 Regression results of ratio of investment to total assets (LINV1): Local firms with <10 employed, 1983–94

Variable/ Year	1984	1986	1987	1989	1990
LRAW	–0.28	–1.06	0.032	2.66*	0.58
	(–0.41)	(–1.58)	(0.049)	(1.88)	(0.123)
LINTER	1.71	–1.66***	–0.052	–1.39***	0.43**
	(1.34)	(–2.91)	(–0.026)	(–5.15)	(2.14)
LLIBB	2.52***	–1.57**	–2.45***	4.88*	1.28
	(5.45)	(–2.29)	(–4.17)	(1.91)	(1.48)
LLOC	1.11*	1.6**	0.242	–7.43***	–.61
	(1.84)	(2.3)	(0.67)	(–3.09)	(–0.5)
LBFIXASC	1.05	0.89**	–0.19	–1.92**	–1.77***
	(1.44)	(2.35)	(–0.756)	(–2.189)	(–4.99)
LNEW1A	0.67	–9.91	–6.75	–62.4	–28.7***
	(0.21)	(–0.82)	(–1.327)	(–1.31)	(–2.51)
Constant	5.0**	8.97	7.04	87.5	44.6**
	(2.3)	(0.45)	(0.85)	(1.12)	(2.24)
N	28	34	67	19	38
Adj-R Sq.	0.66	0.30	0.21	0.74	0.42
F	9.91	3.36	3.96	9.71	5.53

	1991	1992	1993	1994
LRAW	0.21	0.268	0.35	–0.77
	(0.146)	(0.81)	(0.616)	(0.61)
LINTER	2.0***	–0.62	0.648***	–0.76*
	(2.7)	(–0.81)	(2.736)	(–1.8)
LLIBB	–0.14	1.14	–0.153	1.33
	(–0.27)	(1.078)	(–0.303)	(1.11)
LLOC	0.53	–2.59**	–0.364	1.04
	(0.90)	(–2.42)	(–1.106)	(1.12)
LBFIXASC	–1.9**	–0.106	–0.637	1.34***
	(–2.5)	(–0.01)	(–1.514)	(2.66)
LNEW1A	56.8	54.84***	–37.09**	–43.69
	(1.58	(2.98)	(–2.51)	(–0.76)
Constant	–91.4	–0.97***	58.9***	67.4***
	(–1.58)	(–3.16)	(24.6)	(2.68)
N	33	31	39	29
Adj-R Sq.	0.58	0.39	0.39	0.33
F	6.05	3.796	4.54	3.26

Table 8.13 Results of ratio of investment to total assets (LINV1): Local firms with 10–24 employed

Variable	Food, drink, tobacco	Textiles garments etc.	Printing, paper converters	Chemicals & related	Assembly & related	Miscel-laneous
LRAW	0.50	0.28	1.036***	0.18	–0.029	1.16
	(1425)	(0.44)	(2.89)	(0.48)	(–0.091)	(1.643)
LINTER	0.36**	–0.074	0.012	–025	–0.008	–0.12
	(2.44)	(–0.364)	(0.81)	(–1.61)	(–0.50)	(–0.37)
LLIBB	–1.19*	0.52	–0.27	0.715**	0.227	–0.219
	(–2.52)	(1.02)	(–0.79)	(2.27)	(–.824)	(–0.347)
LLOCC	0.51	–2.003**	–0.12	–1.88	–0.35	–0.52*
	(1.11)	(–2.50)	(0.32)	(–0.57)	(–1.37)	(–1.72)
LBFIXASC	–0.33	–0.33	–0.87	0.53***	0.077	0.77***
	(–0.78)	(–0.78)	(–0.42)	(2.77)	(0.38)	(2.95)
LNEW1A	40.19**	–14.7	0.02	–2.93	–11.08	21.6
	(2.11)	(–1.32)	(0.39)	(–0.41)	(–0.84)	(1.0)
Constant	68.6**	19.23	–9.9	1.57	14.7	–36.96
	(2.19)	(1.04)	(–0.67)	(0.13)	(0.68)	(–1.035)
N	46	44	64	80	77	27
Adj-R Sq	0.27	0.16	0.06	0.13	–0.02	0.22
F	3.83	1.50	1.66	2.92	6.63	2.23

Table 8.14 Regression results of investment to total assets (LINV1): Local firms with 25–49 employed

	LRAW	*LINTER*	*LLIBB*	*LLOCC*	*LNEW1A*
Coefficients	0.12	–0.38**	0.074	–0.61***	17.4***
t-Statistic	(0.42)	(–2.50)	(–0.27)	(–3.02)	(2.69)
	LBFIXASC	*D11LLIBB*	*D12LLIBB*	*D21LINTER*	*D31LRAW*
Coefficient	–0.18*	0.23	0.22	0.15*	0.27
t-Statistic	(–1.88)	(0.23)	(0.86)	(1.73)	(1.08)
	Constant	N	Adj-R.Sq.	F	
Coefficient	–33.8	273	0.10	4.10	
t-Statistic	(–3.17)				

Table 8.15 *Regression results for investment to total assets (LINV1): Local firms with 50–99 employed*

Variable	Food, drink etc.	Textiles, garment s etc.	Printing, paper converters	Chemicals etc.	Assembly and related
LRAW	0.13	0.039	0.73	0.39	–0.59**
	(0.37)	(0.32)	(0.71)	(0.8)	(–2.16)
LINTER	0.2	–0.48	–0.25	–0.31	–0.38*
	(0.78)	(–0.66)	(–0.95)	(–1.24)	(–1.66)
LLIBB	–1.17**	1.20	1.55	1.63*	0.24
	(–2.01)	(1.06)	(1.38)	(1.83)	(0.55)
LLOCC	0.19	–2.3	–1.30*	–1.55**	0.79
	(0.31)	(–1.56)	(1.42)	(–2.43)	(1.9)
LBFIXASC	0.01	–0.29	0.37	–0.38	0.44*
	(0.32)	(–0.58)	(0.90)	(–1.57)	(1.71)
LNEW1A	46.8**	–27.9	26.2*	21.8	28.9*
	(1.98)	(–0.87)	(1.67)	(0.81)	(1.92)
Constant	–80.4**	40.9	–48.2	–39.6	–52.6**
	(–2.08)	(0.77)	(–1.92)	(–0.89)	(–2.11)
N	37	33	28	22	57
Adj-R Sq.	0.27	0.02	0.43	0.24	0.11
F	3.07	1.10	4.32	2.11	2.18

Note: Because of the small number of firms in the activities wood and related products and miscellaneous manufacturing, these regressions were not reported. These sectors are not noted for a large number of large firms.

Table 8.16 Regression results for investment to total assets (LINV1): Local firms with 100+ employed

	LRAW	*LINTER*	*LLIBB*	*LLOCC*	*LBFIXASC*
Coefficient	0.11	–0.42***	0.69***	–0.80***	0.18*
T-statistic	(0.47)	(3.65)	(2.68)	(–2.73)	(1.68)
	LNEW1A	*D11LLIBB*	*D12LLIBB*	*D22LINTER*	*D31LRAW*
Coefficient	41.6***	–3.33***	–0.24	0.15***	0.12
T-statistic	(4.64)	(.2.51)	(–0.93)	(2.30)	(0.64)
	D41LLOCC	*D51LNEW1A*	*D52LNEW1A*	Constant	
Coefficient	0.46***	0.21	–0.34*	–73.9	
T-statistic	(2.42)	(0.80)	(–1.62)	(–5.0)	
	n	Adj-R.Sq.	F		
	246	0.20	6.05		

Note: D11LLIBB=1 if LIB>=1 else 0. D22LINTER=1 if INTER <0.01 else 0.

Table 8.17 *Regression results for investment to total assets (LINV1): Foreign firms, by size group*

Variable	Size group				
	<10	10–24	25–49	50–99	100+
LRAW	−1.24**	1.66	1.1***	0.05	0.45**
	(−1.98)	(1.36)	(2.85)	(0.32)	(2.2)
LINTER	0.43	−0.43**	0.016	0.0	−0.06
	(1.41)	(−2.12)	(0.11)	(−0.01)	(−0.71)
LLIBB	0.73	0.13	−0.01	0.31*	0.28**
	(1.56)	(0.25)	(−0.02)	(1.8)	(2..3)
LLOCC	−0.42	−0.47	−0.86	0.19	−0.42
	(−0.57)	(−0.34)	(−1.5)	(1.0)	(−1.21)
LBFIXASC	−0.33	0.48	−0.21	0.11	0.11
	(−0.67)	(1.47)	(−0.8)	(1.02)	(1.3)
LNEW1A	37.9	−15.6	23.4**	22.2**	33.4***
	(0.83)	(−1.4)	(2.2)	(−2.3)	(5.7)
Constant	−64.5	21.4	−41.7	−40.2	−59.1
	(−0.85)	(1.2)	(−2.4)	(−2.54.13)	(−6.2)
N	40	38	47	80	74
Adj-R Sq	0.37	0.23	0.30	0.27	0.41
F	3.21	1.55	2.8	4.44	7.56

Table 8.18 Regressions of total local liabilities to total assets (LLIBB): Selected industries

Variable	Food, drink etc.	Textiles, garments etc.	Assembly & related
LRER	–0.13	0.006	–0.35
	(–0.56)	(0.01)	(–0.83)
LRLEND	0.003	0.005	0.05*
	(0.15)	(–0.102)	(0.09)
LNEW2A	–3.72***	0.20	–1.66
	(–8.6)	(–0.17)	(–4.7)
LINV1	–0.005	–0.11***	–0.03
	(–0.39)	(–3.26)	(–1.5)
Constant	4.7	–3.3	3.0
	(3.8)	(–0.95)	(1.47)
N	198	118	181
Adj-R Sq.	0.32	0.09	0.14
F	22.1	2.65	7.39

Note: *LRER* and *LRLEND* are logs of previously defined variables *RER* – the bilateral real exchange rate with the US, and *RLEND* – the real lending rate of interest.

Table 8.19 Regressions of total interest payments to total expenses (LINTER): Selected industries

Variable	Food, drink etc.	Textiles, garments etc.	Assembly & related
LLIBB	0.87***	0.40***	0.66***
	(6.15)	(2.6)	(4.1)
LRER	0.70	–1.05	–0.97
	(0.73)	(–1.38)	(0.95)
LRLEND	–0.03	0.11*	–0.04
	(–0.44)	(1.81)	(–0.48)
D11*LLIBB*	0.91	0.99	–0.03
	(1.38)	(1.26)	(–1.5)
Constant	–6.9	2.5	1.5
	(–1.4)	(0.68)	(0.31)
N	183	155	207
Adj-R Sq.	0.26	0.17	0.19
F	15.6	4.9	11.5

Figure 8.1 *Scatter of predicted versus actual values of* LNEW2A*: Local firms >10, food processing/drink/tobacco industry*

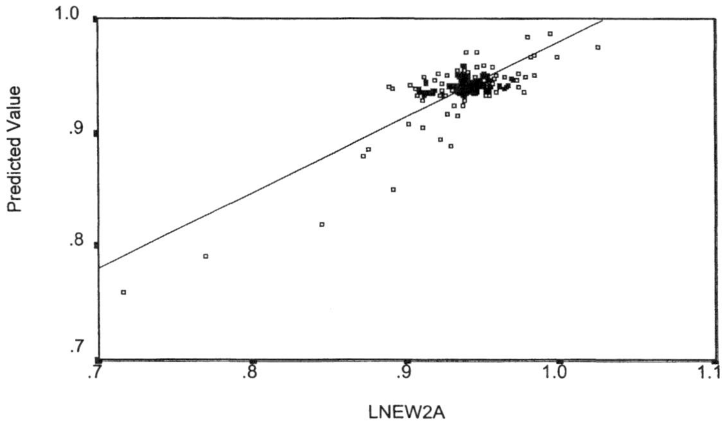

Figure 8.2 *Scatter of predicted versus actual values of* LNEW2A*: Local firms >10, textiles/garments industry*

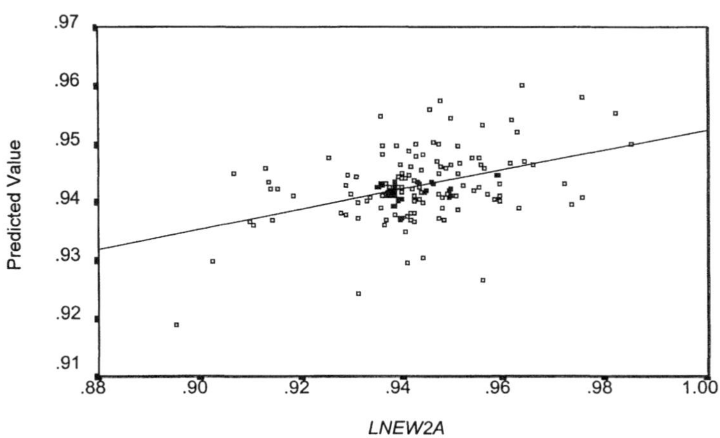

Figure 8.3 *Scatter of predicted versus actual values of LNEW2A: Local firms >10, printing and paper converters industry*

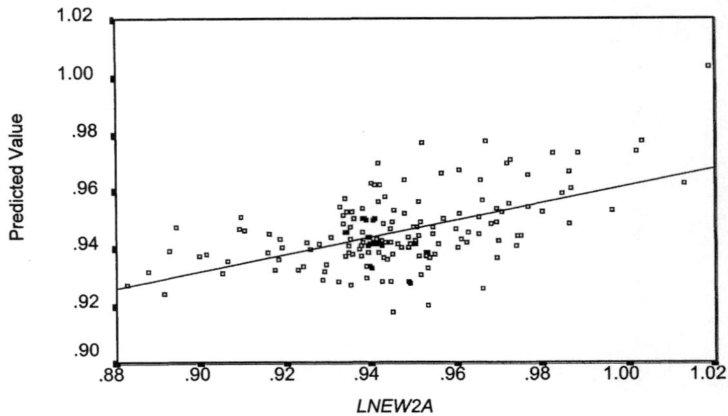

Figure 8.4 *Scatter of predicted versus actual values of LNEW2A: Local firms >10, wood and related industry*

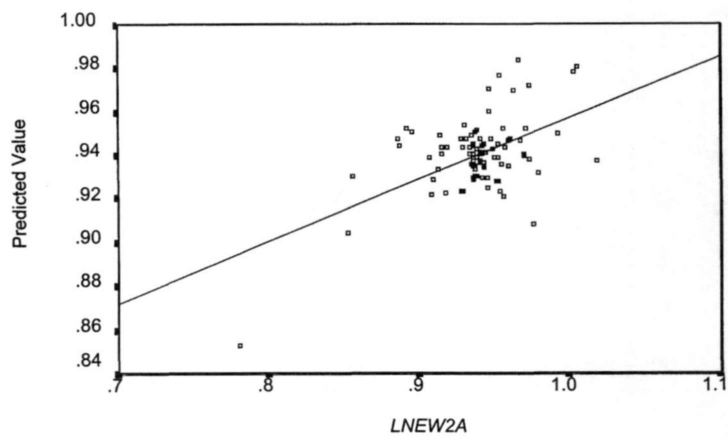

Figure 8.5 *Scatter of predicted versus actual values of* LNEW2A*: Local firms >10, chemical and related industry*

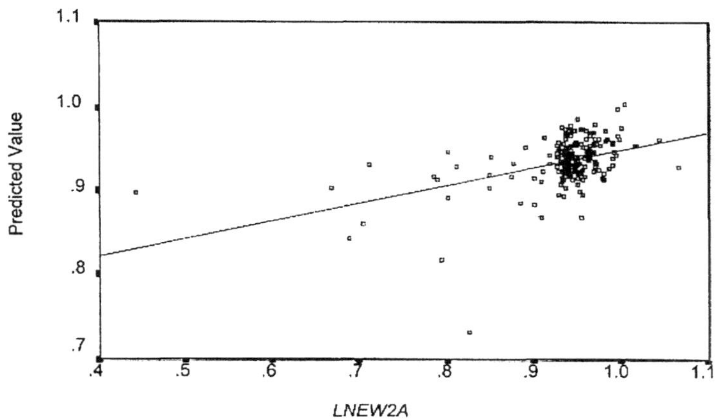

Figure 8.6 *Scatter of predicted versus actual values of* LNEW2A*: Local firms <10, 1987*

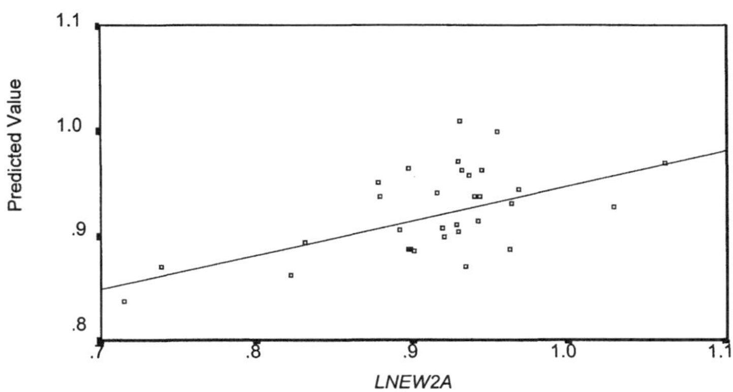

Note: Cases weighted by W1

Figure 8.7 *Scatter of predicted versus actual values of* LINV1: *Foreign firms 25–49*

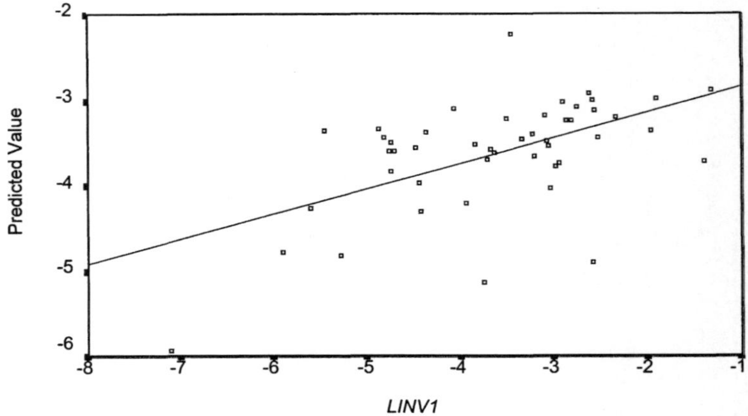

Figure 8.8 *Scatter of predicted versus actual values of* LINV1: *Foreign firms 50–99*

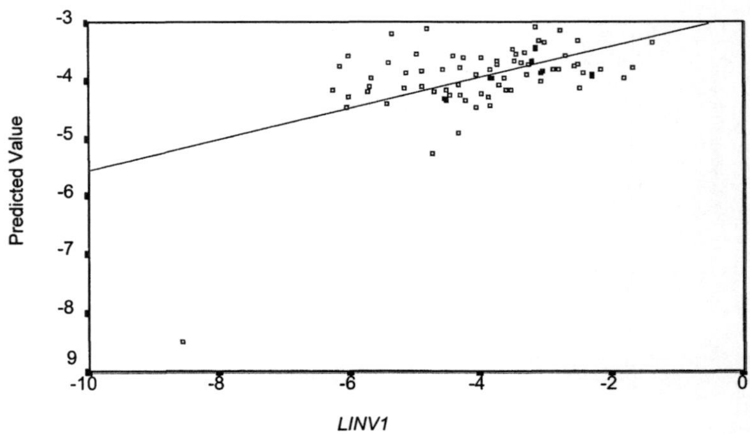

Figure 8.9 *Boxplot of studentized residuals of LINV1: Foreign firms 50–99*

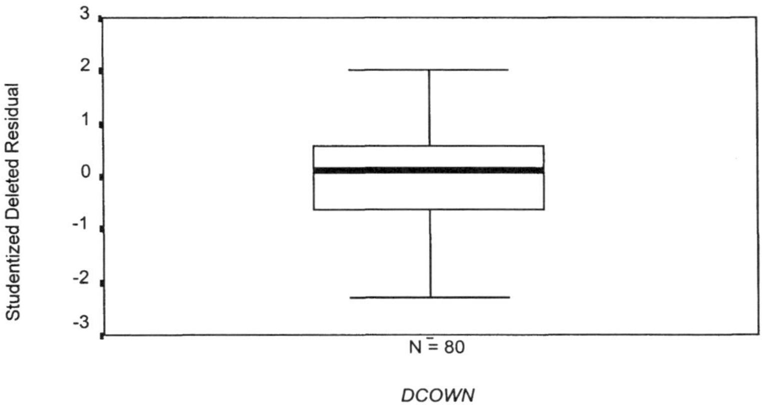

Figure 8.10 *Scatter of predicted and actual values LINV1: Foreign firms 100+*

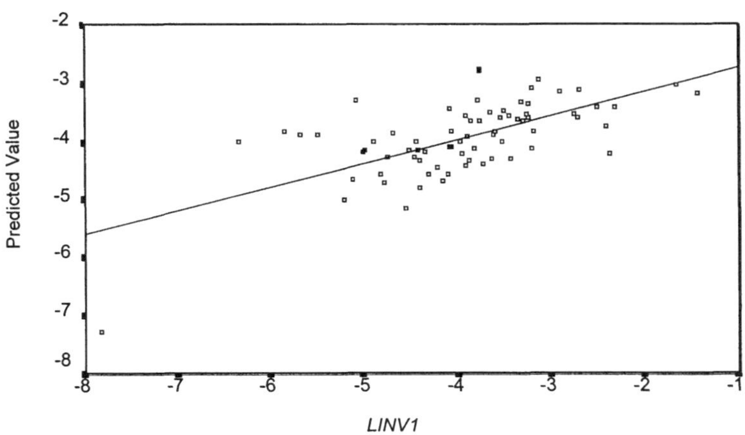

Notes

1. This survey will be referred to as the 'qualitative survey' or the 'survey of establishments, 1995/96'.
2. The frequencies within some of these characteristics proved to be an obstacle in the implementation of some of these tests, i.e. these tests may not be feasible for very small number of firms within these groupings.
3. For some ratios, it was not necessary to deflate.
4. The *DFBETAS* are new variables created for each term in the regression equation representing the change in the coefficient of that term if a specific case is deleted. The studentized deleted residual is the residual when a specific case is deleted from the calculation of the regression equation.
5. These traders got their name through their manner of importing garments from North America, Margarita, Curaçao etc. in large suitcases at a minimal duty, for resale on the streets or in makeshift malls. Invariably, some of these operators are sometimes funded or assisted by relatives abroad – some of whom do the actual transportation of the items.
6. Although the same firms are not being compared in the two periods – i.e. a panel – the firms are of the same employment size group and activity, in line with the comparisons performed in Chapters 5–7.
7. These percentages do not add up to 100 since firms may have indicated more than one effect.
8. As mentioned in Chapter 5, the sample was biased in favour of larger firms, with approximately 84% of the sample employing 10 or more persons on average in 1988 and 1994.
9. These responses also do not add up to 100 since one firm might have carried out more than one strategy.
10. One small firm had 100% exports through the CBI programme, which partly changed garment manufacturing into garment assembly.
11. *Trinidad Guardian*, 30 December 1994, p. 4.
12. *Trinidad Guardian*, 1 January 1996.

9 Conclusions: Private Sector Adjustment

9.1 Introduction

This chapter summarizes the findings of the study, discusses its limitations and strengths, and derives implications for future policy decisions. Section 9.2 recaps the main focus of the study and offers a discussion of its limitations and strengths. Section 9.3 presents a summary of the findings and section 9.4 presents the main policy implications. Concluding remarks follow in section 9.5.

9.2 Adjustment and Private Sector Development: Focus, Weaknesses, Strengths

9.2.1 Main focus of the study

The thematic thrust of the argument is that structural constraints arising from the historical development of the economies of developing countries can lead to results that are contrary to those suggested by the macro policies of adjustment. The main systemic features that have been identified include: financial market segmentation characterized by discriminatory credit allocation by banks against firms based on the criteria of size, ownership and family connections; an import-dependent manufacturing sector; an inherited liability structure of firms; and economic openness with a reliance on the petroleum/energy sector for growth. These features affect the allocation of resources and the structure of production creating in the process conditions that lead to differential effects and responses of firms. Within industries, dualism emerges relative to the production/asset structures, since these features cut across firm activity.

The notion of a heterogeneous private sector was explored by evaluating structural factors based on differences in size, ownership, and industrial activity. The hypotheses of the research distinguished the effect of changes in relative prices (due to adjustment policies) such that the resulting changes in the cost/asset structures may not necessarily lead to an improvement in profitability and investment, given the notion of heterogeneity.

The important role given to the private sector and private investment in economic recovery in adjustment focused the discussion on the history of enterprise development and the justification of the private sector's role, as well as the emphasis on the market over the state. Also important was an understanding of the private sector's capacity to fulfil its role through an awareness of the determinants of private investment.

The study sought to investigate the microeconomic context of the macroeconomic policies of adjustment firstly through laying bare the historical/structural factors in the economy that have influenced the operations of firms and markets in a developing country. Secondly, there was an investigation of factors in the costs and asset structure of firms as the means through which the effects of the macroeconomic policies are felt by firms. The entry point of the research was therefore directed at the assumption of a homogeneous private sector – specifically the concept of a representative firm capable of flexible response to price incentives with equilibrium being achieved in product and factor markets. The review of elements of the microeconomic aspects of adjustment aimed to look at the concept of the firm and micro-level restructuring to the macro policies, given that all firms face similar conditions relative to market price incentives in the quest to maximize profit.

Distinctive features of the Structuralist/Post-Keynesian framework used in the research are: a departure from the assumption of homogeneity, a focus on the historical, social, and institutional processes in capital accumulation, and an understanding of the market and the macro effect through a study of micro-level dynamics.

The nature and processes of micro-level restructuring in a developing country and the differential situations faced by firms were used to give validity to the exploration of heterogeneity in the private sector of

Trinidad & Tobago. Hence, aspects of the economic history that still influence the process of restructuring and affect the capacity of the private sector to respond were identified, partly forming the foundation of the hypotheses of the research.

9.2.2 Weaknesses and strengths of the study

The study represents an approach to analysing the impact of adjustment on firms through a basic understanding of the historical, institutional, and structural perspectives of a developing country. Approaches that seek to understand linkages between firms relative to formal or informal contractual arrangements or to analyse strategic firm behaviour were not explored in this research. Nevertheless, in so far as some elements of strategic responses by firms were articulated, some insights into these approaches can be gleaned.

In addition, it was not feasible in a single study to fully explore all aspects of firm heterogeneity, thus other aspects such as the degree of capital/labour intensity and the degree of export orientation were not covered. The rationale behind these exclusions were in part the limitations of the data and the practicality of the workload. However, it should be pointed out that characteristics such as ownership, size of firm and type of industry in so far as they reflect access to resources, have implications relative to issues such as choice of technology and so forth. Hence the rationale for the use of size groups, foreign/local ownership, and type of industry go beyond a mere representation of these characterizations themselves but are intricately linked to concerns of resource allocation.

The separateness of conventional macro and microeconomics and the lack of clarity in the adjustment process by which firms restructure posed limitations on the theoretical basis of the research. This theoretical limitation led to an exploratory approach which attempts to integrate with the context of heterogeneity, key price relatives in product and factor markets with structural aspects of the firm, using a mix of Structural/Post-Keynesian economics. To the extent that one is able to grasp the processes involved in micro-level restructuring to macroeconomic changes, this approach has been successful in contributing or giving added focus to the necessity of linking macro and microeconomic frameworks in economic analysis.

On the question of the representativeness of the data, very small firms of <10 employment size are not 'well-represented' in the research given the sampling procedure. For the <10 employment size firms, it was not possible to obtain sampling fractions for the past survey data. Hence, there were problems in the weighting of the data for this group due to the unavailability of sampling fractions. A method described in Chapter 4 was used to find approximate weights for this size group.

Some of the main strengths of the research are: the availability of firm-level data (repeated cross-section) of satisfactory quality for both real and financial variables, the use of the above theoretical framework, the method of data analysis which allowed exploration of structural changes over time as well as econometric modelling, and the availability of qualitative information from personal interviews of accountants, managers and owners.

In the exploratory data analysis, the median values were used to assess differences across various categories, and variability analysis was used to identify differences around the median values themselves. The combination of the medians with macroeconomic data such as the real exchange rate and the real lending rate of interest was another method for integrating the micro and macro aspects of the data. The median as the best point estimate was used to represent the various subgroups while the graphical display of inter-quartile range represented by the heights of the boxplots gave vivid representation of variability about the median and over time. While numerous graphs were represented, there were many others which could not be incorporated for reasons having to do with the length of the research.

In the regression analysis, the use of cross-section data over time meant that it was necessary to carry out tests for the pooling of the data over time. These tests were performed for selected characteristics. In the investigation of profitability and investment, it was necessary to organize the results by ownership (foreign/local) and within this classification by size groups. For the smallest size group (those with <10 employment), it was not possible to group the data by year. In general, this was possible for the remaining size groups, though in one case it meant the exclusion of data for one year. It was possible to check for pooling of industries in some subgroups but not in others. For example, among the smaller firms for which data was disaggregated by year, small frequencies meant that no further tests were possible. In addition, for a couple of years regression results were not possible. Thus, the question of sample size was evidently a problem for firms in the <10 size group. The relatively small number of foreign firms implied that beyond size group disaggregation, it was not possible to check for the pooling of the data by activity.

Consistent with the argument of the study, in the regression analysis the structural factors (leverage, interest payments, etc.) were assumed to be directly affected by relative prices in product and factor markets. In turn, these variables were used to assess changes in profitability and investment of firms. For selected industries/size group, an analysis was performed to assess the impact of relative prices on these structural factors (debt, interest payments). While this second approach allows for a direct link of key price relatives to firm-level data, the advantage of the former approach is the ability to use actual changes in costs/asset structure which strikes at the root of the thesis relative to heterogeneity. That is, firms do not necessarily face the same market prices in developing countries due to reasons outlined earlier relative to historical experiences and the ensuing practices and structures that evolve.

Thus the advantages of the regressions are:

1. based on the question of firm differences in costs and access to credit, regression allowed for an investigation of the actual costs of changes in raw material and interest expenses, and of the historical conditions with respect to liabilities and local assets in the assessment of firm profitability and investment;

2. the supplemental regressions on selected sectors which linked the actual relative prices with the structural factors in turn established a direct link between the macroeconomic policies through relative prices and the microeconomic unit, the firm.

Based on the above considerations, the main findings of the study are discussed in the next section.

9.3 Presentation of the Main Findings of the Study

This section discusses the main findings of the study starting first with a brief summary of the macroeconomic trends and then proceeding to the micro-level results based on firm size, ownership and industry.

9.3.1 Summary of main macro policy trends

The macroeconomic trends were analysed using four time periods: 1966–73, the pre-oil boom period; 1974–80, the oil boom period; 1981–87, the post-oil boom and pre-adjustment period; and the adjustment period, 1988–94. These periods will be referred to as such in this chapter. Appreciation of the real exchange rate occurred on average in the oil boom period and in the pre-adjustment period, with a depreciation recorded for the period of structural adjustment. The terms appreciation and depreciation are loosely used since a system of fixed exchange rates was in place except for the years 1993/94, during which a managed floating exchange rate policy was exercised. On average, for the period of adjustment, the exchange rate policy achieved its goal, even though for some individual years a real devaluation may not have been realized during this period.

While the minimum wage rate increased throughout the various phases of the economy, the increase in the adjustment years was offset by a larger percentage real devaluation for that period. The average real lending rate (median) which was negative in the oil boom period was raised to positive levels in the pre-adjustment and adjustment period. However, real deposit rates remained negative due to wide differences in nominal lending and deposit rates of commercial banks and other financial institutions. During the adjustment period, inflation decreased from the oil boom high while unemployment rates increased.

The GDP growth rate increased during the oil boom period, fell in the pre-adjustment period and had a mild recovery in the adjustment period. There were differentials by industry in GDP growth rates. Problems in the textile/garments industry surfaced in the oil boom period because this sector in general found it difficult to become competitive. In the pre-adjustment years, periods of protection, which involved restrictions on garment importation, were necessary; though they resulted in a plunge in GDP. There was a declining growth rate in the assembly sector from the pre-oil boom, oil boom, and pre-adjustment periods, with positive growth rate in the adjustment period at which time an entire activity had disappeared (motor-vehicle assembly). Firms that went out of operation may have been a contributing factor to the positive rate of growth in this industry.

The petroleum sector (the energy sector, which includes petrochemicals, ammonia, urea and natural gas) still remained the largest single contributor to GDP, even though there was some measure of resource-based industrialization (production of methanol, urea, and so forth), which, implies that the contribution of petroleum itself dwindled. However, these industries tend to move together because (1) petroleum is a major input in the manufacturing processes and (2) like petroleum they are also subject to instability in commodity prices. Such external factors as the mildness of the winter or economic fallout in Asia contributed to the movement of earnings in this sector. Hence, this form of economic diversification has left the economy largely dependent on the occurrences in the petroleum/energy-based sector.

Government and private investment fell from the oil boom to the pre- adjustment to the adjustment period. After a decrease in private savings from the oil boom period to the pre-adjustment period, there was an increase in the adjustment period. Government savings continued to decline becoming negative in the adjustment period. As a result, the fiscal deficit remained negative for all periods even though it was less negative in the adjustment than the pre-adjustment period by virtue of lower investment in the former period. However, the current account deficit improved in the adjustment period due to increased private sector balance – improved private savings but decreased private investment.

Debt ratios increased from the pre-adjustment to adjustment period. While the United States remained the major trading partner, some inroads were made in the CARICOM (intra-regional) market. Against the above macroeconomic backdrop, adjustment policies were officially introduced in 1988 in response to a failing economy. Given the largely negative macroeconomic picture, the results of the micro-level analysis are discussed in brief below.

9.3.2 Summary of exploratory analysis on firm heterogeneity

Selected features of the results on the structural factors such as leverage, interest payments, and raw material expenses as well as on profitability and investment are summarized in this section. The summary of trends will be presented relative to size, ownership and industry.

Size

Based on size group, key differences in leverage use over time were noted in the initial response of firms in the first year of the increase in the real lending rate of interest to a positive value. The smallest firms (<10 employment size) and the largest firms (100+ employment size) initially experienced declining leverage, with a longer period decline in the case of the largest firms. The other size groups had increasing leverage with the appearance of positive real lending rates. Explanations offered for the decline in these two groups were based on the difficulty and differentials in costs of credit for smaller firms, or acute indebtedness and/or the ability to operate by lowering their leverage use in the case of the largest firms.

For the larger size group (100+), credit would have been available and cost of credit could have been more uniform due to more favourable interest rates offered by banks. This feature might have led to problems of indebtedness for these firms due to excessive and continuous borrowing as reflected in their consistently high leverage (median) ratios.

With the exception of the smallest firms, interest expenses increased with increasing interest rates for all other size groups. Thus, borrowing by the smallest firms seemed to have been discouraged with the initial increase in interest rate. The more pronounced increase of interest expenses in some of the adjustment years for the 100+ group suggests that these largest firms were experiencing debt accumulation problems.

The trends in raw material expenses were mixed for all size groups. The one key trend was declining raw material expenses in the initial years of the data for the largest firms which suggests that restructuring (perhaps bankruptcy) occurred in this size group.

Declining profitability was common to all size groups in the pre-adjustment years, with a profusion of high and low outliers illustrating the inequality in the effects of adjustment. The 50–99 size group showed the most variability in profitability over time. Little evidence of recovery in profitability was observed in the adjustment period across size groups.

There was also declining investment across size group with the exception of the smallest firms, which exhibited major fluctuations throughout, indicating either major variability among the firms in this size group over time or limitations relative to the sampling of these firms. There was some evidence of an inverse relationship for the larger size groups (10+ firms) between investment and the real lending rate during the adjustment period, which was more pronounced for the 100+ group. Overall, there is little evidence of sustained increase in investment across size groups, with fluctuating trends for some size groups.

An interesting result was the extent to which declining average wages or declining rate of growth of average wages was used to counter the effects of increasing costs of adjustment such as devaluation of the exchange rate. The smallest and the largest firms showed the most consistent inverse patterns between the changes in the average wage and changes in the real exchange rate.

Another interesting result was observed in productivity increases among the smallest firms. In this case, adjustment did appear to achieve the aim of forcing these small firms to be more efficient, given that this was their only recourse if they were to survive. Differences in firms in specific size groups that stood out as outliers (high and low) for successive years (all or some years) were traced to differences in ownership, use of short-term versus long-term leverage, and use of foreign versus local leverage.

Ownership: Foreign/local firms

In the process of following high and low outliers when exploring trends by size groups, the question of foreign versus local ownership and leverage use emerged. The difference in leverage use based on firm ownership was further emphasized by the observation that, in general, foreign-owned firms tended to use lower levels of leverage, and relative to local liabilities, they tended to use more short-term rather than long-term liabilities.

The initial post-oil boom response showed increasing leverage use for local firms reflecting the crisis in this period. In the adjustment period, leverage use showed little variability at this higher level. Foreign firms actually increased their use of leverage during adjustment contributing to a narrowing of the gap between the two groups.

There were differences in the initial response to increasing real lending rates in 1983/84, with interest payments falling for foreign firms but increasing initially for local firms. However, beyond this period, the increasing use of leverage by foreign firms was reflected in an increasing trend in interest payments, which declined in the pre-adjustment and early adjustment period for local firms, contributing to the narrowing of the variability between these groups.

In the post-oil boom period, differences were observed in raw material expenses which declined for foreign firms. Initially, variability in this expenditure item was higher for local than for foreign firms, but the 1988 devaluation year saw increasing variability in these expenses for the foreign firms exceeding that of local firms. By 1993, also a devaluation year, there was little difference in the median or variability of raw material expenses for both groups. As was the case with other structural factors (leverage use and interest expenses), adjustment had the effect of bringing both groups of firms closer together relative to raw material expenses.

Declining profitability and investment were observed in the initial post-oil boom/pre-adjustment periods. Profitability was generally higher for foreign firms but the decline in profitability in this group brought it in line with that of the local firms in the early part of adjustment. However, profitability increased in the latter stage of the adjustment period for foreign firms even though there were some fluctuations. While there was increasing investment for both groups, in the case of local firms this rate remained below the early pre-adjustment level; and then, at the end of the 1993/94 period, investment started to show a declining trend once again. Hence, by 1994 investment for foreign firms was higher than for local firms.

Output to employment was always at a higher rate for foreign than for local firms. Compared to the foreign firms, there was little change in output to employment throughout the period of the data for the local firms. For the foreign firms, output to employment declined in the initial years 1983/84, but the tendency was for an increasing rate despite fluctuations throughout the period. The pattern in declining wages showed declining rates of change and some years with no change for local firms. The changes in the average wage fluctuated for foreign firms with years in which there were declining rates and years in which there were increases. Generally as a means of maintaining competitiveness, local firms seemed to have utilized wage suppression to a greater extent than foreign firms.

Industry

The initial response of leverage use to increasing real lending rates differed for all three industrial activities which were analysed: assembly, food processing and textiles/garments. After the initial increase in leverage use in the assembly industry, there were little changes throughout the period implying that leverage use in this industry was raised to a higher rate with increasing real lending rates and this new rate persisted throughout the adjustment period. In the case of food processing, the consistency in leverage use was at a lower rate. For textiles, the leverage rates fluctuated throughout the period showing some measure of instability in the debt situation of this sector.

All three industrial activities showed increasing interest expenses in the initial part of the pre-adjustment period, with a sharper increase in the case of textiles. In general, the interest expenses ratio tended to be lowest for food processing, followed by assembly. While there was some measure of similarity in these ratios for assembly and textiles, a gap was noticed in the median values in the early part of the adjustment period when this ratio increased to a higher value in textiles/garments. For the food processing industry, there was a clearer inverse association between the median interest expenses ratio and the real lending rate of interest. Such an association was less apparent in the case of the other two industries.

Variation in raw material expenses was more apparent in assembly and textiles/garments than in food processing. For the three nominal devaluations which occurred during this period (with the exception of the 1993 devaluation, when the raw material expenses ratio declined for all three industries), there were differences in the changes in this ratio, as recorded earlier in Chapter 7.

Profitability declined for all three activities in the pre-adjustment period, but in 1987 a special government policy which banned the importation of garments for commercial sale led to increased profitability of the textiles/garments industry in that year. There was fluctuating profitability in all three sectors during the adjustment period with a definite post-1991 decline for the assembly industry. The positioning of firms with high and low extreme values showed a greater concentration of loss-making firms in textiles and assembly than food processing.

Initially in 1983/84, there was an increase in investment in textiles/garments, followed by a decline in 1984/86. For the other two sectors, investment declined from about 1983 to 1986. In all three industries, investment fluctuated for the remaining period, showing no distinct pattern of recovery.

The food processing industry had higher rates of output to employment than assembly and textiles in that order. There was little variation in output to employment in the assembly and textiles/garments industries throughout the period.

There was some evidence of declining output to employment in food processing in the pre-adjustment period, resulting in an equalization of the ratios in 1989 during adjustment. For the remainder of the adjustment period, there were phases of increasing or decreasing output to employment in food processing, showing that productivity in this sector was affected sometimes positively, sometimes negatively during adjustment.

Declining rates of growth in average wages indicate that wage decrease/freezing was a measure used in all three activities in the pre-adjustment period. During the adjustment period, there were signs of declining real average wage in the case of assembly for 1993, a devaluation year. However, in the initial period (1983/84), the textiles and assembly industries recorded no change in wages. Wages in the textiles industry are traditionally low but falling wages in assembly were a reflection of the problems in this sector. For assembly, reduction in average wage occurred during the early part of adjustment.

9.3.2 Summary of regression results

Local firms: Profitability and investment results

< 10 size group

Profitability and investment. Negative results on profitability due to changes in raw material expenses were recorded for the smallest firms. These results fell both in years of adjustment and, in one case, the immediate post-oil boom period. With respect to investment, raw material expenses only returned a significant result in one year (1989), which was a year of greater liquidity in the system enhancing economic activity overall.

The results of interest payments expenses and profitability were mixed with negative results in the pre-adjustment years but positive in the adjustment periods. This latter result was interpreted as not necessarily reflecting the effectiveness of the interest rate in improving profitability relative to financial efficiency since a more plausible explanation seems to be that the profitable firms were the ones who were able to borrow, in the process reflecting increasing interest payments.

For the investment variable, interest expenses also showed mixed results. Except for the adjustment years 1989 and 1994, the results for investment in this period were significant and negative, though there was also a positive result in 1986. The years 1989 and 1994 were explained through greater liquidity in the financial system, which facilitated loans for investment purposes to those firms that could borrow.

In general, there was a negative effect of the use of leverage on profitability with the exception of the devaluation years 1988 and 1993. The positive impact of liabilities on profitability in these two years must be measured against the negative effect of raw material expenses and the positive effect of interest expenses in 1988. For 1988, it appears that the net effect of adjustment policies on profitability was positive for this size group. On the other hand, it can also be concluded that debt was used to bail out firms facing extinction. For the investment variable, no significant results of liabilities on investment were recorded for the adjustment period except for 1989 (positive effect) which was explained relative to increased liquidity. In the pre-adjustment period, there were mixed results with liabilities having a positive impact on investment in 1984 but negatively affecting investment in 1986 and 1987.

The local assets structure was not a significant factor affecting profitability but was significant and positive with respect to investment during two of the pre-adjustment years and negative during two years of adjustment. The composition of local assets in these years is possibly a decisive factor in explaining these results. In the years of negative impact (adjustment period), the accumulation of inventories was greater than the pre-adjustment years. The status of inventories as a guide to investment might have influenced this result. Within this group of smaller firms, size was an important factor determining profitability and investment.

10+ size group

Profitability. Differences were observed in the results of these firms based on industry type. Raw material expenses, while showing negative impact in food processing and manufacturing, showed positive impact in textiles and chemicals. In the case of textiles, this was explained through the ability of these firms to remain competitive by wage suppression, while in chemicals it was the ability to pass on costs to the consumers. Firms with a low ratio of raw material expenses also returned a positive result.

The assembly sector had negative results for liabilities to total assets, interest payments, and output size, showing that these factors were decisive in determining a negative impact on the profitability of this sector. Interest payments had positive results in food processing firms with a higher and positive impact on those with very high interest payments suggesting that increasing and high interest payments did not stop this sector from being profitable.

However, while the liabilities to assets variable was not significantly different from zero for the food processing sector as a whole, this variable was significant and negative for highly indebted firms and those with low leverage use. This last result on leverage reflects on the one hand problems of heavy indebtedness of firms and, on the other, problems with lack of access to credit. In textiles, assembly and chemicals, highly leveraged firms were also more adversely affected by their liabilities position. In printing/wood and related, highly leveraged firms were the ones experiencing a more positive or a less adverse impact on profitability. In these sectors (which possibly receive the lowest proportion of loans among the manufacturing sectors, based on the end of year loans outstanding), the firms that receive loans are probably the more profitable ones.

Investment. The increase in interest payments by itself did not stop the investment thrust of the food processing industry for the second largest size group of firms (10–24), with the use of leverage showing a negative impact and profitability being positive. In this same size group, results for other industries showed that local assets had a negative impact on investment for textiles/garments and miscellaneous. Liabilities had a positive effect on investment in chemicals, with size of firm being a significant factor in this sector as well as in miscellaneous manufacturing. Changes in raw material expenses showed a significant effect on investment in printing.

In the 25–49 size group, interest payments and local assets negatively affected investment. However, firms with a higher percentage of interest payments felt a less adverse impact on investment. Size of firm also mattered: the larger the firm relative to fixed assets the more negative the effect on investment.

In the 50–99 size group, profitability was a significant and positive factor determining investment in the food processing, printing and assembly industries. Local assets had a significant negative impact in printing and chemicals. Liabilities to assets was significant and negative in food processing but had a positive impact on investment in chemicals. In the assembly sector, changes in raw material expenses and interest expenses negatively affected investment, with size of firm being a significant and positive factor. Thus, there were industry differences related to problems of raw material inputs, indebtedness, the composition of local assets, and the cost of credit.

Among the largest size group (100+), the investment thrust was enabled by the use of leverage, profitability, and the size of the firm; but for highly profitable firms there was a tapering impact of profitability on investment. Interest payments and local assets had negative effects on investment. Highly levered large firms had their investment thrust negatively affected, with firms who used a lower ratio of leverage experiencing a less positive impact. Firms with lower interest expenses and local assets experienced a less adverse impact on investment.

Investigation of interest payments and liabilities. Increasing real lending rate was associated with increasing liabilities in the assembly sector, a result which is not surprising given the problems experienced by this industry after the oil boom. Profitability had a significant and negative effect on liabilities in the food processing sector, implying that improvement in the asset position of the firm will diminish the need for increasing liabilities.

In the textiles/garments industry, increases in investment did not lead to increased liabilities. These results lend some support to our argument that relative prices can affect the firm through the effect on structural factors such as liabilities, interest payments, raw material expenses, and so on.

With respect to interest payments, liabilities were a significant and positive factor in food processing, textiles, and assembly. Increases in the real interest rates led to increasing interest payments in textiles.

Foreign firms: Profitability and investment

Changes in raw material expenses had a positive effect on the profitability of the smallest (<10) foreign firms but a negative impact on investment. Interest expenses had a negative impact on profitability among the smallest and largest (100+) foreign firms and a negative impact on investment in the 10–24 category. Leverage use negatively affected profitability in the 10+ category with the exception of the 50–99 group (where there was no effect) and positively affected investment among firms with 50+ employment.

Local assets had a positive impact on profitability in the 50–99 size group with size of firm being important within the 100+ category. Profitability had a positive effect on investment for firms in the 25+ size group. The positive relationship between profitability and investment was expected. However, the unexpected negative results on leverage use and interest payments under the argument that foreign firms do not borrow locally are consistent with the conclusions of the exploratory data analysis. This analysis showed decreased variability in leverage use for foreign firms and a narrowing of the gap in interest payments between foreign and local firms.

Issues arising from qualitative survey: Patterns of adjustment to financial and exchange rate policy

Unequivocally, exchange rate policy had the effect of increasing the costs of imported raw materials. However, proactive responses by the larger and foreign firms such as the penetration of export markets, the replacement of traded aspects of their product lines by non-traded, quality improvements, and the passing on of costs to consumers led to offsetting positive effects. It was argued that the search for export markets was not necessarily led by the devaluation but was part of a firm strategy employed in response to falling domestic demand.

On the other hand, firm response to the devaluation also implied wage reduction, employment reduction, reduced purchasing of raw materials or the search for alternative sources by firms that had the capacity to employ such a strategy. Thus, there were specific responses which bordered on survival strategies to offset extinction.

Differences in foreign/local ownership and firm size relative to factors such as the ability to hold foreign accounts or the possibility of obtaining loans from parent or group companies were contributory factors in determining the effects of adjustment policies.

The question of differential access to and cost of credit emerged as a feature that affected firm operations under adjustment. Invariably, the smaller firms were the ones who complained about the inability to access credit or about the high cost of credit available. The larger firms (foreign or local) normally had traditional and well-established relations with banks. In some cases, this factor might have led to excessive borrowing in the oil boom period and to severe indebtedness in the post-oil boom period, which resulted in firm closures and activity changes.

From the banks' point of view, small firms were seen as high credit risks in the repayment of loans where the safety of depositors funds are concerned, leading to the favoured positions of firms with well-established relationships.

9.4 Policy Implications

This research faced the difficulty of trying to link changes in macro policies with changes in the performance of microeconomic units, firms in this case, specifically as it pertained to profitability and investment. In approaching this problem a few implications arose relative to the methodological approach, the nature of firms/markets in developing countries, and the macro-policies applied. Methodological issues surround the importance of historical and structural factors versus the market and of heterogeneity versus homogeneity in analysing adjustment. These issues are reflected mainly in the Structuralist, Post Keynesian and Neoclassical traditions. The need to distinctly identify the firm in a developing country context and also the conditions of the markets are issues brought out in this research. The macro policy implications that were considered pertain to financial liberalization and exchange rate policies. These issues are discussed below.

9.4.1 The efficacy of analysing structure and history in adjustment

While Agenor & Monteil (1996: 11–12) promoted the view of the Structuralists that 'structure matters', their promotion of this idea is firmly entrenched within the belief that 'economic agents in developing countries behave no differently than those in industrial economies' and in ways that are consistent with the rational, optimizing behaviour of neo-classical microeconomics.

The research perspective on this issue is twofold.

1. Structure matters – not just structure of the economic environment but also the historically determined structure of the firm, as it can influence its ability to deal with external changes.

2. Related to (1) – the processes by which change is achieved bears relation to the underlying features that evolve in the economy and the firm, and the nature of these processes must be understood in context.

Historically determined structures that came out in the research related to the following:

(i) an economy which has historically developed along the lines of import-dependent industrialization, a feature which is pervasive in firms today with implications for the real exchange rate to affect the cost structure,

(ii) a financial market structure that was notably segmented as manifested through the credit rationing behaviour of financial institutions that discriminate between loan applicants in the allocation of credit and the charging of interest rates leading to differential effects of interest rate policy.

This feature of dependency reflected in (i) poses cost constraints on firms and limits the cost-cutting options that firms face. In the face of relative price changes, these options may even imply cost cutting through reduced purchasing of the input itself.

In (ii), a reliance on debt for investment and/or working capital purposes is reflected in changes in the cost and asset liability structures of the firm. Variations in these structures reflect the ability of the firm to adjust its debt and/or the availability of credit or the capacity of the firm to continue to borrow differing by firm size, ownership and industry.

Thus, these historical and structural factors engendered firm behaviour under conditions such that expected results to relative price changes of productive and/ or financial efficiency were not necessarily achieved. In this respect, under conditions of market segmentation and import dependency, structural features of the firm and markets may limit the options of some categories of firms relative to successful economic restructuring.

The other aspect of structure related to finance is the liability structure of the firm over time. In general, the variable representing leverage use was significant in most of the regressions dealing with profitability for the larger firms. In some cases, the consistency of leverage use over time showed some measure of rigidity in the debt structure of the firm. Movements in leverage before and during the adjustment period reflected changes in aspects of the firm costs that were consistent with the percentage of leverage use. Thus, the patterns and statistical significance of factors in the cost and asset structure clearly show the importance of the debt/asset structure relative to the profitability of the firm.

Investment and profitability generally tended to show a declining pattern from the pre-adjustment to the adjustment period as a result of changes in the cost/liability structure of the firm. There were, however, variations based on firm size, ownership and industry as well as interactions of these characteristics over time

It can be concluded that an understanding of the historical structural features and how they manifest themselves relative to patterns of production and financing at the micro level in Trinidad & Tobago is crucial to effecting change through macroeconomic policies. The results of this study suggest that the Structuralist tradition in its preoccupation with structure, history, and institutions offers a better framework to analyse adjustment behaviour in Trinidad & Tobago than does the neo-classical tradition.

9.4.2 Heterogeneity and micro-level restructuring during adjustment

The analyses confirmed that heterogeneity is important in assessing the impact of macroeconomic policies relative to structural features of the firm. The use of firm size, ownership and activity produced results to support and/or substantiate this dimension of heterogeneity. This is another reflection of the importance of the Structuralist/Post-Keynesian tradition over Neo-Classicism as discussed in the early theoretical chapter of this study. The depiction of a representative firm capable of flexible and predictable patterns of behaviour to prices with a tendency towards a mean response does not seem to be substantiated when one considers the heterogeneity that is inherent in the private sector and the differential conditions faced in markets that lead to structural constraints during adjustment.

The inability to pool foreign and local firms, or firms of different sizes or activities relative to the structural factors analysed reinforces the need to investigate heterogeneity as a factor in determining how a private sector responds to relative price changes.

Hence, the expectation that getting the prices right will automatically and unequivocally lead to the recovery of private investment and private sectors is not entirely assured if one takes into consideration the results of this research and the differing outcomes based on ownership, size of firm, and industry along with the historical experiences and structural factors discussed above.

9.4.3 The firm and the market in a developing country context

From a broader perspective, the rationale for adopting a framework of market determined relative prices had to do with the belief that these prices lead to a socially optimal allocation of resources, through a process of profit and utility maximizing behaviour of economic agents, who operate under a series of assumptions relative to the achievement of a competitive equilibrium.

However, the results of the research suggest in practical terms that there is a need to rethink these issues relative to the firm and the market in developing countries. This analysis has shown that historically and institutionally determined problems militate against the effectiveness of policies which have relative price changes as their basis.

The research demonstrates that the assumption of the uniformity of firms and markets regardless of countries and within countries (which is in tune with the Neo-classical tradition) should be substituted by a more realistic approach. By seeking to understand the nature and historical experiences of firms and markets in a developing country, the research has brought into focus a more practical interpretation of the impact of macro-economic policies on the micro-level units, as reflected in the Structuralist approach discussed in the opening chapter. The study also raises the question as to the nature of the firm in a developing country context and suggests that Structuralism provides a better interpretation in this regard. *Nevertheless, this study does not mean to suggest that the achievement of a competitive exchange or interest rate that can target efficient firms is therefore not worth pursuing. However, the context in which these policies are being applied render them inappropriate to bringing about their expected results*. The determination of the effects of these policies should therefore be considered in a particular historical, social, and institutional context reflecting a more realistic picture of the firm and markets in developing countries. Below, additional detailed policy implications are discussed.

9.4.4 Financial liberalization

The structural and historical features of financial markets in Trinidad & Tobago specify a form of credit-rationing which is linked to the historical development of the economy. More specifically, the orientation of the banking sector towards lending to specific 'groups' of firms in the economy is not necessarily related to considerations of efficiency. In this respect, financial institutions have notoriously discriminated against specific economic agents, withholding available resources under the justification of their obligation to depositors and ability to pay.

Financial repression, while not noted for interest rate ceilings in the case of Trinidad & Tobago, did occur through indirect means based on policies on the rediscount rates, moral suasion, threatening legislation, restrictions on credit, and so on. This was manifested by the presence of low and negative real interest rates, deviations from the world interest rates, and occurred in the context of severe credit-rationing and discriminatory interests rates based on historical, ethnic, size, ownership or other similar reasons. As a result, financial repression was not of the conventional variety.

Hence, the functioning of the interest rate in a process of financial liberalization did not lead to improved credit access/greater availability of credit for small firms as should have been the case based on a criteria of efficiency. With financial and trade liberalization in general, the closer integration of the domestic and international financial markets may imply that the domestic interest rate may better reflect the market rate *vis á vis* the international rate in Trinidad & Tobago. Because of the the functioning of financial markets, the interest rate will be ineffective in increasing or improving the efficiency of private investment under the conditions of existing credit-rationing by the commercial banking sector.

Hence, polices which guarantee credit by government agencies to small firms are not likely to be sufficiently effective, given the orientation of the bank and its bias against lending to small businesses. In this respect, in addition to the creation of credit guarantee schemes, there is need for a policy to be stated on the small business sector directed towards the encouragement of sustainable growth, incorporating dimensions such as adequate provision of finance and entrepreneurial education in finance, management and other business techniques.

9.4.5 Exchange rate

The use of exchange rate policy as a means of increasing international competitiveness would not be achieved unless the roots of the production structure of different types of firms are first exposed relative to the effects on economic agents. Thus, industrial policy that seeks to address these issues should form the initial thrust of adjustment policies through mechanisms that aim to reduce import dependency.

In addition, conditions that can enable firms that do not have the experience in export markets to achieve such a status should form part of the industrial policy thrust. Consequently, the question of product quality, provision of information about export markets, and the establishment of market contacts for businesses that do not possess the capacity and the finance to do so should be part of a strategic planning process aimed at provisioning enterprises with the resources needed for development.

More importantly, the establishment of an integrated network of public and private sector agencies is a requirement that can eliminate bureaucratic bottlenecks. Without these measures, the devaluation of the exchange rate may just facilitate the firms in the private sector that already have foreign market exposure and the finance and business contacts to make further foreign market penetration. Yet even in the case of easier market penetration, the availability and cost of finance also poses a problem.

9.4.6 Macroeconomic policies for the promotion of private investment and sustainable growth

The results have shown that the outcome of exchange rate devaluation and financial liberalization may in some circumstances be counterproductive in promoting investment and sustainable growth. The study clearly recognizes the need for a competitive exchange rate and an interest rate that can target efficient investment. However, based on the historical and institutional features that negatively influence the outcome of these policies, there is a need to have supporting policies and agencies that can reverse these negative outcomes. This section seeks to reinforce some of the suggestions given above.

Devaluation of the exchange rate and increasing the real interest rate in order to increase savings for investment may lead to the following unintended outcomes: (1) Savings/productive investment in tradeables does not necessarily increase, (2) higher real interest rates prove to be burdensome to small firms and may cause excessive borrowing and bankruptcy in others, (3) the burden on small firms and those large firms that are not export-oriented leads to decreasing profitability and investment through increasing the costs of imported intermediates. The outline of policies that can be implemented as part of a programme of structural reforms are itemised below. Some of these suggested measures have been articulated elsewhere in medium term and multisectoral development plans but were not necessarily implemented.

Financial measures

1. Prior to liberalization of the interest rate, the lending/deposit interest rates should be set at levels that will address the gap between do-

mestic lending and the deposit interest rates differentials as well as between foreign and domestic interest rates.

2. The containment of inflation through an appropriate mix of interest rate policy as in (1), and the direction of credit to productive uses.
3. Increased financial sector supervision.
4. An expansion of guaranteed credit to enable small firms to borrow for investment purposes.
5. An intensive programme of education and training in financial management for small firm owners in order to enable their financial viability and capability to access loans.
6. Support and expansion of the system of monitoring and evaluation of small entrepreneurs as per the last two points above.
7. An income and wages policy to target increased savings.
8. The provision of export financing by banks and other financial institutions that can facilitate the expansion of the export thrust of small/medium businesses.
9. Development of other financial instruments that further strengthen the financial sectors and encourage savings.
10. Re-orientation of the banking personnel with regard to international financial banking concerns.

Increased investment in traded goods/reduced import dependency

11. The prioritizing of specific activities with regard to selective and *temporary* incentives/protection to firms. These would include firms that are initially attempting to enter export markets as well as those in the following activities: capital goods, technology enhancing/engineering, the production of components and other industrial raw material inputs in selected small scale industries.
12. Provision of assistance in research, development, quality control functions to target increased domestic sourcing of industrial inputs

and the development of training in research, science, and technology.

13. Encouragement of downstream industries in the traded sector other than petroleum/natural gas resource-based industrialization.

14. Education and training geared to the development of capability in technology.

Export development

15. Provision of information, financial assistance, and export incentives to enable market penetration by non-exporting firms willing to enter foreign trade.

16. Conducting studies on industry performance, foreign and domestic markets, and potential for new products particularly exports.

9.5 Concluding Remarks and Implications for Further Work

The approach to the investigation of the research problem has emphasized the significance of looking for differences in conditions faced by firms in a private sector as fashioned by its historical experience. Hence, an awareness of the history and the structural heterogeneity that gives rise to differences among firms and markets can contribute to a more realistic understanding of the processes of adjustment than that provided by the concept of a representative firm, and market equilibrium conditions in the context of a developing country.

Relative to the above point, a more plausible representation of the nature of the firms and the workings of markets in developing countries can be derived that can better equip firms to survive in the world economy. Thus policies that rely on relative price changes, such as financial liberalization and exchange rate devaluation, may not necessarily lead to productive and financial efficiency without taking into consideration historical, socio-economic and other factors that impinge upon the production and asset structure of firms and the market conditions within which they operate.

This is just one dimension in the research of private sector development during periods of adjustment. Further work entails 1) a closer look at other factors that can contribute to heterogeneity in firm response such as practices of innovation, choice and availability of technology, use of information, the question of agency, and 2) a closer look into the reasons behind differentials in results of structural factors which requires in-depth analysis at the micro level. The current study is best viewed as a preliminary enquiry into the understanding of the process of adjustment in the private sector. From this preliminary work, other facets or dimensions of the problem can evolve for future analysis.

References

Adam Christopher, William Cavendish and Percy S. Mistry (1992) *Adjusting Privatization – Case Studies from Developing Countries*. London: Villers Publications.

Addison, Dough (1989) 'The World Bank Revised Minimum Standard Model – Concepts and Issues', *Policy and Planning and Research Working Papers,* WPS 231, Country Economic Department. Washington, D.C.: The World Bank.

Agenor, Pierre-Richard & Peter J. Monteil (1996) *Development Macroeconomics*. New Jersey: Princeton University Press.

Allahar, Haven & Deryck R. Brown (1995) 'Trinidad & Tobago's Credit Guarantee Programme – Lessons from Five Years' Experience', *Small Enterprise Development*. Vol. 6, No. 3: 45–53.

Aoki, Masahiko, Bo Gustafsson & Oliver E. Williamson (eds.) (1990) *The Firm as a Nexus of Treaties*. London: Sage Publications.

Aoki, Masahiko (1984) *The Co-operative Game Theory of the Firm*. Oxford: OUP.

Arestis, Phillip (ed.) (1988) *Post-Keynesian Monetary Economics – New Approaches to Financial Modeling*. Aldershot, UK: Edward Elgar.

Arestis, Philip & Thanos Skouras (1985) *Post-Keynesian Economic Theory – A Challenge to Neo-Classical Economics*. Sussex, UK: Wheatsheaf Books.

Argawala, A.N. & S.P. Singh (1959) *The Economics of Underdevelopment*. Oxford: Oxford University Press.

Arndt, Heinz W. (1988) ' "Market Failure" and Underdevelopment', *World Development*. Vol. 16, No. 2: 219–29.

Arndt, H.W. (1985) 'The Origins of Structuralism', *World Development*. Vol. 13, No. 2: 151–59.

Arrieta, Gerardo M. Gonzales (1988) 'Interest Rates, Savings and Growth in LDCs: An Assessment of Recent Empirical Research', *World Development*. Vol. 16, No. 5: 589–605

Aryeetey, Ernest, Amoah Baah-Nuakoh, Tamara Duggleby, Hemamala Hettige, & William F. Steel (1994) 'Supply and Demand for Finance of Small Enterprises in Ghana', *World Bank Discussion Papers–African Technical Department Series* 251, Washington D.C.: The World Bank.

Balassa, Bela (1984) 'Adjustment Policies in Developing Countries: A Reassessment', Discussion Paper Report No. DRD 79, San Francisco.

Balassa, Bela (1978) 'Exports and Economic Growth: Further Evidence', *Journal of Development Economics*, 5 (June): 181–89.

Balasubramanyam, V.N. & Sanjaya Lall, (eds.) (1991) *Current Issues in Development Economics*. Macmillan.

Barzel, Yoram (1989) *Economic Analysis of Property Rights*. Cambridge: Cambridge University Press.

Bauer, P.T. (1991) *The Development Frontier – Essays in Applied Economics*. London: Harvester, Wheatsheaf.

Bauer, P.T. (1984) *Reality or Rhetoric – Studies in the Economics of Development*. London: Weidenfeld and Nicholson.

Bauer, P.T. (1976) *Dissent on Development*. London: Weidenfeld and Nicholson.

Beckford, George (ed.) (1975) *Caribbean Economy: Dependence and Backwardness*. Jamaica: Institute of Social and Economic Research (ISER), University of the West Indies.

Beckford, George (1972) *Persistent Poverty: Underdevelopment in Plantation Economies of the Third World*. New York: OUP.

Beckford, George & Michael Witter (1980) *Small Garden…Bitter Weed – The Political Economy Struggle and Change in Jamaica*. Morant Bay, Jamaica: Marron Publishing House.

Bell, D. & I. Kristol. (1981) *The Crisis in Economic Theory*. New York: Basic Books.

Benjamin, Nancy (1992) 'What Happens To Investment Under Adjustment: Results From a Simulation Model', *World Development*. Vol. 20, No. 9: 1335–44.

Bernanke, Ben S. (1983) 'Irreversibility, Uncertainty and Cyclical Investment', *Quarterly Journal Of Economics*. 98: 85–106.

Bernal, Richard, Mark Figueroa & Michael Witter (1984) 'Caribbean Economic Thought: The Critical Tradition', *Social and Economic Studies*. Vol. 33, No. 2: 5–96.

Best, Lloyd (1996) 'Concepts of Disillusion', Comments from a workshop on 'The Management of Field Co-ordination' at ILO Centre and UN Staff College, Turin, Italy, *Trinidad Express Newspaper, Trinidad* (Internet).

Best, Lloyd (1980) 'International Co-operation in the Industrialization Process – The Case of Trinidad & Tobago', in *Industry 2000 New Perspectives* – Collected Background Papers. Vol. 6: Industrialization Strategies and Country Case Studies, Vienna: UNIDO.

Best, Lloyd (1968) 'The Mechanism of Plantation-Type Economies – Outlines of a Model of Pure Plantation Economy', *Social and Economic Studies*. Vol. 17, No. 1: 283–349.

Bienfeld, Manfred (1991) *The Legacy of Karl Polyani: Market, State and Society at the End of the Twentieth Century*, Maguerite Mendell & Daniel Salée (eds). UK: Macmillan.

Bird, Graham (1981) 'Should Developing Countries Use Currency Depreciation as a Tool of Balance Of Payments Adjustment? A Review of the Theory and Evidence and a Guide for the Policy-maker', *The Journal Of Development Studies*. (Nov.).

Bleaney, Michael & David Fielding (1995) 'Investment, Trade Liberalisation and Structural Adjustment', *Journal of Development Studies*. Vol. 32, No. 2: 175–94.

Blejer, Mario & Moshin Khan (1984) 'Government Policy and Private Investment in Developing Countries' *Staff Papers, International Monetary Fund.* 31 (June): 379–403.

Blomstrom, Magnus & Bjorn Hettne (1984) *Development Theory in Transition – The Dependency Debate and Beyond: Third World Responses*. London: Zed Books Ltd.

Bobb, U. (1986) 'Money and Capital Development in Trinidad & Tobago', *Quarterly Economic Bulletin*. Vol. VIII (1) March 1983, Central Bank of Trinidad & Tobago.

Brett, E.A. (1988) 'State Markets and Private Power: Problems and Possibilities' in *Privatization in Less Developed Countries,* Paul Cook & Colin Kirkpatrick (eds). New York: Harvester Wheatsheaf.

Caballero, Richard J. (1993) 'On the Dynamics of Aggregate Investment', in *Striving for Growth After Adjustment – The Role of Capital Formation*. Washington D.C.: The World Bank.

Camejo, Acton (1971) 'Racial Discrimination in Employment in the Private Sector in Trinidad & Tobago: A Study of the Business Élite and Social Structure', *Social and Economic Studies*. Vol. 20, No. 3: 294–318.

Canavese, Alfredo J. (1982) 'The Structuralist Explanation in the Theory of Inflation', *World Development*. Vol. 10, No. 7: 523–29.

Chakravarty, Sukhamoy (1987) Post-Keynesian Theorists and the Theory of Economic Development. *World Institute for Development Economic Research* (WIDER) of the United Nations University.

Chenery, H.B. (1975) 'The Structuralist Approach to Development Policy', *Papers and Proceedings of the American Economic Association*. Vol. 65, May 1975: 310–16.

Chenery, H.B. & T.N. Srinivasan (1988) *Handbook of Economics*, Vol. I. Amsterdam: Elsevier Science Publishers.

Clark, Peter K. (1979) 'Investment in the 1970s: Theory, Performance and Prediction' *Brookings Paper on Economic Activity*. Vol. 1: 73–113.

Clarke, Thomas & Christos Pitelis (eds) (1993) *The Political Economy of Privatization*. London: Routledge.

Cline, William R. & Sidney Weintraub (eds) (1981) *Economic Stabilization in Developing Countries*. Washington D.C.: The Brookings Institution.

Colclough, Christopher & James Manor (eds) (1993) *States Or Markets? Neo-liberalism and the Development Policy Debate*. Oxford: Clarendon Press.

Commander Simon & Tony Killick (1988) in Cook & Kirkpatrick. *Privatization in Less Developed Countries*. New York: Harvester, Wheatsheaf.

Connolly, Michael & John McDermont (eds) (1985) *The Economics of the Caribbean Basin*. New York: Praeger.

Cook, Paul & Colin Kirkpatrick (eds) (1988) *Privatization in Less Developed Countries*. New York: Harvester Wheatsheaf.

Corbo, Vittorio, Stanley Fischer & Steven B. Webb (eds) (1992) *Adjustment Lending Revisited – Policies to Restore Growth*. Washington D.C.: The World Bank.

Cosci, Stefania (1993) *Credit Rationing and Asymmetric Information*. Aldershot, UK: Darthmouth.

Crotty, James R. (1992) 'Neoclassical and Keynesian Approaches to the Theory of Investment', *Journal of Post-Keynesian Economics*. Summer 1992. Vol. 14, No. 4: 483–97.

Crotty, James R. (1980) 'Post-Keynesian Economic Theory: An Overview and Evaluation', *American Economic Association*. Vol. 70, No. 2: 20–25.

Cyert, Richard M. & James G. March (1992) *A Behavioral Theory of the Firm* (second edition). UK: Blackwell.

Dailami, Mansoor & Marcelo Giugale (1991) 'Reflections on Credit Policy in Developing Countries – Its Effect on Private Investment', *Policy Research and External Affairs Working Papers*-WPS-*654*, Country Economics Department: The World Bank.

Dale, Angela & Richard B. Davis (1994) *Analysing Social and Political Change – A Casebook of Methods*. London: Sage Publications.

Davidson, Paul (1991) 'Uncertainty and Money', in *Controversies in Post-Keynesian Economics*. Aldershot, UK: Edward Elgar..

Davidson, P. (1981) 'Post-Keynesian Economics' in Bell & Kristol.

Davis, J.B. (1987) 'Three Principles of Post-Keynesian Methodology', *Journal of Post-Keynesian Economics*. Summer, Vol. IX, No. 4: 552–565.

Dawson, Johnathan (1994) 'Responses to Adjustment – The Marginalization of Small Enterprises in Nigeria' *Small Enterprise Development*. Vol. 5, No. 2: 18–24.

Deane, Phyllis (1978) *The Evolution of Economic Ideas*. Cambridge: Cambridge University Press.

de Melo, Jaime & James Tybout (1986) 'The Effects of Financial Liberalization on Savings and Investment in Uruguay', *Economic Development and Cultural Change*. Vol. 34, No. 3: 561–87.

Dornbusch, Rudiger & Stanley. Fischer (1990) *Macroeconomics* (fifth edition). New York: McGraw-Hill.

Dow, Alexander C. & Sheila C. Dow (1989) 'Endogenous Money Creation and Idle Balances', in Pheby.

Dutt, Amitava Krishna & Ajit Singh (1994) *The State, Markets and Development: Beyond the Neoclassical Dichotomy*. Aldershot, UK: Edward Elgar.

Dutt, Amitava Krishna & Kenneth P. Jameson (1992) *New Directions in Development Economics*. Aldershot, UK: Edward Elgar.

Earl, Peter E. (ed.) (1988) *Behavioural Economics*, Vol. I & II. Aldershot, UK: Edward Elgar.

Eckaus, R.S. (1955) 'The Factor Proportions Problem in Underdeveloped Areas', *The American Economic Review*. 55(1): 539–65.

Eggertsson, Thráinn (1990) *Economic Behaviour and Institutions*. Cambridge: Cambridge University Press.

Eichner, Alfred S. (ed.) (1979) *A Guide to Post-Keynesian Economics*. London: Macmillan.

Eichner. Alfred S. & J. Kregel (1975) 'An Essay on Post-Keynesian: A New Paradigm in Economics', *Journal of Economic Literature*. 13: 1293–314. Reprinted in Sawyer (1988).

Eshag, E. (1983) *Fiscal and Monetary Policies and Problems in Developing Countries*. Cambridge: Cambridge University Press.

Evans, Michael K. (1969) *Macroeconomic Activity Theory, Forecasting and Control*. New York, Evanston, & London: Harper & Row, and Tokyo: John Weatherhill.

Faini, Riccardo, Jaime de Melo, Abdelhak Senhadji & Julie Stanton (1991) 'Growth-oriented Adjustment Programmes: A Statistical Analysis', *World Development*. Vol. 19, No. 8: 957–67.

Faini, Riccardo, & Jaime de Melo (1990) 'Adjustment, Investment and the Real Exchange Rate in Developing Countries', *Economic Policy*. 11: 492–519.

Farrell. T.W. (1989) *Central Banking in a Developing Economy – A study of Trinidad and Tobago*, 1964–1989. Central Bank of Trinidad & Tobago.

Farrell. T.W. (1989) 'The IMF and Trinidad & Tobago Letter of Intent' (mimeo).

Farrell, Terrence & Crichton (1986) 'Market Structure and Concentration Within the Manufacturing Sector', *West India Collection, University of the West Indies Library*, Trinidad.

Fazzari, S.M., R.G. Hubbard & B.C. Petersen (1988) 'Financing Constraints and Corporate Investment', *Brooking Papers on Economic Activity*. 1: 141–95.

Fazzari, Steven M. & Tracy L. Mott (1986–87) 'The Investment Theories of Kalecki and Keynes: An Empirical Study of Firm Data, 1970–1982', *Journal of Post-Keynesian Economics*. Vol. IX. No. 2: 171–87.

Feiwel, George R. (1975) *The Intellectual Capital of Michael Kalecki – A Study in Economic Theory and Policy*. Knoxville, USA: The University of Tennessee Press.

Ferguson, Paul R. & Glenys J. Ferguson (1988) *Industrial Economics – Issues and Perspectives* (second edition). London: Macmillan.

FitzGerald, E.V.K. (1993) *The Macroeconomics of Development Finance – A Kaleckian Analysis of the Semi-industrialized Economy*. New York: St Martin's Press in association with the Institute of Social Studies, The Hague.

FitzGerald, E.V.K. (1992a) 'Hamlet Without the Prince: Structural Adjustment, Firm Behaviour and Private Investment in Developing Economies', *Development Economics Seminar Paper* No. 92-1/1. Institute of Social Studies, The Hague.

FitzGerald, E.V.K. (1992b) 'Beyond Adjustment: Promoting Sustainable Growth in an Uncertain World' (mimeo), Institute of Social Studies, The Hague.

FitzGerald, E.V.K. (1989) 'The Impact of Macroeconomic Policies on Small-scale Industry: Some Analytical Considerations', *Working Paper Sub-Series on Money, Finance and Development*, No. 29. Institute of Social Studies, The Hague.

FitzGerald, E.V.K. & Rob Vos (1989) *Financing Economic Development – A Structural Approach to Monetary Policy*. Aldershot, UK: Gower.

Foxley, Alejandro (1981) 'Stabilisation Policies and their Effects on Employment and Income Distribution – A Latin American Perspective', in Cline & Weintraub, pp. 191–233.

Frattianni, Michele U. & Dominick Salvatore (eds) (1993) *Monetary Policy in Developed Economies – Handbook of Comparative Economic Policies* (Volume 3). Westport, Connecticut: Greenwood Press.

Friedman, Milton & Rose Friedman (1980) *Free To Choose*. London: Secker & Warburg.

Froyen, Richard T. (1993) 'Monetary Policy and Economic Activity', in Frattianni & Salvatore.

Fry, Maxwell J. (1988) *Money, Interest, and Banking in Economic Development*. Baltimore, USA: The John Hopkins University Press.

Galbraith, Kenneth John (1978) 'On Post-Keynesian Economics', *Journal of Post-Keynesian Economics*. Vol. 1, No. 1: 8–11.

Gersovitz, Mark (1988) 'Savings and Development', in Chenery & Srinivasan.

Giovannini, Alberto (1985) 'Saving and the Real Interest Rate in LDCs', *Journal of Development Economics*. 18: 197–217.

Giovannini, Alberto (1983) 'The Interest Elasticity of Savings in Developing Countries: The Existing Evidence', *World Development*. Vol. 11, No. 7: 601–7.

Girvan, Norman (1973) 'The Development of Dependency Economics in the Caribbean and Latin America: Review and Composition', *Social and Economic Studies*. Vol. 22, No. 1 (Special edition: Dependence and Underdevelopment in the New World). Jamaica: (ISER) University of the West Indies.

Girvan, Norman & O. Jefferson (1971) 'Readings in the Political Economy of the Caribbean', *New World*. Kingston, Jamaica.

Glade, William (ed.) (1991) *Privatization of Public Enterprises in Latin America*. San Francisco: ICS Press.

Gordon, M.J. (1992) 'The Neoclassical and a Post-Keynesian Theory of Investment', *Journal of Post-Keynesian Economics*. Vol. 14, No. 4: 424–43.

Greene, Joshua & Delano Villanueva (1991) 'Private Investment in Developing Countries – An Empirical Analysis', *IMF Staff Papers*. Vol. 38, No. 1 (March): 33–58.

Greenwald, B. & Joseph E. Stiglitz (1990) 'Asymmetric Information and the New Theory of the Firm: Financial Constraints and Risk Behaviour', *AEA Papers and Proceedings* (May), pp. 160–65.

Harcourt, G.C. (1972) *Some Cambridge Controversies in the Theory of Capital*. UK: Cambridge University Press, reprinted by Gregg Revivals, USA (1991).

Harrison, Philomen (1994) 'The Impact of Oil on Trinidad & Tobago, 1966–1973' *Working Paper No. 171*, Institute of Social Studies, The Hague.

Hay, Donald A. & Derek J. Morris (1991) *Industrial Economics and Organization Theory and Evidence* (revised second ed.). New York: Oxford University Press.

Hilaire, Alvin (1994) 'Initiatives in Monetary Policy – On the Brink of a New Beginning', *Central Bank Supplement*, Sunday Guardian newspaper: 8–9.

Hodgson, Geoffrey M. (1988) *Economics and Institutions: A Manifesto for a Modern Institutional Economics*. UK: Polity Press.

Hunt, E.K. & Howard J. Sherman (1972) *Economics: An Introduction to Traditional and Radical Views*. New York: Harper & Row.

International Monetary Fund (1987) *Theoretical Aspects of the Designs of Fund-Supported Adjustment Programs – A Study by the Research Department of the International Monetary Fund*, Occasional Paper No. 55, September 1987, Washington D. C.

International Monetary Fund (1977) *The Monetary Approach to the Balance of Payments*, Washington D.C.

Jansen, Karel (1990) *Finance, Growth and Stability – Financing Economic Development in Thailand, 1960–86*. Aldershot, UK: Avebury.

Jensen, Michael C. & William H. Meckling (1976) 'Theory of the Firm: Managerial Behaviour, Agency Costs and Ownership Structure', *Journal Of Financial Economics*. 3: 305–60.

Jorgenson, Dale W. (1971) 'Econometric Studies of Investment Behaviour: A Survey', *Journal of Economic Literature*. Vol. IX, No. 4: 1111–47.

Jorgenson, Dale W. & Calvin D. Siebert (1968) 'A Comparison of Alternate Theories of Corporate Investment Behaviour', *The American Economic Review*. Vol. LVIII, No. 4: 681–711.

Kaldor, Nicholas (1983) 'Devaluation and Adjustment in Developing Countries', *Finance and Development*. Vol. 20, No. 3: 35–47.

Kaldor, Nicholas (1982) *The Scourge of Monetarism*. New York: Oxford University Press.

Kaldor, Nicholas (1972) 'The Irrelevance of Equilibrium Economics', in *Economic Journal*. 82: 1237–55.

Kaldor, Nicholas & J. Trevithick (1981) 'A Keynesian Perspective on Money', *Lloyds Bank Review* (Spring), pp. 1–19. Reprinted in Sawyer (ed.) (1988).

Kalecki, Michael (1971) *Selected Essays on the Dynamics of the Capitalist Economy 1933–1970*. Cambridge: Cambridge University Press.

Kenyon, Peter (1979) 'Pricing', in Eichner (ed.).

Keynes, John Maynard (1957) (reprint of 1936) *The General Theory of Employment Interest and Money*. London: Macmillan.

Khan Moshin S. & Malcolm D. Knight (1991) 'Stabilization programs in Developing Countries: A Formal Framework', in Khan, Monteil & Haque.

Khan, Moshin S., Peter J. Monteil & Nadeem U. Haque (eds) (1991) *Macroeconomic Models for Adjustments in Developing Countries*. International Monetary Fund.

Khan, Moshin, P.J. Monteil & N. Haque (1990) 'Adjustment with Growth: Relating the Analytical Approaches of the World Bank and the IMF', *Journal of Development Economics*. Vol. 32 (Jan.): 155–79.

Khan, Moshin S. & Carmen M. Reinhart (1990) 'Private Investment and Economic Growth in Developing Countries', *World Development*. Vol. 18, No. 1: 19–27.

Killick, Tony (ed.) (1984) *The Quest for Economic Stabilization: The IMF and the Third World*. London: Gower in association with Overseas Development Institute.

Knight J.B. (1991) 'The Evolution of Development Economics', in Balasubramanyam & Lall.

Kregel, J.A. (1976) 'Economic Methodology in the Face of Uncertainty: The Modelling Methods of Keynes and the Post-Keynesians, *Economic Journal*. 86: 209–25. Reprinted in Sawyer (ed.) (1988).

Kregel, J.A. (1973a) *The Reconstruction of Political Economy – An Introduction to Post-Keynesian Economics*. London: Macmillan.

Kreuger, Anne O. (1990) *Perspectives on Trade and Development*. New York: Wheatsheaf.

Kreuger, Anne O. (1985) 'How to Liberalize a Small Open Economy', in Blonnolly & McDermont.

Kreuger, Anne O. (1981) 'Interactions between Inflation and Trade Regime Objectives in Stabilization Programs', in Cline & Weintraub.

Kreuger, Anne O. (1974) 'The Political Economy of the Rent-seeking Society', *American Economic Review*. Vol. 64, No. 3: 291–303.

Kriesler, Peter (1987) *Kalecki's Microanalysis – The Development of Kalecki's Analysis of Pricing and Distribution*. Cambridge: Cambridge University Press.

Krugman, Paul & Lance Taylor (1978) 'Contractionary Effects of a Devaluation', *Journal of Development Economics*. 8: 445–56.

Lal, Deepak (1984) 'The Real Effects of Stabilisation and Structural Adjustment Policies: An Extension of the Australian Adjustment Model', *World Bank Working Paper* 636, Washington D.C.: World Bank.

Lal, Deepak (1983) *The Poverty of Development Economics*. UK: The Institute of Economic Affairs.

Lamberte, Mario B., Gilberto M Llanto & Aniceto C. Orbeta Jr. (1992) *Micro Impacts of Macroeconomic Adjustment Policies (MIMAP): Phase II Integrative Report*, Working Paper Series No. 92-13, Philippine Institute of Development Studies.

Layard, P.R.G. & A.A. Walters (1978) *Microeconomic Theory*. New York: McGraw-Hill.

Lensink, R. (1996) *Structural Adjustment in Sub-Saharan Africa*. London: Longman.

Levitt, Kari & Lloyd Best (1975) 'Character of Caribbean Economy', in Beckford (ed.).

Lewis, W.A. (1988) 'The Roots of Development Theory', in Chenery & Srinivasan.

Lewis, W.A. (1980) 'The Slowing Down of the Engine of Growth', *The American Economic Review*. Vol. 70, No. 4: 555–64.

Lewis, W.A. (1976) 'The Diffusion of Development', in Wilson & Skinner (eds).

Lewis, W.A. (1955) *The Theory of Economic Growth*. London: Allen & Unwin.

Lewis, W.A. (1954) 'Economic Development with Unlimited Supplies of Labour', reprinted in Argawala & Singh, (1959).

Lim, Joseph (1987) 'The New Structuralist Critique of the Monetarist Theory of Inflation – The Case of the Philippines', *Journal of Development of Economics*. 25: 45–61.

Lipsey, R.G. & Kelvin Lancaster (1956/57) 'The General Theory of Second Best', *Review of Economic Studies*. 6: 11–32.

Little, I.M.D. (1982) *Economic Development*. New York: Basic Books.

Little, Ian, Tibor Scitovsky & Maurice Scott (1970) *Industry and Trade in Some Developing Countries – A Comparative Study*. London: OUP.

Lizondo. J. Saul & Peter J. Monteil (1989) 'Contractionary Devaluation in Developing Countries – An Analytical Overview', *IMF Staff Papers* 36, No. 1: 182–227.

Maharaj, Susheila (1991) 'Structural Adjustment, Labour and Labour Relations: A Comparative Study Of Trinidad & Tobago and Venezuela', unpublished research paper, M.A. *Development Studies*, The Institute of Social Studies, The Hague.

Marris, Robin (1964) *The Economic Theory of 'Managerial' Capitalism*. New York: Basic Books.

McKinnon, Ronald I. (1973) Money and Capital in Economic Development. Washington D.C.: The Brookings Institution.

Meier, Gerald M. (1984) *Emerging from Poverty – The Economics That Really Matters*. New York: OUP.

Meier, Gerald M. & William F. Steel, assisted by Richard J. Caroll (1989) *Industrial Adjustment in Sub-Saharan Africa*. New York: World Bank, OUP.

Mendell, Maguerite & Daniel Salée (1991) *The Legacy of Karl Polanyi – Market, State and Society at the End of the Twentieth Century*. UK: Macmillan.

Mills, Cadman Atta & Raj Nallari (1992) 'Analytical Approaches to Stabilization and Adjustment Programs', The International Bank for Reconstruction and Development.

Minsky, Hyman P. (1985) 'The Financial Instability Hypothesis – A Restatement', in Arestis & Skouras (eds).

Mishan, E.J. (1960) 'A Survey of Welfare Economics, 1939–59, *The Economic Journal*. June 1960, Vol. LXX, No. 278: 197–265.

Moore, Basil J. (1979) 'Monetary Factors' in Eichner (ed.).

Musalem, Alberto R. (1989) 'Private Investment in Mexico – An Empirical Analysis', *PPR Working Paper* WPS 183, World Bank.

Myers, Robert J. (ed.) (1987) *The Political Morality of the International Fund*. New Brunswick, USA: Transaction Books.

Nath, S.K. (1969) *A Reappraisal of Welfare Economics*. London: Routledge & Kegan Paul.

Nell, E.J. (1996) 'Transformation Growth and the Long Period Method', *Review of Political Economy*. Vol. 8, No. 4: 379–401.

Nell, Edward (1984) *Free Market Conservatism – A Critique of Theory and Practice*. London: George Allen & Unwin.

Nowzad, Bahram (1981) 'The IMF And Its Critics', *Essays in International Finance*. No. 146 December. New Jersey: Princetown University..

Norusis, Marija (1996) *SPSS-SPSS 6.1 Guide to Data Analysis*. Prentice Hall New Jersey.

Olivera. Julio H.G. (1970) 'On Passive Money', *Journal of Political Economy*. Vol. 78, No. 4, Part II: 805–14.

Oser, Jacob & Stanley L. Brue (1988) *The Evolution of Economic Thought* (fourth edition). San Diego: HBJ, Publishers.

Oshikoya, W. Tempitope (1994) 'Macroeconomic Determinants of Domestic Private Investment in Africa: An Empirical Analysis', *Economic Development and Cultural Change*. (April 1994) Vol. 42, No. 3: 574–96, The University of Chicago.

Palley, Thomas I. (1996) 'Inside debt, aggregate demand, and the Cambridge theory of distribution', *Cambridge Journal of Economics*. 24: 465–74.

Penrose, E. (1959) *The Theory of the Growth of the Firm*. Oxford: Basil Blackwell.

Pheby, John (ed.) (1989) *New Directions in Post-Keynesain Economics*. Aldershot, UK: Edward Elgar.

Pindyck, Robert S. (1991) 'Irreversibility, Uncertainty, and Investment', *Journal of Economic Literature*. Vol. XXIX: 1110–48.

Pindyck, Robert S. & Daniel L. Rubinfeld (1992) *Microeconomics* (second edition). New York: Macmillan.

Pirie, Madsen (1988) *Privatization*. UK: Wildwood House.

Pollin, Robert (1991) 'Two Theories of Money Supply Endogeneity: Some Empirical Evidence', *Journal of Post-Keynesian Economics*. Spring 1991, Vol. 13, No. 3: 366–96.

Ramsaran, D. (1992) *The Future of the Caribbean Culture and Entrepreneurship in the Caribbean – The Sociology of Enterprrise: A Survey of Entrepreneurs in Trinidad & Tobago*. Trinidad & Tobago: Institute of Social and Economic Research, University of the West Indies.

Reddock, Rhoda (1980) 'Industrialization and the Rise of the Petty Bourgeoisie in Trinidad & Tobago', M.A. thesis, The Institute of Social Studies, The Hague.

Rider, Christine (1994) 'Privatization in the Transition Economics: A Critique', *Journal of Post-Keynesian Economics*. (Summer) Vol. 16, No. 4: 589–603.

Robinson, Joan (1980) 'Time in Economic Theory', Kyklos. 33: 219–29. Reprinted in Sawyer (ed.) (1988).

Robinson, Joan (1978) *Contributions to Modern Economics*. Oxford: Basil Blackwell.

Robinson, Joan (1973a) foreword to Kregel.

Robinson, Joan & John Eatwell (1973b) *An Introduction to Modern Economics* (revised edition). London: McGraw Hill.

Rodrik, Dani (1991) 'Policy, Uncertainty and Private Investment in Developing Countries', *Journal of Development Economics*. 36 (October): 229–42.

Ryan, Selwyn & Lou Anne Barclay (1992) *Sharks and Sardines – Blacks in Business in Trinidad & Tobago*. Jamaica: ISER, The University of the West Indies.

Ryan, Selwyn & Taimoon Stewart (eds) (1994) *Entrepreneurship in the Caribbean – Culture, Structure and Conjucture*. Trinidad & Tobago: Multimedia Production Centre, Faculty of Education, St. Augustine, University of the West Indies.

Ryan, William (1971) *Blaming the Victim*. USA: Random House.

Sachs, Jeffrey D. & Felipe Larrain B. (1993) *Macroeconomics in the Global Economy*. New York: Harvester Wheatsheaf.

Samuelson, Paul A. (1955) *Foundations of Economic Analysis*. Cambridge: Harvard University Press.

Savas, E.S. (1982) *Privatizing the Public Sector – How to Shrink Government*. Chatham, New Jersey: Chatham House Publishers.

Sawyer, Malcom (1991) *The Economies of Industries and of Firms – Theories, Evidence and Policy* (second edition, reprint). London: Routledge.

Sawyer, Malcolm (ed.) (1988) *Post-Keynesian Economics*. Aldershot, UK: Edward Elgar.

Schumpeter, J. (1934) *The Theory of Economic Development*. Cambridge, Mass.: Harvard University Press,.

Seers, Dudley (1964) 'The Mechanism of an Open Petroleum Economy', *Social and Economic Studies*. Vol. 13, No. 2 (June). Jamaica: ISER, University of the West Indies.

Sen, Amartya (1983) 'Development: Which Way Now?', *Economic Journal*. 93: 745–62.

Servén, Luis (1996) *Irreversibility, Uncertainty and Private Investment: Analytical Issues and some Lessons for Africa*. Washington D.C.: The World Bank.

Servén, Luis & Andrés Solimano (1993) *Striving for Growth After Adjustment – The Role of Capital Formation*. Washington, D.C.: The World Bank.

Servén, Luis & Andres Solimano (1992) 'Private Investment and Macroeconomic Adjustment: A Survey', *The World Bank Research Observer*. Vol. 7, No. 1: 95–113.

Setterfield, Mark (1995) 'Historical Time and Economic Theory', *Review of Political Economy*. 7(1): 1–27.

Shaw E.S. (1973) *Financial Deepening in Economic Development*. London: OUP.

Solimano, Andrés (1989) 'How Private Investment Reacts to Changing Macroeconomic Conditions – The Case of Chile in the 1980s', *Policy, Planning and Research Working Papers* WPS 212, The World Bank, Washington D.C.

Sikorski, Trevor M. (1996) Financial Liberalization in Developing Countries. Cheltenham: Edward Elgar.

Singer, H.W. (1950) 'The Distribution of Gains between Investing and Borrowing Countries', *American Economic Review* (Proceedings). (May) 40: 473–85.

Steel, William F. & Leila M. Webster (1992) 'How Small Enterprises in Ghana Have Responded to Adjustment', *The World Bank Review*. Vol. 6, No. 3: 423–38.

Stein, Howard (1992) 'De-industrialization, Adjustment, the World Bank and the IMF in Africa', *World Development*. Vol. 20, No. 1: 83–95.

Stewart, Taimoon (1994) 'Caribbean Entrepreneurship in Historical Capitalism', in Ryan & Stewart (eds).

St Cyr, Eric (1981) 'Industrial Development Strategies in the Caribbean Countries – The Case of Trinidad & Tobago', The University of the West Indies, St. Augustine: Trinidad & Tobago (mimeo).

St Cyr, Eric (1980) 'On Lewis' Theory of Growth and Development', *Social and Economic Studies*. Vol. 29, No. 4: 16–24, Institute of Social and Economic Research, University of the West Indies: Jamaica.

Stiglitz, Joseph E. & Andrew Weiss (1981) 'Credit Rationing in Markets with Imperfect Information', *American Economic Review*. 71: 393–410.

Stiglitz, Joseph E. (1988) 'Why Financial Structure Matters', *Journal of Economic Perspectives*. Vol. 2, No. 4: 121–26.

Studart, Rogerio (1995) Investment Finance in Economic Development, London: Routledge.

Studart, Rogerio (1993) 'Financial Repression and Economic Development: Towards a Post-Keynesian Alternative', *Review of Political Economy*. 5(3): 277–98.

Sundrum, R.M. (1983) *Development Economics A Framework for Policy Analysis*. Chichester: John Wiley & Sons.

Taylor, Lance (1992) 'Structuralist and Competing Approaches to Development Economics', in Dutt & Jameson.

Taylor, Lance (1990) (ed.) *Socially Relevant Policy Analysis – Structuralist Computable General Equilibrium Models for the Developing World*. Cambridge, Mass.: The MIT Press.

Taylor, Lance (1987) 'IMF Conditionality: Incomplete Theory Policy Malpractice', in Myers (ed.).

Taylor, Lance (1983) *Structuralist Macroeconomics – Applicable Models for the Third World*. New York: Basic Books.

Taylor, Lance (1981) 'IS/LM in the Tropics: Diagrammatics Of the New Structuralist Macro Critique', in Cline & Weintraub.

Tenjo-Galarza, Fernando (1995) 'Corporate Finance Under Adjustment – Firm Behaviour, Private Sector and Economic Policy in Colombia 1970–90', Ph.D. thesis, Institute of Social Studies, The Hague.

Thom, Basil W. (1992) 'Financial Repression and Efficient Resource Mobilisation: The Case of Trinidad & Tobago 1972–1984', research paper, M.A. in Development Studies Economic Policy and Planning, Institute of Social Studies, The Hague.

Thomas, Vinod, Ajay Chibber, Mansoor Dailami & Jaime de Melo (1991) *Restructuring Economies in Distress – Policy Reform and the World Bank*. OUP for the World Bank.

Toney, Hayden (1995) 'A Critical Review of the Manufacturnig Sector in Trinidad & Tobago', prepared for the Economic Commission for Latin America and the Caribbean (mimeo).

Toye, John (1987) *Dilemmas of Development – Reflections on the Counter-Revolution in Development Theory and Policy*. Oxford, UK: Basil Blackwell.

Tybout, James R. (1983) 'Credit Rationing and Investment Behaviour in a Developing Country', *The Review of Economic and Statistics*. (Nov.) Vol. 25, No. 4: 598–607.

Van Wijnbergen, Sweder (1986) 'Exchange Rate Management and Stabilisation Policies in Developing Countries', *Journal of Development Economics*. (Oct.) Vol. 23: 227–47.

Van Wijnbergen, Sweder (1983) 'Credit Policy, Inflation and Growth in a Financially Repressed Economy', *Journal of Development Economics*. 13: 45–65.

Varian, Hal (1978) *Microeconomic Analysis*. New York: W.W. Norton.

Walsh, Vivian & Harvey Gram (1980) *Classical and Neo-classical Theories of General Equilibrium – Historical Origin and Mathematical Structure*. New York: OUP.

Warman, Fanny & A.P. Thirlwall (1994) 'Interest Rates, Saving, Investment and Growth in Mexico 1960–90'. *Journal of Development Studies*. Vol. 30, No. 3: 629–49.

White, Howard (1996) 'Adjustment in Africa' (a review article), *Development and Change*. 27(4): 785–815.

Williamson, Oliver E. & Sidney G. Winter (1991) *The Nature of the Firm – Origins, Evolution, and Development*. Oxford: Oxford University Press.

Wilson, Thomas & Andrew S. Skinner (eds) (1976) *The Market and The State – Essays in Honour of Adam Smith*. Oxford: Clarendon Press.

Wolfson, Martin H. (1996) 'A Post-Keynesian Theory of Credit Rationing', *Journal of Post Keynesian Economics*. (Spring) Vol. 18, No. 3: 443–70.

Worrell, DeLisle (1985) 'Monetary Mechanisms in Open Economies: A Model for the Caribbean' in Connolly & McDermott.

Yip Choy, Wayne (1995) *Sunday Guardian* (newspaper) Trinidad & Tobago Manufacturer's Association (TTMA) Supplement, p. 3.

Zamagni, Stefano (1987) *Microeconomic Theory – An Introduction*. Oxford, UK: Basil Backwell.

Reports and Other Publications

Government of Trinidad & Tobago: First Five Year Plan, 1958–1962.

Government of Trinidad & Tobago: Second Five Year Plan, 1964–1968.

Government of Trinidad & Tobago: Third Five Year Plan, 1969– 1973.

Government of Trinidad & Tobago: Budget Speeches, several years.

Government of Trinidad & Tobago: Review of the Economy, several years.

Interim Report of the Commission Enquiry into Racial and Colour Discrimination in the Private Sector, October 1970 (mimeo).

IMF Staff Papers, several years.

Republic of Trinidad & Tobago: Medium-term Policy Framework, 1994–96 (November 1993).

Republic of Trinidad & Tobago: Medium-term Policy Framework: From Stabilisation to Growth 1993–95 (November 1992).

Republic of Trinidad & Tobago, National Planning Commission: Restructuring for Economic Independence – Draft Medium-term Macro Planning Framework (July 1988).

Republic of Trinidad & Tobago, Ministry of Finance: Trinidad & Tobago Government's Relationship with the International Monetary Fund and the Paris Club (1990).

Republic of Trinidad & Tobago, The Imperatives of Adjustment-Draft Development Plan 1983–1986-Report of the Task Force appointed by Cabinet to formulate a multi-sectoral development plan for the Republic of Trinidad and Tobago-Volumes I&II

Republic of Trinidad & Tobago: Central Statistical Office Business Surveys Report, 1974.

Republic of Trinidad & Tobago: Central Statistical Office Business Surveys Report, 1978

Republic of Trinidad & Tobago: Central Statistical Office Business Surveys Statisitics, unpublished, several years.

Republic of Trinidad & Tobago, Central Statistical Office: The National Income of Trinidad & Tobago, 1966–1985.

Republic of Trinidad & Tobago, Central Statistical Office: The National Income of Trinidad & Tobago, 1981–1991.

Republic of Trinidad & Tobago Central Statistical Office: The National Income of Trinidad & Tobago, 1990–1994.

Republic of Trinidad & Tobago, Central Statistical Office: Annual Statistical Digests, several years.

Republic of Trinidad & Tobago, Central Statistical Office: Economic Indicators Reports, several years.

Report No. 10417-TR, Trinidad & Tobago Policy Agenda for Sustained Development, June 23, 1992–country Department III–Latin America and the Caribbean Region–Document of the World Bank.

Report No. 9818-TR, Staff Appraisal Report–Trinidad & Tobago Business Expansion and Industrial Restructuring Project–November 22, 1991–Trade Finance and Industry Division–Department III– Latin America and the Caribbean Region–Document of The World Bank.

The World Bank (1992) *Adjustment Lending and Mobilization of Private and Public Resources for Growth 22* (Policy and Research Series) Country Economics Department.

World Bank Policy Research Bulletin (1993) 'The Making of the East Asia Miracle' Vol. 4, No. 4: 2.

World Debt Tables, several years.

World Development Report (1997) The World Bank, OUP.

World Development Report (1991) The World Bank, OUP
World Development Report (1987) The World Bank, OUP.
World Development Report (1983) The World Bank, OUP.

Index